ANTHONY NORRIS GROVES

ANTHONY NORRIS GROVES

SAINT AND PIONEER

*A Combined Study of a Man of God and of the
Principles and Practices of the Brethren*

BY

G. H. LANG

KingsleyPress

Shoals, Indiana

Anthony Norris Groves

PUBLISHED BY KINGSLEY PRESS
PO Box 973
Shoals, IN 47581
USA
Tel. (800) 971-7985
www.kingsleypress.com
E-mail: sales@kingsleypress.com

ISBN: 978-1-937428-26-6

Scripture quotations are usually from the Revised Version.

Printed in the United States of America.

Contents

A. N. GROVES

Born at Newton, Hants. . . . . 1st February, 1795
Commenced practice as dentist at Plymouth . . 1st February, 1814
Converted to God at Plymouth, probably in 1814
Married his cousin, Mary Bethia Thompson,
and removed to Exeter. 1816
Suggested the principles of the Brethren, at Dublin . . . 1827, 1828
Resigned his profession and means to serve
in the gospel in dependence upon God 1828
Left England for Bagdad. . . . . 12th June, 1829
Mrs. Groves died in Bagdad . . . . 14th May, 1831
Reached Bombay, India. . . . . July, 1833
In England (and visited Germany) .1835
Married Harriet Baynes. . . . . .25th April, 1835
Reached India . . . . July, 1836
Reached England . . . . 20th March, 1848
Left England for India . . . . 20th June, 1849
Reached England . . . . 25th September, 1852
Died at Bristol, aged 58. . . . . 20th May, 1853

". . . the simplicity of Groves' faith, the depth of his humility, the energy and purity of his zeal, the fervour and comprehensiveness of his charity, have rarely been equalled in the Church of God." (*Neatby*, 38).

Notes to the Reader

The reader will please note:—

1. Numbers in brackets (220) refer to the pages of the *Memoir of the late Anthony Norris Groves* by his widow, 2nd edition, 1857.
2. *Narrative* means *A Narrative of Some of the Lord's Dealings with George Müller,* Vol. I, 1850.
3. *Neatby* or *History* is *A History of the Plymouth Brethren* by W. Blair Neatby, 1901.
4. In quotations all italics are those of the author quoted.
5. My quotations of Holy Scripture are usually from the Revised Version.
6. All matter in square brackets [ ] is mine.
   -G.H.L.

Note to Second Edition

Apart from a very few minor corrections, and the addition of notes on pp. 206, 392 and 393, this is a reprint of the first edition.

F. A. Cox, D.O., upon C. M. Du Veil, D.O., in his *Historical Introduction* to the latter's *Commentary on the Acts of the Apostles*, Hanserd Knollys Society's edition, 1851.

Among the various classes of knowledge, that which relates to what may be denominated the biography of the mind must be regarded as one of the most important. By this expression it is intended to make a clear distinction between the mental and physical phenomena, which are in general blended together in the term biography. Where a man was born, in what schools he was instructed, what profession or trade, if any, he followed, what connexions he formed, in what sphere he lived, where he died, with many other particulars respecting any notorious individual, possess a certain degree of interest; but incomparably less than what concerns the habits of his mind, the processes of his thought, and the formation of his character.

In contemplating some minds we look upon a dead level, a sort of quiet lake, so enclosed and contracted as never to have been ruffled by the inward stirrings of anxious thought, or the winds and storms of controversy. There is little to discover and little to instruct. There is a surface smooth enough, but too flat and tame to be truly interesting; and though they may excite to approval and even some admiration, they fade from the memory. Others there are whose peculiarities are such, or who have passed through such courses of thought and action, as to awaken the utmost attention, and claim a scrupulous enquiry. We ask, What led them to the extraordinary changes they underwent—what influenced at this or that time, their decisions—what altered their decisions—what fixed and unfixed them in their revolutions of sentiment—by what motives were they urged, and where at last they landed?

There may be a great apparent similarity between caprice and principle; yet are they widely different. Both admit of great changes; but changes upon different grounds; and nicely to distinguish these differences is a progress in the science of mental philosophy. In regard

9

to religion this is of the utmost importance, and must necessarily regulate our contempt or admiration. The researches of a mind really engaged in the pursuit of truth are worthy of the greatest attention; its struggles claim our sympathy; its progress upon this great voyage of discovery, as we may say, may assist our own enquiries, or strengthen our own faith.

Few persons, we believe, hold important truth firmly who have not experienced some, it may be very considerable, alterations of opinion. Light has broken gradually upon them, errors have been for a time tenaciously held; but the day of their knowledge has often been the brighter for the mists of the early morning. All minds indeed are not thus, or similarly constituted; but we must make allowance for those that are, and gain this general instruction from their history, to look well and often to the foundations, that we may secure the stability of our faith.

1

The Spring

A passage in Herodotus, the father of history, shows that in the fifth century before Christ inquiring minds were busy upon a question that was answered by other inquiring minds only in the nineteenth century after Christ, namely, the course and the source of the Nile.

This habit of the mind to trace things to their source has been very fruitful in the gaining of knowledge and its consequent advantages. It can be turned to excellent account in the spiritual realm as in the material, which is our present task.

Throughout almost the whole of the nineteenth century there lived a man who attained to colossal and commanding spiritual stature—George Müller of Bristol. His perception of the will of God in matters practical became extraordinarily accurate; he seems seldom to have missed that will through seventy years of intensely active Christian life. His confidence in God that that holy will could be accomplished, without appeal for human aid, advanced to proportions that were phenomenal, though doubtless it ought not to be so unusual. Among other activities he made himself the father of orphans. At one time, and over a long period, he was personally responsible for the maintenance of some two thousand persons, orphans and helpers. It will help to estimate what this means if we suppose that a man, with no means, should walk into a country town of 2,000 inhabitants and propose to assume personal and permanent responsibility for all the material needs of the whole community, and to see all those needs met without informing any person but God that the needs existed.

This overwhelming burden George Müller carried with an easy mind, and carried it for long, long years. He was known in his old age to say: "I am a happy, a very happy old man." Such was his child-like faith in God his Father.

Now if we seek in his *Narrative* to trace this broad and placid stream of faith up to its source, we shall find that source described on page 44. In the March of 1829 he had come from Germany to London to be trained in the seminary of the London Jews Society for service as a missionary to Jews. He writes:

Soon after my arrival in England, I heard one of the brethren in the seminary speak about a Mr. Groves, a dentist of Exeter, who, for the Lord's sake, had given up his profession, which brought him in about fifteen hundred pounds a year, and who intended to go as a missionary to Persia, with his wife and children, simply trusting in the Lord for temporal supplies. This made such an impression on me, and delighted me so, that I not only marked it down in my journal, but also wrote about it to my German friends.

It is true (as he stated in 1837) that in 1826, two and a half years earlier than he heard of Mr. Groves, he had

...lived for about two months in free lodgings, provided for poor students of divinity in the Orphan House, built in dependence upon God, by that devoted and eminent servant of Christ, A. H. Franke, Professor of Divinity at Halle, who died 1727.

But he adds:

I mention this as some years afterwards I was benefited myself through the faith of this dear man of God (*Narrative* 23).

This "some years afterwards" is to be noted. It is not till after ten years (April, 1835) that he mentions Halle again (*Narrative* 131), and in October of that year says:

I found Franke's life. I have frequently, for this long time, thought of labouring in a similar way (*Narrative* 145).

But it was early in 1829, six and a half years before this, that Groves' step of faith had so arrested and delighted him; and by the end of that same year, December 12th, 1829, he had himself resolved to leave the Society, on grounds of Scripture principles concerning gospel service, and to go about the work of the Lord under His immediate direction and with an immediate faith in Him as to earthly needs; and of this momentous step of faith he wrote:

The Lord most mercifully enabled me to take the promises of His word, and rest upon them, and such as Matt. 7:7–8, John 14:13–14, and Matt. 6:25–34, were the stay of my soul concerning this point. In addition to this, the example of brother Groves, the dentist before alluded to, who gave up his profession, and went out as a missionary, was a great encouragement to me. For the news, which by this time had arrived, of how the Lord had aided him on his way to Petersburg, and at Petersburg, strengthened my faith (*Narrative* 52).

On October 7th next year, 1830, Mr. Müller married Mary Groves, A. N. Groves' sister, and in 1835 we find him accompanying Groves on a tour in Germany.

It therefore seems clear that the river of George Müller's faith took its rise from the spring of A. N. Groves' faith; and if the latter had done nothing more than inspire and give direction to the faith of George Müller this alone would have been a memorable service to the cause and church of God. But he did, or rather God did through him, very much more. For He made him a rare saint and a brave and inspiring pioneer in matters spiritual, whose teaching and example have affected, directly and indirectly, the whole church of God for a hundred years, and the spread of the gospel over vast areas of the earth. In simple fact he was one of the most influential men of the nineteenth century.

Another who owed to him the chief spiritual impetus of his life was the ripe and saintly scholar, Henry Craik, George Müller's most intimate fellow-worker for thirty-six years. During the years 1826–1828 he had lived in Groves' house in Exeter while the latter's mind was deeply exercised on church truths and practical godliness; and Craik said to Groves' son, Henry:

> …it was not at St. Andrews [his university], it was not at Plymouth [the scene of the early ministry in England of B. W. Newton and J. N. Darby], it was at Exeter that the Lord taught me those lessons of dependence on Himself and of catholic fellowship, which I have sought to carry out (Henry Groves, *Darbyism* 25).

And we shall learn of other notable men who were powerfully influenced by him.

Let us glance at the spiritual condition of England a century ago. In 1837 one wrote publicly:

> We question whether there is one dissenting body which would permit their members *occasionally* to break bread with another body of believers in the same place (*Christian Witness* 1, 306).

What a flash-light is this remark upon the narrowness, alienation, bitterness, and bigotry that then characterized Nonconformity. What separations, what heart-burnings, what hardening of heart sectarianism has caused.

An extreme example was that of two small Irish sects who nearly arranged to unite, but at last did not, because one party could not accept a declaration upon which the other party insisted, that John Wesley is in hell! (*Neatby* 27). How largely this spirit has passed away is well known. Today the general tendency is towards the opposite extreme and evil, an amalgamation of denominations reached too largely by the elimination of positive truth. Yet in itself the salvation of true Christians from that former pride-nourishing, love-slaughtering spirit is blessed.

The principal agency used by God to effect this change (shall we call it revolution?) was the testimony and practice of individuals, and groups of believers, who about the year 1828 commenced to gather to build one another up with no other guide than the Spirit of Truth and no other rule than the Word of God. As the ground of reception to their fellowship they demanded nothing more than that a person could show that he, by a new birth, possessed the life of God by faith in the Son of God. The uniting, inspiring energy of their fellowship was divine love. So evident to all were these two features, the life and the love of God, so plainly were they one family as children of the one God and Father, that they became known simply as "brethren." Inevitably perhaps, at any rate by a persistent tendency of the human mind, the common name, embracing all children of God, became a proper name, the small "b" a large "B," and the movement was termed "The Brethren." But this was not by their own act or wish.

Their influence upon the spiritual life of the whole century was immediate, profound, permanent. An acute outside observer, Robert

Govett, thought that early period was the mightiest movement of the Spirit of God since Pentecost. The writer of the article "Plymouth Brethren" in the *Popular Encyclopedia* says "it seemed at first to be a movement great enough to threaten the whole organization of the Christian Church." One who was within said that the meetings of those early times were as days of heaven upon earth.

In the course of years thousands were converted; believers innumerable entered into joyful assurance of their salvation and their riches in Christ; the plans of God in Christ for heaven and earth, for the church, for Israel, for the nations were opened up as never since apostolic days; the allied theme of the return of the Lord to the earth was made again the living and blessed hope of believers; and a mighty impetus was given to the spreading of the gospel in all the world, which impetus is by no means yet exhausted. All evangelical Christianity in all lands has been enriched. One of America's most celebrated bishops and preachers is said to have pointed to books of the early Brethren and to have declared he would rather lose all the rest of his library than those works.

The first of these gatherings arose in Dublin by several Christians of various denominations meeting to edify one another, Christians who did not find in the Established or Nonconformist Churches what their souls craved. But at that time they had no distinctive Bible truths or Bible practices, and the gathering might very well have come to an end in the course of years, as other such beginnings have done. But this was far from being the purpose of God, and through A. N. Groves His Spirit shortly introduced to them those original apostolic principles of Christian fellowship, worship, and ministry which, being joyfully accepted, practised, and propagated, made them so great a blessing to the whole church.

On page 259 of the *Memoir* of Groves we read his words written in 1833:

> I was almost forgetting, till a letter from Mr. Bellett of Dublin reminded me, that I was the first to propose that simple principle of union, the love of Jesus, instead of *oneness* of judgment in minor things, things that may consist with a true love to Jesus. Little did I then think to see that dear

brother, and many others, united in a holy, loving fellowship on these blessed principles, and to see that they are extending.

A. N. Groves was as the one small hole in the hillside through which the waters of heaven begin their expanding flow that shall make a continent fruitful. It is to be noted that neither he nor the others of that first group had any intention of starting a new movement: that was in the mind of God, but not in their minds.

A century earlier than the period before us England was not only dead spiritually, but in consequence was blighted morally. To change this on a large scale the Spirit of God, Who was brooding over the chaos and darkness, used the Wesleys, Whitefield, and their co-workers. If Wesley and Whitefield had recognized the principle that in divine things the divine Word should alone be followed, and had founded churches that were to be ordered in all things by that Word alone, perchance the Brethren movement would not have been needed. But those great preachers, like the great Reformers before them, while they accepted the truth so well stated in the sixth Article of the Book of Common Prayer, that "Holy Scripture containeth all things necessary to salvation," failed to apply that truth to matters that accompany salvation. They followed human wisdom in church organization and in arrangements for the ministry of the Word. They adopted virtually the assertion of Article 20 that "the Church hath power to decree rites or ceremonies," which is as false as Article VI is true.

On this account the spiritual impetus of their work, like that of the Reformers, and for the same reason, failed comparatively soon, a matter for profound sorrow. Upon this declension, and its spiritual causes, Groves, in 1845, wrote as follows, kindly and searchingly:

> I trust McCheyne's life will refresh you: it is so deeply spiritual and true, free from all those questions of doubtful disputations, which wither the soul's sweetest affections, and make every man the judge of his brother, and in reality, if not in word, say, "stand by, for I am holier than thou." I have also been reading a rather interesting paper on the general stagnation of Methodism in all its divisions, or rather going back from its original design. It seems as though love of refinement, love of power

and consequent love of money, were sapping its spiritual strength. How plainly we can see everywhere that the absence of spiritual enjoyment of God, and finding all sufficiency in Him, is the real source of all declension: spiritual affections must be *cultivated,* for they grow not, so as to render their fruits to the careless husbandman; warm and true affections toward God, are indeed, a spring of unmixed joy, yet how seldom with most are they in lively exercise (408).

Let all, Brethren as well as Methodists and others, note the word "everywhere," for a universal truth is declared in this statement.

Nevertheless out of the increased piety that became prevalent in century eighteen there came a strong and gracious activity for the spread of the gospel through the unevangelized world, and some of the oldest missionary societies, as well as the Bible Society, had been at work some thirty years by the time of A. N. Groves' service. But their activities were hampered, and the natural growth of churches hindered, by the fact that they worked on the plan of Western organization, and transplanted the organized church systems of the West instead of planting churches of the apostolic type shown in the New Testament. This plan also involved for the workers, godly persons as in those times they all were, dependence upon man, rather than directly upon the Lord Himself, for financial support and for control of their work.

These limitations have been in some considerable measure lessened for half a century by the arising of societies less highly organized and giving a larger place to real faith in God for funds. Such commonly make no direct appeals for money, do not guarantee to the workers a salary, and often allow the individual worker far more real freedom of action than do the older missionary societies. All this is to the good of the work as to spirituality, expansion, and permanence. In his not well known but instructive book *Forward Movements of the Last Half Century,* issued in 1901, Dr. A. T. Pierson gave one chapter to this growth of faith missions.

But before Hudson Taylor, through the China Inland Mission, had set the example in this better way of working, a number of godly men and women had already found a still better method, that of the Lord and His apostles, and had gone forth in actual dependence upon God for both leading and support. And alongside of the development of faith missions there has continually increased a flow of workers of this other order, and the work God has done through them is truly marvellous. Lord Radstock and Dr. Baedaker began that testimony which greatly stimulated the vast Stundist movement in Greek Orthodox Russia. R. C. Chapman led the way to what has become extensive work in Roman Catholic Spain. F. S. Arnot pioneered vast unknown tracts of Central Africa, and hundreds of churches and thousands of Christians from the heathen testify to the blessing of God. In India, China, the Americas, and Europe, in other parts of Africa and elsewhere such servants of the Lord have gone, and the grace of God has been with them in great power.

Now of this mighty stream of active gospel labour on these—the original—apostolic principles, A. N. Groves appears to have been the modern pioneer. He was the direct forerunner of the great host of workers last mentioned, and the indirect inspirer of the modified form of faith enterprise before mentioned. For Hudson Taylor was greatly influenced by the faith and example of George Müller, and, as we have seen, George Müller had been guided and stimulated by A. N. Groves.

In the world spiritual, as well as in the world geographical, scientific, or commercial, there have been pioneers; and of those of later times we think Groves was the greatest in his influence. It is with the desire and prayer that God may be glorified, and His work on earth be strengthened, by others following Groves as he followed Christ, that these pages are written.

2

The Channel: Its Cleansing

1. IN ME, THAT IS, IN MY FLESH, DWELLETH NO GOOD THING. ROM. 7:18

The river of the water of life, which is the life-giving energy of the Spirit of God, issues out from the throne of God and of the *Lamb* (Revelation 22:1), that is, it comes from God to His universe through the sacrifice of the Son of God, the Lamb of God. So when the river is seen flowing on earth it comes from the house where God dwells, past the altar, the place of sacrifice (Ezekiel 47:1). But water needs a channel along which to pass from its source to the region it is to enrich. In the spiritual world holy angels, and on earth holy men, are such a channel. Therefore to be holy is the chief condition for diffusing the grace of the Holy Spirit. The channel must be clean.

> How then can man be just with God?
> Or how can he be clean that is born of a woman?
> Behold, even the moon hath no brightness,
> And the stars are not pure in His sight:
> How much less man, that is a worm!
> And the son of man, that is a worm!
> Job 25:4–6

> For:
> Behold, I was brought forth in iniquity;
> And in sin did my mother conceive me.
> Psalm 51:5

> What is man, that he should be clean?
> And he that is born of a woman
>   that he should be righteous?
> Job 15:14

19

> Of a truth I know that it is so:
> But how can man be just with God?
>   Job 9:2.

These are some of the most ancient utterances that are on record, words of men who thought deeply upon the deepest problems, and amongst these upon the actual moral state of the heart of man. And to be deeply convinced that these descriptions are utterly and terribly true is the prime necessity for attaining to holiness. The biography of every true saint testifies to this, including the *Memoir* of A. N. Groves.

From a distance of twenty-five years he wrote thus of his youth, fastening upon one kind of sin as a revelation of the attitude of his heart toward God:

> When I was between thirteen and fourteen, I used to attend Fulham Church with the school to which I was sent, and all I recollect of my general religious state then was, that it was a common practice with us, to take the smaller novels, such as Fielding's and Smollett's, *within* our prayer-books, to read at church;

and of this he speaks as indicating a

> ...state of open rebellion against God and walking in open defiance of His holy will (23).

Such strong sentences concerning a boyish act of deception may astonish those who have never been blessed with that view of the hatefulness of sin expressed by the speakers above quoted from the book of Job. But the writer will never forget the shame that flooded his whole soul in adult life when a playmate of his boyhood reminded him of what had left no impress upon his own memory, so callous are we to sin, that he too had been guilty of the very deceit that Groves deplored, only with the aggravating details that he already knew Christ as his Redeemer, which Groves did not, and that he had used the Word of God itself as the cover. He could not have felt more wretched had he been a felon standing convicted in the dock. Indeed, to stand consciously beneath the all-searching eye of the God of truth produces a deeper conviction and more desperate distress than can result from being found guilty by fellow-mortals. Such can understand these words that Groves adds, speaking still of his school days, after having heard a sermon by John Owen:

> I recollect the thought arising in my dark soul, "Surely it would be a worthy object to die for, to go to India, to win but one idolater from hopeless death to life and peace." Little did I then think that I was ten times worse than he, as great a sinner with none of his excuses (24).

Nor was this sombre view of his human nature (which nature is shared by us all) a passing and over-darkened opinion; rather was it a conviction that deepened and strengthened to the close of his life, for in his last, his fifty-eighth year he wrote:

> The more I see of natural life, the more I see that there is no refuge but in God for personal peace, or quiet resting (477);

and of one of his very last days one wrote:

> This morning when he was reading that verse—
> "Lord, I believe thou hast prepared,
> Unworthy though I be,
> For me a blood-bought free reward," etc.,

> he said, on the reading of the second line, "unworthy, unworthy, unworthy"; and in the reading of the third line, "yes, that's it, blood-bought and free, *blood-bought and free*" (503).

Groves, like Job, had been brought into the presence of God, and for long years had lived there, wherefore he said:

> There is something in Jesus so unspeakably forbearing and kind, that when faith fairly reveals Him, I can say with Job, "I abhor myself in dust and ashes" (436).

He knew, what all who study to be holy are taught by God, the experience of soul expressed in the lines:

> And none, O Lord, have perfect rest,
> And none are wholly free from sin;
> And they who fain would serve Thee best
> Are conscious most of wrong within.

Nor was it that sin ever ruled him in his outward conduct. "He had been, from the testimony of those still alive, a strictly moral character from his youth," writes his biographer (26); but he had been granted the inestimable blessing of a divine revelation of the depravity of human nature, of himself; and he who receives and bows to this says with the unblamed Daniel:

"My *comeliness* was turned in me into *corruption*" (Daniel 10:8), and with the Chrysostom—the "golden-mouthed"—of the Old Testament, "I am a man of unclean lips" (Isaiah 6:5). Thus from his deathbed we have this scene:

> One day, looking at his tongue, which was exceedingly parched with fever, he said: "Naughty tongue! but Jesus has forgiven all; I shall have a new tongue, which will never dishonour Him" (504).

Yet with that tongue he had proclaimed the high praises of God for thirty-five years.

There is a state of mind greatly to be pitied: it is never to have been convicted of one's sinfulness, or to have quenched that conviction. There is a state of mind greatly to be feared: it is to imagine that sin no more dwells in me: "Let him who thinketh he standeth take heed lest he fall," is the warning given by a great saint (1 Corinthians 10:12). But blessed is he who becomes ever more keenly sensitive as to what sin is, especially in its subtler forms, ever more deeply humbled as to himself, and ever more dependent, confident, triumphant in the keeping, sanctifying power of Christ, indwelling by the Spirit.

Groves learned that the channel was blocked and foul, which was the first, the necessary, step to it being opened and cleansed, that the river of the water of life might flow through it.

2. BEING JUSTIFIED FREELY BY GOD'S GRACE, THROUGH THE REDEMPTION THAT IS IN CHRIST JESUS. ROMANS 3:24.

Because each of us is an *individual* God graciously gives to each individual education, and our spiritual experiences differ. In his incomparable spiritual autobiography *Grace Abounding to the Chief of Sinners*, Bunyan has described the flagrant godlessness of his youth; his almost violent arrest by the Spirit of God on Elstow Green, as "a Voice did suddenly dart from heaven into his soul" and challenge him with the question: "Sinner, wilt thou leave thy sins and go to Heaven, or have thy sins and go to Hell?" at which, he says: "I was put to an exceeding maze" (para. 22). He tells further of his decision to turn from sin, of how a measure of light came to him, of how he was fairly harassed by Satan (unrecognized) into giving up Christ, and thus was plunged into black despair and wallowed in the Slough of Despond for years. And his moving narrative reveals that, among other passages which at last brought him into liberty and assurance, the one above quoted had an important place. For as he meditated upon it he heard again that heavenly Voice speak, with equally arresting power but this time with healing unction, as it said:

> Sinner, thou thinkest that because of thy sins and infirmities I cannot save thy soul; but behold, My Son is by me, and upon Him I look, and not on thee, and deal with thee according as I am pleased with Him (para. 257, 258).

What more could God give or man desire? To be treated, not as I deserve, but as Christ deserves, grants to faith *all things,* as Bunyan rejoiced to learn and feel.

Groves was educated differently in many respects; and yet with him, and with all who come to present assurance of salvation, both the essentials of the process and its goal are the same.

Even in his youth he was "a great observer of external *forms* of religion" (26), and when, at about thirty-three years of age, he was asked by his intimate friend, Miss Bessie Paget, "to take charge, on Sundays, of her little flock, at Poltimore," he could scarcely bring himself to consent:

> I cannot, perhaps, convey to you the repugnance that I had; first, because I really disapproved on principle; and, secondly, because I saw that it would stand in the way of my procuring ordination.

He went, but says:

> Yet I only allowed this going to Poltimore as a particular exception, in consequence of the notorious inadequacy of the clergyman there. I had never yet gone near a dissenting place of worship (40);

and he speaks elsewhere of

> …being so high a churchman that I never went to a dissenting place of worship, nor intimately knew a dissenter, except Bessie and Charlotte [Paget] (38).

Like all who are "great observers of the external *forms* of religion" Groves was hindered thereby from reaching the *heart* of religion, the enjoyment of the love of God and the grace of our Lord Jesus Christ. But not by a startling challenge by a voice from heaven, as with Bunyan, was he shaken from this false confidence in externals. As with many others, it was a poignant and long-enduring sorrow that was used. He loved dearly his cousin, Mary Bethia Thompson, and the affection was returned, but the peremptory refusal of her father to sanction their union blighted his hopes. He writes:

> I now became supremely miserable, and the more so because I could not help hearing of her, and that she was silently but uncomplainingly sinking. My slight thoughts about religion now became my solace (25).

He had before written of his cousin:

> Her mind, like my own, had a *certain tincture* of religious feeling, which even at that time endeared us to each other; and as we walked to church, or round the garden at Fulham, the subject of religion often engaged our thoughts, and one of the very few presents I recollect ever making her, was a Bible (24).

The picture should be studied. It portrays many a soul. A *tincture* of religion, enough to *tint* the life without changing its essential qualities; enough to lead to religious conversation, to choose a Bible as a present, to constrain to zealous performance of external forms, to prompt a thought of becoming a missionary, to being "absorbed in plans of service for the Lord" (26); yet all the time no personal acguaintance with God, no knowledge of personal salvation by faith in Christ, no *new* life by a birth from above by the Spirit; and, of course, this self-deception induced and perpetuated in him as a high churchman by the soul-blinding falsehood that one was born again by baptism.

A friend of mine had opportunity to press upon a monarch of the continent that he must be born anew or he never could see the kingdom of God. Troubled by such news, he, as is reported, sent for his chaplain, who sought to wipe away the impression the truth had made by saying: "All that your majesty needs was done at your majesty's baptism." Of this soul-destroying doctrine Groves, when afterwards labouring for the souls of Mohammedans and Armenians wrote:

> We cannot help feeling that the difficulties among the Mohammedans and apostate Christian churches, are great beyond anything that can be imagined previous to experience. The difficulties of absolute falsehood are as nothing to those of perverted truth, as we see in the confounding of infant baptism with the renewing of the Holy Ghost. In everything it is the same—prayer, praise, love—all is perverted, and yet the name retained (88).

This statement I can but endorse, sorrowfully and emphatically, after forty-five years of labour for souls, in many lands, and among all the churches, eastern and western, that teach regeneration by baptism. The doctrine is one of the most deadly opiates in the pharmacy of the father of lies, and myriads who have taken the clerically dispensed draught have never awakened from it.

Thus it was the shock of a great and sudden sorrow that awakened Groves from this slumber, and many others likewise.

An Englishman abroad, also reared a high churchman, but at last immersed in the irreligious world, suddenly lost his young wife, leaving him with an infant. He said to me: "It taught me what an insect I am, and that the world can give a man nothing when he is most in need." And he learned to bless the bitter cup of grief that sent him to Christ for satisfaction. Thus it was with Groves. Writing of that time of disappointment, he says:

> My slight thoughts about religion now became my solace. I made the acquaintance of dear Mr. Joseph Richards, and Mr. Hitchins, of Plymouth. They did all they could for me; yet my soul had much and deep sorrow to go through before it knew either the peace or the *power* of Jesus' blood (25).

His biographer adds:

This was evidently the great turning point in his spiritual history: he does not enter upon any particulars of the "much and deep sorrow" he had to go through ere he found peace in the blood of the Lamb: but, in comparison of the light he gained through the ministry of Mr. Joseph Richards, he looked on his former *thoughts* about religion as having had no real foundation; he now speaks after a season of much conflict, of the "peace and power of Jesu's blood," and labouring, as he then did, under a deep natural disappointment, doubtless the gospel of glad tidings must have been, from the relief it brings, a pleasant sound; but it is evident, by his own account, it was at this time more the burthen of natural sorrow than a sense of sin, which made him seek peace out of himself in Jesus. The *full* gospel was not yet known by him, as it was a few years after, through the instrumentality of a dear friend in Exeter (25).

But he reached this most desirable knowledge of the *full* gospel, and on January 1st, 1828, he wrote to a friend:

Nothing seems to me more truly lamentable than the very low standard the Church takes and is satisfied with; it so undervalues that redemption by the blood of Christ, by which we live before the Lord of hosts (46);

and in 1847 he said:

…peace with God rests only on the *covenant,* ordered in all things and sure, and on the blood that cleanseth from all sin (431);

and this confidence and testimony he closed on his deathbed with the words before quoted:

Yes, that's it, blood-bought and free, *blood-bought* and *free* (503).

Thus a good part of the rubbish that blocked the channel was now cleared away. Groves had ceased from the dead works which were all that a man dead toward God can do, had received a new life in Christ, and so could serve the living God (Hebrews 9:14). But why, some may ask, this extraordinary emphasis upon the "blood"? What does he mean exactly when he speaks of the "peace and *power* of Jesus' blood"?

No one can understand this to a greater degree than he who has felt the sinfulness of sin, as Groves had begun to feel it. And as that conviction deepened all through life so did his appreciation of the precious blood of Christ heighten. It is always thus. Has the reader who so inquires ever realized that he has simply no vestige of a right to be alive—that his right to live has been forfeited by sin against God? The law recognizes that certain penalties may justly be compounded by a money payment; but the penalty of death cannot be. History tells that Arion, the celebrated lyric poet, having amassed much wealth in Italy, decided to return to Corinth, and hired a Corinthian ship. But on the high seas the sailors ordered him to destroy himself that they might seize his riches. He offered to surrender all but begged that his life might be spared. Why is it that a man will thus give all that he hath for his life? Does he not thereby testify that life is of infinitely greater value than the greatest possible wealth? And does he not thereby acknowledge that a forfeited life can only be redeemed by the sacrifice to justice of an unforfeited life? But which of the sons of men has not by sin forfeited his right to live except Jesus Christ alone? Is not therefore Peter's assertion self-evidently true that "in none other is there salvation"? (Acts 4:12).

> There was no other good enough
> To pay the price of sin:
> He only could unlock the gate
> Of heaven, and let us in.

Now the outpouring of the blood is visible proof that life has been given up, "for as to the life of all flesh the blood thereof is all one with the life thereof ... for the life of the flesh is in the blood" (Leviticus 17:14, 11). A savage chief need not require that the corpse of his slaughtered foe be produced; it would be sufficient proof of his death that a bowl of his blood be brought.

Death, as penalty for sin, was to enter each house in Egypt (Exodus 12). If blood enough were available to be smeared all round a doorway that was proof enough that death had already entered that house, and that so the penalty had been there executed and justice satisfied. When the spear pierced our Saviour's side and blood and water poured forth, that was visible and certain proof of His death, proof therefore that the penalty of our iniquities had been met by Him, and that the believer on Him has thereby acquired a legal right to live.

Thus mighty, to repeat Groves' words, "is the power of Jesus' blood"; it effects legally the deliverance of the believer from eternal death and secures for him the right to eternal life, "for the wages of sin is death, but the free gift of God is eternal life in Christ Jesus our Lord" (Romans 6:23). Hence his further words that it is "by the blood of Christ we live before the Lord of hosts"; and hence the reason he gives that the "low standard the Church takes and is satisfied with" is that "it so undervalues redemption by the blood of Christ." Since his day that standard has, in general, fallen yet lower proportionately to the deeper general devaluating of the blood of Christ. It cannot but be so.

As the debt that has been fully paid is thereby cleared, cancelled, and ceases to exist, so in strictest fact "the blood of Jesus, God's Son, cleanses (clears) us from all sin," if, that is, we are among those who have turned from darkness and have begun to walk in the light of God (1 John 1:7). By grace on the part of God, by faith on his own, Groves had been brought to share the ecstasy of David when he sang:

Oh, the happinesses of the man whose transgression is forgiven,
    Whose sin is covered [by atonement, by blood shedding, as the word means].
    Oh, the happinesses of the man unto whom Jehovah imputeth not iniquity [because it was imputed to his Substitute],
    And in whose spirit there is no guile [because he has honestly confessed all sin unto God] (Psalm 32).

No one can advance with Groves into the life of intimate, sanctifying communion with God as his Father that he knew, or into the life of God-blessed service that he lived, who does not begin with Groves in these two experiences of the depravity and helplessness of human nature and of peace with God through the blood of Jesus. Therefore have we enlarged upon them. May God bring the reader into the power of them.

3. WE ARE GOD'S FELLOW-WORKERS. 1 CORINTHIANS 3:9.

It is instructive and encouraging to observe the great use that the Lord made of a woman in the preparation of this chosen instrument.

Of Miss Bessie Paget's gracious, powerful influence upon him we read:

> The *full* gospel was not yet known by him, as it was a few years after, through the instrumentality of a dear friend in Exeter. At first his views were decidedly Arminian: he thought more of what he was to do for the Lord, than of what the Lord had done for him (25).

And again we read of

> ...the Misses Paget, of Exeter, two sisters long known as eminent and devoted Christians; one has fallen asleep [i.e. in 1857 when the *Memoir* (2nd edition) was published]; the elder, who still lives, had, as it will be seen, a most powerful influence over Mr. Groves' history, and continued to the end of his life his attached friend, and one to whom he was indebted much for spiritual counsel (38).

Of the year 1829 he himself writes:

> Dearest B. had, for some time, sunk the keen controversialist[1] in the tender and kind friend. She felt how ignorant I was, and treated me accordingly; yet so sweetened it by a lively and real interest, that I never could doubt she loved me; and the more I saw into her holy, unselfish soul, the more I regretted I ever felt alienated from her; and, by a natural sort of revulsion of feeling, now drew to her so much the more. She kept instructing me, as my obstinacy and self-will would allow, yet always bore most gently and lovingly with me; and I look up to her, and love her now as my mother, in the things of God; and to this day, when others have disappointed me, her love has never failed.

Groves was at this time a man of thirty-four years, well educated, very able, a strong, if tender, character. Let those who would help and change such an one, no easy task, study the above paragraph as to the way to succeed. The avoidance of keen controversy, the tenderness, kindness, sweetness, patience, and aptness to teach as the pupil could bear it, are noteworthy.

It was evidently the excellence of this "dissenter" that weaned him from bigoted devotion to the Establishment as the only sphere of spiritual life; it was she who led him into the wider sphere of service

---

1. This refers merely to his Arminian views, from which she was at last the means of delivering him (40).

to the whole church of God by inducing him to preach in her hall at Poltimore (40); it was in her house that his wife obtained full rest in Christ (29); it was there that they stayed for a year after he had resigned his profession and before they left for Bagdad, in which time their little girl died (34); and it was Miss Paget who had accompanied him on a journey to Dublin which was to have the momentous results for the church of God and its service in the gospel before mentioned (38). Her part in those events is not recorded, save in the books on high.

If we have rightly traced George Müller's life primarily to the influence of Groves, it would almost seem that his own life may find its chief impulse and direction in the influence God exerted upon him through this spiritually powerful, winsome woman. Yet we may presume that at first she could have had no conception of *how great* a work the Lord was doing through her. Let each of us, man and woman, do our utmost to serve well each person we touch, for Christ's sake. Priscilla may still expound unto Apollos the way of God more accurately (Acts 18:26), and his influence become far mightier in the work of God, and she share in the reward in the day of Christ. And blessed is the eloquent, learned Apollos who is humble enough to receive instruction in the Word from a woman.

Lines written by Miss Paget when her sisters and friends wished her to leave Barnstaple, November, 1857, to reside in Exeter.

> I cannot now return to thee,
> I cannot leave my rest;
> For here God's children comfort me,
> And here I find I'm blest.
> We worship not neath fretted dome,
> Or organ's feeling sound,
> Nor where the dim light streams athwart
> The long aisle's sculptured round;
> But simply, as of old they came,
>
> According to the Word,
> They met in Jesus' sacred Name,
> And called upon the Lord.
> No priests adorned with priestly pride,

No altar railed around,
No multitude of mixed race
Are meeting on the ground;
But worshippers sincere are there,
And there the wine and bread,
Mysterious emblems of their Lord
Who for them groaned and bled.
Mysterious! for by faith we look
Beyond the outward sign
To Him, who now will come again
In glory all divine;
To Him, Who said, Take this and eat,
Drink and remember Me—
We do it, Lord, for thy dear sake,
And long Thy face to see:
We do it in sweet fellowship.
Communion with each other;
Not as a stranger alien host,
But brother now with brother.

Then, loved one, call me not away
From this dear chosen band;
I've much to learn, here let me stay,
That I may understand
More perfectly the will of God,
The love of God to me,
That love which changed to sunny calm
Life's dark and troubled sea;
That love which drew me nearer Him.
My portion and my stay,
My port in storms,
My light in clouds,
My Lord, my life, my way!

3

Dominant Qualities

Why was Mary chosen from among all the virgins of Israel to be the mother of the Lord's Anointed? What had the grace of God produced in this young woman that she was known among the angels as one highly favoured, one with whom their Lord was? Her song of praise unto the Lord is also an unconscious revelation of herself (Luke 1:46–55). She knew God as her own Saviour; she owned her own low estate; she knew God as He truly is, mighty, holy, merciful, the helper of His servants, faithful to keep His word to Abraham and his seed. She knew that to fear Him is a condition of His blessing; that He abhors the proud, exalts the lowly, fills the hungry. And that He so filled and exalted her proves that these qualities were hers.

It is to him that hath that abundance shall be given (Matthew 25:29). To him that hath what? Obviously the capacity to use what may be entrusted[1] and readiness to be faithful and diligent in the trust. A sinner's salvation is not here in the question: that is a "free gift" without conditions precedent or consequent. But the privileges of service are contingent upon the qualities found in the servant.

What had the grace of God produced in A. N. Groves that such special service could be entrusted to him?

Like Mary, he too, as we have seen, knew his "low estate" as a son of Adam; like her he trusted in the mercy of the Lord that exalts the lowly; he also, and perhaps with richer meaning than Mary, could say "God *my* Saviour," for he was deeply assured of the *eternal* favour of God in Christ Jesus.

Upon this solid foundation the Spirit of truth built into his character, by means of the new spiritual nature, other vastly important qualities most necessary to make him, or others, vessels fit for the Master's use in high and uncommon degree.

---

1. "To each according to his several ability," ver. 15.

1. The Will of God

I delight to do Thy will, O my God (Psalm 40:8).

The holy God is perfectly good, therefore is His will perfectly good. To move in perfect harmony with that will is to be assured that "all things work together for good" (Romans 8:28); to be out of that harmony is to secure to oneself the uncertainty and misery that ever attend disorder. David endured years of outlawry, exile, danger, privation, and all manner of hardship. Yet he was "suffering according to the will of God" (1 Peter 4:19) for him, in preparation, the indispensable preparation, for his task of lifting God's people from humiliation to triumph. Reviewing that period of his life he could see and say that "as for God, his way is perfect. . . and he maketh my way perfect," which testimony the Spirit of God thought good to record twice for our instruction and encouragement in patient endurance (2 Samuel 22:31, 33; Psalm 18:30, 32).

A first secret of A. N. Groves' rapid advance in godliness and usefulness is given by this sentence of his biographer concerning the period after his conversion:

> He grew rapidly in the knowledge of God, having, as his own narrative will show, a desire to fulfil *all* the will of God, as soon as it was revealed to him (4).

In like manner could George Müller write as to his state of heart in the year 1830:

> It had pleased God, in his abundant mercy, to bring my mind into such a state that I was willing to carry out into my life whatever I should find in the Scriptures concerning the ordinance [baptism], either the one way or the other. I could say, "*I will do his will*," and it was on this account, I believe, that I soon saw which "*doctrine is of God*," whether infant baptism or believers' baptism (*Narrative*, 65).

Mr. Müller had taken the full theological course for the ministry of the Lutheran Church, which practises infant baptism, but in simple obedience to the will of God he was now baptized as a believer, as Mr. Groves had been in the preceding year (36).

On page 479 of the *Memoir* Mr. Groves mentions a visit to "R.C." at Barnstaple. This was R. C. Chapman, of whom, in a memorial notice, Dr. A. T. Pierson said there were men who brought to mind the words "there were giants in the earth in those days." The same attitude to the will of God marked him also. The late Mr. E. S. Pearce, who lived with him and knew him intimately, wrote to me:

> It was Mr. Chapman's desire that, by so walking with God and by obedience to His Word in *all* things, he might not shut himself out from the honour of reigning with Christ. He saw no authority from the Scripture for saying that all the children of God would. Revelation 20:4, "And they sat upon them" Mr. Chapman considered were distinguished persons, not *all* the saints."

The *Memoir* abounds with striking sayings upon this vital matter.

> I am happy when I can do my Lord's will, and unhappy when I fail; not because I fear, but love Him (250). . . . My Lord seems to assure me He will uphold His poor servant, notwithstanding all his unimaginable weakness, because He knows I have told him He shall do as He lists with me, and I would not rebel, though it should involve ten times more unhappiness in this world than I have ever yet felt, and that I am fully prepared, by His grace, to follow His way and not my own. I know I have been very unsubdued to that will, and the Lord therefore dealt with me as a Father, who knew where my disease was and the remedy (259).

The last sentence refers to the terribly severe afflictions of the preceding year (1832) in Bagdad, including the death of his wife and infant daughter, which will be noticed later. In the same year he wrote:

> In reading today the third of Matthew, verse 15, I am much struck with the humility of our great Exemplar. He does not say, what can baptism do? or what can it not do? but, if it be His Father's appointment, the least thing is as much an act of "righteousness" as the greatest. Indeed, it is these things that very much manifest a child-like spirit. To obey, when you see a plain and palpable reason, is nothing; but to obey, because He hath enjoined it, though we see nothing to issue from it, is true obedience.
>
> I often feel how blessed that simple faith is that realizes all His will as a sufficient source of joy, and accepts all His ways with *thankfulness*. I

feel I have only yet attained *submission* (264). . . . O, may I arrive among you, with a sweeter savour of Jesus, and with a heart and all its will and affections more simply identified with, and consecrated to, the will of Him, whose will is at once the rule, liberty, joy, and glory of all unfallen creation (324). . . . Today I addressed the little company here on God's love; and I do not know that I ever before felt so thankful for God's great indignation against disobedience to His blessed will; seeing that in it is wrapped up the essence of mercy. I see so much love in it; and having been able to see how ineffably hateful sin is to God, my soul desires to loathe it in its least goings forth (352, 353). . . . I sometimes think God is leading me by the golden thread of His chastening grace, out of where I am, to where I ought to be. Indeed, I trust He is teaching me more to love His will, though it crosses mine. I do truly desire to bend before His gracious hand, however heavy, for I feel I have deserved it all (413). . . . I leave all external circumstances with the Lord; as He decides, so I shall arrange my affairs, and I know it shall be well. I am content with bread and water, if only we are flourishing in grace; without that, all the world would be to me as nothing. O, that all His will may be more and more the aim and the end of life (419).

From the literary point of view, as well as the spiritual, Romans 12:1–2 is a singularly beautiful passage:

I beseech you, therefore, brethren, by the mercies of God, to present your bodies, a living sacrifice, holy, well-pleasing to God, which is your reasonable service. And be not fashioned according to this age: but be ye transformed by the renewing of your mind, that ye may prove what is the good and well-pleasing and perfect will of God.

Constrained by the marvellous "mercies of God" the believer, out of gratitude, is to dedicate his *body* unreservedly to God. It does not say "yield," as of a passive submission to superior right or to force; but "present," that is actively, with full intelligence and intention, the will deliberately granting to another possession of the article so presented; for the full property right in a present is given up to the receiver, and no more belongs in any degree to the giver.

It is the body that is to be so dedicated. But it is in the body that the man himself, the ego, the soul, with all his powers, dwells. Now he who presents to another a purse gives also all that may be in it, and thenceforth the receiver alone owns and may use both purse and contents. His right is indefeasible.

This surrender to God on the part of man is but "reasonable." God created the body and granted it to man to use for its Creator's glory. Man misuses this instrument; the first act of human sin was a misuse of ears, listening to the tempter; of eyes, doting upon the thing forbidden; of feet, moving toward it; of hands, taking it; of mouth, eating it; of feet and hands carrying it to Adam to do the same. Thus we sin "by means of the body" and for this must be judged (2 Corinthians 5:10). In the body we receive already much chastisement; in a resurrection body eternal punishment must be endured. Deliverance from this sinful misuse can come only by the wholly right and reasonable act of dedicating the instrument of all action to God, to do only His will.

Moreover, through the divine mercy, the Son of God took a human body, prepared for Him by the Father, that in it He, being thus man, might do the will of God on earth. In that holy body "He bore our sins upon the tree" (1 Peter 2:24), suffering in body and soul the pains and penalties due to us in body and soul. By this redemptive work He secured for us exemption for the body from that eternal penalty due, and opened the prospect that the believer may attain to a body of glory, such as Himself has received through the glory of the Father. But by redemption all proprietary rights in the thing redeemed pass inalienably to the redeemer. "Ye are not your own; for ye were bought with a price: glorify God therefore in your body" (1 Corinthians 6:19–20). Thus the creative right of God over our body is doubled by the redemptive right of Christ.

But he who sets out to live upon the principle of admitting in practice the rights of God has adopted an exactly contrary principle to that of the world, and thenceforth he may not be "fashioned according to this age." The word "fashioned" has at its basis the word "scheme," and Anglicized would read "be not syschematized to this age." Beneath all the diversities of races and climates there runs a scheme which unifies the whole human race. It was introduced by the prince of this world at the fall, and has as its main feature that man shall alienate himself from God, serve himself by his body, and thereby serve the end of Satan to rob and dishonour God to his own aggrandisement. Evidently he who dedicates his body to God must wholly disregard the world's ways and opinions as far as they further this scheme. And so quite early Groves wrote:

> As to the opinions of men, I feel they have their place and value in the things of the world, but, in the things of Christ, they are of no value but in proportion to their accordance with that Word [of God], and to that they must be brought as to the scales in which they are to be weighed (47).

And again:

> Let your eye simply rest on the truth of God, and not on man's opinions. What they may think is of little consequence, what He says is of infinite moment (205).

And of missionary work in India, as he found it on arriving, he wrote in 1834:

> From my arrival in Bombay to the day I reached Jaffna [Ceylon: it was a period of seven months, July 1833 to January 1834], I had been continually hoping to find missionary institutions carried on with that simplicity which, I think, so highly becomes us, but I have been deeply disappointed. Wherever I have been, the system of the world and its character of influence have been adopted, instead of the moral power of the self-denial of the gospel. I trust the Lord has allowed my coming here to be of some little use in eradicating this baneful system (274).

To maintain outward nonconformity to the world and conformity to God the believer needs ever more to be "transformed by the renewing of the mind," for what rules in the mind is displayed in the actions of the body. How blessed to be able to say with Paul, "We have the mind of Christ" (1 Corinthians 2:16). A man narrated to another an injury that had been done to him, and asked, "Do you not think it would be manly to resent such conduct?" "Yes," was the reply, "it would be manly to resent it, but it would be godly to forgive it!"

Truly this was a new mind to be found in a human heart, and it is by the dominance of this new mind over conduct that the sinner is "transformed" into a saint.

The word "transformed" is that which is used of the Lord on the holy mount, "He was transfigured before them." By the response of our heart to the revelation His Spirit gives of His moral glory we are morally "transfigured into the same image" (Matthew 17:2; Mark 9:2; 2 Corinthians 3:18). The scientist uses this word when he speaks of the caterpillar being *metamorphosed* into the handsome moth, or the seed into the gorgeous flower. It is the life within developing its full possibilities.

There can be no metamorphosis unless life lies in the seed or cocoon; the sinner must be born of God before the new life, with its new mind about matters, can develop. But this development may, alas, be hindered, thwarted. Paul knew his Galatian converts had the divine life, but he could not yet see Christ being formed in them, which defect pained him deeply (Galatians 4:19). For the Ephesian saints he prayed fervently that Christ might dwell in their hearts, by the powerful working of the Spirit, and on their part by faith (Ephesians 3:16–17); and to the Colossians he stated that "Christ in you is the hope of glory" (1:27). He does not say that Christ dying *for* you is the hope of glory, but Christ *in* you; for it is the advance of a process of manufacture that gives ground for confidence that there will be a finished article. The purchase price that buys the materials is the necessary basis of all, but the process of manufacture is equally necessary, for without the latter the former cannot reach its full purpose.

But in the believer who dedicates his body wholly to the Lord the Spirit can work freely, and will do so increasingly; and the sure and soul-harmonizing result will be that such an one will prove by blessed experience that the will of God is "good and well-pleasing, and perfect." He will be enabled in his measure to say with the Son of God on earth, "I delight to do Thy will, O my God; yea, Thy law is within my heart" (Psalm 40:8). Groves had been brought to this happy state and could say:

> I do so desire to deal with my Father with that love and loyalty that hate rebellion against the *least* intimation of His will. . . . I think I can call God to witness, that I desire to know the whole of His holy will (333).

This attitude of heart to the will of God is so fundamental to life and progress in His fellowship, and so characteristic of those who have been greatly used of Him, that it will be well to resume the quotation from George Müller commenced above:

> the passage to which I have just now alluded, John 7:17 ["If any man willeth (intendeth) to do His will, he shall know of the teaching, whether it is of God"] has been a most remarkable comment to me on many doctrines and precepts of our most holy faith. For instance: *"Resist not evil: but whosoever shall smite thee on thy right cheek, turn to him the other also. And if any man will sue thee at the law, and take away thy coat, let him have thy cloak also. And whosoever shall compel thee to go a mile, go with him twain. Give to him that asketh of thee, and from him that would borrow of thee turn not thou away. Love your enemies, bless them that curse you, do good to them that hate you, and pray for them which despitefully use you, and persecute you,"* Matthew 5:39–44. *"Sell that ye have, and give alms,"* Luke 12:33. *"Owe no man anything, but to love one another,"* Romans 13:8. It may be said, surely, these passages cannot be taken literally, for how then should the people of God be able to pass through the world. The state of mind enjoined in John 7:17, will cause such objections to vanish. WHOSOEVER IS WILLING TO ACT OUT these commandments of the Lord LITERALLY will, I believe, be led with me to see that, to take them LITERALLY, is the will of God. Those who do so take them will doubtless often be brought into difficulties, hard to the flesh to bear, but these will have a tendency to make them constantly feel that they are strangers and pilgrims here, that this world is not their home, and thus to throw them more upon God, who will assuredly help us through any difficulty into which we may be brought by seeking to act in obedience to His word (*Narrative* 65, 66).

Nor should any think that such entire acceptance of the will of God is something that no doubt is seemly to those of older years and possible to those advanced in grace, but too exacting and too difficult for younger men and women. At the time in view George Müller was twenty-four, and Groves about thirty. It never can be too early to give unto God what is simply His right.

Nor let anyone suppose that so full and early an agreement with God impoverishes life and makes it melancholy. Of that very time we read:

> It was at this period the Editor first became acquainted with Mr. Groves; and the happy state of his mind was such, that all who came in contact

with him received a blessing. Very many trace to this period the beginning of undertakings for the Lord, which to this day are monuments
of the blessedness still found in trusting in God, and in unreserved
surrender of our all to Him. . . it was his own happy testimony of the
enjoyment of giving up all for His sake, which so impressed her [the
Editor] with the reality of that truth, "His service is perfect freedom";
so that, could she have obtained the consent of her only remaining parent, she would gladly have formed one of their missionary party—so
precious and glorious a thing did it seem to forsake all for Jesus (35).

This desire was granted later when she became Mr. Groves' second
wife.

Thus infectious is the gladness of a life wholly harmonized with
God. Surely this acceptance of the will of God was the yoke which
the Son of Man carried and which He invites us to bear with Him.
In the will of God He found rest, and He promises that rest to those
who bear the same yoke. For the yoke on the ox, which looks so
heavy, in reality makes light the hard toil of the plough or laden cart.
In that yoke Christ found joy and satisfaction, even when the will of
God brought to Him base ingratitude, callous rejection, bitter opposition from the very cities He had most graced with His presence and
blessed with His gifts. And so Luke's painstaking inquiries enabled
him to record of the occasion when Jesus upbraided the ungrateful
cities, that "in that same hour He rejoiced in the Holy Spirit, and
said: I thank thee, O Father. . . . Yea, Father; for so it was well pleasing in thy sight" (Luke 10:21–22 with Matthew 11:20–30). Paul
describes the almost incredible toils and sufferings of twenty long
years in the service of Christ as being but "light" and momentary
(2 Corinthians 4:17). He uses the same word as the Lord when He
said: "My burden is light," and thus from deep experience sets his
seal to the truth of his Master's statement.

Oh, to sing with full understanding and resolute intention:

> I worship thee, sweet will of God,
> And all thy ways adore,
> And every day I live I seem
> To love thee more and more;

or with another deeply tried and experienced saint:

Thy wonderful, grand will, my God,
With triumph now I make it mine:
And faith shall cry a joyous, Yes!
To every dear command of Thine.

It is but our reasonable service; let us render it; that we too may find it the entrance to a life of rest, power, usefulness.

The following letter by George Müller, hitherto unpublished, is too notable a testimony to be lost. It shows very strikingly how the principle of devotion to God and to His Word operated in and sustained that man of faith throughout his long and blessed course. The letter was addressed to Mr. J. Gordon Logan, at one time working in the gospel in Egypt. My copy was taken by me from the original when staying with Mr. Logan there in 1910.

New Orphan Houses,
Ashley Down,
Bristol,
July 17th, 1895

Dear Sir,

I became a believer in the Lord Jesus in the beginning of Nov. 1825, now 69 years and eight months. For the first four years afterwards, it was for a good part in great weakness; but in July 1829, now 66 years since, it came with me to an entire and full surrender of heart. I gave myself fully to the Lord. Honour, pleasure, money, my physical powers, my mental powers, all was laid down to the feet of Jesus, and I became a great lover of the Word of God. I found my all in God; and thus, in all my trials of a temporal and spiritual character it has remained for 66 years. My faith is not merely exercised regarding temporal things; but regarding everything: because I cleave to the Word. My knowledge of God and His Word is that which helps me.

Yours sincerely,
George Müller

Now, as shown on p. 18 above, July 1829 was the very time when he first came under the influence of Mr. Groves, and by December of that year he had taken the step of faith in God as to service and earthly support. No one can become an imitator of such men who does not wholeheartedly adopt their inner life of unreserved devotion to the will of God as revealed in His Word. But each who does this can say: "Thy statutes have been *my songs* in the house of my pilgrimage" (Psalm 119:54). Yet this singing pilgrim will meet much to exercise his heart. It is one deeply experienced in the ways of the Lord who will say: "My faith is exercised regarding everything *because* I cleave to the Word"; for that divine Word directs the soul into circumstances which test it, for its purifying and enriching and perfecting for royal service to God and man. The heartlessness of his brethren, the cunning of Potiphar's wife, the weight and cruelty of Potiphar's fetters were the instruments of Joseph's testing and perfecting, but in deeper spiritual reality it was "the word of Jehovah tried him" (Psalm 105:19). Had he disregarded that word and broken the seventh commandment he might not have been in prison, but obedience to the Word of his God cost him his freedom, which tried his fidelity, but it saved to him his moral freedom and a good conscience, and fitted him for his noble future.

2. The Word of God

The writer once pressed a high church clergyman to justify the use of the pagan-derived practice of worshipping toward the east, seeing that the Word of God uniformly rejects and denounces it.[1] The discussion raised the question of how we can ascertain the will of God. The churchman said it was by prayer. It was answered that both of us prayed, but each reached an opposite conclusion upon the point in hand and many others. It was urged that in prayer we speak to God, but that it is in His Word that He speaks to us, upon all matters with which that Word deals, and that therefore it is from that Word that the mind of God must be learned. It follows that obedience to it is a first duty, and an essential condition of communion with God and

---

1. Egyptian temples usually faced west and worship was towards the east, as part of the worship of the sun. Moses, taught of God, reversed this, and the tabernacle faced east and worship was toward the west (Numbers 3:38). It was so with the temple of Solomon. Apostates who worshipped the sun had to turn their backs on the temple of Jehovah (Ezekiel 8:16), and this was the culminating iniquity that brought the wrath of God and the destruction of the temple. It will be so in the future temple: "the forefront of the house was toward the east" (Ezekiel 43:1–4; 47:1).

of co-operation with Him in His affairs. Failing such knowledge so gained, or such obedience, we can only follow human intelligence, or human folly, and our best intended labours may be rather working against God than with Him.

A. N. Groves early saw this principle. One of the many to whom he was made a great blessing was the afterward celebrated Bible scholar Dr. Kitto, whom he greatly befriended in his youth, and who was a member of his household for a great while. Of Mr. Groves he wrote:

> You ask "is Mr. Groves an Arminian, a Calvinist, a Papist, a Lutheran?" He is one of those singular characters, a Bible Christian, and a disciple of the meek and lowly Jesus; not *nominally*, but practically and really such. A man so devotedly, so fervently, attached to the Scriptures, I never knew before. This is the best criterion I can furnish you of his character and disposition (5).

And his biographer adds:

> Truly may it be said that this devoted love of God's Word was that which distinguished him to the end of his course.

To this his own statements bear abundant witness, and deserve the closest consideration, as revealing a chief secret of his saintliness and spiritual power. Writing to a friend preparing for the ministry of the Word he said:

> If I might be allowed to rejoice in one thing more than another, it is in the singleness of heart and eye which I trace growing within you... I am sure it is the way to find the largest measure of happiness even earthly things can yield; besides, and above all, being the key that unlocks those things in the Divine Word which are hard to understand, and for this reason, that we come to the consideration of them with hearts preoccupied by a ready-made decision, more in union with the worldly systems by which we are pressed on every side. And, against all this overwhelming influence, there is but one remedy, to read the word of God with a single view to know His will, by whom it was inspired; and then the baseless nature of all systems but the one that has a single and undivided reference to the glory of God, and the advancement of His kingdom appears as clearly as if it were the subject of material vision (10, 11).

The penetrating insight into spiritual affairs here shown is unusual in one but thirty years of age and a believer of some ten years. The necessity for singleness of heart to please God as the secret of coming to understand the deeper truths in the Word; the blinding influence, the block upon progress in knowledge, of a heart preoccupied with a ready-made decision; the hindering power of harmony with worldly systems; the baseless nature of all that has not sole reference to the glory of God; that there is a spiritual vision that can make spiritual objects as clear as material vision makes material objects; that the one remedy against those spiritual dangers is to read the Word of God with the single view to know His will—these momentous matters are seen distinctly, and in their relations to one another, as by a divinely enlightened mind, and are set together in one short statement as by a master hand.

But three years before he so wrote he had been made to see something which, seen and practised in theological halls, would revolutionize preparation for the ministry of the gospel, as it did in fact his own preparation. To feel the full significance of his words it must be remembered that he was possessed of an active and versatile mind; was well educated; had mastered not only his own profession of dentistry, so as in a very few years to have an income of £1,500 a year (worth then very much more than now), but had studied chemistry with a leading London firm, and had walked a hospital and acquired considerable skill in surgery. At Plymouth, when only twenty years of age, he devoted himself to scientific objects, and was a leading member of the Athenaeum Literary Society, in which his talents were much appreciated. It was such a one, gifted and brilliant, and no dullard, who says to us:

> About this time [his twenty-seventh year] I was led to see that the plan I had been pursuing of making myself acquainted with *general literature,* in order to gain influence over those I came in contact with, *was founded in error,* and I was led to believe, that if I laid aside these false grounds of Christian influence, and gave myself up to the study of His holy Word, the Lord would lead me to learn such principles from it, that I should *see* its sufficiency. From this moment the Lord began to bless me, and was about to commence that great work of stripping off from our united

hearts the thick clog with which we [himself and his wife] had been cumbering ourselves so many years, and to show us that nothing is too hard for Him (27, 28).

It appears that this adoption of a sound and reverent attitude to the Word of God as *sufficient* was the next great advance in his spiritual experience after his conversion about seven years earlier. How different is such a preparation for the ministry of the Word to that generally sought and given. Sitting with an aged Doctor of Divinity, the learned principal of a theological college, one found that his whole mind ran philosophically and not really theologically. He dilated fluently upon Kant, Hegel and Schleiermacher, but all my attempts, as much his junior, to draw upon him for instruction from Paul and John were fruitless. Yet we dare assert confidently that only by such a concentration upon the Holy Scriptures as *sufficient* can there be the slightest hope for a fulfilment of the wish expressed by Dr. Hatch in his Hibbert Lectures (114, 115):

> The hope of Christianity is that the class [of rhetorical sermonizers] which was artificially created may ultimately disappear; and that the sophistical element in Christian preaching will melt, as a transient mist, before the preaching of the prophets of the ages to come, who, like the prophets of the ages that are long gone by, will speak only "as the Spirit gives them utterance."

Ere long Groves writes:

> What little leisure I have for reading is confined to God's Word, the book of our Father's wisdom. I have very little confidence in man; my great desire has been to cast myself on the Word of God, that every judgment of my soul, concerning all things, may be right, by being, in all, the mind of God. For exactly in proportion as this is the case, shall we be a blessing to others (43).

Let the reader test the state of his own mind against this self-revelation. Every judgment formed is to correspond with exactness to the mind of God, and no subject of thought whatever is to be an exception. Such phrases, therefore, are entirely ruled out as, "I think so and so," "I have a right to my own opinion." Human judgment distrusted; the mind of God sought from His Word, and the whole

inward man subjected thereto: what a wholesome, correcting, illuminating principle.

Yet it was not that he claimed to have reached perfection, though
he longed after and aimed at it; for twenty years later, in 1847, he
wrote:

> I sometimes for a moment feel as though I might one day experience
> the Spirit's power in bringing every thought into obedience to Christ. I
> *know* now it is the only pathway of service (452).

We are reminded of two contrasted statements of a true master
mind, even judged naturally. The deep springs of action in Saul of
Tarsus are given in this one sentence: "I verily *thought with myself*
that I ought to do many things" (Acts 26:9). The profound, all-pervading, inward revolution that changed Saul, the sincere but blinded
bigot, into Paul, the receiver and revealer of the secrets of the Most
High God, he himself states in this one sentence: "not that we are
sufficient of ourselves to account [to reckon, to form a judgment
about] anything as from ourselves; but our sufficiency is from God"
(2 Corinthians 3:5).

Yea, we are reminded by Paul and by Groves of those words by
which the Son of God drew back the veil that we might look within
His perfect heart: "Meek am I, and lowly in heart" (Matthew 11:29);
even as He had before said: "I can of myself do nothing: as I hear I
judge: and my judgment is righteous; because I seek not mine own
will, but the will of him that sent me" (John 5:30). Groves' words are
an echo of these; for Christ was being formed in him, by the Spirit,
and that was becoming true with him, which had been seen perfectly
in the Lord Jesus, that He knew and heeded all that was written in
His Father's Book.

Thus we read again, words written in 1828, perhaps two years
after the former:

> My very constant prayer is that the Lord would lead my poor wandering
> heart into all truth, and make His holy Word my light and comfort. I
> feel how much I need very humble and patient waiting for the Lord's
> manifestation of His will, that I may not fall into any error. I walk very
> fearfully, and the more I feel I differ from most about me, the more

sensible I am of the very great need of the light of the Lord to guide me through the difficulties which surround me. My firm purpose is, by the grace of God, to follow simply the word of God, contending for what it plainly reveals with boldness, and with respect to those things not so plainly revealed, to remain in doubt; this must, doubtless, expose me to much from those I love, that I would not willingly incur, but I fear I cannot help it (45, 46).

It was by maintaining this humble spirit that he, in due time, penetrated far into the present experience and enjoyments of things divine, and inherited the promise: "Blessed are the poor in spirit: for theirs is the kingdom of the heavens" (Matthew 5:3). In 1847, his fifty-second year, he wrote: "What a hard lesson it is to learn to be 'poor in spirit' as well as 'pure in heart'; yet these are lessons that must be learnt, if we would enjoy spiritual peace"(449). Is not John Newton's verse an admirable description of this true poverty of spirit?

> As a little child relies
> On a care beyond his own,
> Knows he's neither great nor wise,
> Fears to stir a step alone,
> Let me thus with Thee abide
> As my Father, Guard and Guide.

This attitude to the Word of God characterized Mr. Groves' whole career.

Of their life in Bagdad in 1832, four years later than the above lengthy extract, his eldest son wrote:

In nothing was this period more marked than for the earnest study of the Word: it was regarded truly as "the light unto the feet and the lamp unto the path" of the child of God; obedience to it in everything being the one thing needful to those who would love the Lord (218).

In the next year, 1833, he himself writes:

Wherever I can literally follow Scripture, I feel easy as to the act; where I cannot, or fancy I cannot, I feel weak in proportion to my distance from it (229).

And again:

Remember our old rule, to judge according to God's Word; let us be neither frightened nor allured from it: believe me, my dear brother, it will be the rock on which our battle with infidelity must be fought; therefore now learn to *trust* your sword, for it will cut deep if well wielded under the power of the Spirit (249).

Such words have proved prophetic. When he wrote them infidelity was still outside of the churches; now it is very widely within them. As Begbie in his life of William Booth sarcastically but truly said of a great English Abbey: If the Bible is still in the lectern, the *Origin of Species* is in the pulpit! And no one can do anything to withstand this devastating tide except he be firmly set upon this rock, the Word of God as sufficient, authoritative, binding, permanent. To hear those Nonconformist orators, who have thrown away such faith in and submission to the Word of God as Groves had, declaim against the Roman Catholic Church, or any other spiritual foe, would be ludicrous were it not so solemn and dangerous. The trained battalions of evil smile at wooden swords, with whatever shouting they are flourished; but they still dread the sword of the Word "well wielded under the power of the Spirit." It is idle to shout "The sword of Jehovah and of Gideon" if it be a paper sword.

He spoke above of differing from most about him. Perhaps in nothing did he more radically differ from the majority of persons around him than in this fixed principle to follow the Word of God only. Certainly in this he was in his day very much of a pioneer. In 1834 he writes from India:

Sometimes my heart seems bewildered in the labyrinth of thoughts and difficulties that lie before me; it does seem so hard simply and fully to follow the word of the living God. Most persons you meet will hardly look at even the picture of it; and if we will not, how can God fully bless us? for it must be His own ways, His own plans, His own principles, that He will honour, and not ours (280).

And in 1838 he adds:

Dear Caldecott well says that the struggle now is between the Word and tradition. It ever has been, it ever was among the Jews, and is among the Gentiles. We take our stand on the Word; and in proportion to our practical inconsistency with it, will our testimony be weakened (385).

In his quite unique and fascinating survey of church history, *The Pilgrim Church*, Mr. E. H. Broadbent has shown that, all through the Christian age, as spiritual life declined, God has again and again quickened the testimony to the truth by turning godly minds away from human tradition and opinion to His Word, strengthening them to search for His mind, to follow it as far as they perceived it, and to suffer for doing so. The Brethren movement was such a quickening, and in marked degree displayed this dominant feature. In his *History* (3) Neatby says justly:

> The Brethren sought to effect a fresh start without authority, precedent, or guidance beyond the letter of Holy Scripture. For them, essentially, the garnered experience of eighteen Christian centuries was as though it were not. Such an experiment in the hands of eminent men could scarcely fail to yield a considerable harvest of interest and instruction; and it has actually shed, if I mistake not, a flood of light on many of the obscurities and incredibilities of the history of the Church.

The addition which needs to be made to this statement is that these men did not rely upon their eminence in natural talents or acquirements to explain the Scriptures. They believed in the Spirit of truth; and so Groves speaks of guidance "by the Word and Spirit of God, which is always promised to us for asking" (420).

As a further example of how this attitude to the Word of God, and conjoint dependence upon the Spirit of God, was as a tap root that nourished the spiritual life of the mighty men of God of that period, we may again listen to George Müller.

Speaking of his first intercourse in 1829 with that learned scholar and theologian, Henry Craik, with whom he was later associated closely for many years, and of the influence at once exerted upon him, Mr. Müller writes:

> I will mention some points which God then began to show me. 1. That the Word of God alone is our standard of judgment in spiritual things; that it can be explained only by the Holy Spirit; and that in our day, as well as in former times, he is the teacher of his people. The office of the

Holy Spirit I had not experimentally understood before that time... the Holy Spirit alone can teach us. . . it was my beginning to understand this latter point in particular, which had a wonderful effect on me; for the Lord enabled me to put it to the test of experience, by laying aside commentaries, and almost every other book, and simply reading the word of God and studying it. The result of this was, that the first evening I shut myself into my room to give myself to prayer and meditation over the Scriptures, I learned more in a few hours than I had done during a period of several months previously. *But the particular difference was, that I received real strength for my soul in doing so.* I now began to try by the test of the Scriptures the things which I had learned and seen, and found that only those principles which stood the test were really of value (*Narrative* 46).

Here, then, was a man of ability, who had taken a full theological course for the ministry, who knew Hebrew, Greek, Latin, German, and English, but did not know experimentally that the Holy Spirit alone can teach us the truth of God or that the Word of God is the only standard for things spiritual. And seeing how general this, alas, is, it is no wonder that the severe comparison of that mighty evangelist, C. G. Finney, remains true, when he said of the men sent out in his day from the colleges to the pulpits, that they were like men who should leave a naval college knowing everything except how to navigate a ship!

Similarly R. C. Chapman, speaking in 1854 to two lately converted children of another leading man in that circle, H. W. Soltau, said:

Never forget how blessed it is to have the heart stored with the Word of God. Before I was brought to the Lord I slept with my copy of Homer under my pillow, but in the year 1823 the Lord brought me to Himself [it was his twentieth year] and gave me a vision, the only vision in my life. I distinctly saw an arm and a hand pointing with a finger to an open Bible and I believe the Bible was open at Psalm 119. Ever since, this has been my meat and drink (Cable, *A Woman Who Laughed* 40).

And H. W. Soltau himself said of the first Brethren:

They cast away all traditions, and read the Bible without note or comment. Many of them were men of understanding and learning, but they laid aside all traditions and commentaries, and resolved, by the help of God, to search for themselves (*Who are the Brethren* 7).

It was not that men like Groves, Craik, Müller, or Darby under-rated general or special learning. On the contrary, they used it to the full. As another scholar, G. H. Pember, said to me: "I took honours in classics at Cambridge, but I did it in my unconverted days for my own glory. Since I have known the Lord, however, I have tried to use it for the spread of the truth."

Nor should it be thought that Groves, Müller, or other such despised the writings of other godly men. That would have been to despise the use the Spirit had made of those men and their books. Groves' *Memoir* contains reference to various books read and express-es a desire for the preparation of good writings for use in India (429), and George Müller, through his Scriptural Knowledge Institution, distributed vast quantities of spiritual literature. And Darby in the Introductory Notice to his New Translation of the Bible says: "all available helps have been used, different versions and commentaries having been laid under contribution." Their statements that they read little but the Bible come from the opening period of spiritual life and when they had first come to see that they had been giving too large a place to the books of men and too little to the Book of God, and commenced to reverse this proportion. This being accomplished, and the Scriptures having gained their proper dominance, they could use safely and worthily what God had given other godly men to teach to His church, yet ever preserving to the divine oracles their pre-eminent place. Of a five months' voyage from Calcutta to England in 1834 Groves wrote:

> I allow myself an hour or two of retirement every day, which tends to compose my spirits into a patient waiting on the mind and ordering of Christ. Just at the end of this time, before I leave my cabin, Arundoo, the Hindoo, comes in, and we have a little prayer together: besides this, I do little but write, and read God's word: thus my days pass on (332).

A very different, and far more profitable, sea voyage this, than what some of us know too well on a modern liner, with its quin-tessence of worldly, time-wasting folly, amidst which the spiritual man is in daily danger and conflict! Prayer, the Word, and writing filled the quiet days; the last showing that he did not discountenance others reading more than the Bible, or he would not have written anything for others to read. But what he wrote he sought to draw from the Word, so as to help others to understand it. And this is the true test of other books: do they illuminate the Holy Scriptures? If so, let us be thankful for them and use them, especially if we are of the majority who cannot ourselves study the Word in the original tongues. A thousand allusions to the then common life of men cannot be understood without some knowledge of that ancient and oriental life, and preachers and teachers especially do well to read works which explain that life.

Yet it remains to emphasize that to these men the Bible was the *only standard* and *test* in things spiritual. Many children of God shrink from this. In present-day declarations of faith by evangelical bodies it is not seldom stated that the Word of God is the *supreme* standard of doctrine and practice. This is far below the position that Holy Scripture is the *sole* standard. The other allows to the Book of Common Prayer, or the Westminster Confession, or a denominational text-book, or a trust deed of a building, or to human reason, *some* right to be heard, *some* degree of authority, even if less than attaches to the Word of the living God.

This simply falsifies the position and stultifies action. In *practice* men tend to follow the lower standard, because it is necessarily easier to nature to do so. Of the written Word and its requirements even good men, disciples, say what men said of the demands made upon them by the living Word: "This is a hard saying, who can hear it?" and still many of His disciples go back and walk no more with Him (John 6:60–66). But blessed, thrice blessed, are all the family of Caleb; they "follow the Lord fully and wholly," they conquer the wilderness, they win their inheritance, they have repeated and honourable mention in the records of God, and when they are old they still have the vigour of their youth (Numbers 14:24; Deuteronomy 1:36; Joshua 14:6–15).

God has said, "to this man will I look, even to him that is poor and of a contrite spirit, and that trembleth at my word" (Isaiah 66:2).

Groves could write: "O for a meek, lowly, and contrite spirit, that trembles at God's word, whilst fearless of all besides" (407), and God indeed "looked" upon him, that is, gave him His divine attention and favour.

How very great is the loss of such as are of a class he describes:

Christians here feel the truth of these and other principles that I hold, but they dread them and their consequences (311);

and again :

I spent last evening with some who desire the truth, yet dread the price. O! that they knew the preciousness of Him whose service, to those who love Him, is perfect freedom (323).

3. THE SON OF GOD

Christ our life. Colossians 3:4.
To me to live is Christ. Philippians 1:21.

The last quotation spoke of "the preciousness of Him whose service, to those who love Him, is perfect freedom." A. N. Groves loved Him with all his heart, soul, mind, and strength, or at least, as himself would have said, he longed and sought to do so.

Heart attitude to Christ, the Son of God, is the highest and surest test of a soul. The ultimate end of God in all the universe is that the Son shall inherit it (Hebrews 1:2); for this it was intended before it was made. In Christ as man it is at last to be headed up, to find its apex, as the top stone of a pyramid (Ephesians 1:10). Pursuing this purpose, the Father, out of divine, ineffable love to the Son, has committed all things into His hand, a fact frequently emphasized (John 3:35; 5:19–29; 13:3; etc.). Whoever therefore would be in fellowship with the Father must of necessity give to the Son that place in his own heart and conduct which the Father has given to Him in all the universe; he must study how to honour the Son even as he honours the Father, and "he that honoureth not the Son honoureth not the Father who sent Him" (John 5:23). And thus Christ laid down the test: "If God were your Father ye would love me" (John 8:41), and the Spirit of truth added: "Whosoever denieth the Son, the same hath not the Father: he that confesseth the Son hath the Father also" (1 John 2:23).

But this devotion to Christ must spring from love to Him personally, otherwise it is neither acceptable nor enduring (1 Corinthians 13). Hence the chief reason why early energy in service or in suffering may presently flag and finally die. Devotion to a body of philosophy, to a creed, a denomination, a cause may prove unequal to the strain of persecution, or to the lapse of time with its hopes deferred and its disappointments. But love to a person, and that Person the Son of God, this is the love that is stronger than death, that many waters cannot quench.

In A. N. Groves this love was a passion, a flame that glowed the brighter the longer it burned. How did he gain it? How was it fed with fresh oil? He shall tell us himself:

> June 26, 1834. Yesterday, I received a letter from a very dear sister, whom I have before mentioned, the wife of a missionary in Jaffna. Her heart seems sadly cast down because she has not all the love of Jesus that she desires. How I pity all who are thus distressed; for indeed I have known the sorrows of this cup; and hope I shall never cease to praise God for raising me out of the horrible pit and the miry clay, by showing me that the way to love *Him* with all my heart was not by contemplating my want of love, but by looking at *His* unspeakable fulness, till my heart was won; and though I feel an immeasurable deficiency of the love and service my soul desires, yet I do love, and am happy, and find all service delightful, compared with anything I ever knew before. I feel indeed He is worthy of our whole hearts, and sometimes He enables me to state this so clearly, that those who call me the greatest enthusiast are obliged to acknowledge that the words I speak are the words of truth and soberness (321,322).

Or again, a few days earlier, he had written:

> June 18, 1834. O, how blessed is that knowledge of Jesus, which, having won the heart by its manifestations of inconceivable tenderness and love, lays the soul prostrate before the least, as well as the greatest, act of obedience, to receive the precious charge from Him, whose very charges are only renewed opportunities, given by Himself, to endear Himself to the soul by breathing into our little services the breath of His own life

and love, till the very labour itself becomes a pleasure, because it is for Him whom the soul loves. I cannot tell you how precious and gracious God has been to me, in enabling me to understand the operations of divine love in the soul. I have been much, very much, exercised of late, in finding out how true love ought to act; this led me to Jesus, and in Him, indeed, I found a feast of fat things. At this moment, I cannot describe the intense feelings I have of His holy character; and at times I feel a little more, and this body could not bear the intensity of its joy; and I find myself obliged to cast away for a time even these most endeared thoughts. The view of His unselfish, self-sacrificing love, does so encourage me to beseech every heart on which love rests, to love as He did who spared not Himself, but gave Himself up *only* for the objects of His love; repaid enough, if He won the confiding love of those He sought to win (318).

The application of this principle of love to everyday life he shows in a letter of again a few days earlier:

June 15, 1834. I have received an interesting note from a lady, requesting from me some directions how to lead a holy life.

I will copy what I have written to her.

"My dear Mrs. C.,

"You know the old adage relative to natural affection, that love is the best casuist; when you really love, you soon find out what will please; and thus it is with Christ; if your love glows towards *Him,* you will have almost an *instinctive* sense of what will please *Him,* and that will prove to be a holy life, when followed on from day to day. Yet when you think to please one whom you truly love, till death, you do not plan a life of service, but the fruits of love, in sweet and anxious service, rewarding as they flow, spring from the heart fresh and fresh, as from an exhaustless spring; and so it is with Christ; think not on a holy life, but on a holy moment as it flies; the first overwhelms the heart by its immensity, the other sweetens and refreshes by its lightness and present stimulus; and yet a succession of holy moments constitutes a holy life. I know your anxious heart will say, how is the love to be obtained, that makes the yoke so easy and the burden so light? I will endeavour to explain to you. During my first visit among you, neither to yourself nor to your dear daughter did I feel particularly drawn. I did not feel assured of your interest in the truth, nor of your kind feelings towards me; but at the conclusion of my second visit, all was changed, and I feel now that to do you a service would not be merely a duty, but a pleasure, bringing its own reward, as done to a sister and a daughter. Why? Because I have felt *your* kindness and its power. Thus it is with Christ: believe His love and all service is sweet: and that you may know Him, and how much He deserves all your love, pay Him not hasty visits, but *dwell* with Him. The more we were together, the more we loved each other; and thus it will be in heaven, and should be always with the saints even here; but it may so happen (for so abounding is our natural weakness) that we fail to find love in one another; but thus it cannot be with *Him;* for whosoever finds Him finds love; for it is His *very nature* towards us, as all His holy dedication of Himself to our service proves. And I am sure you will see, if you reflect, how much more blessed such a principle is, than any *scheme* we could draw out; it takes into consideration every situation and circumstance, and allows for the ever-varying relative duties, in every family. For it must never be forgotten, that we have often (especially as wives or children), to serve Christ through our duties to others; and we must look through all that is pleasant or sad to Him, to take away our selfishness in those we delight in, as well as our sorrow in those who oppress us. As a principle to guide the heart, I would say, seek such a deep acquaintance with Christ's mind, as revealed in His holy life, and life-giving word, in order that when any little circumstance arises that requires instant decision, you may have Himself, as it were, present to the memory of your heart, to give you counsel; and that you may fully understand this mind seek above all things the guidance of that Spirit that alone can guide you into all the truth" (315, 316).

The reader who would understand and not misunderstand A. N. Groves' life and service must ponder these utterances of his heart. And if he further wishes to reach in heart-experience the same elevated state as is here portrayed, and to know a similar life of communion and usefulness, let him seek with undivided zeal that "knowledge of Jesus which. . . *lays the soul prostrate* before the *least,* as well as the greatest, act of obedience, to receive the precious charge from Him"; for the true lover of Christ will say, "I love Thy commandments above gold, yea, above fine gold. Therefore I esteem *all* Thy precepts concerning *all* things to be right. . . . Oh how I *love* Thy law! It is my meditation all the day" (Psalm 119:127–8, 97).

And, oh, the Son of Man is fair!
And he who shares His love
Rejoices in Him everywhere,
All other joys above;
And finds with Him, e'en though they climb
A long and rugged road,
His cup o'erflowing all the time,
And light life's heaviest load.

4

Christian Devotedness (1)

Present yourselves unto God, as alive from the dead. Romans 6:13.

With the will of God his easy yoke, the Word of God his only rule, the Son of God his passion and his joy, a man is in harmony with the whole Godhead, Father, Son, and Spirit, and to him the whole counsel of God concerning him is possible. The development of that counsel in and through Anthony Norris Groves is a deeply profitable study.

Love and sacrifice are as inseparable as the sun and sunshine. Sunshine is the sun sacrificing itself. Love is measured by sacrifice, by its gifts. "The Father loveth the Son, and hath given all things into his hand" (John 3:35); "God so loved the world that He gave his only-begotten Son" (John 3:16); "Christ loved the church and gave himself up for her" (Ephesians 5:25); "the Son of God loved me, and gave himself up for me" (Galatians 2:20).

Sacrificing love claims, begets, and enjoys responsive sacrificing love: "We love, because He first loved us" (1 John 4:19). Thus is God in His essential nature, which is love, reproduced in His creature ruined by selfishness, and His lost empire is reestablished, which is righteousness and peace and joy in the energy of the Holy Spirit (Romans 14:17). This is a foreign realm, indeed, to the citizen in Satan's kingdom of darkness, but a world of light and gladness to him who is actually a follower of the Lamb. For the Lamb is He who sacrificed His all, yea Himself, to the will of God and the good of man, and thereby entered into His glory, the glory of the Lamb that was slain. And he who surrenders himself unreservedly to that same principle, the sacrifice of love, shall share that glory.

Groves was granted a glimpse of the loveliness of *the Lamb*, and to know Him *thus* became a passion.

> For ah, the Master is so fair,
>   His smile so sweet to banished men,
> That they who meet it unaware
>   Can never rest on earth again;
>   (*Ezekiel and Other Poems,* B.M.)

and so of himself and his wife, when he was perhaps thirty-two or three years of age, we read:

> We were to the heart of a natural parent *indeed* prospering [his income was about £1,500 a year]; we had a little circle of natural blessings seldom equalled, and rarely surpassed, and we knew them, and we were peculiarly capable of enjoying them; but we had found something better—*to suffer with Christ* (33).

Property. The sufferings of Christ included poverty: "For ye know the grace of our Lord Jesus Christ, that, though he was rich, yet for your sakes he became poor, that ye through his poverty might become rich" (2 Corinthians 8:9). Of course, poverty does not necessitate rags and dirt, but it does involve the lack of reserves and of the means to be luxurious. On the one hand our Lord wore an under-robe too good to be torn and the pieces divided among the soldiers (John 19:24); on the other hand, on two occasions when a coin was needed He appears to have been without one (Matthew 17:27; 22:19). Some thirty or more years ago, in a telling S.A.G.M. booklet, Andrew Murray pointed out that the Lord and His apostles could not have accomplished the work *they* had to do had they not been actually poor. He who would lift up another must descend, like the Samaritan, to where he lies, and the infinite majority of mankind always have been and still are poor. It was no marvel that by a mind so keen as that of Groves this feature of the Life he was resolved to follow should be early perceived, nor that a heart so eager for intimacy with his Master should embrace this element of His experience.

It is not that the possession of property is in itself sinful or the Creator would be the chief of sinners, for, as Wesley said justly: "God is, and must remain, the inalienable proprietor of everything that He has created; it is a right of which He cannot divest Himself." As a mighty king said truly: "All that is in the heavens and in the earth is Thine. . . . Both riches and honour come of Thee" (1 Chronicles 29:11–12). It could not be wrong for Solomon to own wealth God granted to him without his having even asked for it (2 Chronicles 1:12). The denial of the right of private property is the denial to God of the right to do as He likes with His own and to bestow it on whom He pleases. Man has indeed no right of ownership as against God, but is only a steward; but, by the act of God himself, he may have such a right as against his neighbour, otherwise God could not impose the law, Thou shalt not steal, nor even wish to steal, anything that is thy neighbour's.

But there is something far nobler than the right to own, even the right to give up one's right. The Son of God counted not His right to be on an equality with God a thing to which He must hold on, but divested Himself of it, emptied Himself, became poor; for the work that Love longed to do, and in doing which it should acquire a richer moral glory and a fuller joy, demanded this sacrifice, and Love made it gladly. To Groves and his wife had come the vision of living only and wholly to further the ends of that Love divine, and right gladly did they share the sacrifice involved.

His account of their course in this important matter may be studied by the humble of heart with much profit. Meditation on the Scriptures was the spring of his conduct; but he made no haste in decision or in action, still less in pressing his wife thereto. Beginning with the consecration of a tenth of their income, they increased this later to one-fourth, and afterward surrendered the whole, which presently, upon the death of Mrs. Groves' father, included some £10,000 or more.

In the education of His children God our Father gives light by degrees; with successive steps of obedience He increases the faith to trust Him; tests faith by larger claims upon it, and so develops and strengthens it to meet yet larger claims and further advance. And each forward step of obedience and sacrifice is rewarded by a fuller freedom of soul from bondage to things earthly and a richer gladness by enjoyment of things heavenly. Thus does the disappointment inherent in things that are transitory, even the lawful things, fade out of life, and is replaced by the satisfaction ministered by the things eternal and unfailing.

And the foreseeing wisdom of God begins betimes the training of His chosen servants. Of a series of business reverses endured by Groves' father while Groves was young his biographer writes:

> These trials early associated his son with loss and discipline, as also three surviving daughters, who, being unmarried at the time, were made to feel with their brother the vanity of human expectations; and are still spared to witness to the blessing of those higher possessions, which have many years enabled them to account the glory of the world as dung and dross, that they may win Christ (2).

Graciously prepared thus to face trials of circumstances Groves was at the due time led further. Of the year 1822 or 1823 he writes that the Lord taught him the sufficiency of His Word. His words have been already quoted (pages 53, 54), and he continues:

> Soon after this, my mind became exercised about the right use of *property,* from the study of God's word, and I soon saw that we had been greatly to blame, and as I was walking round the garden at Northernhay [Exeter] one day, underneath that great elm tree near the gate, I said to Mary, "My love, I think we ought to lay by something regularly for the Lord, for you recollect when we commenced our career we often said, if we ever possessed a thousand a year, it would be the height of our wishes; now, we have much more than this, therefore, let us begin to give some." She replied, "Well, my dear, do as you like," and I fixed that it should be a tenth (28).

After a period which ended in his wife being led into a deeper and distinctly richer enjoyment of God, a preparation needed for what was to come, he felt able to carry further the subject of money and said:

> "Dearest M., since the Lord has so graciously received our little dedication of a tenth and made it the means of so blessing us, perhaps He would graciously also receive more at our hands." "Well," she said, "it shall be so; we have now three little children, let it stand as one, and be a fourth:" the more we gave the more we were blessed. My dearest M. threw aside all superfluous articles of dress, and put by all the things we had in our, or rather her, worldly days" (19).

And of yet a little later he continues:

With respect to property, we had only yet gone a certain way; some may think it far enough, others too far; but my heart, which had been so blessed that it could not contain its blessing, felt that so long as anything was kept back from so gracious a Lord who had dealt so bountifully with us, it was as though nothing were given; and this led me to propose one day to my dearest M. that as the Lord had blessed us more and more, in all that we had given up for Him, perhaps He would accept all from our loving grateful hearts, which, at that time at least, they were; but I recollect the tear coming into her eye, when she said, "My dear, I think it would be most wicked; consider the dear little children."

I saw the time was not come, and I only added, that I thought not so, but that the Lord would receive it. The thought rested on her mind, and I think she proposed that Kitto, who was then staying with us, should search out the mind of the Lord, from the New Testament and say what he thought, and then, if we, on examination, found the Lord would graciously accept it, we would thankfully use these base things to testify our sense of the value of the true riches He had given us. The result was as might be expected, seeing Kitto had no interest in the question, and he said, he felt we were more than free (30).

At this point in the narrative Groves' biographer writes:

That Kitto was not an indifferent spectator to what was going on, or to the devotedness which prompted the desire to give up all to God, and which finally led to Mr. Groves' missionary course, is evident, from the following passage in his memoir, page 103:

"During the period of my abode with Mr. Groves, I was enabled to imbibe a measure of those principles and opinions by which he is known to be actuated. For this I have more cause to be thankful than for any other circumstance of my life. In the whole world, so far as I know it, there is not one man whose character I venerate so highly. And I am free to confess, that my veneration is greatly increased by that very measure, which, as he foresaw and expected, does and will expose him to the opprobrium and the stigma of enthusiasm. When I first became acquainted with Mr. Groves' design, words can but poorly describe the feelings it inspired. The step was so opposed to the selfish calculations of human policy and interest, and indicated so warm and intense an appreciation of the supreme importance of unseen realities; there was so much to relinquish, so much opposition and injurious treatment to encounter, and so heavy a cross to be borne, that I contemplated it as the most exalted exhibition of devotedness to the cause of a crucified Saviour, that in the present state of the world in general, and European society in particular, can possibly be made. It manifested a martyr's energy, and fortitude, and zeal" (30, 31).

No doubt many had taken this, or a similar, step before him, but Groves does not seem to have known of them, for of this period he writes:

Just at this time, Bishop Chase came over from Ohio, and we were deeply interested in him, from hearing he had *given up all* for the Lord's cause in Ohio. Sir T. A. brought him to us, or rather to me, and said, "Here is a man after your own heart." I can only say, I was confirmed and strengthened by my intercourse with him (31).

This interest and invigoration would hardly have been so marked had Groves known of many who had already so acted. He was treading a, to him, untracked path; he was pioneering; and in the light of this fact Dr. Kitto's estimate of the step seems not extravagant.

Of the result of Kitto's examination of the New Testament upon his wife, Groves continues:

After the deepest thought and most earnest prayer, M., without reserve, gave it all up, and till the day of her death, only rejoiced in it more and more. When this great burden was once got rid of, we began to feel other than before; we had no object now in life, but living to the Lord and the Church, and in thus doing we were really living for our dear little ones ten times more effectually than in laying up poisonous heaps of gold (31).

The truth of this was evidenced by the faith and godliness his children displayed.

Nothing is more worthy of admiration or imitation than the gentle, patient manner in which this spiritually-minded man waited for his wife to be brought to his mind in this matter. The testings of faith, the actual trials that must be endured in this path must fall as heavily, if not more heavily, upon the wife than the husband, and only in the rarest and most exceptional of supposable cases would a husband be justified in involving her in them without her most unconstrained and heartiest consent. Here in quite especial degree must they be "*joint*-heirs of the grace of life," or united prayer will be hindered (1 Peter 3:7), and tension culminating in contention in the family life be all but inevitable. When God means two to walk and work under the same yoke He guides their hearts in the same direction at the one time, His predetermined time. To act before that time is to court disaster, and oft-times He graciously prevents premature action by the one party through delaying willingness in the other.

His own parents being dead Groves had no opposition to his course to meet from them, but from the parents of his wife, who were also his own aunt and uncle, it was otherwise. They did everything possible to dissuade and to hinder, which to his sensitive nature was very painful; but the manner in which he endured this trial was truly spiritual and commendable; and again we may see how obstacles serve godly ends in our training, and how they are removed when those ends have been reached. Of the year 1826, when he was thirty-one, speaking of this determination to give up his profession and possessions, he says that,

> We had come to the point when it became necessary to communicate this strange, this heart-rending choice, to those we loved, especially to dear M.'s family, whose wounded affections and disappointed hopes, after all their love and kindness, were naturally shown to us. My heart bleeds, even to this day, while I am writing, to think of what I know her dear father suffered. At first everything that kindness and love could do to induce us to stop, was done; when this failed, less kind, but equally well-intentioned efforts, were made to deter us; besides our being cut off from the sweets of family intercourse, dear M.'s father alluded to a mortgage of £1,000 he had lent, out of kindness, to my father. I was deeply wounded by the way he alluded to it, for I had never asked it of him, and I wrote back to say, I would never leave England [that is, on missionary work as was by now announced] till I had paid it (33). . . .
> I soon made up my first £100 towards the £1,000, and sent it off, and not many months after, dear M.'s father died suddenly. . . . [He] had made a new will, and signed it only two or three days before his death: with respect to property it was all divided *as before,* equally; and as to the mortgage for £1,000, it was *given to me,* and the £100 I had paid, *given back,* so that I now became ten times freer than I had ever been; in fact, nothing comparatively remained but one trial; all our dear family

gathered round us on that day, and offered all that love could offer to induce us to stay. The Lord gave us strength, and we overcame this last trial, simply saying, that if there had been a human being living to whom we could have yielded when the Lord said "go," it would have been to him who was gone. They felt its force, and kindly desisted (34).

The matter of A. N. Groves' call to go abroad with the gospel will be noticed later. The subject here is their dedication of all their substance to Christ, as a complete surrender, involving as a natural consequence that, when they went forth, they did so without personal resources and without guaranteed funds.

The following remarks of June 26th, 1825, should be pondered, for they go down to the true basis of the whole matter:

> Since we parted, I have had on many occasions to stand in defence of those views which I feel to be so essentially connected with that great characteristic of the gospel dispensation, love and simple *reliance* on God. Every review of the Word of God, as well as the steps by which I have arrived at my present conclusions from that Word, convince me, that self-devotion, in the largest sense, is the indisputable claim of Christ from His members; and, as a corollary, that, therefore, it is the highest happiness of a Christian, and the instrumentality by which God will most essentially bless His Church.
>
> The soul that, in very deed, casts all cares for the future on Him who careth for us, and has told us that our Heavenly Father knows our necessary wants, so that He would not have us careful or anxious about them, is of all created beings the happiest upon earth. . . . The state of mind most to be avoided by a searcher after truth, is deciding with the understanding that a course is right, but with the will and affections determining against pursuing it: it destroys all honest dealing with God (12, 13).

Every sentence here is pregnant; every thought is basic.
  (1) Love and reliance upon God are of the essence of the gospel dispensation.
  (2) They are the root of dedication of our means unto God.
  (3) The Word is the guide as to how this dedication is to be made.
  (4) Conclusions are not to be jumped at hurriedly, but to be

reached by patient reviewing of all the steps of reasoning that lead to them. Let this be remembered by any one prompted inwardly to give up hastily their business, home, and life and go out as a "missionary."

(5) Dedication of property is only part of the larger matter of self-devotion. This is of the deepest importance. Many give of their means to a "good cause" who have never "first given their own selves to the Lord" (2 Corinthians 8:5). In this case their giving, like all other actions, is self-centred, and therefore unacceptable to God, not arising from pure love to Him; and it is restricted in extent, part—and usually the far larger part—being held at the disposition of self, in dispute of the right of God to dispose of the whole as He may wish.

(6) Happiness and whatever is essentially blessed are a result of such self-devotion.

(7) Dependence upon God as to temporal wants brings freedom from anxiety—a state of heart as delightful as rare.

(8) Thorough honesty in dealing with God is indispensable.

In the same year that he so wrote, 1825, he had published a pamphlet entitled *Christian Devotedness,* advocating the views he shortly exemplified. Of this paper Dr. Morrison, the well-known pioneer missionary in China, wrote in his private journal, November 20th, 1827:

A tract entitled "Christian Devotedness" has appeared, a little in my way, with views as some deem them fanatical, of devoting all to God and not laying up treasures in the earth. The Eclectic has opposed it fiercely. . . but my principles go to lending to the Lord. He will provide. . . . Let us pray for enlarged hearts and strong faith, and heavenly hopes. . . . Oh! I abominate that mode of reasoning: "O yes, this is all very well in theory, but it won't do in practice!" Christ's precepts high spun impracticable dogmas? Oh! no, let it not be said. I think them the words of truth and soberness (16).

And in April, 1834, Groves wrote of the celebrated Dr. Alexander Duff of Calcutta:

he speaks of his first glow of devotedness, as having arisen from my little tract on "Christian Devotedness" (295).

And these were but some of its direct results. In the preceding December he had written:

> I had the other day a letter from a dear young civilian, in which he tells me his purpose of devoting all he has to God. The little tract on "Christian Devotedness" has been once published in India, and there is to be another edition; a dear *native* minister of Christ offered ten rupees towards it [then £1] and he is a poor man (259).

Mr. Neatby affirms of George Müller's earliest days in England, that "Groves' early pamphlet on Christian Devotedness fell into his hands, and influenced him powerfully" and "gave a real impulse to his mind" (*History* 54, 55). It may well have been so, though Mr. Müller does not mention this in the early part of his *Narrative* upon the period in question.

Groves claimed for Christ all things from all disciples. Who will declare the claim excessive, unjustified? His own surrender to the claim was uncompromising, complete, and he deemed this to be the duty of all. Yet in the practical application of the matter to others he was neither fanatical nor tyrannical. A few months after the publication of the tract he wrote:

> I am much gratified to hear you think my little pamphlet is true: about this I am more concerned than about any thing else connected with it; because it is from this source that good must arise to any who peruse it. As to the application of it to another man's conscience, it cannot be so applied; for though I think it is not only a great loss of present comfort, but a great sin, not to trust God's promises, let them relate to what they will, and not to obey His injunctions, let them involve what they may; yet as all acceptable obedience of this sort must be willing and free, it will be a snare and a temptation to enjoin the body, when you cannot give the spirit, which alone gives it worth in the sight of God. But while it is fully admitted that we are not capable of applying the principle to every man's conscience, so as to specify what he should do, because we cannot tell how far he goes without grudging or of necessity, and therefore how far he is capable of offering up the service acceptably; yet our ignorance does not alter the nature of his obligations, for his not having faith to trust God is his sin, for faith has no respect to *what* is commanded, but *who* commands. If God says, "Slay thy son," faith obeys just as readily as when it is said, "Believe on the Lord Jesus Christ, and thou shalt be

saved." Neither does it matter to the eye of faith, whether it be said, "Lay not up for yourselves treasures upon earth," etc.; or, "Come, buy of me gold tried in the fire," etc. Therefore I would say, if the principles contained in my little book be according to the plain and obvious meaning of the Lord, it is the duty of all to embrace them; though it may not be my duty to urge any to the external act, without a fuller knowledge than one man can have of another, as to the actual state of the heart; I am not, however, sure that this limitation is sound, for if no man is to be urged to a duty until he is in a state to perform it acceptably, the great end of all preaching is at an end. The Lord exhorted the young man to give up all, though He knew his heart was after his covetousness, and promised him great blessings if he obeyed. My present impression is this, that it is the duty of everyone to give up all for Christ, absolutely and unreservedly, though the precise mode must be left to individual conscience. I think the command to pray and to give up, stand on the same authority, and may be urged on the same grounds; and if you would feel it your duty to urge a man to pray, though a known sinner, you may exhort a man to give up all, though a known miser; and if you would feel yourself at liberty to hope, that if a man began to pray from a sense of duty, it would terminate in the sense of privilege; so, on the other hand, he who gives up all, from the conviction that it was the command of his Lord, though he felt no present sense of delight, would, I have no doubt, be blest in his surrender. Think this over, and let me know the result; and remember, I regard truth, not my book (17, 18).

Into this path of dedication and faith some have hastened impetuously without searching thoroughly into its grounds or weighing adequately its consequences. It was plainly not so with Groves. He knew the power of that promise: "The meek will He guide in *judgment*" first, and then "will He teach His *way*" (Psalm 25:9); and when the path of God is thus walked with intelligence, the soul, amidst all the trials that are met upon that way, can affirm readily that "*All* the paths of Jehovah are lovingkindness and truth unto such as keep His covenant and His testimonies" (Psalm 25:10). Whereas if the mind be unintelligent in the ways of God the heart is often first surprised, and at last stumbled, by the barrenness or ruggedness of the road and turns out of it as hurriedly as it turned into it, to find only too often that Bypath Meadow leads to Doubting Castle and to the cruel grip of Giant Despair.

It was the opposite with Groves. These convictions deepened with practical experience in obeying what he had learned from the Word of God of the will of God in this matter, and he was given a rich measure of the peace and joy that come through believing. His testimonies to this are many and clear and stimulating. He says:

> I know no state where such close communion with God is necessarily kept up, as where you are almost placed, like the ravens, to be fed day by day from your Father's hands (12).

In Bagdad, with the cholera, which had devastated neighbouring towns, sweeping upon them, he wrote:

> Oh, who would not live a life of faith in preference to one of daily, hourly satiety—I mean as to earthly things; how very many instances of happiness should we have been deprived of, had we not trusted to, and left it to, His love to fill us with good things as He pleased, and to spread our table as He has done, year after year, and will do, even here in this wilderness [Mesopotamia] (106).
>
> But all our past experience has led us to look to the Lord alone for profitable help. Those whom we think promise everything [as helpers in the work of the gospel], often occasion us nothing but anxiety, and those from whom we expect the least, we have reason abundantly to bless God for having sent us—so wisely, so graciously, and yet in so sovereign a way does the Lord bring to pass His purposes, and bless His servants, that every thought of confidence in any creature may be destroyed, and that the soul, by a thousand disappointments, when it has reposed elsewhere, may at last be compelled to learn only to repose on the bosom of its Father, where love and faithfulness eternally dwell, and may be convinced of the vanity of its past expectations from any other source (111).

At the beginning of his second year in Bagdad (1831) he wrote:

> I have this day settled all my accounts, and find, after everything is paid, including the expenses of my baggage from Bushire, and of the house and school for another year, that our little stock will last us, with the Lord's blessing, two months longer, and then we know not whence we are to be supplied, but the Lord does not allow us to be anxious; He has so wonderfully provided for us hitherto, that it would be most ungrateful to have an anxious thought. . . . That we may many times be

in straits I have no doubt, but the time of our necessity will be the time for the manifestation of our Lord's providential love and munificence (112, 113).

And this he proved.

A journey to Bagdad is now [in 1935] a simple affair, but a century ago it was a formidable undertaking; and when there, one was dreadfully isolated. Upon news reaching him of money being available he wrote on March 4th, 1831:

> Surely the Lord has most graciously seen fit to dry up those sources from whence we anticipated supply, that we might know we depend on Him alone, and see how He can supply us even here; we were ashamed of every little anxious feeling we had ever had, and were much encouraged to trust Him more and more. My soul is led to abhor more and more that love of independence which still clings to it, when I see how it would shut me out from these manifestations of my Father's loving care. O! how hard it is to persuade the rebellious will and proud heart, that to depend on our Father's love for our constant support is more for the soul's health than to be clothed in purple and fare sumptuously every day from what we call our own resources; and yet how plain it is to spiritual vision (114).

And two years later he wrote in India:

> The little carpet I sit on by day serves as my bed by night, and a cloak covers me. *I cannot tell you how comfortable it is to be independent of everything but the sunshine of the Lord's countenance* (238).

But perhaps none of the testimonies to the spiritual blessedness of this manner of life is more striking or convincing than the following. Bagdad was ravaged by the plague, and his wife was attacked, when he wrote:

> All the conversation of my dear dying wife, for these twelve months past, but especially as our difficulties and trials increased, was on the peace she enjoyed in the Lord. Often and often she has said to me, "notwithstanding the disparity of everything external, I never in England enjoyed that sweet sense of my Lord's loving care that I have enjoyed in Bagdad." And her assurance of her Lord's love never forsook her, even after she felt herself attacked by the plague (146).

The sweetness of honey can be appreciated by those only who taste it, and the peace of God by those only who enjoy it. It is one thing to be at peace *with* God through our Lord Jesus Christ, reconciled by the blood of His cross; it is another and further experience to have the peace *of* God guarding the heart from anxiety (Romans 5:1; Philippians 4:6–7). Many have the former who lack the latter. Anxiety arises from a sense of insufficiency, a knowledge that, or a fear that, one's resources are inadequate to meet circumstances existing or anticipated. God knows Himself absolutely sufficient for all events, and therefore He abides eternally in unbroken tranquillity of heart. It is the privilege of the believer to enjoy this same inward tranquillity, and it is one of the essential elements of power. Fretfulness and fearfulness dissipate energy of spirit. How then may the child of God acquire the peace of God? It may be helpful if I give my own experience.

Fifty years ago, at the age of twenty-four, I was in business. The calling was one to which a man of diligence and ability, if he were disposed to live for this world and not for eternity, might expect to attain a good position and large salary. But from such short-sightedness God, in His great grace, had already saved my heart. One day, by a sudden illumination, I saw that in that business there was a regular transaction that could neither be eliminated nor be reconciled with the holiness of God. For weeks I pondered the matter and searched the Scriptures. My duty was settled by Colossians 3:17, "Whatsoever ye do, in word or in deed, do all in the name of the Lord Jesus, giving thanks to God the Father through him."

It was a question of indirectly supporting the drink traffic by arranging their fire insurances, and my heart said instantly: You dare not go to that vile public-house in that slum, which you surveyed three weeks ago, where men and women are helped to hurry to hell faster than they need go, and say to that poor bloated barman, In the name of the Lord Jesus I am come to arrange to rebuild this place, if it be burned down, so that you may carry on this business, and I thank God my Father that I am able to do this!

It was the sharp issue of either searing my conscience, and thereby forfeiting fellowship with God, or forfeiting my earthly prospects. I had no reserves of money. From my youth I had been brought up, thanks be to God, to live economically, and, though my salary was not large, it more than met my needs, and the balance I had always given away. With the poor always at hand, and with the work of the gospel needing support, my heart's heavenly affections would have been crushed had I laid up treasure on earth. So I faced life afresh with a month's salary, *and* the promises of God.

The whole affair and its consequences had naturally been a source of deep and anxious concern; but the ink of the signature to my letter of resignation was not yet dry when there stole softly into my heart a restful, all-pervading quietness and not the least sense of care was left; it might henceforth have been someone else's affair and not mine, so richly was the promise fulfilled: "Thou will keep him in perfect peace whose mind is stayed on Thee" (Isaiah 26:3). And throughout the long succeeding years of dependence upon my faithful God and Father for daily supplies, for my home, and for long journeys in the gospel in many lands, that peace has guarded the heart from anxious care. And thus are all the energies of the soul preserved from distraction as to ways and means, and can be concentrated on high ends, in the power of the Holy Spirit.

The psychology of such an experience is really quite simple. A man with legal tangles, that baffle and harass him, goes to a lawyer, in whose skill and integrity he has full confidence, places the matter in his care, and feels relieved, believing that his affairs are now in competent hands. Peter exhorts troubled saints to commit the keeping of their souls (lives) unto a faithful Creator by doing what is right in His eyes (1 Peter 4:19); and doing this, the heart receives the comfortable assurance that all must be well. How can it be otherwise when God is ordering all?

Isaiah and Paul use similar military figures to teach and to explain this. The former pictures a countryside overrun by a cruel foe, and the people fleeing from their unprotected homesteads to the fortified city. Once within its walls and gates fear gives place to peace. "We have a strong city; salvation will he appoint for walls and bulwarks. Open ye the gates that the righteous nation which keepeth faith may enter in. Thou wilt keep him in perfect peace whose mind is stayed on Thee; because he trusteth in Thee. Trust ye in Jehovah for ever; for in Jah, even Jehovah, is an everlasting rock" (Isaiah 26:1–4). The word "mind" may be read "imagination." Many of our anxieties come not from actual circumstances but from events we fear may arise; they are fictions of the imagination. "I have had a great many troubles in life, but most of them never came." Faith fills the future, the morrow, not with phantoms but with God, and is at peace.

Paul looks upon our own inner life as the city, whereinto fear and care seek to rush and to work havoc, and the peace of God is the garrison that defends our heart and thoughts. The Lord personally is at hand, that is, nearby; turn to Him, tell Him your needs and trials, thank Him for ten thousand mercies, past and present; and the sense of His nearness, faithfulness, sufficiency will fill you with the peace of God. (Philippians 4:5–7).

Groves and his wife reached this blessed experience by doing the will of God in a matter that was shown to them by His Spirit through the Word, the matter of laying up treasure in heaven and not on earth. The same path to the same enrichment of soul is open to every obedient heart, though the door to that path may vary in different cases. Since their time and example, thousands have entered by that same door, to their great spiritual advantage and advancement. It is one of the most valuable of all preparatory steps for those especially who are called, as Groves was, to spread the gospel as the whole work of life, but it bestows its riches of peace and joy indiscriminately in every walk and calling. Many a care-spoiled home, many a care-filled business would become a place of rest and radiance were trust placed in God, instead of in His gifts, these being habitually used up for Him, under the leading of His Spirit, instead of being laid up on earth in defiance of His directions. For, as Wesley justly said in his sermon on Stewardship, to lay up treasure on earth is as plainly forbidden by our Master as adultery and murder.

I have lived and worked in happy fellowship with workers in the gospel in many lands through fifty years and am satisfied that a guaranteed or regular income, because it dispenses with direct and constant faith in God as to temporal supplies, is certainly a spiritual loss, not by any means a gain. And it is the same in degree with all believers. If trust is placed on anything but God himself the heart is impoverished. I wrote this in Egypt, the land of all lands to see the force of Jeremiah 17:5–8. As far as the waters of the Nile can overflow or be diverted the trees flourish: a few yards only beyond that limit the dwarfed shrubs struggle to exist and presently succumb. "Blessed is the man that trusteth in Jehovah and whose trust Jehovah [really] is. For he shall be as a tree planted by the waters, that spreadeth out its roots by the river, and shall not fear when heat cometh, but its leaf shall be green; and shall not be careful in the year of drought, neither shall cease from yielding fruit."

I knew intimately a Christian of fine quality with a flourishing business. He commenced in a very small way, and at his conversion prayed God to prosper him enough to give to His cause £100 a year: an unusual and noteworthy request. This sum he soon trebled. With the financial responsibilities of a growing business he rightly kept in hand reserves enough to meet all liabilities; which was not laying up *treasure,* but merely providing things honest in the sight of all men. In due time the income from this necessary reserve sufficed for his personal needs, and from that time he laid by nothing, but gave away the whole of his income. He told his two sons that he would educate them for any profession they wished, or they could join him in the business, but they need expect nothing more from him. This constrained them to qualify thoroughly for life and saved them from the evils so often attendant upon inherited fortune. They both walked after his Christian faith and example. We were passing the house of a Christian who had lately died leaving £30,000. My friend remarked: I would think the Lord had a controversy with me were I going to leave £30,000 behind me! He might easily have done so, but his estate was not a third of that sum, simply, I suppose, the value of his business and house. He was a tree planted by the river, and brought forth fruit to the end.

Such living is not reckless, nor is such giving indiscriminate. In 1831 George Müller wrote words which throw light on the outworking of these principles which he had lately seen in his brother-in-law, A. N. Groves, and himself practised:

I notice one more false report which has been spread concerning our mode of living. It has been often said, since we have been in Bristol, that if more money were given to us than we needed during the week, we at once gave away the rest. The truth, however, is this. We never give away for the sake of giving; but when our Lord sends us opportunities for communicating of what he has been pleased to bestow on us, we desire to have grace to give, without reckoning as to the future (*Narrative* 78).

The last sentence is the crux of the matter for perhaps the majority: they reckon upon the future, and seek to provide against its imagined conditions and contingencies. Next year's crops may be poor; business may take a bad turn; sickness may attack me or my family; I must provide against a rainy day, or my old age; and so forth. Their divine Lord cries to them in vain: "Be not anxious for *tomorrow*"; they take anxious thought for the distant future, perhaps ten thousand morrows away. Their heavenly Father's precious and exceeding great promises are not security enough, they must have some promises from the Bank of England also or they cannot sleep in peace. By such distrust the heart of their Father is pained, their own heart is impoverished, their willingness to give withers, they remain earth-bound, for "where thy treasure is, there will thy heart be also" (Matthew 6:21).

All these perils necessarily beset Groves, with his flourishing worldly affairs, and he too might easily have been reduced to a mere respectable, earthly-minded Christian, giving, perhaps, his dole to Christian efforts, but with eyes downward, wings clipped, hands hanging down and feeble knees, a slave in golden fetters, setting on mammon a higher value than on heaven. Nothing more truly denotes the freedom with which Christ sets free than liberation from the thraldom to money, much or little. Groves knew its true value as a servant, and its unreal value as a tyrant. So he was able to write such sentences as those before quoted, describing possessions as "a great burden" of which they had got rid, and speaking of money as "poisonous heaps of gold"; and using these further words:

The death of Mrs. Groves' father...has put some of that deadly corrupter of the human heart—money—in our way, under circumstances we have no control over. Pray for us, therefore, that we may glorify Him with every farthing of it (19).

And again:

> Do you think that any become really richer in the *world* by following the Gospel? It appears to me, if they do, it must be by listening to precepts by halves: for instance, when the Apostle says, "Let him that stole steal no more: but labour, working with his hands the thing which is good"; here they would stop, or say, that he may become a respectable member of society, instead of adding, "that he *may have to give to him that needeth*." And they would be ready to say, "Not slothful in business"; but forget, "fervent in spirit, serving the Lord." Indeed, the Gospel impoverishes you in the things of earth; but overwhelms you, in return, with the things of heaven; it empties, that it may fill you with the fulness of Him who contains the treasures of God (351).

Wealth a "great burden," gold "poisonous," money a "deadly corrupter of the human heart"—this is the vision and the verdict of heaven, not of earth; that it is unpopular does not make it less true; and he only who has this judgment about it can safely handle it. Groves was its master, not its slave. Is the reader this? From this point his inner man and his outer life could move *forward*. Alas, how easy it is to sing with great energy, "*Onward*, Christian soldiers!" and yet to remain stuck in the mud, making no progress in heart fellowship with God, no advance in Christian experience.

> Oh, bliss to leave behind us
> The fetters of the slave;
> To leave *ourselves* behind us,
> The grave clothes and the grave;
> To speed unburdened pilgrims,
> Glad, *empty-handed,* free;
> To cross the trackless deserts
> And walk upon the sea.
> (Mrs. Bevan, *Hymns of Tersteegen*, 5).

How Groves moved onward we shall see: let us also press on.

5

Christian Devotedness (2)

After the foregoing chapter was written I was enabled, by the kindness of a friend, to read the tract mentioned. It is entitled:—

> CHRISTIAN DEVOTEDNESS,
> Or
> The Consideration of Our
> Saviour's Precept,
> "Lay not up for yourselves
> treasures upon earth,"
>
> By A. N. Groves
>
> Second Edition, London,
> James Nisbet, Berners Street,
>   1829

Before this second edition was issued Groves had taken the step which he here had advocated. The tract is a revelation of the man, and affords an insight into the spirit and the glow which made his ministry attractive to sincere souls, and effectual. It being long since unobtainable we give it in full. By it he, being dead, may yet speak, and other hearts be enlarged and enriched to the glory of God. It reads:

PREFACE

In sending a second impression of the following little work into the world after a lapse of four years from the publication of the former edition, it may be right to state, that my views on the subject of it, have undergone no change in the way of relinquishment; but on the contrary, the experience of every day in my own history—every observation I have been able to make on the history of those with whom I have come into the closest contact, and who have either received or rejected the view, and in whatever degree, has tended exceedingly to strengthen the conviction on my mind, of the infinitely deep knowledge of the human heart, and springs of human action, which these injunctions of our Blessed Lord manifest: and that He means simply what He says in "Lay not up for yourselves treasures upon earth, etc." There is an eye-salve in this doctrine, when received by faith, that wonderfully clears the field of our spiritual perceptions; therefore, he that can receive it, let him receive it. Many more, certainly, have been influenced by it, and some to a much greater extent than I had expected; and the clusters that have adorned their branches seem to be of the true Eschol grapes; however, of these, and many other things, time will be the manifester and the Lord the judge.

The principal objections urged, seem to arrange themselves under *three* heads: The influence of which this principle would rob the Church; the children it would leave without a provision; and that it would require those having estates to sell them, and would not be satisfied with the dedication of the interest or profits arising out of such property. My business, however, is not with the consequences of the precept, but with the precept itself. Yet still I would say, there is in this reasoning as deistical a disregard of the Lord's especial government of his Church and people, as could be expected from an infidel.

I purpose publishing, the Lord sparing me, a few remarks separately, in relation to the first of these subjects—that of *Influence;* the nature of that which is Christian, and its distinction from that which is worldly, and which operates either upon worldly men, or that worldliness which still adheres to every one of us. And I shall endeavour to show, that a grain of the pure gold of Christian influence, which is the exhibition, in truth, of the mind of Christ, springing from the love of Christ in the soul, is no wise increased in value by being beaten out into plates as thin as imagination can conceive, and employed to gild the brassy admixture of earthly influence—the titles, honours, rank, wealth, learning and secular power of this world. It looks indeed like a mighty globe of gold; and the eyes of the inexperienced may be caught by it; but the least scratch proves its brassy character. If this simple principle had been perceived, how differently would many public religious bodies have been constituted for the purpose of extending the influence of Christ's Kingdom.

With regard to the other two points, I feel they may be disposed of under one general argument, which is this: That the principle of God's government is paternal; and therefore its primary object is the development in us of the character of *dear children,* the essential feature of which is unlimited dependence. But, of course, this relation implies its co-relative, the Fatherly character of God; and the least entrenchment upon daily dependence for daily provision, either for temporal or spiritual supplies, affects God's honour in this character. Then, as to our children, David knew that they shall not beg their bread—at least, that he, who had been young and then was old, had not seen such a thing; and to suspect such a thing, is to suspect the perfection of the Fatherly character of God; of whom our blessed Lord said, "Your Father knoweth you have need of all these things," and, therefore, "all these things shall be added unto you." As to capital and estates, after knowing that our loving Father will supply us in every need, the sooner we are disencumbered by disbursement, for His honour, and His service, the better; for then we shall have the happiness of seeing it spent for the glory of Him *whose it is,* and for whom we are *only stewards;* whereas were we to die tomorrow, we do not know whether the capital and estate may fall into the hands of a wise man or a fool, so that we may be cut off after spending part of a year's income for God—say one hundred, out of a thousand pounds, and this, I think, would be called Christian devotedness by many— and the fool comes in and spends the whole residue, twenty thousand pounds perhaps, for Satan and the corruption of the world. But some may say, Are not all things given us richly to enjoy? Yea; but it would be degrading indeed to the members of the Kingdom of Christ, to make their rich enjoyment appear in consuming on their own lusts, like the members of the kingdom of Satan, those things which they are permitted to apply to the exaltation of their Lord and Redeemer. Be assured, my dear friends, the sooner we can see it appropriated to God's service and glory the better. For then it is gone for the Lord; and the world, the flesh, and the devil, cannot, though combined, bring it back, and the Lord will not allow us to wish it were, so graciously will He receive our weak services, and so kindly and overwhelmingly repay them with the light of His countenance, and the secret assurance in our own souls, that our dedication has been acceptable at our hand.

A.N.G.

London, May 16th, 1829.

Christian Devotedness, etc.

The writer of the following pages has been deeply affected by the consideration of the strange and melancholy fact that Christianity has made little or no progress for fifteen successive centuries: and having, as he trusts, perceived, in an attentive perusal of the Gospel History,[1] that primitive Christianity owed much of its irresistible energy to the open and public manifestation by the early disciples, of their love to their Redeemer and King, and to one another, by the evidence which they gave of it in their conduct, and being moreover convinced that the exhibition of this love tends directly and most powerfully to augment the prosperity of the Church of Christ within its own bosom, and to extend its influence throughout the world in all ages; he ventures to lay the result of his reflections open to the candid consideration of the sincere disciples of that Saviour, "who, though he was rich, yet for our sakes became poor, that we through his poverty might be rich" (2 Corinthians 8:9).

This manifestation of love he believes to have been made by the entire and real (not figurative) devotion of themselves, their property, time and talents to Christ, their Lord and King. The subsequent remarks, however, more especially relate to the bestowment of property, and that whether of capital already possessed, or of income to be acquired by industry.

The object proposed by the writer is to prove that such a Dedication is *invariably* enforced by the commands of our Saviour and that

---

1. The author would not be understood as insinuating that this manifestation was the efficient cause of the success of the Gospel, but merely as asserting that it was the means by which the all-powerful Spirit of God accomplished the wonderful extension of Christ's Kingdom during the early ages. It may be right here also to point out the reason why cautions are not more abundantly introduced to prevent the mind from resting on the Dedication, treated of in this Essay, as a ground of Justification before God. The reason is simply this—that the author wrote it particularly for the eye of those who make the fulness and freeness of salvation the very incentive to obedience in all things. He himself believes the Dedication, spoken of, to be a part of this obedience; and, in urging it, it is not his design to turn away the eye of the believer from those glorious objects which a full and free salvation presents to his view: but, supposing the eye already directed towards those objects, he would hold them up as affording the only efficient motives to live in all things unto Him who died for us.

it is illustrated by the practice of his Apostles and their immediate cotemporaries:[2] and he entreats of all the sincere disciples of Christ, that they will weigh what is written in the balance of the Sanctuary, and not in the balances of this world; that they will pray earnestly to the "Father of lights" to have, in their search after truth, a single eye to the glory of Him whose they are and whom they ought to serve, and to the extension of His Kingdom—that they will, while they search and pray, have a tender regard both to their own souls; and to those of the millions of "Jews, Turks, Infidels, and Heretics," whose ignorance and wretchedness they profess to deplore. If, in our enquiry into the meaning and extent of our Saviour's words: "Lay not up for yourselves treasures upon earth," we should be led to the persuasion that he *meant* them, and that the Apostles and their companions *received* them, in their most unrestricted sense; may the Holy Spirit of God enable us to lay firm hold on the most comfortable and consolatory permission thence arising to cast all our cares upon Him, because we know that He careth for us. All that is, or that can fairly be, claimed, in investigating the question before us, is, that the various precepts and arguments, along with the uniform practice, of our Saviour and his Apostles, be allowed to explain His meaning in this particular instance. I shall, therefore, consider in the *first* place, the direct Scriptural account of the Principle, to which we have alluded, as it is enforced by precept and illustrated by example; and I shall *next* consider its important bearing upon other momentous commands, which, without it, are rendered exceedingly difficult, nay, impossible, to be understood and received. I shall then *conclude* with a few arguments to prove that, if the extension of the *spirit* of Christ's Kingdom be the proper object of the churches pursuit, these views are as consonant with reason as they are with revelation.

I.

I shall begin with the passage from which the motto is taken. "Lay not up for yourselves," says our Saviour, in his Sermon on the Mount,

---

2. The texts which seem to give another aspect to this question, such as, "He that provideth not for his own, etc."—"The parents ought to lay up for the children, etc."—"Provide things honest in the sight of all men," are considered together in a note at the end of the Pamphlet [see page 111].

"treasures upon earth, where moth and rust doth corrupt, and where thieves break through and steal: but lay up for yourselves treasures in heaven, where neither moth nor rust doth corrupt, and where thieves do not break through nor steal: for where your treasure is, there will your heart be also. The light of the body is the eye: if therefore thine eye be single, thy whole body shall be full of light; but if thine eye be evil, thy whole body shall be full of darkness. If therefore the light that is in thee be darkness, how great is that darkness! No man can serve two masters: for either he will hate the one, and love the other; or else he will hold to the one, and despise the other. Ye cannot serve *God* and *mammon*. Therefore I say unto you, Take no thought for your life, what ye shall eat, or what ye shall drink; nor yet for your body, what ye shall put on. Is not the life more than meat, and the body than raiment? Behold the fowls of the air: for they sow not, neither do they reap, nor gather into barns; yet your Heavenly Father feedeth them. Are ye not much better than they? Which of you, by taking thought, can add one cubit unto his stature? And why take ye thought for raiment? Consider the lilies of the field, how they grow; they toil not, neither do they spin; and yet I say unto you that even Solomon, in all his glory, was not arrayed like one of these. Wherefore, if God so clothe the grass of the field, which today is, and tomorrow is cast into the oven, shall he not much more clothe you, O ye of little faith? Therefore take no thought, saying, What shall we eat? or, What shall we drink? or, Wherewithal shall we be clothed? *(for after all these things do the Gentiles seek;)* for your heavenly Father knoweth that ye have need of all these things. But seek ye first the Kingdom of God and his righteousness; and all these things shall be added unto you. Take therefore no thought for the morrow: for the morrow shall take thought for the things of itself. Sufficient unto the day is the evil thereof" (Matthew 6:19, etc.).[1]

    The principal points to be attended to, in the above passage, are: The importance attached to a "single eye" and the clear declaration of our Saviour that riches disturb the clearness and simplicity of its vision; God's care of the lowest of his creatures, and his provision for

---

1. It should be remembered that in this passage the words "take no thought" should have been rendered "Be not anxious." See the Revised Version.

those which have neither storehouse nor barn; the inference thence deduced by our Saviour, that He will much more care and provide for those who singly and earnestly seek the Kingdom of God and His righteousness, though they have neither *storehouse nor barn;* and the source of all our distrust and doubt, clearly intimated in the expression "O ye of little faith."

The parallel passage in St. Luke is almost verbally the same. It is, however, more striking, as it is introduced by a practical warning derived from the conduct of the "rich man,"[2] who cries out, on the contemplation of his security from want, "Soul, thou hast much goods laid up for many years," and to whom God replies: "Thou fool, this night shall thy soul be required of thee: then whose shall those things be which thou hast provided" (Luke 12:13–21). It also concludes with an exhortation somewhat different from that in St. Matthew. In the latter, it is said: *"Lay not up";* whereas in St. Luke it is said: *"Sell all that thou hast,* and give alms; provide yourselves bags which wax not old, a treasure in the heavens that faileth not."

To all arguments drawn from passages of this description, the usual answer is, That the exhortations contained in them are not to be taken literally, but are to be considered merely as loose general statements, strongly, and only in *appearance* absolutely, made, with a view of producing greater effect. In endeavouring, therefore, to ascertain their true meaning, let us examine the evidence supplied by the remarks and conduct of our blessed Lord and his Apostles, in those cases which bear upon the point in question.

When the young man came to enquire what good thing he should do to inherit eternal life, after having mentioned several duties, our Lord says: "Yet *lackest* thou one thing: sell all that thou hast, and

---

2. "He could not tell into whose hands his wealth would pass: nor would it be any comfort to him, even for his children or friends to possess it, when he was torn from all which he loved and idolized, and plunged into the pit of destruction; and perhaps they too were preparing by it for the same dreadful end."—Scott

"Though possessions are useful to sustain life, yet no man is able to prolong life, and to make it any thing more happy and comfortable to him, by possessing more than he needs or uses, that is, by any superfluity of wealth. The only way to be the better for the wealth of the world, is to dispose and distribute it to the service of God, and benefit and comfort of others." —Hammond

distribute to the poor, and thou shalt have treasure in heaven; and come, follow me. And when he heard this, he was very sorrowful, for he was very rich. And when Jesus saw that he was very sorrowful, he said, 'How hardly shall they, that *have riches,* enter into the Kingdom of God! For it is easier for a camel to go through a needle's eye, than for a rich man to enter into the Kingdom of God.' And they that heard it said, 'Who then can be saved?' And he said: 'The things that are impossible with men are possible with God.' Then Peter said: 'Lo, we have left all and followed thee.' And he said unto them, 'Verily I say unto you, there is *no man* that hath left house, or parents, or brethren, or wife, or children, for the Kingdom of God's sake, who shall not receive manifold more in this present time, and in the world to come life everlasting'" (Luke 18:22–30).

If then this is the judgment of Him in whom we believe to be "hid all the treasures of wisdom and knowledge," who "Knew what was in man," who was acquainted with all the secret influences by which his heart is governed; shall we, in opposition to His solemnly recorded judgment, that "it is easier for a camel to go through the eye of a needle, than for those who have riches to enter into the Kingdom of God," strive, by the amassing of wealth, effectually, as far as in us lies, to stop our own heavenward course, as well as that of those dear little ones, whom our heavenly Father may have committed to our peculiar and tender care? We may, without anxiety, contemplate the circumstance (I shall not say the *misfortune)* of dying and leaving our families to struggle with many seeming difficulties in this world, should obedience to the Divine Commands bring us and them into such a situation; because our faith could lay hold, for support and consolation, on the well-known declarations and the acknowledged truths: that the Captain of our Salvation was made *"perfect through sufferings,"* and *"learned* obedience by the things that he suffered" (Hebrews 1:10, and 5:8); that the Apostle "gloried in tribulations, knowing that tribulation worketh patience, and patience experience, and experience hope—even a hope which maketh not ashamed" (Romans 5:5); that he could describe himself "as sorrowful, yet always rejoicing; as poor, yet making many rich; as having nothing, and yet possessing all things" (2 Corinthians 6:10). But a family left, by our labour and contrivance, in a situation in which, as our blessed Lord himself declares, it is all but impossible that they should be saved,[1] presents an object of contemplation widely different. Faith can only lay hold of the fearful declaration, "It is easier for a camel to go through the eye of a needle, than for those who have riches to enter into the Kingdom of God"; and if the situation of such a family is irretrievably fixed, and that by our exertions, the contemplation of it may well bring alarm and sadness and distress upon the last hours of a Christian parent. And these feelings may well rise to anguish, if he is conscious that his system of accumulation was carried on in defiance of solemn admonitions; and if he is persuaded that the wealth he has amassed—as it were to shut out heaven from the hopes and prospects of his children—if it had been dedicated day by day, as God had prospered him, as a manifestation of his love, and a tribute of his gratitude to his Lord and King, might have been the means of feeding with the bread of life some of the hundreds of millions who lie in darkness, hopelessness, and sin, because the Son of Righteousness has not arisen on them with healing in His wings.

Such are the views and feelings which an unbiassed consideration of the words of our Saviour is calculated to produce. Some, however, may be prepared to assert that His words give no encouragement or allowance to any such conclusions; and this assertion they may support by another—that a *love of riches* was the peculiar failing of the young man, whose conduct suggested the observations of our Saviour. It ought, however, to be remarked that he does not say, How hardly shall this rich man enter into the Kingdom of God!—but in the most general terms, "How hardly shall *they that have riches* enter into the Kingdom of God!"—it may be desirable for those who consider the expression "Trust in riches" used in the parallel passage of Mark 10:24 as mitigating considerably the severity of our Saviour's

---

1. The argument is not distinctly affected, but it is to be observed that the Lord did not here speak of being "saved," but of entering the Kingdom. That the disciples at that time thought the two ideas were the same does not establish it, for prior to the gift of the indwelling Spirit of truth they misunderstood other things that the Lord said. Matthew 16:22; Luke 22:36; Acts 1:6. For the same thought compare Matthew 5:20; 18:1–3; 1 Corinthians 6:9–10; Galatians 5:19, 21; Ephesians 5:5; all addressed to persons already "saved."

declaration to view the connexion of the several parts of the passage in which the expression is found. "Jesus looked round about, and saith unto his disciples, 'How hardly shall they that have riches enter into the Kingdom of God.' And the disciples were astonished at his words. But Jesus answered again and saith unto them, 'Children, how hardly shall they that trust in riches enter into the Kingdom of God! It is easier for a camel to go through the eye of a needle, than for a rich man to enter into the Kingdom of God.' And they were astonished out of measure, saying among themselves, 'Who then can be saved?'" Our Lord, in the 23rd verse, asserts it to be almost impossible for those who have riches to enter into the Kingdom of God. When he observes the astonishment of his disciples, he explains to them the reason of his passing a judgment so severe, by stating the cause of that difficulty, of which he spoke as amounting almost to an impossibility. It is next to impossible for a rich man to enter the Kingdom of God, because he *trusts* in his riches. So that the expression is not introduced with a view of making riches appear less dangerous to the possessor, but rather with a view of explaining *why* they are so dangerous. The repetition of the general declaration in the strongest terms, as it is found in the 25th verse, shows that this is the meaning of our Lord; and the increased astonishment of the disciples plainly gives the same intimation. It is evident that they were not led, by this explanation, to consider the case of the rich less hopeless or deplorable; for they cry out: "Who then can be saved?"— evidently the expression of men whose difficulties were confirmed, not removed, by the answer they had received. The simple meaning, therefore, of the passage seems to be this: The danger of riches is their being trusted in; and the difficulty of possessing them, and not trusting in them for happiness and protection, is as the difficulty of a camel's going through the eye of a needle: therefore, "lay not up for yourselves treasures upon earth, for where your treasure is, there will your heart be also."

But the man whose soul the love of Christ has touched, does not look on the question as one merely involving danger to himself: he looks on wealth, as well as every other gift, as an instrument of bringing glory to his Lord, by feeding the little ones of His kingdom, or in some way extending the savour of His name. It is not a matter of law, but a golden opportunity on which affection seizes, to bring a leaf to the wreath of praise and honour, that crowns *Him* Lord, to the glory of God the Father, who has won the hearts, and is entitled to the uncontrolled dominion of His own saints.

From the observations suggested by the conduct of the "young man," let us pass on to the memorable comment of our Lord on the charity of the poor widow, as recorded in Mark 12:41–44. "Jesus sat over against the treasury, and beheld how the people cast money into the treasury: and many that were rich cast in *much*. And there came a certain poor widow, and she threw in two mites, which make a farthing. And he called unto him his disciples, and saith unto them, 'Verily, I say unto you, that this poor widow hath cast more in, than all they which have cast into the treasury: for all they did cast in of their abundance; but she *of her want* did cast in *all that she had, even all her living*.'" In the world's estimation nothing could be more improvident or more improper than her conduct; and I fear that few of us would have the heart to commend one who should go and do likewise. But how does our blessed Lord judge, who judges not according to appearance, but righteous judgment? Observing that she acts quite according to His precept of giving up all, He does not call His disciples round him, to warn them, by her example, not to take His words literally, as He did Peter on the use of the sword; but, on the contrary, points out carefully the peculiarity and unequalled greatness of her sacrifice, and holds her up to admiration on account of it. The rich cast in of their *abundance much;* she, of her *penury,* cast in a *little;* but it was *all that she had, even all her living.*

We have now only to go one step farther in order to ascertain in what sense the apostles understood that command of our Saviour now under consideration. The conduct of them and their adherents is thus recorded by St. Luke (Acts 2:44, etc., and 4:32, 34 and 35): *"All that believed* were together and had *all things common:* and sold their *possessions and goods,* and parted them to all men, as every man had need. And they, continuing daily with one accord in the temple, and breaking bread from house to house, did eat their meat with gladness and singleness of heart. The *multitude* of them that believed were of one heart and of one soul: neither said *any of them* that ought of the things that he possessed was his own; but they had all things common. Neither was there any among them that lacked: for as many as were *possessors of lands, or houses, sold them,* and brought the prices of the things that were sold, and laid them down at the apostles' feet: and distribution was made unto every man according as he had need."

By what arguments can it be shown that such a "union of heart and of soul," as is here described, is not just as important to us now, as it was to the primitive Christians? If this community of hearts and possessions was according to the mind of the Spirit *then*, why not *now?* We have the general precept enforcing the conduct of our blessed Lord himself; a particular exhortation to it in his conversation with the "young man"; and a most pointed approbation of it in the case of the poor widow. We have, moreover, to encourage and urge it, not only the example of the apostles, but that of all those who believed in Jerusalem. The former truly said, "Lo we have left all and followed thee"; and of the latter it was also truly written, "Neither said *any* of them that ought of the things which he possessed was his own."

I would just remark that such conduct does not essentially involve the institution of a common stock, but will be effectually secured by each individual blending himself with the whole household of faith, feeling their wants, and rejoicing in their welfare, as his own. This sympathy of the members of the holy family toward each other is strongly enforced and beautifully illustrated by the Apostle Paul: "Ye know the grace of our Lord Jesus Christ, that though he was rich, yet for your sakes he became poor, that ye through his poverty might be rich. I mean not that other men may be eased, and you burdened; but by an equality, that now at this time your abundance may be a supply for their want, that their abundance also may be a supply for your want, that there may be equality; as it is written: *'He that gathered much had nothing over; and he that had gathered little had no lack'*" (2 Corinthians 8:9, 13–15). As then here, the superabundance of him, who had gathered much, ministered to the deficiency of him who had gathered little; so now, whatever the bounty of God may bestow upon *us,* above a sufficiency for our present necessities, is to be esteemed a blessing in proportion as it is *distributed* to relieve the temporal and spiritual wants of others.

Again I ask, How do we evade the application of all these precepts and arguments and exhortations and warnings and examples to our own times? Is there in the Holy Scriptures any limitation as to the time when the love which distinguished the primitive church was to be in exercise? Is not humiliation and suffering, the very character of this dispensation, as of the life of Him who introduced it? Are there no farther ends to be obtained by the crucifixion of self and selfish interests, and manifesting the mind that was in Christ Jesus? Let the disputes and divisions in the Church of God, and the 600,000,000 who have never heard the name of salvation by the blood of Jesus declare. Let the agents of our societies declare, who travel from one end of the land to the other, to gather a scanty pittance from half-reluctant Christians—nay, who are often led to sharpen their goads at the Philistines' grindstones, to the dishonour of the cause of God. What then is the ground of evasion? Why, that those were apostolic times and apostolic men. Could there be a stronger reason urged for following their steps? Their having *supernatural aids,* in addition to *moral,* makes the obligation to use *moral* more imperative on our part, if possible, than on theirs; for we have now only the silent and unobserved influences of the Spirit of God operating by them. Those who may be inclined to ask, Were not the miraculous powers, entrusted to the apostles for the advancement of Christianity, also subservient to their personal comfort, amidst their want and pain and distress? We would refer those who enquire to the words of the Apostle Paul. "Even unto this present hour," says he (1 Corinthians 4:11 and 2 Corinthians 11:27), "we both hunger, and thirst, and are naked, and are buffeted, and have no certain dwelling-place. I have been in weariness and painfulness, in watchings often, in hunger and thirst, in fastings often, in cold and nakedness." It was, indeed, the very ground of the apostles' glorying and rejoicing that they were counted worthy to suffer for the sake of Him who had died for them; and it was these very sufferings which they endured, and sacrifices which they made, that proved most effectual in converting others to the faith, by drawing their attention to Him whom they loved, and for whom they suffered gladly the loss of all things. They felt the beneficial effects of suffering on their own souls, and they saw it blessed to the conversion of the souls of others: and, looking beyond things which are seen and temporal, they beheld that "exceeding and eternal weight of glory" which their sufferings were working out (2 Corinthians 4:17); they knew that, if they suffered with their Master, they should also reign with Him.

Considering the preceding remarks to establish the sense in which the apostles received the command of our Saviour in regard to giving up all, as well as the meaning of our Saviour Himself, it may appear superfluous to state anything farther; particularly as my only desire is to open the eyes of those who love their Lord and Master with a pure heart, fervently, to the understanding of His mind on the subject of this little book; for it is not money, time, and talents that I desire to see brought into the external service of Christ, as such; but only as the incense of praise and thanksgiving to Him "who has loved us, and washed [properly "loosed"] us from our sins in His own blood, and hath made us kings and priests unto God the Father," from His own redeemed, yea, the ransomed of the Lord, not the extorted, but voluntary homage from those hearts which would crown Him Lord of all. And certainly, any further statement would be superfluous, if we were called upon to sit in judgment on the meaning of writers, whose opinions laid us under no practical obligation, or whose sentiments were in unison with our whole nature. Here however, the case is widely different; we have an old nature for this earth, as well as a new nature for heaven; and therefore, things require to be stated as fully as may be, that Satan may be stopped at every turn by "it is written." To admit an opinion is to admit a truth; and to admit a truth is to admit the obligation to act upon it, against our earthly constitution. And as the admission and reception of the particular truth now under consideration, strikes at the very root of many of nature's most fondly cherished feelings, and of many apparently so amiable, that we scarcely allow ourselves to doubt that they are of God; it may be necessary to enlarge still more upon the subject, and show that the reception of this truth prepared the way for the success of the apostles, by leaving them free to follow Him who had called them to be soldiers, and that it will, by the grace of God—promised to us as well as to them—accomplish as great things in our days as it did in theirs, springing, as it did, and ever will, from this one source, Christ in us the hope of glory, dwelling in us richly in all wisdom and spiritual understanding; yea, in those cases where the world think we fail, as well as in those in which we seem to succeed: for if Christ and the spirit of His Kingdom be manifested, we are a sweet savour of Christ unto God, whether they receive our testimony or reject it; yea, though we preach as Noah did, an hundred and twenty years, and no man regard us.

2.

I come, therefore, *secondly,* to consider the important bearing of the principle, I have endeavoured to establish and illustrate, on several momentous commands which, without the reception of it, are rendered exceedingly difficult, nay, impossible, to be understood and received; notwithstanding that the import and object of these commands are abundantly obvious, and the performance of them tends most directly and most powerfully to promote the highest good which the church is capable of enjoying.

"Go ye into all the world and preach the gospel to every creature" (Mark 16:15), was the parting command of our blessed Saviour; and it was on the literal reception of this command that the momentous alternative hung of *our* knowledge or ignorance of the only Name under heaven given among men whereby we must be saved; for "how shall they hear without a preacher, and how shall they preach except they be sent," still is the order of God's government. Had there been the same doubt of the meaning and obligation of this precept in the infancy of Christianity, which these last ages have exhibited, it would scarcely have extended its influence beyond the confines of Judea. But, thanks be to God, the first Christians felt the gospel, committed to their trust, to be "the power of God unto salvation to everyone that believeth"; and they felt it to be the mind of Him who had loved them with an everlasting love, and given Himself for them, that this great act of surpassing love should be published to every creature, for His own glory, and for salvation to the ends of the earth; and therefore they counted all things but loss, that they might fulfil His will, and advance His Kingdom. Why has this spirit for so many centuries been slumbering? Because men have been seeking, every one his own things, and not the things of Christ. Let anyone ask his own heart, as in the presence of God, in which state he should feel most disposed to embrace the command: "Go into all the world and preach the Gospel to every creature"—whether, when he is labouring for, and enjoying the comforts and conveniences of life, and providing against the future possible wants of himself and his family; or when, like the apostles and first Christians, he has laid aside every earthly encumbrance, and waits ready to go or to stay, as the Spirit of God may appoint. To the enquiry "Who will go for us?" can there be a doubt whose heart would be most ready to reply "Here am I, send me" (Isaiah 6:8)? The one, having the eye single, since to glorify his Lord is the only object of his life, will be ready to answer, "Here am I"; while those who are surrounded by the cares and comforts of this world, have so many earthly claims and relations to adjust, that the general result will be that of standing still, and the enquiry, "Who will go for us?" will sound unwelcome to the ear, will chill, not animate, the noblest sympathies of the heart, and set the seal of silence on the lips. It is not meant absolutely to say that every man should become a missionary, in the proper sense of the term. "There are diversities of gifts, but the same Spirit; and there are differences of administrations, but the same Lord" (1 Corinthians 12:4). While one has that ministration of the Spirit which leads him to go and preach the gospel in person, another shows that he is guided by the same Spirit in carefully supplying the wants of him who thus goes —"taking nothing of the heathen" (3 John 7), from the abundance yielded by devoted diligence in his honest vocation, and by rigid habits of self-denial.[1]

---

1. Although this essay seems to have respect rather to those who have much to bestow, than those who have little, yet what the apostle says as an encouragement to labour, may be applied to every man however humble. "Let him labour, working with his hands the thing which is good, that he may have to give to him that needeth" (Ephesians 4:28). "I have coveted no man's silver, or gold, or apparel. Yes, ye yourselves know, that these hands have ministered unto my necessities, and to

Again, consider the important command, "Love thy neighbour as thyself" (Leviticus 19:18). Can we, with any truth, be said to love that neighbour as ourselves, whom we suffer to starve, while we have enough and to spare? May I not appeal to any, who have experienced the joy of knowing the unspeakable gift of God, and ask, Would you exchange this knowledge, with all the comforts and blessings it has been the means of imparting, for a hundred worlds, were they offered? Let us not then withhold the means by which others may obtain this sanctifying knowledge and heavenly consolation. Is it a profitable employment of our wealth, to raise it as a bulwark against those difficulties, which, if they meet even the children's children of the servants of God, are sent as especial proofs of their Father's love—for what son is he whom the Father chasteneth not?—and are designed to work out for them a far more exceeding and eternal weight of glory? Are not these very difficulties, dangers, and afflictions, against which we so anxiously desire to provide, the very marks by which Jesus Christ himself, His Apostles and Prophets, and all the chosen servants of God, have ever been distinguished, and the means by which they have been perfected?[2] Can then our wealth be so beneficially employed, either with reference to our own advantage or that of others, in removing from our Christian course these means of advancement, and characteristics of our profession, as in helping on the Kingdom of Christ with all that energy which a single eye

---

them that were with me. I have showed you all things, how that so labouring ye ought to support the weak, and to remember the words of the Lord Jesus, how he said, 'It is more blessed to give than to receive'" (Acts 20:33–35).

2. "What shall I more say? for the time would fail me to tell of Gideon, and of Barak, and of Samson, and of Jephthae; of David also, and Samuel, and of the Prophets: who through faith subdued kingdoms, wrought righteousness, obtained promises, stopped the mouths of lions, quenched the violence of fire, escaped the edge of the sword, out of weakness were made strong, waxed valiant in fight, turned to flight the armies of the aliens. Women received their dead raised to life again; and others were tortured, not accepting deliverance; that they might obtain a better resurrection: and others had trial of cruel mockings and scourgings, yea, moreover, of bonds and imprisonment: they were stoned, they were sawn asunder, were tempted, were slain with the sword: they wandered about in sheepskins and goat-skins; being destitute, afflicted, tormented; (of whom the world was not worthy:) they wandered in deserts, and in mountains, and in dens and caves of the earth (Hebrews 11:32–38).

can impart to the most limited powers, when directed and sustained by the Spirit of God?

It has been remarked that some pious men have, from their imprudence, left their children a burden upon the Christian public, and thus disgraced their profession. If, however, the unprovided state of these children was owing to an enlarged view of devotedness to God on the part of these parents, accompanied by frugal appropriations to themselves, and that strict honour and honesty, which must ever precede beneficence to others; all the disgrace, and ultimately all the loss, must rest on those that survive, who are so dead to the privileges of the Gospel, as either to forget that it was ever said, "Whosoever receiveth one such little one in my name, receiveth me" (Matthew 18:5), or to neglect the opportunity, despise the honour, and spurn away the blessing, of entertaining such a guest. Oh! if we really believed our Saviour's declaration, how dearly should we value, and how warmly embrace, such an opportunity of glorifying our Master, of blessing ourselves, and of showing again to the world "how these Christians love one another!"[1]

All our misconceptions on this subject seem to arise from one deeply-rooted opinion, learnt of Satan and the world over which he presides, that *riches* and *comforts* are better for our children, than *poverty* and *dependence*. The whole tenor of the New Testament, however, pronounces the opinion to be false; and were a hundred individuals appointed to the office of choosing a portion for their children, in accordance with the obvious principles of Christianity, and with the declarations of its Author and His apostles—such a portion as bore the most favourable aspect on the acquisition of the prize of the high calling of God in Christ Jesus; and were they conscientiously to perform their office, they would all unite in choosing a portion poor and dependent.[2] Yet whilst our Lord says: "How hardly shall

---

1. In 1841 Mr. and Mrs. Groves adopted a child of eight as daughter, "an orphan who was commended to their care by her father on his *deathbed*. This charge was a source of *great comfort* to them: they undertook it as unto the Lord, who truly gave them their hire. The child, being early converted to God, grew up to be a very efficient help in their mission work when other labourers were withdrawn; and she became to them, in every way, as a beloved daughter" (400).

2. "I see here parents who are toiling night and day. 'What are you doing?' 'I have a

they that *have* riches enter into the Kingdom of God!" we act just as though He had said, "How hardly shall they enter in, who are *without* them!" Here I would leave the sovereignty of the Lord unlimited. It is doubtless the same thing to Him to work by many or by few—by the rich or the poor: but still "*how hardly* shall they that have riches enter into the kingdom of heaven" must stand.

If there had been an *unerring* physician of the body sent to a consumptive family, who left it as his prescription: "How hardly shall they survive the climate of the North; it is easier for a camel to go through a needle's eye than your children escape destruction in the blasts of the North"; if after this you saw the parents struggling for northern climates, you must say they either did not believe the physician, or they were deliberately doing what they could to destroy their children. . . .

Again I say, let me not be misunderstood, as though I wished to make all Christianity consist in giving up money, time, and talents. Unless they are the expressions of love to the Lord, and flow from a desire to meet His mind and promote His glory, they are but sounding brass and tinkling cymbals. Yet surely, they are the natural external expressions of internal love; and although they be insincerely assumed by hypocrisy, it is her homage to truth; and although the self-righteous Pharisee may present the semblance of devotion, as a vain and hateful barter for heaven, yet it requires very little spirituality of mind to discern that this arises in a different source and terminates in a different object; the one begins in self, and ends in self; the other begins in Christ, and ends in Christ. When, therefore, the Lord requires his Church to be careful for nothing, it is only that He might display His watchfulness and carefulness over her. Surely it is a most unspeakable privilege to be allowed to cast all our cares

---

large family of children; and I am endeavouring to lay up a portion for them." Why then do you not in truth lay up a portion for them! What! will you lay up a little dust and call that a portion? Is that a portion for an immortal soul? You *are rather hanging a millstone about the neck of your children which may sink them deeper into ruin. You may thereby tempt them to plunge into the world: and there they may scatter what you have treasured up and called a portion.* 'The Lord is my portion, saith my soul,' is the declaration of David; and till you lead your children to this portion, you are making no real provision for them'" (Rev. Richard Cecil).

upon God; and to feel that we are thereby delivered from the slavery of earthly expectations, and made free to speak the truth in love, without fear or apprehension? What is the glorious liberty of the children of God, but to be dependent only upon One, "who giveth liberally and upbraideth not," who says, "Ask, and ye shall receive; seek, and ye shall find; knock, and it shall be opened unto you: for everyone that asketh, receiveth; and he that seeketh, findeth: and to him that knocketh it shall be opened." God, in pity to our weakness and unbelief, condescends to reason with us thus: "What man is there of you, whom, if his son ask bread, will he give him a stone? or if he ask a fish, will he give him a serpent? If ye then, *being evil,* know how to give good gifts unto your children, how much more shall your Father, which is in heaven, give good things to them that ask him?" (Matthew 7:7–11). Let us therefore do the will of such a Father to the utmost of our ability now, and trust Him for the *future:* "for he hath said, 'I will never leave thee, nor forsake thee'; so that we may boldly say, 'The Lord is my helper, and I will not fear, what man shall do unto me'" (Hebrews 13:6). "Trust therefore in the Lord, and do good; and verily thou shalt be fed" (Psalm 37:3). Oh! if everyone who believed himself ransomed by the precious blood of Christ, felt himself so entirely the purchased possession of Him who thus so dearly bought him, as to determine henceforth to know nothing save Jesus Christ and Him crucified; not to labour for anything but that the unspeakably glad tidings of salvation through Him might be spread throughout the world, till every heart of the ransomed family drank of the same overflowing cup of consolation; how soon would the wants of the whole habitable earth be answered by thousands crying out: "Here am I, send me"; while those sheep to whom the glad tidings would be borne, would discern the shepherd's voice, receive with thankfulness such messengers of peace, seeing by their fruits "that God was in them of a truth."

Think not that this is carrying things too far. Our blessed Lord says, "This is my commandment, that ye love one another, as I have loved you. Greater love hath no man than this, that a man lay down his life for his friends. Ye are my friends, if ye do whatsoever I command you" (John 15:12). Here our blessed Lord tells us to love one another, as He has loved us; and then points to the laying down His life, as the most exalted proof of that love which could be given. If then, as the example of our Saviour and the exhortation of the Apostle testify, "we ought to lay down our *lives* for the brethren,"[1] how much more ought we to impart to them our substance.

We all know what a persuasive power the deaths of the martyrs exerted on the minds of those who witnessed them; and, in its just measure and proportion, would the dedication of property, time and talents, have a similar effect at the present day. It would convince those, whom we are anxious to convince, of the reality of our faith in that redeemer and that inheritance, which they now think only a name, in consequence of the secular spirit that disfigures the Christianity of too many of its professors. How differently would the heathen look on our endeavours to publish the mercy of our glorified Lord, if the hardy and suffering spirit of primitive times were to descend again on the silken age into which we are fallen! and if they perceived in us that love which led them to endure all things for the elect's sake, that they may also obtain the salvation which is in Christ Jesus with eternal glory. Example is a far more fruitful source of self-denial than the influence exerted on the mind by precept. If we call on those, who know nothing of the savour of that name which is as ointment poured forth, to give up all for Christ, and this you literally do to every Hindoo and Mahomedan; let us, who thus call, and who profess to know much of the power of His Name, do so likewise; that they may catch a kindred spirit from a living exhibition. Let us evidence, in very deed, that we love not the world, neither the things of the world, but that the love of the Father is in us. "For all that is in the world, the lust of the flesh, the lust of the eyes, and the pride of life, is not of the Father, but of the world. And the world passeth

---

1. "Hereby perceive we the love of God, because he laid down his life for us; and we ought to lay down our lives for the brethren; But whoso hath this world's good, and seeth his brother have need, and shutteth up his bowels of compassion from him, how dwelleth the love of God in him?" (1 John 3:16–17). And "how dwelleth the love of God in him" who can behold his fellows, by millions, perishing with ignorance—that hunger of the soul—without putting forth every effort, and making every sacrifice, that they may receive the bread of life.

away, and the lust thereof; but he, that doeth the will of God, abideth for ever" (1 John 2:15).

3.

I shall now conclude with a few arguments to prove, that if the extension of the *spirit* of Christ's kingdom be the proper object of the Church's pursuit—which is, on earth, essentially a spirit of self-denial for others' good—the entire surrender contended for is as consonant with reason as it is with revelation; and consequently the great end of our existence should be the extension of this spirit; and the most important enquiry in which we can be engaged is: how this may be most effectually accomplished.

Let us, therefore, begin with the consideration of our children, as it regards their apprehension of this spirit of our Lord's kingdom. There is no one calling himself a Christian, who does not *profess* to desire, and there is no one really a Christian, who does not in *earnest* desire for his children, both the apprehension and attainment of this blessing. The *lips* of all, and the *hearts* of the saints continually declare it as their wish that their children may receive the word of truth, "not as the word of man, but as it is indeed the word of God"; that they may esteem and receive it as "a lamp unto their feet and a light unto their paths"; that they may prize it as the greatest and best gift of God, next to Him of whom it bears testimony and to whom it owes its preciousness. How then is a Christian to direct, most powerfully and practically, the opening and susceptible minds of his children towards this Word of truth? Is it to be done by exhibiting to them a life devoted to the study of that Word, as revealing the will of Him whom he loves, and Him of whom it testifies, so that they may attach true ideas to true words, following simply its precepts as judging them concerning all things, to be right for himself, and promoting the extension of this knowledge as equally essential to others; by a dedication of time and talents to this end; by habits of continued self-denial, having for their object the acquisition of greater means towards the accomplishment of a work for which he would have them to believe that Jesus their Lord left the bosom of his Father and descended to earth, and for the furtherance of which apostles and martyrs regarded all temporal advantages as loss, and were ready to suffer the privation of them all? Or is it to be done by speaking, in very high terms, of the excellence and importance of the work; by accompanying the words with a gift of one, five, fifty, or a hundred pounds a year for the promotion of it, but, in other respects, providing for temporal conveniences and enjoyments like the world? As long as the human mind is capable of being influenced by example, the first of these two exhibitions must exert the most powerful influence on the youthful mind. It must have a direct and almost invincible tendency to impress that mind with a conviction of the sincerity of our love of the truth, of the reality of our devotion towards its great Author, of our deep feeling of its necessity as the only guide to purity and happiness, and of our ardent desire that all men may know and receive and embrace it. And although all this is infinitely removed from a work of grace on the soul, the almighty work of the Spirit of God; yet they may be, and continually are, the instruments He uses for arresting the sinner, and turning his attention to Jesus, and leading beyond the apprehension of the truth—in the understanding, to the Author and Finisher of faith for the realization of it in the heart. But, on the contrary, every appropriation towards providing temporal comforts and conveniences, and pleasures, either for them or for ourselves, has a tendency directly the reverse. It shows that there is, in this value for the world, a rival interest in the heart; it weakens their conviction of our sincerity; and lessens, in exact proportion to its amount, the *practical* conviction on their minds—that there is but "one thing needful" in our estimation.

The true servant of God knows, better than any man, the real value of money, the value of time, the value of talents of whatever order. He is accordingly the most assiduous in his vocation, the most parsimonious of his time, the most anxious to improve his talents, so far as they are subservient to the interests of Christ's Kingdom.[1] He knows that the mysterious dealings of God have most intimately connected us in the ways of His providence, with the salvation of one another. He knows also that there is no means, humbly laid at

---

1. The Christian motto should be: Labour hard, consume little, give much, and all to Christ.

the foot of the cross, which He who hung there does not bless and send forth, with the blessing resting on it, to accomplish purposes of mercy.

As to laying up for children,[1] believing it to be contrary to the letter and spirit of the Gospel, and therefore to the best interests of the children themselves, I have no hesitation in saying that, on these grounds, I am persuaded it ought to be relinquished—as much so, as spending our means on the selfish indulgence of our own inclinations. The reason indeed of the commands, exhortations, and encouragements to abstain from all such provision, appears as obvious, from every day's experience, as that of any single command in the Scripture; so that it manifestly would be the happiness of a child of God to pursue the conduct thus enjoined by his Lord, even if revelation was far less explicit on the subject, than it clearly and undeniably

---

1. "Wherefore should I fear in the days of evil, when the iniquity of my heels shall compass me about? [Revised Version "iniquity at my heels," that is, enemies who would work iniquity.] They that trust in their wealth, and boast themselves in the multitude of their riches; none of them can by any means redeem his brother, nor give to God a ransom for him (for the redemption of their soul is precious, and it ceaseth [faileth] for ever); that he should still live for ever, and not see corruption. For he seeth that wise men die, likewise the fool and the brutish person perish, and leave their wealth to others. Their inward thought is that their houses shall continue for ever, and their dwelling-places to all generations; they call their lands after their own names. Nevertheless, man being in honour abideth not: he is like the beasts that perish. This, their way, is their folly; yet their posterity approve their sayings. The upright shall not be ashamed in the evil time; and in the days of famine they shall be satisfied. I have been young, and now am old; yet have I not seen the righteous forsaken, nor his seed begging bread" (Psalm 49:5–13, and 37:19 and 25). "God hath fed me," says Scott, "all my life long. I die, but God can provide for my children, and children's children without *me;* I cannot without *Him.* I have not, since I came here, allowing for my house, cleared £100 a year: yet the Lord hath provided; and I live in plenty, and can give something, and, if more money were good for me, He would give it." What he farther says, in speaking of the "carnal" anxiety of parents for the temporal welfare of their children, though applied by himself to the clergy in particular, is equally applicable to the laity. "I often think what St. Paul would say to ministers in our days, on this ground; when of those in his days he says, 'All seek their own, not the things of Jesus Christ.' (See my note on the passage.) I have long lamented that we cannot serve God by the day, and leave it to him to provide day by day for us and ours" (*Scott's Letters,* London, 1824; pages 296–7).

is. A "single eye" can alone secure our fidelity in the discharge of a stewardship so peculiarly trying as that with which the wealthy[2] among us are entrusted. The circumstances of such a stewardship have a remarkable power in directing and drawing our affections toward improper objects; in fixing them upon others in an inordinate degree; in leading us to misapprehend the nature of true happiness, and to estimate things by a standard entirely at variance with the plainest and most frequently reiterated declarations of the Gospel. If, therefore, under such circumstances, personal conveniences and indulgences, the elevation of self in the world, under the thousand alluring masks which Satan provides for those who wish to wear them, as means, he tells them, of influence, be allowed any weight in the argument, we may easily determine the judgment which will go forth; you will see every man looking on his own things, not on the things of others. Nay, is not this now the aspect even of the professing Church of Christ? Should anyone rise, and say, However this may be with others, it does not apply to me. I give a guinea to this, and a guinea to that, and a guinea to another; I might say, Yes, and as many hundreds, it may be thousands to self, whose desires were to be mortified and solicitations curtailed.

How much would the judgment of the Christian world be modified with regard to the leadings of providence if the eye had always the glory of God as the single object on which it rested! If that glory were our only aim, we should be all led to press forward in the path to affluence and honours with a more faltering step and chastened energy. How slowly would a servant of Christ, who profitably labours among many thousand souls with a bare subsistence, be led to interpret the possibility of obtaining a more abundant provision (if with a less extensive sphere of usefulness) into a leading of providence which encourages and demands his removal. He might, on the other hand, be led sometimes even to suspect the possibility of its being only a temptation of Satan, laid in his way, with a view of limiting the field of his usefulness. That malicious and powerful

---

2. By wealthy, I mean those who have large incomes, as contrasted with those who have a hare subsistence from their labours, or those who have inheritances entailed upon them, so that they cannot enjoy the privilege of disencumbering themselves.

spirit doubtless now tempts the servant, as he once did his Lord, by saying: "All this power will I give thee and this glory: *for that is delivered unto me: and to whomsoever I will, I give it.* If thou therefore wilt worship me, all shall be thine" (Luke 4:6). We should never forget that this power of Satan over the world and the things of the world is acknowledged by our Saviour himself when He calls him "the prince of this world" (John 14:30). With the solicitations of this "Prince of Darkness" coming, as he often does, in the form of "an angel of light," there concur affections of our nature, called tender and amiable. The whole heart is misled; the judgment is biassed; and the understanding darkened. He, on the contrary, who considers and uses an increase of means only as a sacred deposit, committed to him for the extension of Christ's Kingdom, and not for individual aggrandizement, is liable to no such deception with respect to the leadings of providence. He has no personal interest in the pecuniary advantages attendant on any situation; and his only question is whether it be one in which he may best serve and glorify his Master. When his heavenly Father sends him prosperity beyond what is sufficient for his immediate wants, he does not ask himself, May not I possibly need this superabundance at some future period? or, If I never require it myself, may not my wife, or children, or relatives? He dares not to ask a question so full of unbelief, nor presumes to turn the very abundance of the past mercies of God into an argument against trusting Him for the future. He knows that the best security for all spiritual blessings and all temporal mercies, both to himself and to his friends, lies in doing the will, and trusting unreservedly in the promises, of that God who hath said: "Can a mother forget her sucking child; that she should not have compassion on the fruit of her womb? Yea, she may forget; yet will not I forget thee" (Isaiah 49:15). What, therefore, he has freely received, he freely gives; and trusts for the future the promises of his Heavenly Father, with a sincere, filial, and ingenuous confidence.

The view here taken may naturally lead the minds of many enquirers after the truth to ask, "Is not this tempting God?" To this difficulty Scripture supplies us with many very interesting and striking answers; from which I shall select a few.

When Abraham was called to quit his kindred and country and to put his trust under the shadow of the Almighty's wing, his going, notwithstanding that he knew not whither, and that he was perfectly unacquainted in what manner or to what extent he was to be provided for, constitutes that peculiar feature in his obedience, which all Christians feel and appreciate, and the spirit of which they profess to desire to have animating their own. The same is also observable in the sacrifice of his son. Compliance in this case seems the death-blow to his fondest hopes; and to trust that, notwithstanding his compliance, the promises which God had made to him would be fulfilled, was a confidence resting on somewhat beyond the bounds of all human probability. Yet he does not hesitate to obey (and the author of the Epistle to the Hebrews tells us why), because he believed that God was able to raise his son up from the dead. Was this then tempting God? What says His Word? "The Angel of the Lord called unto Abraham out of heaven the second time, and said, 'By myself have I sworn, saith the Lord; *for because thou hast done this thing, and hast not withheld thy son, thine only son;* that in blessing I will bless thee, and in multiplying I will multiply thy seed as the stars of the heaven, and as the sand which is upon the seashore: and in thy seed shall all the nations of the earth be blessed; *because thou hast obeyed my voice*'" (Genesis 22:15, etc.).

Again, in the 34th chapter of Exodus it is written: "Thrice in the year shall all your men-children appear before the Lord God, the God of Israel. For I will cast out the nations before thee, and enlarge thy borders; *neither shall any man desire thy land when thou shalt go up to appear before the Lord thy God thrice in the year.*" Now, would obedience to this precept be tempting God? Doubtless not. Yet surely there is a much greater natural difficulty in the way of protecting the defenceless wives and families of a whole people during the absence of all the males at Jerusalem, than there is in providing subsistence sufficient for those who daily labour; for by this means the great mass of mankind are, and ever have been provided for.

The institution of the sabbatical year appears to afford another very apt illustration. Let us therefore for a moment consider the commands and promises annexed to its observance, as well as the threatenings pronounced, and the punishments inflicted in case of disobedience. "Six years thou shalt sow thy field, and six years thou shalt prune thy vineyard, and gather in the fruit thereof; but in the seventh year shall be a sabbath of rest unto the Land, a sabbath for the Lord; thou shalt neither sow thy field, nor prune thy vineyard. And if ye shall say, 'What shall we eat the seventh year? behold, we shall not sow, nor gather in our increase'; then I will command my blessing upon you in the sixth year, and it shall bring forth fruit for three years. And ye shall sow the eighth year, and eat yet of old fruit until the ninth year; until her fruits come in, ye shall eat of the old store. If ye will not for all this hearken unto me, but walk contrary unto me, I will bring your land into desolation, and I will scatter you among the heathen: and your lands shall be desolate, and your cities waste. Then shall the land enjoy her sabbaths, as long as it lieth desolate, and ye be in your enemies' land: even then shall the land rest, and enjoy her sabbaths. As long as it lieth desolate it shall rest: because it did not rest in your sabbaths, when ye dwelt upon it" (Leviticus 25:3, 4, 20; and chapter 26.).

We see afterwards the execution of this threat: "Them that had escaped from the sword carried he away to Babylon; where they were servants to the King and his sons until the reign of the kingdom of Persia; to fulfil the word of the Lord by the mouth of Jeremiah, until the land had enjoyed her sabbaths; for as long as she lay desolate she kept sabbath, to fulfil threescore and ten years" (2 Chronicles 36:20).[1]

Now these illustrations of the nature of the divine government are very instructive, whether we contemplate Abraham's obedience and reward, or the disobedience and punishment of his posterity. Abraham appears to pursue a line of conduct which must end in the loss of everything dear to him; yet in the way of obedience, unimagined mercies and favours meet him. His posterity, by neglecting to go

---

1. Now many may say, these commands are so clear that none could misunderstand them, but not so these under consideration; perhaps if we were to analyze a little deeper our hearts, we should find that the one owes its clearness to our freedom from any consequent burden on finding them clear; the other its indistinctness from the reverse, not having yet learnt the glorious liberty of depending on and yielding all to Christ. In heaven they are seen to be, I have no doubt, equally clear, equally commands, or rather privileges of the saints of God.

thrice in the year to Jerusalem, or to obey the command respecting the observance of the sabbatical year, seem to the natural eye to be in the way of safety and abundance; yet their enemies brought famine and desolation on their land, and they themselves, their wives, and their little ones, were carried away into captivity. Now the anxieties which led the Jews to ask, "What will become of our wives and our children during our absence at Jerusalem?" or, "What will become of our households during the seventh year?" are natural anxieties, as strong and as amiable as can influence the decision of the human heart. Yet these very anxieties were the immediate cause of their doubts, their distrust, and their disobedience. If then the following even these strong dictates of the heart against a command of God has proved perfect foolishness to those who have presumed so to do, let us take warning by their example; for to this end were these things written.

There is one inference which, guided by the analogy of faith, I would draw from the preceding observations. If trusting against the natural appearance of things was demanded under the comparatively dim light of the Old Testament—a dispensation which, considered nationally, had peculiar respect to temporal prosperity—much more might we expect it to be required under the bright light of the Gospel—a dispensation in which temporal prosperity and all temporal distinctions are cast entirely into the shade: and as the disobedience of the Jews cut them off not only from the direct blessings promised to obedience, but also from the striking manifestations of the divine providence over them, which the three years' corn in one year, and the protection of their families and possessions during their absence at Jerusalem would have afforded them; so we, by our want of confidence in God, lose those endearing evidences of His love, which a simple trust in His promises is the appointed means of drawing down from His open and bountiful hand.

What preachers of righteousness would these Jews have been had they obeyed the commands of their God! What a sermon on God's providence over His chosen would the three years' provision in one year, and the miraculous protection of their coasts, have been to the heathen around!

It may be of importance for us to remember that it is *God* alone whom we are afraid to trust. Where we have no doubt of the integrity or ability of *man,* we fearlessly trust. If one of the Princes of this world has an arduous undertaking to accomplish, which requires the undivided care and attention of those to whom it is committed; and if he says to his servants, "Pursue steadily and singly the business entrusted to you, without distraction about personal provision, of which I will take sufficient care"; how many are the candidates, how eager the contention, how secure the confidence! Nay more, the obvious tendency of such a plan toward the attainment of the end in view is seen and its wisdom appreciated. Yet when the King of Heaven, after manifesting His unspeakable love toward us in the sacrifice of His Son, demands of us a similar confidence, we make no scruple to withhold it. When our Blessed Lord says, "Lay not up for yourselves treasures upon earth," that your eye may be single in my service, that your whole body may be full of light to discern between good and evil: when He expressly says, "Take no thought, saying, 'What shall we eat?' or, 'What shall we drink?' or, 'Wherewithal shall we be clothed;' but seek ye first the Kingdom of God and his righteousness, and all these things shall be added unto you"; we see neither the wisdom nor goodness of His design. We begin to explain away His instructions concerning it; we hesitate about the meaning of His promises; we put far from us the privilege of believing that He, who neither slumbers nor sleeps, watcheth over us. Whence then this confidence in man, whose breath is in his nostrils, who is absent in the moment of calamity; yet diffidence in God,[1] who is the

---

1. How different the spirit and conduct of our blessed Lord! Did He fear to leave, without temporal provision, his widowed mother to the promises and providence of God? No; He left her unprovided to an unprovided (Acts 3:1 and 6) disciple: and this He did, not at a time when probabilities were greatly in favour of a comfortable competence being easily procured, but when He knew that difficulties and dangers would beset them at every step. Surely had laying up *beforehand* been the duty of a child, our Saviour would have exhibited this virtue among that constellation of virtues which shone forth from His character; for He knew that we were to follow His example. Why then did He act thus, while we hesitate to follow His steps? Because He knew the truth, nature, and extent, of the promises of God, which we doubt or deny. Some will say, "But this was a provision!" Yes, the very provision which God will ever make for those that trust in Him … a provision at the moment of necessity.

omnipotent, the very present help in every time of trouble? Does it not arise from a fear, lest, if we trust Him with our provision, He might choose for us and ours the portion He chose for *the Son of His love?* Does it not arise from a secret desire that our *own* wills may be done, and not *His?* Yet we may rest assured that, as it is not for the interest of a wayward child to be independent of the salutary control of an excellent father, neither is it for ours to be able to say: "Soul, thou hast much goods laid up for many years."

So intensely am I convinced of this truth that I can, with my whole heart, pray for myself and all who are nearest and dearest to me, that we may be so circumstanced in life as to be compelled to live by faith on the divine promises day by day.[2] "Godliness with contentment," says the Apostle, "is great gain. For we brought nothing into this world, and it is certain we can carry nothing out. And having food and raiment, let us be therewith content. But they that will be rich fall into temptation and a snare, and into many foolish and hurtful lusts, which drown men in destruction and perdition. For the *love of money is the root of all evil* [a root of all evils, Revised Version]; which while some coveted after, they have erred from the faith, and pierced themselves through with many sorrows. But thou, O man of God, *flee these things;* and follow after righteousness, godliness, faith, love, patience, meekness" (1 Timothy 6:6–11). Let us therefore "endure hardness, as good soldiers of Jesus Christ," knowing that "no man that warreth entangleth himself with the affairs of this life; that he may please him who hath chosen him to be a soldier" (2 Timothy 2:3).

Now that all this may not appear irresistible to many, I am fully aware; and having been myself, in times past, led to wish that a few passages, such as 1 Timothy 5:8; 2 Corinthians 12:14, had admitted of clearer explanation, or, rather, required none, I shall now, in a few words, endeavour to explain what appears to me to be the principle of the New Testament revelation, which is not to supply the logician with an irresistible chain of premises and conclusions, but the child with a light to his Father's mind; therefore, on the divinity of

---

2. "I will also leave in the midst of thee an afflicted and poor people, and *they shall trust* in the name of the Lord. They shall feed and lie down, and none shall make them afraid" (Zephaniah 3:12 and 13).

our blessed Lord, the Lord's day, the principle of communion, of church discipline, and of literally giving up all—if a man wishes to be disputatious and escape the easy and blessed yoke of Christ's love he may, and therefore will walk in darkness, whilst the child is, in his simplicity, surrounded by a flood of light.

I shall, therefore, briefly recapitulate the reasons why it appears to me that our Saviour spoke *literal* truth, and meant to be understood as so speaking, when He used such expressions as these: "Lay not up for yourselves treasures upon earth," and, "Sell all that thou hast":

(1) Because He commanded the young man to do so;

(2) Because He commended the poor widow for doing so;

(3) Because the apostles, and all who believed at Jerusalem, did so, by selling their goods, houses, and lands;

(4) Because without this dedication, it is impossible to receive the command, "Love thy neighbour as thyself";

(5) Because, while it obviously tends to the general extension of Christ's Kingdom upon earth, it does also, in an equal measure, contribute to the happiness and usefulness of the individual, by extirpating carefulness and sloth, and causing to grow in abundance the peaceable fruits of righteousness and love.[1]

---

1. He which soweth sparingly shall reap also sparingly; and he which soweth bountifully shall reap also bountifully. Every man according as he purposerh in his heart, so let him give; not grudgingly, or of necessity: for God loveth a cheerful giver. And God is able to make all grace abound toward you; that ye, always having all sufficiency in all things, may abound to every good work: (as it is written, He hath dispersed abroad; he hath given to the poor; his righteousness remaineth for ever. Now he that administereth seed to the sower, both minister bread for your food, and multiply your seed sown, and increase the fruits of your righteousness:) being enriched in everything to all bountifulness, which causeth through us thanksgiving to God. For the administration of this service not only supplieth the want of the saints, but is abundant also by many thanksgivings unto God; (whiles by the experiment of this ministration they glorify God for your professed subjection unto the Gospel of Christ, and for your liberal distribution unto them, and unto all men:) and by their prayer for you, which long after you for the exceeding grace of God in you" (2 Corinthians 9:6–14).

[I cannot refrain from inviting any candid and careful reader to compare the rendering of this passage as given with the rendering in the Revised Version, as an instance of the real need there was for a revision of the English version. Especially

Should I be asked, what I understand by *giving up all for Christ*, my reply would be that I believe this surrender to be made, when any individual, following whatever lawful vocation he may, labours and contrives therein, with all the assiduity and indefatigable diligence of which he is capable, to accomplish the known—the recorded will of his Lord and Saviour. If that will requires that he should labour for the souls, as well as the bodies of men; that he should strive to make his fellows happy in time, and in eternity; that he should impart to them the knowledge of Him who is "the way, the truth, and the life"; he will labour with time, talents, means, and prayers, for the attainment of these ends, as diligently as others labour from motives of simple coveteousness, or with a view of making provision against future contingencies for themselves or for their families. If any object to selling "houses or lands," it remains for themselves to distinguish[2] between the motives which induce them to retain *their* property, and those which induced the "young man" to retain *his*. If they retain it from any private affection unsupported by the Word of truth, and if it is not their own full conviction that, in so doing, they are pursuing the path most directly tending to fulfil the mind of Christ; neither the myriads of those who embrace their views and follow their plans, nor the learning and authority by which they are supported, will prove them to be wise, or true, or eligible, in that day when the judgment shall be set, and the books shall be opened. The principle I have here endeavoured to establish from the sacred volume, demands of no man the relinquishment of a present sphere of usefulness, till he is himself conscientiously convinced that he is

---

is this seen from verse 10 and onward. Let him notice the words—ministereth and administration, experiment, professed; the change from "both"—expressing a desire, to "shall"—making a promise or assurance. And if he can compare the Greek he will notice the opening of verse 10, where the construction of the Greek was missed, "bread for food," being connected wrongly with the words following instead of with the words preceding, and "your" was inserted; and then the last clause quoted (verse 14) made clear and emphatic in the Revised Version.]

2. It might be an examination of not less importance to ascertain why provision for future possible wants is almost the only point in which the Christian and the man of the world stand on the same ground, pursue the same ends, and govern themselves by the same maxims; and how it happens that this part of our duty, if it indeed be such, coincides so exactly with our natural propensities.

called to another, where he may accomplish more for the great cause for which he lives—the exaltation of Jesus, and the gathering his sheep. But though it does not require a relinquishment of present occupations, it is most uncompromising as to the *end* to which they must be directed.[1]

That the hearty reception of this principle may be connected, by natural consequence, with many and great difficulties in this life, no one, who knows anything of human nature, as opposed to the nature of Christ's kingdom, or the gospel history, can doubt. In this world's history, great things are not accomplished but by great sacrifices. A life free from sufferings and sacrifices our Lord has not promised, and the apostles did not enjoy. Such a portion they did not even expect, but were always prepared to live on the remembrance of the "faithful saying, If we suffer with Him, we shall also reign with Him." It should therefore be no question of ours whether, in literally fulfilling our Saviour's command, we shall be subjected to many sufferings and privations, or not. The question is, Is it the command of Him who loved us too well to enjoin any thing but for our good; and whether in His sovereign arrangement, the embracing of it may not be connected with the advancement of His Kingdom and promotion of His glory? It would at least elevate the church from the disgraceful

---

1. What is here meant is that the principle contended for by no means precludes the carrying on such pursuits as require a large stock. But, as he who had ten talents used them as a servant, and brought the interest to his master, so the Christian merchant lives and labours as a servant purchased by his Lord, and considers his gains as designed for his Master's service, not his private emolument. If he so acts, whatever his station may be, he has given up all for Christ. He remains where he is, not for his own private advantage, but that, as a faithful steward, he may pour forth the rich abundance which God grants to his labours, to nourish and build up the Church, and enlarge the confines of his Master's kingdom, and the only personal advantage he has above his poorer brother is, he has more anxieties (but for Christ, who sweetens them) every step he advances up, and therefore would have no personal inducement to get up but the sense of duty, that he may have more abundantly to give to him who needeth, and the guinea dedications and speeches from the rich would pass out together as no longer needed; for one *action* of real dedication would contain more argument than a thousand *speeches* about it, from those who are living in all the luxuries of life, and yield more help than a thousand guineas, and there would be left for the poorer, and the *poorest* would bring in their blessed two mites.

position in which she now stands, striking hands with Geshem and Sanballat, to raise up the walls of Jerusalem. She would then rejoice to say: "We will do the Lord's work ourselves." Another question is, whether the gathering in the sheep of Christ out of a lost world, or even of a single one, be not worthy of all the sacrifices we are called upon to make; and whether the means we have pointed out have not, in the appointment of the Lord, a tendency to the accomplishment of this end? If, from the word of truth, we can answer "Indisputably"; troubles, dangers, and difficulties should be as nothing. "Not my will but thine be done."

If the world esteem this madness, we must say with the Apostle, "Whether we be beside ourselves, it is to God; or whether we be sober, it is for your cause. For the love of Christ constraineth us: because we thus judge, that if one died for all, then were all dead [therefore all died]: and that he died for all, *that they which live should not henceforth live unto themselves but unto him who died for them and rose again*" (2 Corinthians 5:13).

Thus I leave the question to those who love the Lord Jesus Christ in *sincerity;* who desire that His name may be a praise in the earth; and who, seeing that the harvest is truly plenteous, but the labourers few, are constant in prayer to the Lord of the harvest that He would send forth more labourers into it, and that He would more abundantly pour out His Holy Spirit upon His Church, that it may more fervently desire, and more assiduously labour for, the coming of that day, when the Lord shall come to be glorified in His saints, and to be admired in all them that believe. And may the Lord direct all our hearts into the love of God, and patient waiting for Christ, that if we should be alive and remain at His coming, we may be caught up to join the saints who are to come with their Lord in the clouds; and so be ever with the Lord; or if we go before, may we come with Him in the day of His glory. Amen.

NOTE, REFERRED TO IN PAGE 3 [SEE P. 81].

It may be necessary to notice the only preceptive passage in the New Testament which apparently bears a different aspect. This we shall do for two reasons:

First, to meet the readiness with which it is pleaded as a counterpoise to the otherwise clearly universal doctrine of the New Testament; and secondly, to prove that, far from its being in opposition to the principle for which we contend, it is another illustration of it. The text alluded to is contained in 1 Timothy 5:8, where St. Paul is giving general directions relative to the provision to be made for widows, making a distinction at the same time between such as are to be relieved by the Church, and such as are to be relieved by their relatives. In reference to the latter he says, "He that provideth not for his own, and especially for those of his own household, hath denied the faith, and is worse than an infidel [unbeliever]"; which Hammond thus paraphrases, "But if any man or woman do not maintain those that belong to them, especially those of their family—as their parents clearly are, having a right to live in their house, and a propriety to be maintained by them (or that they take care and relieve them) supposing *that they are able to it*,—that man or woman doth quite contrary to the command of Christ, and indeed performs not that duty to *parents* that even infidels think themselves obliged to do." And in his note he adds, "To *provide* here does not signify laying up by way of *careful, thoughtful providence* beforehand, but only taking care of for the present, as we are able, *relieving, maintaining, giving to them* that want." Whitby in his annotation on the same verse says, "Some here are guilty of a great mistake, scraping together great fortunes, and hoarding them up for their children, with a scandalous neglect of that charity to their Christian brethren which alone can sanctify those enjoyments to them, and enable them to lay up a good foundation against the time to come; pleading these words to excuse their sordid parsimony and want of charity; that 'he that provideth not for his own household, hath denied the faith, and is worse than an infidel'; *whereas these words plainly respect the provision which children should make for their parents, and not that which parents should make for their children."* See also Doddridge, Scott, and Poole's *Synopsis*, in loco. The meaning of the text then is simply this: he who ministers not to the necessities of his aged relatives, having the means so to do, is to be esteemed worse than an infidel; for even the heathen acknowledged this to be a duty. The precept, therefore, is to *give* and not to *lay up,* and consequently is in perfect accordance with the command, "Lay not up for yourselves treasures upon earth."

For the meaning of the passage, "Provide things honest in the sight of all men" (Romans 12:17) (which some for want of more efficient support are anxious to press into their service) see the above authorities; where it will be seen to have reference only to the beauty of character becoming and attractive in a Christian. See, as a Scripture comment, Philippians 4; 8. 2; Ch. 8 and 21. [There appears a mistake in the reference here. It may be 2 Cor. 8. 21].

I shall now make a few remarks on the passage contained in 2 Corinthians 12:14, that I may bring under one point of view all the evidence the New Testament seems to me to afford, either in fact or by possible construction, against the view taken in this essay. And this passage we more particularly notice, as it really appears to present some difficulty. "Behold," says the Apostle, "the third time I am ready to come to you; and I will not be burdensome to you; for the children ought not to lay up for the parents, but the parents for the children." Now the difficulty alluded to consists in determining the meaning of the Apostle in this illustration. In the first Epistle to the Corinthians, just before the close of it, he gives the Corinthian Church a precept, similar to the one he had given all the other Churches he established—that they should lay by every Lord's Day, as God had prospered them, for the relief of the poor saints. It appears, by the Apostle's remarks in the second Epistle to the same Church, that there were some who desired to impute base motives to him, as though he wished to share in this bounty. He accordingly evinces his disinterestedness by declining all provision for himself. He tells them, however, that he did not decline receiving anything from them because he loved them less than other Churches by whose liberality he had been once and again supplied, but that he might cut off occasion from those who desired occasion to malign his motives. And he once more excuses himself, in the next chapter, from being a participator of the bounty which they had laid up, and to which he had encouraged them for the purpose of supplying the wants of the poor saints in Judea; and he employs an illustration drawn from the common practice of mankind. "The children," says he, "ought not to lay up for the parents, but the parents for the children." And this illustration he employs as he does many others; just, for example, as he illustrates the Christian race by circumstances and practices attendant on the Olympic games. It is essential to the illustration of this passage to consider that the whole argument of St. Paul does not refer to the providing against his future possible wants, with which alone this essay has to do, but to the relief of his present actual necessities. It is evident indeed that the words cannot be taken strictly. The Apostle begins with asserting that children ought not to lay up for their parents, that is, ought not to provide for their present necessities; for, if this be not his meaning, the words have no reference to the question between the Apostle and the Corinthians, and therefore cease to be an illustration at all; since that question referred to present necessity on the one hand, and to present supply on the other. His simple object appears to be to decline their bounty without giving pain; for it is clear from this very epistle that he was in the habit of receiving assistance from other Churches, of which he was as much the spiritual parent as of the Church of Corinth. The former he highly commends for the anxiety which they felt and the assistance which they afforded: from the latter he declines receiving any pecuniary aid, as if it were not incumbent on them to give, and would be improper for him to receive. He seems unwilling to recall to their minds the special reason of his refusing to accept of their bounty, and endeavours to find one in the general relation in which he stood to them, as their spiritual father. Let anyone read from the eighth chapter to the end of the Epistle, and he will be fully satisfied that the idea of laying up in store for future and possible wants never entered into the mind of the Apostle. Let him read especially that part of the eighth chapter beginning with "For you know the grace of our Lord Jesus Christ, that though he was rich, yet for your sakes he became poor," and ending with "As it is written, He that had gathered much, had nothing over; and he that had gathered little, had no lack."

6

The Church of God (1):
Its Principle of Union

Christ loved the church, and gave himself up for it, that he might sanctify it. . . that he might present the church to himself (Ephesians 5:25–27).

"We had no object now in life, but living to the Lord and the Church" (31).

There are those who live unto the Church (that is, their own organized church system), and have no devotion to the Lord Jesus. There are those who wish to live unto the Lord but have little concern for His church—such as devout but misled anchorites in their desert cells or monasteries; or evangelists who are satisfied to save souls as individuals but neither form nor build up churches. To the heart of Groves both were dear; the Lord first, and then the church of God as precious to the Lord; and his contribution to the well-being of the latter was signal.

As we have seen from his own words he was at first a thorough high churchman. The force of this term is not to be measured by the elaborateness of the ritual practised, or the degree to which it is Romish in character. It is said that a leading atheist of the nineteenth century was asked with what Church he thought he would associate were he to join any. He answered it would be the Roman Catholic Church or the Exclusive Plymouth Brethren. And it has been suggested that the probable point of similarity which led to this curious conjunction of the two in his mind is that they both make everything of "the Church." Of the maker of Exclusivism, J. N. Darby, Neatby rightly says: "Darby was nothing if not an ecclesiastic, and all his operations subserved ecclesiastical ends," (*History,* 76). This is essential high churchism, and is not of necessity a reproach.

Of course, different high churchmen have different conceptions of "the Church." The Roman Catholic thinks of that organized system of which the Pope is the head. To Groves, as to Wesley before him, it meant in practice the Church of England as by law established. Wesley has told us that in his earlier years he would have thought it almost wrong for a sinner to be saved elsewhere than in a church, that is, a Church of England edifice, and even after his conversion it was some while before he could bring himself to be "yet more vile" and preach in the open air. Similarly, as we have read, it was with nothing less than "repugnance" that Groves heard Miss Paget's proposal that he should help in her hall at Poltimore, for he "had never yet gone near a dissenting place of worship" (40).

This unloving state of heart, thus baneful in its effects on gospel effort and Christian communion, was rampant a century ago, and its influence was almost as great and as evil in the dissenting as in the State Churches. Thus of the Baptist church in Stuttgart, Germany, in 1843, George Müller relates that:

> ...the brother who appears to take the lead among them, and who is the only one who speaks at their meetings, told me that the time was drawing nigh when the church would take the Lord's Supper, and that they had a rule which they considered to be Scriptural, which was, neither to take the Lord's Supper with anyone who was not himself baptized by immersion after he had believed, nor with anyone who, (though thus baptized himself) would take the Lord's Supper with any who had not thus been baptized. Nor did they take the Lord's Supper with any brother who would take it with any yet belonging to the state church (*Narrative* 530);

and this Baptist Church had refused to baptize certain persons

> ...except they would promise never to take the Lord's Supper any more with unbaptized believers, or with those who belonged to any State Church (517, 518).

This attitude was not exceptional in Germany, as it was not in England. Nor is the same spirit and practice extinct, nor are the grounds of exclusion confined to the matter of immersion. At this day there are godly persons who will not take the Lord's Supper if the bread be leavened or the wine fermented, nor will break bread with any person who would use those elements in another place, nor with believers who, though themselves using unleavened bread, would receive anyone who elsewhere would break bread with those who use leavened bread. The conscientiousness of such Christians can be respected; schism in the body of Christ on such grounds can only be deplored.

That such divisive sentiments and such separatist spirit is not now practically universal, as it was a century ago, is mainly a result, under God, of the diffused influence of the teaching and example of those who became known as "Brethren." High churchism received its most powerful and evil stimulus through the Tractarian Movement initiated by J. H. Newman. At the same period Biblical views of the church of God were developed out of suggestions as to the Scriptures made by A. N. Groves. These were dominating phases of the age-long conflict between the kingdom of darkness and the kingdom of God in the nineteenth century.

Should anyone think this contrast too severe a condemnation of Newman let him compare the subtle, jesuitical casuistry of the Appendix to Newman's *Apologia* (Sections 7 and 8), with its virtual justification of lying, and the simplicity and transparency of Groves' statements scattered through the *Memoir.* The two men, the two biographies, reveal the essence of the two systems: the one a servile, degrading surrender to the authority of "the Church," which is *thorough* high churchism; the other a humble, confiding, enlightening, ennobling submission to the Word of God. The one is a miasma-spreading swamp, the other is a branch of the river of the water of life. Men of noble character have survived the influences of the former system; men of ignoble character have lowered the influence of the other; but the opposed nature of the systems is not affected.

It was by degrees that Groves changed completely from the one system to the other. As has been remarked, his attachment to "the Church" was first weakened by the gracious, godly influence of the only dissenters with whom he was intimate, the Misses Paget. Another influence which he himself mentions was the intercourse had in Dublin. Trinity College there granted examinations to students who did not reside in that city, but went up only for the examinations.

This Groves did with a view to ordination as a clergyman. He says:

> From my first going to Dublin, many of my deep-rooted prejudices
> gave way, I saw those strongly marked distinctions that exist in England
> little regarded; the prevalence of the common enemy, Popery, joined all
> hands together;

and he adds:

> ...my connexion with Dublin...answered the purpose of breaking down
> the high church feelings which I had carried there (38, 41).

Thus Groves went to Dublin for a purpose of his own; God used
it for a purpose of *His* own: "There's a Providence that shapes our
ends, rough hew them how we will."

It was no doubt to some extent the case that in Ireland there
was more intercourse between Christians than in England; yet the
general difference was not great. Edward Cronin, a medical student, went from the south of Ireland to Dublin. Formerly a Roman
Catholic, he was then with the Independents. He was received to
occasional communion by various dissenting churches

> ...till it was found that I became resident in Dublin. I was then warned
> that I could no longer be allowed to break bread with any of them with-
> out special membership with some of them. That was the starting point
> with me. With the strong impression on my soul, though with little
> intelligence about it, that the Church of God was one, and that all that
> believed were members of that one body, I firmly refused membership.
> ...This left me in separation... (*Neatby*, 18, 19).

His name was publicly denounced from one of the Nonconformist pulpits, a clear evidence of the sectarian bitterness that obtained.
An Edward Wilson, who protested against this, presently withdrew
from the church. These two met in one of Wilson's rooms for breaking bread and prayer, and out of this tiny rift in the hard rock of
sectarianism first trickled the stream that was to diffuse so widely
a rich supply of the grace of God for the beautifying and rendering
fruitful of many barren tracts in His church.

This seems to have been in 1826. The company grew, and from
May, 1830, met in a hired room in Aungier Street. It was into this

circle that Groves came in 1826, or early in 1827. His biographer writes:

> …he became acquainted with many sincere Christians, chiefly members of the Establishment, who, with him, desired to see more devotedness to Christ, and union among all the people of God. To promote these objects, they met continually for prayer and reading the word (38).

We shall not pursue the history in detail, for we are not attempting a history of the Brethren movement, but only of A. N. Groves' influence upon it at its commencement. Other Christians, and other little companies of Christians, in various places in Ireland and England, were at the same time seeking after that same increase of union among the people of God. The inquirer must peruse Neatby's painstaking *History* if he wishes to follow the subject farther. His conclusion is justified that

> Brethrenism was indeed formed out of a variety of little meetings of a more or less similar character, and these must be accepted as its ultimate elements; but Brethrenism, as we know it, is a synthesis, and the synthesis has a history; and I do not believe that its history can be truly told without locating its original force in Dublin, and in Aungier Street (*History* 24).

Groves was *not* an ecclesiastic and did not set out any formal scheme of ecclesiastical life. But certain major truths connected with the church of God and its working he saw and suggested to others.

1. THE TRUE GROUND OF CHRISTIAN FELLOWSHIP.

His biographer writes:

> The views that he, to his death, so *strongly* held, both of the entire unity of the family of God and their liberty to unite together in worship, were, he often said, first opened to him while searching the Scriptures in Dublin. After one of their happy prayer-meetings, already mentioned, it was asked by one of the party, "Are there no principles in the Word of God which would unite all believers in worship, whatever might be their various views or attainments in the divine life?" Mr. Groves replied, "Yes, there are: we are evidently called to know nothing among our fellow-Christians, but this one fact: Do they belong to Christ? Has Christ

received them? then may we receive them, to the glory of God."To what happy results would these simple truths lead, among God's people. Even where they did not overthrow any mere human systems, they would help forward fellowship and intercourse among all Christians (39, 40).

This was in 1827. In 1836 he wrote to J. N. Darby a letter which will be given later, and said:

> It has been asserted. . . that I have changed my principles; all I can say is, that as far as I know what those principles were, in which I gloried on first discovering them in the Word of God, I now glory in them ten times more. . . . I ever understood our principle of communion to be the possession of the common life or common blood of the family of God (for the life is in the blood); these were our early thoughts, and are my most matured ones (539).

That this was a correct statement of the first principle of communion held and practised by those believers is very abundantly witnessed by the writing of those early years. A collection of extracts therefrom, from the years 1833 to 1840, showing this, has been published.[1] Nothing can be more emphatic than Mr. Darby's own statement to Rev. J. Kelly of the year 1839, three years later than Groves' letter last quoted. It agrees verbally with Groves' words first above cited:

> But our principle is this, sir: whenever the first great truth of redemption—in a word—whenever Christ has received a person—we would receive him ... as our table is the Lord's, not ours, we receive all that the Lord has received, all who have fled as poor sinners for refuge to the hope set before them, and rest not in themselves, but in Christ as their hope. We do not make a creed, but Christ, the ground and term of union (*Collected Writings of J. N. Darby*, vol. 14, pp. 332–4).

In his pamphlet *The "Brethren," A Historical Sketch*, issued in August, 1899, Mr. William Collingwood, who united with them in 1844, testified to the same principle:

> The chief aim was to exhibit, in a Scriptural way, *the common brotherhood of all believers.* They recognised no special membership. That they

---

1. *The Remedy for Division.*

belonged to Christ was the only term of communion; that they loved one another was the power of their fellowship. In principle, it embraced all whose faith and walk showed that they had spiritual life; in practice, all such of these as would avail themselves of it (9).

To the end Groves adhered to this.

The family life of the children of God, their oneness in Christ, was thus the ground of communion. It is worthy of remark that, later, the Exclusive Brethren stressed the phrase "meeting on the ground of the one body." The earlier practice was the safer. For the purpose of communion it is wiser to build upon the *fact* of the family relationship than upon the *figure* of the body. The latter, because it is a figure of speech, is more susceptible of different and controversial interpretation; and when fellowship is sought controversy must be avoided as much as possible.

2. DENOMINATIONALISM.

This ground of fellowship of necessity excluded denominationalism as a principle of Christian union. In 1828 Groves wrote:

> My full persuasion is, that, inasmuch as anyone glories either in being of the Church of England, Scotland, Baptist, Independent, Wesleyan, etc., his glory is his shame, and that it is antichristian; for, as the Apostle said, were any of them crucified for you? The legitimate ground of glorying is that we are among the ransomed of the Lord, by His grace, either in ourselves or others. As bodies, I know none of the sects and parties that wound and disfigure the body of Christ; as individuals, I desire to love all that love Him. Oh! when will the day come, when the love of Christ will have more power to unite than our foolish regulations have to divide the family of God? (49).

Believers of the apostolic days did not unite on the ground that they were members of a nation and therefore of the Church of a nation; for the only church then known was being gathered out of "*every* tribe, and tongue, and people, and nation" (Revelation 5:9), and therefore, of necessity, in it all national distinctions lapse, being foreign to its essence and genius, and there "*cannot* be Greek or Jew or Scythian" (Colossians 3:11).

The assemblies of the apostolic days were in no sense or degree a group of affiliated churches, but each assembly was administratively a unit.[1] But they did not gather because of, or on the ground of, this undoubted feature: there was no Independent or Congregational body.

Each such assembly was ruled by presbyters, elders, the "bishops" of the New Testament. Episcopal government by bishops, as now known, was then unknown, Yet this fact of government was not the basis of those churches or their fellowship: they were not Presbyterians, but simply Christians.

Each and every member of those apostolic churches had been immersed in water to own his union by faith with the death and resurrection of Christ; but neither was this baptism the basis of their union or worship: they were not Baptists, though baptized.

The church was (and is, and ever will be) built upon the bedrock fact and truth that Jesus is the Son of God; consequently each who can honestly confess to this truth is on the rock and is of the church. But this confession is by no manner of means the mere acknowledgment of a creed; it is the genuine, unreserved submission of the man to the Lordship of Christ, his surrender to a revelation of the Son made to his heart by God the Father (Matthew 16:13–20). It was those who were "added to the Lord" that were added to one another (Acts 5:14; 2:41, 47). And therefore the principle of reception laid down was: "Wherefore receive ye one another, even as Christ also received you, to the glory of God" (Romans 15:7).

It was this that Groves had pointed out in 1827 and which those early seekers after true union had accepted, and this Darby had stated in 1833, in a letter to one at Plymouth:

> I do trust that you will keep infinitely far from sectarianism. The great body of the Christians who are accustomed to religion are scarce capable of understanding anything else, as the mind ever tends there ... You are nothing, nobody, but Christians, and the moment you cease to be an available mount for communion for any consistent Christian, you will go to pieces or help the evil (*Letters* 1, 21).

---

1. See Hatch, *Organization of the Early Christian Churches*; Hort, *The Christian Ecclesia*; or my own *The Churches of God*.

3. LIFE NOT LIGHT THE BASIS OF UNION.

This followed naturally and necessarily from the family life and relationship being the principle of reception, for every child is welcome at the family table (so long as family affection rules) without regard to age, learning, or differences of opinion.

Of those earliest years Groves wrote in 1836:

> What I mean is, that then, all our thoughts were conversant about how we might *ourselves* most effectually manifest forth that life we had received by Jesus (knowing that that alone could be as the Shepherd's voice to the living children), and where we might find that life in others; and when we were persuaded we had found it, bidding them, on the Divine claim of this common life (whether their thoughts on other matters were narrow or enlarged) to come and share with us in the fellowship of the common Spirit, in the worship of our common head; and as Christ had received them, so would we to the glory of God the Father (539).

And in 1845 he wrote:

> One point only is fixed on my mind; to receive all, as Christ receives them, to the glory of God the Father. More than twenty years this point has been deepening in my mind; and all I hear and see makes it more precious: indeed amidst so much weakness and infirmity, with such partial and imperfect views of truth, I see no other way but committing all judgment to the Son, to whom the *Father* hath committed it (409).

And again:

> The power of a union in a common life is so strong, that evils, endless in variety, and often intense in character, are not sufficient to divide, when this life is felt to exist. This, surely, is the nature of the unity of God's love with all the members of the one body; nothing should divide when Christ unites. I shall return to my native land with the very feelings I left it, eleven years ago, only strengthened tenfold by experience (410).

That this was the belief and practice of those first days is fully evidenced. In 1839 or 1840 another wrote:

> The terms "*free* or *open* communion are adopted to indicate the right of all who are known, or supposed, on the best evidence we can command,

to be *sincere believers* in the Lord Jesus, to come to the table of the Lord; however different their degrees of faith and love, *however diverse their judgments upon many points,* which, however important in themselves, are yet not such as to prevent their being recognized by the Lord as His members (Romans 14:1–3; 15:7) (*Collected Tracts* 31).

In the first volume of the first magazine of Brethren, *The Christian Witness,* for 1837, pp. 306–309, it was said:

... a credible profession of faith in the Lamb, and a consistent conversation is all that we have a right to require; if we demand more we are guilty of the sin of schism; we divide those whom Christ has united on purpose that they might strengthen and edify one another. Speaking of "The increased desire for union on the simple ground of Christian brotherhood" the writer adds: "We pray that it may be continued— that all who desire the welfare of the Church of Christ may labour to see themselves and others so circumstanced as not only to love, but to receive into the appointed fellowship of breaking bread, all whom they believe to be brethren in Christ Jesus; not requiring uniformity nor oneness of understanding, but only the possession of the one Spirit."

And of the rigid sectarianism of the dissenting bodies at that time he says:

In refusing to receive their brethren *because they are brethren,* they have shut themselves out from the blessed privilege of seeking to follow the mind of Christ as to His desires for the unity of the one body; and have assumed to themselves a power which Christ never delegated to His Church, of legislating terms of communion.

So well known was this principle and practice as characterizing them, that the official Census report of 1851 said:

The Brethren, therefore, may be represented as consisting of all such, as practically holding all the proofs essential to salvation, recognize each other as, on that account alone, true members of the only Church. A difference of opinion upon aught besides is not regarded as a sufficient ground for separation; and the Brethren, therefore, have withdrawn themselves from all those bodies in which tests, express or virtual, on minor points, are made the means of separating Christians from each other.

The happy tendency of this principle is to reduce causes of separation to the minimum, and therefore to enlarge communion to the maximum. In 1834 Groves wrote:

> I am so sure of the truth of those blessed principles the Lord has taught me, that I glory in their propagation. Simple obedience to Christ alone; recognition of Christ alone in my brother, as the Alpha and Omega of terms of communion; lastly, unreserved devotion to Christ alone (321).

The year before he had enquired:

> What have any gained by making knowledge the sign of a man in Christ? Why, that they sit as critics when they should weep and lament because the gospel is through them maligned and misunderstood throughout the earth (250).

The New Testament is witness that wide differences of judgment existed and were tolerated in the first churches. Paul makes no suggestion of excommunicating those at Corinth who were asserting the annihilation of the dead, searchingly and severely as he dealt with the teaching itself (1 Corinthians 15); nor did the fact of such false teaching in that assembly lessen his intention to go there. They were a church of God in spite of this doctrine (1 Corinthians 11:34; 2 Corinthians 13:1). It was gross moral sin that demanded excommunication (1 Corinthians 5). Unity of judgment was, indeed, the ideal (1 Corinthians 1:10), but large and lasting forbearance was a duty (Romans 14), for whom God has received His people may not reject (Romans 14:3).

It was only to be expected that the blessing of God should abide where the love of God ruled, and that to such gatherings hungry, godly souls should turn. They do so still where the same drawing power is at work. One who knew Benjamin Wills Newton well told me of how he used to say of those earliest years that they were as days of heaven upon earth. Mr. Collingwood says:

It was, moreover, quite a common thing to see the clerical dress at their largest meeting in London (*The Brethren* 11).[1]

---

1. In those days they were too Christlike, wise, and loving, not to say too gentlemanly, to speak sarcastically about a clergyman's dress, and not a few of that order joined the meetings and divested themselves of the dress.

4. SEPARATION FROM OTHER CHRISTIANS NOT A CONDITION OF COMMUNION.

Another consequence of this fundamental principle of fellowship was that no one seeking communion was challenged as to his relationship to any bodies of Christians, nor was required to sever therefrom. This was stated most emphatically in 1838 by a writer who said:

> Though the fullest devotedness and separation from the world are enjoined as a privilege and duty, yet gladly would we have admitted the late emperor of Russia before he died [a member, of course, of the Greek Orthodox Church. That he was a true believer may be seen in the *Memoirs* of Stephen Grellet, chs. 24 and 30], as we would the Archbishop Fénelon [a French Roman Catholic, but a true Christian], without obliging or calling upon either to give up their thrones. The ONLY ground of communion is real faith in Jesus... and I would add, that all of you, who are really Christians, are free to come to the communion in Bridge Street [Hereford], without yielding any of your opinions, and even while continuing to attend any other place of worship.... It is not true that we have "a broad and definite line of separating between our own members (as they are wrongly called) and other children of God"; indeed, if we hold any one truth more prominently than another it is the contradiction of this statement; for, we welcome the lowliest and feeblest real Christian, even though they continue in much worldiness both of worship and practice, though, of course, we would that it were otherwise (*Collected Tracts*, 22, 23).

Precisely the same is W. Collingwood's account:

> The principles thus briefly stated were in full force when in 1844 the writer sought a place with them at the Lord's table. He plainly expressed his intention, at the time, of continuing to attend the ministry of the

---

Dr. Adolph Saphir well said that, "The union of Christians is marred not by giving too much importance to little things, but by not keeping sufficiently prominent the great things. Did it ever strike you that the early Christians also differed on minor points, for which nowadays it would be thought quite necessary to make a new sect? but they were so absorbed in thinking that they knew God as their Father, that Jesus was their Saviour, that they were possessors of the Holy Ghost, that nothing could separate them. Thus it is that when we go to a meeting where Christians meet *as Christians,* we feel as if we lost our asthma—we can breathe" (*Memoir of Adolph Saphir* 362).

clergyman through whom he had received much spiritual blessing. The answer was that this would be no bar to their full and hearty fellowship; that so far as they were concerned—though it was not likely to be profitable to himself—he was free to go to as many of the evangelical communities as he thought fit; but being recognized as a child of God, there would always be a place for him at the Lord's table whenever he would come. And this was not an exceptional case; it was the rule in those early days (*The Brethren* 11).

When Mr. Darby commenced his labours in Switzerland, it commended him to many that he did not require any to separate from the National Church before they could be received to break bread. In principle at least he maintained this position to the end. My father knew him well from about 1858 to the close of his (J. N. D.'s) life in 1882. He told me that the above precise case was put to Darby: A person in the town, known to us as a real Christian, asks permission to break bread for once, saying plainly that he does not propose to come again: What ought we to do? He replied: You ought to thank God that he did the right thing for once!

It is possible that, to this day, all who profess and call themselves "Brethren," of all parties, would acknowledge in theory the right of every believer to a place at the Table, but in practice not a few impose the condition that there must be a severance from other religious associations, the very practice of those Baptists at Stuttgart and of others. It may well be that thereby a church or group of churches may be compacted and inspirited as a fighting unit to wage war against all around; but never have I seen a trace of true heavenly, spiritual influence so gained.

Treated as above Mr. Collingwood was drawn into entire fellowship with those who showed him love and left him his liberty, and he was one of thousands. A Baptist commenced attending the weekly Bible Address at an assembly. By enquiry we learned he was a worthy Christian. Visiting him I asked if he had ever seen the Lord's Supper observed as at the Hall. He had not. I remarked simply that there would be a welcome whenever he thought fit to come. No conditions were imposed. He came; felt the blessedness and saw the Scripturalness of the observance and worship, and never returned to what he thus of himself learned to be less Scriptural.

To be acceptable to God every step must be taken out of love to His will, and therefore unconstrained, save by love. The imposing of our conditions easily violates this essential principle. To a clergyman who of his own will, though through intercourse with Groves, was leaving the Establishment, he wrote from Bagdad in 1831:

> The non-arrival of [your letter] prevents my knowing the progress through which your mind has gone; yet I see the conclusion, that, with all love to all that is true and spiritual in the Church of England, you cannot accept man nor men, however exalted, as the authorized expositors of God's truth. That you would finally, dearest brother, come to this conclusion I never had any doubt, the moment I saw your mind really set to enquire and weigh everything in the balances of the sanctuary. Oh! may the Lord make it the means of abundant blessing to you. To the flesh there is much in this step that will lead to trying results; but if the mind be once set free to follow Christ's truth, wherever it finds it, it is better than a thousand worlds. I prize among my present and happiest privileges, that I can examine God's Word now without reference to man. Those dear brothers and sisters with whom the Lord has led me to act, demand not my submission to them, nor do I *desire* their submission to me; let Christ be all in all, and the true hearty love of Him, *the bond* that binds His members (169).

This further and most explicit testimony to the earliest practice may be cited. Mr. J. E. Howard of Tottenham was associated with Brethren from many years before the 1848 strife, certainly as early as 1838. He is mentioned in Groves' *Memoir,* p. 465, year 1849. In 1850, in *A Caution Against the Darbyites* (21), he quotes from Groves' Letter of 1836 to Darby, and says:

> Such, I believe, were the feelings of many of us when we first met together as "Brethren." We sought to meet, not as hostile to, but as embracing other Christians, and *made no point of their renouncing their different sects,* in order to sit down at the table of the Lord, as our common privilege—*theirs* and *ours.*

Had this happy state and relationship continued, the unhappy dissensions of the Brethren would not have come. Yet even now the Spirit of grace will revive it where humble hearts seek it.

5. On Intercourse with Believers in Religious Systems.

Denominationalism was thus recognized as unscriptural, schismatic, a breach of the family life of the children of God, a frustrating of the expressed purpose of the Lord that His followers should be seen by the world as one. This raised the practical question of the attitude to be taken to such churches and persons as were members of a denomination. It was agreed that believers from them should be welcomed in the new assemblies, but how far, if at all, could fellowship be shown to them in their own associations? Two lines were possible: to abstain from all intercourse with them in those associations, that is, neither to go to their buildings nor to share in their witness or service; or, to show fellowship with what was of God and according to His Word, and abstain only from what was of man.

The evidence is unimpeachable that at first the latter was the course acknowledged to be godly. Groves' statement to Darby, in the 1836 letter, is distinct and was never questioned:

> We were free, within the limits of the truth, to share with them in *part,* though we could not in *all,* their services. In fact, as we received them for the life, we would not reject them for their systems, or refuse to recognize any *part* of their systems, because we disallowed much. . . . Was not the principle we laid down as to separation from all existing bodies at the outset, this: that we felt ourselves bound to separate from all individuals and systems, *so far* as they required us to do what our consciences would not allow, or restrained us from doing what our consciences required, and no further? And were we not as free to join and act with any individual, or body of individuals, as they were free *not* to require us to do what our consciences did *not* allow, or prevent our doing what they did? and in this freedom did we not feel brethren should *not* force liberty on those who were bound, nor withhold freedom from those who were free?
>
> Did we not feel constrained to follow the apostolic rule of *not judging other men's consciences,* as to liberty, by our own; remembering it is written, "Let *not* him that eateth despise him that eateth not; and let not him which eateth not, judge him that eateth; seeing that God hath received" both the one and the other? Now it is one of these two grounds; their preventing me from, or demanding from me, other than the Lord demands, that divides me in a *measure* from every system; as my *own*

proper duty to God, rather than as witnessing against THEIR evils. As any system is in its provision narrower or wider than the truth, I either stop short, or go beyond its provisions, but I would INFINITELY RATHER BEAR with *all their evils,* than SEPARATE from THEIR GOOD. These were the *then* principles of our separation and intercommunion.

And he asserts these to have been Mr. Darby's views when, speaking of two other brethren, he says:

> I cannot be supposed, of course, to know fully *their* grounds of acting, but I thought I knew *yours,* at least your *original* ones (539–541).

That this fastening of these views on Darby was justified is seen from the later as well as earlier practice of the latter, and thus far supports the assertion that they were the views then commonly accepted. Two years later than Groves' letter, when Darby commenced to work in Switzerland, he preached freely in the dissenting churches. Dr. Ironside states that in the seventies Darby held meetings in D. L. Moody's church at Chicago and in Dr. J. H. Brookes' in St. Louis, which shows that to the end he maintained and used this liberty (*The Brethren Movement,* chs. 6. and 8). And my father told me upon this point that Darby had expressed his readiness to wear the gown in the pulpit of an Established Church, were that required, that he might have opportunity there to preach the truth.

But it was urged, and still is urged, against this liberty that its exercise involves a condoning of the evils that are in the religious systems of men so visited. To this Groves answered that no *visitor* in a house was considered responsible for its ordering or arrangements or as approving all that was done. But boldly, and consistently with the fundamental principles of fellowship before stated, he went further, and, in words before quoted, pressed for the toleration of "evils endless in variety, and often intense in character," rather than incur the yet greater sin of unwarranted schism. Perhaps it is only the Roman Catholic Church that displays an adequate sense of the enormity of the sin of schism. In Galatians 5:19–21, it is classed with idolatries, sorceries, drunkenness, and such like excommunicable abominations, and is equally threatened with the disinheriting of the believer.

In support of his plea Groves (in 1837) cited examples hard to set aside, even Christ and the apostles, saying:

You ask me to give you my opinion about separating from evil. I as fully admit as you can desire, *that in my own person*, it is my *bounden* duty to depart from every evil thing; but the judgment of *others*, and consequent separation from them, I am daily more satisfied is *not of God*. The blessing of God rests on those who are separated *by others* from their company, and it is a mark of apostasy to be of those who "separate themselves" from God's own redeemed ones; moreover, if ever there was a witness for God on earth, that witness was Jesus, and He never separated Himself from the synagogues; and this, if it proves nothing more, proves that *separation* is not the *only* way of witness, and yet He was emphatically "separate from sinners," not from their persons nor assemblies, but separate from their sins (373, 374).

In 1834 he had written:

I have been thinking to *whom* it was said, when they asked "shall we pluck up the tares?" "Let them grow together till the harvest, lest, while ye pluck up the tares, ye root up also the wheat with them." Surely the least this means is, "judge nothing before the time"; or, that we should be very wary in the exercise of this dangerous power, in which there is so much room for self-righteousness and pride, under the garb of zeal for what really may be the truth; but there may be a spirit of error, with much truth; and a spirit of truth, with much error. Besides, the Lord has said, "Vengeance belongeth unto me"; every kind and degree of it. Some think this is sacrificing truth; but surely if you proclaim the truth, and condemn error by words of truth and by a life of truth, this would meet the precept, "ye should earnestly contend for the faith." Consider the Church at Jerusalem; consider the Church at Corinth, how much to be questioned, how much to be condemned, yet the Apostles *bore* with and reproved, but separated not. Indeed, the more my soul searches into this matter, the more I feel I cannot *formally* separate from, or *openly* denounce those, whom I do not feel are *separated* from Christ and denounced by Him as His enemies. If I were to give up this principle, I know of none to guide me, but that which I have always seen fail, and which engenders a spirit more hurtful than could arise from a readiness to endure contradiction to your *own* views: this looks more like crucifixion of self, than casting out as *evil*, those who, with whatever faults, we cannot but believe are children of the kingdom (339, 340).

And therefore he said (1837):

I also daily more and more desire to see raised up for God discriminating witnesses, discerning between things that differ; enduring the evil for the sake of the good, rather than fleeing from the good for fear of the evil. I am so fixed in this principle that I could never give it up, even were those I most love to oppose me in it. It is, to my conscience, the breath of God; the image of God's actings and mind (376). What a blessing it is that the Lord's heart is so large, that He can help whenever He sees *some good* thing; whereas man withdraws because he sees *some evil* thing, which is generally found to mean something that wounds his own self-love in the little scheme he had set up as perfection (378).

In 1845, the year in which occurred the first open breach among the Brethren, he wrote to one in England:

I am so glad to hear so pleasant an account of your brother's ministry; may he ever hate strifes, divisions, separations, and all those tendencies of the heart which make a brother an offender for a word. Instead of this being a day in which love "THINKETH NO evil," it seems to me a day in which man glories in paradoxes; shows how love, not only exists, but that it is an eminent proof of it, to think nothing good, but everything evil of a brother; to diminish nought but exaggerate everything; to call nothing by a gentle name, but to designate the most ordinary acts by the most vituperative appellations; and that "separation" is God's principle of *unity*. I am sure, as man now uses it, it is the devil's main spring of confusion (409, 410).

The following year he added upon the same doctrine:

By the Lord's blessing there has been no schism among us [at Chittoor, India]: all seem more and more satisfied that the theory of *unity by separation*—for what has been put forward amounts to nothing less—is false; and so far from its being God's plan, all we see of it in operation convinces us that the unity of God is found in the union of all who possess the common life of Jesus.

I have been reading an interesting publication by an old friend of mine, Morant Brock,[1] Chaplain at the Penitentiary, Bath. It breathes a love to Christ's body, apart from all sects; this is *true* catholicity, an

---

1. Probably Mourant Brock, M.A., author of *The Cross, Heathen and Christian*, 1879; *Worship, What it is Not, and What it Is*; and *Short Papers on the Sacrament*.

infinitely better test of the unity of the Spirit than hatred of other people's systems, or "clericalism" —Socinian quakers may have the latter as intensely as need be; but only Christ's chosen ones can have the former (427).

Of ministry he gave, on Christmas Eve 1852, within five months of his end, when he was already very ill, one wrote:

I felt so thankful that on the evening of the tea meeting he was led to trace a little the history of Brethrenism, and the downfall of *collective* blessing, from the moment that "separation from evil, God's principle of unity," became their standard of communion. I went along with every word he said, and the language of my heart was, "let me live and die with such as occupy themselves with beholding the beauty of the Lord, rather than with detecting and judging evil in their brethren." There is such an unmistakeable savour about those who make Christ their centre, who own His pre-eminence, by receiving all who are owned and accepted by Him (483).

In 1923, a survivor of that early period, W. H. Dorman (Jr.), wrote:

The testimony to the cardinal ecclesiastical truth of the Unity of the Church was the duty committed to the "Plymouth Brethren." It was the divine remedy for the sectarianism that had paralysed every attempt to conform to the New Testament teaching as to the Church since Reformation times. It became, therefore, an object with the Lord's Enemy, by any means, fair or foul, to destroy that testimony, and he laid a most crafty plot to effect this. His objective was not to introduce clerisy, or "system," or false doctrine (however welcome as a side issue), as was generally supposed but was the wrecking of the Testimony of Unity and the kindred truths (*Philadelphia and Laodicea* 5).

And among the influences that signally contributed to the success of this "most crafty plot" the doctrine Groves repudiated was one of the most powerful, for it of necessity prepared minds for division by gendering a sectarian spirit. And the after history of those who adopted it declares this; for having first taken up the attitude of witnessing *against* errors in others, both systems and persons, they were naturally driven to an unscriptural separation from them, were thereby inevitably compacted into a new sect, and then, upon what were deemed to be errors arising within their own midst, were compelled by the same principle to divide from one another again, and yet again. And thus it must ever be until the doctrine be rejected, and believers return to the theory and practice of those earliest days, which Groves was the first to suggest and which he exemplified to the end. Speaking of those first suggestions his biographer wrote:

> This was the beginning of what has been erroneously termed, "Plymouth Brethrenism." With one of the party, who had met together in Dublin, originated a meeting of a similar kind in Plymouth; and among the Christians who took part in it were clergymen, still officiating in the Church of England. The *original* principles of this happy communion are fully detailed, and largely dwelt upon, in Mr. Groves' letters and journals; they tended to nothing less than the enjoyment of union and communion *among all* who possess the common life of the family of God. The realization of these principles enabled Mr. Groves, whether in Ireland, England, Russia, or the presidencies of India, to go in and out among God's people, everywhere, both conveying and receiving refreshment; and, up to the time of his removal, his steadfast adherence to the same blessed principles, made him know nothing among men, save Jesus Christ, and Him crucified (39).

That his liberty of fellowship with all the family of God, in the systems in which he might find them, neither lessened his own adherence to nor dissemination of his own principles of church fellowship will be seen in the sequel. From forty years' observation of travel in the gospel in nearly as many countries I am sure this liberty is a most real asset for spreading the truth as to the church of God. I write [in 1939] in a town in North Africa, 650 miles from the Mediterranean. Beyond to the south stretches only the vast desert. It is a veritable out-post of the three kingdoms, those of man, the devil, and God. To represent the last in this almost wholly Moslem town I find, twinkling amidst the Islamic midnight, a small native Coptic Presbyterian Church, a Lutheran Mission of godly Germans, aiming to reach the Moslems, and a small company of Exclusive Brethren. Upon the principle that witnessing against their errors is the primary duty, I can have fellowship with no one, and must stand before the Mohammedans either as one of the general run of irreligious English tourists, or as claiming that those who seek to represent Christ do not do so. In the first case my influence would be nil; in the other I should so far nullify what testimony to Christ there is.

If separation from evil is my first duty, I must refuse fellowship with the Lutherans because of a relic of ritualism—they light two candles on the Table; to me a childish thing, but to which they seem to attach importance as a symbol of the presence of Christ; I must repudiate the Presbyterians, for they have a "pastor" ordained by men, which I think a rudimentary clerisy; I cannot accept the loving welcome of the Exclusive Brethren because they hold a modified form of church federation, which I judge to be non-apostolic and dangerous; and moreover, all three parties baptize infants, a practice I abhor.

But upon the principle of recognizing and supporting what is of God, I can enjoy and help in the public ministry of the Word, in private study thereof, in prayer, in the remembrance of the Lord at His table, and in personal Christian intercourse. Were they to invite me to help in any of those things which I think not according to the Word, I should refuse, and should use the opportunity to explain what I believe that Word teaches upon those matters, as in fact I have already done as to some of them.

This is not an exceptional situation, but frequent. Now the reason why the Exclusive Brethren receive me is that some years ago, in another town, acting on these principles, I showed to their brethren there all the fellowship they would permit, though they would not then allow me to minister or to break the bread. The leader who then refused me now lives in this town, and grace and love shown then have opened the door fully here.

Is it not of Christ to strengthen what is of Christ, even if it be associated with things not of Christ, as I suppose? Is it not for His glory that, by the exposition of truth, by sympathy, prayer, fellowship, their hearts should be taught and encouraged to glorify Him more? And is not this demanded by any just sense of the unity of the church of God? Am I not responsible to seek the sanctifying of His people in whatever connexions I may find them? If my heart will seek the good of those only who are in my circle I am a sectarian indeed. Warrant for so acting I see in the Word of God, and the love of God in my heart confirms me in this. It is the situation Groves detailed in his letter to Darby, and my judgment and affections concur in what he said:

> Some will not have me hold communion with the Scotts, because their views are not satisfactory about the Lord's Supper; others with you, because of your views about baptism [Darby practised the baptizing of all the children of a believing parent]; others with the Church of England, because of her thoughts about ministry. On my principles I receive them all; but on the principle of witnessing against evil, I should reject them all ... I naturally unite fixedly with those in whom I see and feel most of the life and power of God. But I am as free to visit other churches, where I see much of disorder, as to visit the houses of my friends, though they govern them not as I could wish; and, as I have said, I should feel it equally unreasonable and unkind for any brother to judge me for it, though I leave him in perfect liberty to judge himself (542, 543).

Of the Brethren of those early days Mr. Collingwood says:

> Their attitude toward other Christians was shown, for example, at Hereford, when Mr. Venn, the godly Rector, was holding a public discussion with a Unitarian, and they sent him word that they would spend the time in prayer for him (*The Brethren* 11).

Surely he whose heart would not urge him to do this is lacking in the mind of Christ. But if it be godly to pray for my brother-soldier, how could it be ungodly to stand beside him publicly in the fight and with him contend openly for the faith of the gospel?

Let us seek to penetrate into the inner heart of the divergence of theory and practice now considered. I have before me two pictures: the well-known portrait of John Nelson Darby, as seen in Neatby's *History,* and a photo of Anthony Norris Groves. The former shows a head of massive proportions, the temple of a powerful intellect, steady penetrating eyes, and a mouth revealing an indomitable will. It is the face of one bound to be a leader in any walk in life. Groves also had a penetrating intellect, and a strength of will which met the heroic sufferings of his early missionary life. But his countenance is radiant with love and sweetness. Darby, too, had an element of affection, or he could not have enthralled so many hearts or have won the confidence of children. But intellect and will were more dominant.

Groves had no ordinary intellect or will, but love ruled his whole inner man, breathed in all he said, and impelled or restrained his actions. He aimed to fulfil, and in large degree did fulfil, the exhortation: "Let all that ye do be done in love" (1 Corinthians 16:14).

Speaking of certain Church of England brethren he wrote in 1846:

> Truly I should hate myself, if I allowed any formal differences to rob me of their love, or them of mine.
>
> Dear _____ accuses me of want of sincerity in my principles, but it is because he does not understand them. To make myself one in heart with *all* God's children is one of the principles I have ever held. I love them ten times more, because they belong to Christ, than I feel separated from them on any comparatively lesser ground. My fervent desire is to be enabled to love and fear the Lord my God, to wait upon Him with a humble, lowly, and contrite heart, under the sense of my own unnumbered transgressions; yet with an unshaken sense of the love that has not only covered them, but washed them out, never to appear again. And in all my ministry here [India], my great wish is to produce in the brethren, especially the poor, a distaste for questions that "gender strife rather than godly edifying," which is in Christ Jesus (426, 427).

Is it any wonder that of such a man one could testify: "He found all in confusion and left all in peace"? (240). And though the faithfulness of his exposition of Scripture as to some truths provoked opposition and even resentment, yet a clerical opponent could not but say that they could not have "too much of his spirit," even though he added, "or too little of his judgment" (320).

Love not directed by sound judgment may prove impulsive, feeble, foolish; the intellect uncorrected by love may be severe and hurtful in action. Groves' mind was filled with knowledge from the Word taught to him by the Spirit of truth; but he did not become harsh, separating from his brethren because they could not accept all he knew of truth, for his heart was filled with affection by the Spirit of love, a love that bound his soul to all saints and would not suffer him to injure them. And so in 1845, the year that strife burst into flame among his brethren in England, he could write:

> I bless God, I daily feel more and more able to rejoice in all I see of Christ in any of those systems which my heart grieves over, and which

my own sense of duty keeps me in a measure separated from; but it will be the anxious endeavour of my future life that this separation shall be *limited* by the urgent necessities of conscience (407).

And thus by a combination of love and faithfulness, by speaking truth, but speaking it in love, he showed his care for the church and his zeal for the Lord who loved the church and gave Himself up for her.

Were Groves living now, the area within which the most generous extension of his principles would allow him to visit denominational circles would be greatly restricted as compared with his own time. The Church of England today is most alarmingly and widely saturated with Romish errors and unblushingly displays Romish ritual symbolizing those errors. In very many other of her pulpits, as well as in thousands of Nonconformist pulpits, divine truth as to the Word of God, the Son of God, and His precious atoning blood is denied, and soul-destroying doctrines of men or demons are proclaimed. Groves' own principles of faithfulness and love to God and man would effectually forbid any degree of intercourse within such spheres.

But they would not hinder him from receiving lovingly the Fénelons that may be still in those spheres when such might seek his fellowship, nor from going among such evangelical bodies who may be still where their forefathers were in adherence to the Word of God as their authority, though with confused thoughts as to its meaning in many matters. It will be for the blessing of the whole true church of God, as well as for themselves as part of it, that those believers with whom Groves, were he alive today, would more directly associate shall maintain his spirit and practice in this matter, that so, as Darby put it, they may be "an available mount of communion for any consistent Christian," for otherwise, as he said, they will either go to pieces, or help the evil of sectarianism, by being themselves sectarian.

This last is a most dreadful condition, for the light that was within has become a deeper darkness. It was the manifestation of this in his day that caused Groves, in 1847, to write thus from Ootacamund, a European hill station in South India:

I could not give you an adequate idea of all that might be done here, by a devoted spiritual servant of God. A sectarian of *any* school would be worse than useless; the carrying out of the *earliest* conceptions of that little knot of Christians, out of which the brethren grew, would alone meet the views of this place; it requires a heart that feels it an infinitely higher thing to witness for the work of God in the redeemed family, than *against* the work of Satan; if one bears testimony *for all* God's work and ways, those of Satan are and must be condemned, though indirectly; while testimony against every form of evil in others may leave the Lord's work unmanifested by ourselves. I see in the Establishment a multitude of men who, notwithstanding sectarian institutions, have catholic hearts, ready and willing *actively* to help those from whom their systems separate them in the Lord's work: in others I see the absence of systematic sectarianism; they have a catholic system, but a most sectarian spirit, feeling unable to help any but those who hold their own views: for myself I have infinitely closer communion with the former than with the latter...

The position I have ever maintained, of union with the whole circle of God's redeemed family, without exclusive attachment to any section of it, is daily more precious in my eyes; it certainly gives one something to *bear everywhere;* but then, by becoming habituated to forego one's own will, it becomes at last easy; and we can rejoice, and praise, and love, and intimately associate with the Lord's handiwork in His saints, though they may be associated with much that the heart longs to see away (433).

And of two godly clergymen, who had helped his own more immediate fellow-workers in India, he wrote:

I have such a nice letter from Fox and Noble, a circular in behalf of Bowden and Beer, so sweetly catholic. Their system may be sectarian, but they are not so; and it is ten times better to have to do with those who are catholic in a sectarian system, than those who are sectarian with no system (435).

Yet is it ten times better still to be catholic without any system, and this they are who, themselves separate from systems, can yet say from the heart with Paul: "Grace be with *all* them that love our Lord Jesus Christ with a love incorruptible" (Ephesians 6:24), at the same time heeding John's exhortation, "Little children, let us not love in word, neither with the tongue, but in deed and truth" (1 John 3:18).

The principles involved in such a question are alike for all, but in practice there is a distinction between disciples called of the Lord to minister His word publicly and others. It is the former who will often face the matter: the latter will not so often be placed where there is any real occasion to go where the whole of God's mind for the ordering of His house is not entertained. In both cases there are two features to be kept in view: The maintenance of Scriptural liberty, and then the avoidance of abuse thereof.

Upon the case of the minister of the Word, in *The Witness* for December 1931 Mr. C. F. Hogg wrote the following judicious remarks:

> Occasions may arise when it would be wise to take advantage of an opportunity so provided to proclaim the Gospel, or to open up Scripture. This is the liberty of the servant which no man must take from him. "Who art thou that judgest the servant of another? To his own lord he standeth or falleth. Yea, he shall be made to stand; for the Lord hath power to make him stand" (Romans 14:4).
>
> On such occasions, however, a certain sacrifice of freedom to declare the whole counsel of God may be involved, owing to the claims of Christian courtesy. As a general rule, therefore, it would serve well, in the interests of loyal, happy, and efficient service to associate with those whom we know, in whom we have full confidence, and who have like confidence in us...
>
> As suggested above, and as Scripture strongly asserts, every servant is *answerable to his own Master and to Him alone*. It seems clear to me, however, that one of two courses may be followed, but not both. A man may use what he conceives to be his liberty to the full, going hither and thither to preach, but so doing he dissipates his energies and builds nothing; or he may surrender his liberty of movement, so to speak, and thus preserve his liberty to declare the whole counsel of God, and to build up a Church of God, teaching the saints to observe all things whatsoever he himself has learned of God.

Where these alternatives are clear it is equally clear that a faithful servant will take the latter course. But a considerable number of instances will remain where all the counsel of God could be stated, and saints be led on towards its practice. In every case the individual servant must be free to seek and to follow the leading of the Spirit for each several occasion, and he should be free to do this without resentment or criticism from his brethren.

It is also most important to understand that our true ground of personal separation from churches which profess the truth is that we believe we have been granted more light as to certain aspects of the will of God and that it is an evident duty to walk in all light gained, even if this may involve leaving a little behind those who either have not that light or do not see their way to walk in it. But this does not hinder the equally evident duty to encourage them to receive and to follow light when they may be willing to give us opportunity to do this.

As to the question of general Christian communion apart from the particular matter of public ministry, the following considered and printed statements of Groves may fitly and helpfully close the subject. He wrote in 1834:

> With respect to our communion with congregations, where the chaff and the wheat are mixed in all conceivable proportions between the extremes of the almost unmixed abominations of the apostate churches, where no souls are converted under the public ministrations, to the most pure and spiritual ministry, where sinners are converted and saints edified in love, till they grow up into the stature of perfect men in Christ, it is evident that we must consider ourselves in the double position of individuals who have duties they owe themselves, and, secondly, as members of an immense brotherhood, embracing the universal Catholic Church throughout the world, in all the congregations of the saints, where Christ still walks amidst the golden candlesticks, notwithstanding unnumbered weaknesses and errors. The first duty to ourselves is in selecting the congregation with whom we should stately worship; it should be where the form is most scriptural in our persuasion and the ministrations most spiritual; where there is the sweetest savour of Christ; where our own souls are most edified; where the Lord is most plainly present with those who minister and those who hear. This is what we owe the Lord, the Church of God, and our own souls. Considering, however, agreement in what we think best as to form of worship altogether secondary to heart agreement in the mystery of Christ and of godliness. These, then, appear the principles that ought to govern our selection, as indivuduals, of the place where we stately worship, since personally we cannot be with all. Yet as to our liberty in Christ to worship with any congregation under heaven where He manifests himself to bless and to save, can there be in any Christian mind a doubt? If my

Lord should say to me, in any congregation of the almost unnumbered sections of the Church, "What dost thou here?" I would reply, "Seeing Thou wert here to save and sanctify, I felt it safe to be with Thee." If He again said, as perhaps He may among most of us, "Didst thou not see abominations here, an admixture of that which was unscriptural, and the absence of that which was scriptural, and in some points error, at least in your judgment?" my answer would be, "Yea, Lord, but I dared not call that place unholy where Thou wert present to bless, nor by refusing communion in worship reject those as unholy whom Thou hadst by Thy saving power evidently sanctified and set apart for Thine own." Our reason for rejecting the congregations of apostate bodies is that Christ doth not manifest Himself among them in their public character, though He may save some individuals as brands plucked from the burning. To these churches we cry, standing on the outside, "Come out of her, my people, come out of her." Among the others we stand, as the Son of Man, or rather with Him, in *the midst* of the seven golden candlesticks (Revelation 1:13), telling them to remember their first love, first purity, and first work in all holy doctrine and discipline, lest the Lord take away their candlesticks; but we would rather linger, in hope that the impending judgment may be stayed, or some yet repent, than say, like Edom, in the day of Judah's sorrows, "Down with her, down with her, even to the ground" *(See* also Obadiah 10–14).

To the question, Are we not countenancing error by this plan? our answer is, that if we must appear to countenance error, or discountenance brotherly love and the visible union of the Church of God, we prefer the former, hoping that our lives and our tongues may be allowed by the Lord so intelligibly to speak that at last our righteousness shall be allowed to appear; but if not, still we may feel we have chosen the better part, since we tarried only for our Lord's departure; and as the candlestick retired, and its light vanished, we pronounce our sad farewell; but so long as Christ dwells in an individual, or walks in the midst of a congregation, blessing the ministrations to the conversion and edification of souls, we dare not denounce and formally withdraw from either, for fear of the awful sin of schism, of sin against Christ and His mystical body (534, 535).

7

The Church of God (2): Its Worship and Ministry

LARGELY because of this warm and generous spirit in which he met all Christians, and bore with those things with which he had ceased to agree, Groves was able to commend to many his own beliefs, learned from the Word, new and revolutionary as they were. These his glowing nature advocated with an enthusiasm, yet reasonableness, which made them attractive and infectious. Of these beliefs the first to be now noticed is:

1. LIBERTY TO OBSERVE THE SUPPER OF THE LORD.

Until that time, and still in many quarters, the Feast of Remembrance was observed at considerable, though various, intervals, and, what was more essential, only when an ordained person was present to officiate. In the spring of 1827, in Dublin, Mr. J. G. Bellett said to Miss Paget:

> Groves has just been telling me that it appeared to him from Scripture that believers, meeting together as disciples of Christ, were free to break bread together, as their Lord had admonished them; and that, in as far as the practice of the apostles could be a guide, every Lord's day should be set apart for thus remembering the Lord's death and obeying His parting command.
>
> This suggestion of Mr. Groves was immediately carried out by himself and his friends in Dublin; and how many, who have since followed their example, can speak of the peace and joy they have experienced in thus obeying the Lord's will! (39).

To tens of thousands today this inherited liberty to observe the holy Supper in simplicity is a spiritual common-place, even though prized; they can hardly imagine any other condition. But a century ago the proposal to observe the "sacrament" without an ordained minister to consecrate the elements was, for most, if not all, revolutionary, a direct attack upon one of the central, vital rights of clerisy, indeed, a thorough denial of the whole clerical standing and claims. Because if for this most sacred act no "priest," of some degree or name, is necessary, then is he wholly unnecessary, and can be dispensed with entirely.

It is clear from the writings of Ignatius of Antioch, early in the second century, that clerisy was the first major evil to insinuate itself into the Christian churches. From that time, step by step it was claimed that only men duly consecrated for the purpose by predecessors in holy orders could make certain sacramental acts valid and effectual, and of these acts the consecrating of the bread and wine became in time the chief. By this device the "clergy" became indispensable and dominant, and the "laity" became dependent and enslaved. And only in measure did the Reformed Churches, or Nonconformity, free themselves from this blight. In this slow process of liberation Groves' suggestion was probably as great a step forward as had ever been made.

It is for all who see this to value and preserve their liberty. It is never safe, for Satan knows its vital power, and seeks ever to filch it from the church of God. Thus in one section of Exclusive Brethren there has been made of late years the assertion that only certain brethren have advanced so far spiritually as to be "priestly" in state, and that only these ought to minister the Word or "go to the table," that is, distribute the bread and wine.

With the noble-souled Moses one may truly wish that "all the Lord's people were prophets," and that every Christian man knew *in power* his liberty in Christ and could exercise profitably his privileges. In this connexion may be quoted with advantage several passages from Groves' journal:

> What I long for is what I have always felt my soul so deficient in, the *realization* of the power of the truth I hold (449). Words would fail to convey what I mean, but still it is pleasant to bear testimony to the truth that *Jesus realized* is the same Prince of Peace He ever was (416). I feel what we really need, both to enable us to carry out, and to suffer, all

God's will, is realization of the things we know (408). I do purpose to be more and more close in my communion with God, as the only secret of real power, either in ministry or worship; REALIZATION IS EVERYTHING IN THE THINGS OF GOD (384).

But while this longing is excellent, and even though it is truly salutary to own our weakness, personal and collective, it is quite another matter to differentiate distinctly between this person and that, and to decide and to declare that this one has reached "priestly" condition and the other has not, that the former can perform certain functions and the latter cannot do so. This is essential clerisy, and it is not surprising that the same circle stated in print in 1932 that "The breaking of bread is for a *remembrance* of Christ, and this obviously contemplates His absence, not His presence. He is present spiritually as He is recalled in His appointed way; but this is *after* the bread is broken, not before."

This means that after the due observance of the Supper in the breaking of bread, the Lord becomes present in the gathering, which He was not before that act. These believers would not, I am persuaded, suggest that the bread and wine had become the body and blood of the Lord by the action of one of these "priestly" brethren. The doctrine as stated approximates to the Lutheran consubstantiation, that is, that after consecration by the minister the Lord is present in the elements, but that these remain bread and wine; but it is not far from that to Rome's transubstantiation, that is, that after consecration the elements only appear to be bread and wine, yet are these no longer, but in reality have become the body and blood of Christ; and such descents are slippery.

In 1840 Groves wrote thus from India:

> The fact that our position here puts pastoral work and fellowship on a simple Christian footing among the natives is by no means the least important feature of our work. Until we came, no one but an ordained native was allowed to celebrate the Lord's Supper or to baptize; and when our Christian brethren, Aroolappen and Andrew, partook of the Lord's Supper with the native Christians, it caused more stir and enquiry than you can imagine. The constant reference to *God's Word* has brought, and is bringing, the questions connected with ministry and Church government into a perfectly new position in the minds of many (393).

At the present time there are many thousands of congregations of Christians, in almost all parts of the earth, who enjoy this simple privilege of commemorating the death of their Lord without an "ordained" celebrant. Thus encouragingly great has been the extension of this liberty which caused so much stir and inquiry a century ago. But let us be watchful. It would surely be a deep grief to A. N. Groves could he know that among those who would claim to be his successors in India there are some—I hope and think only a few, but some—who discourage little groups of believers from breaking the bread unless one of themselves is present, or an Indian brother deemed by them to be suitable.

The reason advanced for this is an alleged spiritual immaturity, making for an unprofitable, and sometimes unseemly, observance, and consequent reproach. But this is exactly what was seen at Corinth, yet the apostle did not adopt any such plan to meet the trouble; he did not direct that the Table should not be spread until he, or someone he approved, could be present. Not even the great apostle would arrogate to himself a right and standing so clerical in its essence.

There seems a perpetual tendency to regard baptism and the Lord's Supper as "church ordinances," and this conception leads directly to the idea that "church officers" are required for their due observance. It is a false and pernicious notion, and robs these blessed acts of their real spiritual value by robbing them of the simplicity which is of the essence of their nature and benefit.

We are not told that the apostles personally baptized the three thousand at Pentecost, or, for the matter of that, any other persons. It is clear that Peter left the baptizing of Cornelius and his friends to others: "he commanded them to be baptized" (Acts 10:48). Paul baptized the first one or two of his converts at Corinth, and he must have left them to baptize the rest. He emphasizes this (1 Corinthians 1:14–16). Evangelists baptized a convert immediately, without any reference to a company of Christians, as Philip did the eunuch (Acts 8:39), or Paul the jailor at Philippi (Acts 16:33). It was no church ceremony at all and required no church officer to sanction or perform. The community entered into the matter only when a baptized person sought its fellowship; it did not as such decide for or against his baptism.

It was so with the Supper also. The Jerusalem church from the first numbered thousands, and it was impossible that they could all meet in one place to break bread, for there was no place available, nor probably any one hour suitable for so many. Hence we read (Acts 2:46) that, while they continued attending daily the public prayers and worship in the temple, yet as Christians they observed their own Christian feast of remembrance and of fellowship in their houses, in connexion with their usual meals. The breaking of bread and the taking of food are conjoined yet distinguished: "breaking bread at home, they took food in gladness of heart."

Mr. Groves' original suggestion as to the time for observance of the ordinance needs modifying, or at least should not be deemed conclusive and exclusive. He said: "as far as the practice of the apostles could be a guide, every Lord's day should be set apart" for the feast. Presumably Acts 20:7 was in his mind, where Luke says: "And upon the first day of the week, when we were gathered together to break bread, Paul discoursed (dialogued, held interchange of thought) with them." This is warrant enough for meeting on the first of the week, but, read strictly, the statement refers to *that* first day of the week only: it is but an inference that already it was the regular custom to meet on that day. It may have been so, but Luke does not say as much. It was not on the first of the week that the Lord instituted the Supper, nor, as to the exact fact, did the actual remembrance at Troas take place that evening, for it was after midnight when Paul broke the bread (verses 7 and 11). With these facts before us, and the fact that the Jerusalem church broke bread daily, and in their homes as might be convenient, it is clear that no bondage, no ecclesiasticism, no clergy, no fixed day or hour, but much simplicity and informality, characterized the observance.

Upon this essential matter Groves wrote in 1831 as follows:

The miserable substitute of man's arrangements for the Holy Ghost's, has destroyed the true unison and order of the Church of Christ, by substituting that which is artificial for that which is of God, by appointing man to be the artificer of a work God alone can accomplish. Now the Church presents a disunited aspect; the unity being marred, among other things, by the unscriptural distinction of clergy and laity, which confines ministry to a few, leaving the many without due office or service: this is not of the Spirit (209).

But though the church be low and poor his heart found refuge and strength in God. He continues:

> How blessed it is among all these disorders to know that the Lord cares for His own, and will keep them as the apple of His eye, watching day and night lest any hurt them. Thus were we preserved, when we little thought it, by our Shepherd's care. There is something, I think, in this view of the body being composed of members of various orders, various services, from the most minute to the most important, all tending to the one great end, the glory of the only Head, and the Church's glory in Him, that greatly comforts the weak (209).

In this, and all other matters, it is not the point that so good a man as Groves suggested the thought, but that he brought to light that which was already in the Word of God but generally unnoticed, hidden by human traditional practices.

But this liberty to break bread without an ordained minister involves the wider and deeper question of the validity of human ordination itself. Groves came to see that.

2. Human Ordination to the Ministry of the Gospel is not of God.

This was no new question, but a battle fought through the long centuries, and needing still to be fought in our day.

The Roman Church is sensible and consistent in not attempting to justify many of its claims and doings by the New Testament. It knows that the attempt is perverse and hopeless, and it boldly depends upon tradition, even though it be a mere alleged oral tradition. Episcopal ordination to minister in holy things is *not* in the New Testament, but it is far too powerful a means for exalting the bishop to be neglected or foregone.

John Bunyan, in the seventeenth century, need not have spent twelve years in Bedford gaol would he have consented that he had no right to preach because he had not been ordained. The same battle is now [1939] in progress in some countries in Southeast Europe. The State, in the interests of the Greek Orthodox Church, and of its own power, insists that all preachers and leaders must be licensed by itself, upon its own conditions. These include that such may not be under twenty-five years of age, must not have been convicted of a crime, and must minister only in the area specified in the licence. By the first condition I myself must have been silent for eight years after my heart urged me to make known the good news; by the second, George Müller never could have preached; by the third, the wide and rapid spread of the gospel becomes impossible. The brethren in that region rightly answer that they have no power or right to restrain the Holy Spirit by such means; they cannot dictate to Him, and He will refuse to submit to the dictates of men, in the choice, control, and use of His servants. And so the battle goes on, is indeed rapidly extending in various countries, and must go on, for the point is vital to apostolic Christianity.

Who can conceive of the Son of God applying to Caiaphas or Pontius Pilate for a license to bear witness to the truth? or Paul negotiating with Felix or Festus as to preaching the gospel? The religious authorities at Jerusalem "charged the apostles not to speak at all nor teach in the name of Jesus"; the answer was: "we cannot but speak the things which we saw and heard." Upon this positive, legal prohibition being promptly and openly violated, the high priest said: "We strictly charged you not to teach in this name." The apostles replied: "We must obey God rather than men" (Acts 4:18–20; 5:27–29). Accommodation between the two parties was out of the question from both sides. It is so still, and ever will be. No apostle or evangelists of the first century received any human authorization to preach the gospel or to serve in the church.

But Groves had been reared a high churchman, and his mind was dark and bound upon this matter. He himself shall describe his state and narrate his path to evangelical freedom. We have seen that part of his objection to ministering in Miss Paget's unconsecrated building was that it would stand in the way of his procuring ordination to the ministry of the Church of England. He was intending to become a clergyman.

> During this time, he tells us, dear Hake came and consulted me about certain difficulties, which involved his leaving his wife and children penniless, so far as he knew, or following a course that his conscience disapproved. I gave my opinion clearly; and he, with that holy simplicity which has ever characterized him, acted out what his conscience dictated (41).

This is one more instance of the deep spiritual influence Groves exerted on individuals.

Mr. Wm. Hake had almost a life-long friendship with R. C. Chapman, whose small biography of him, *Seventy Years of Pilgrimage*, is profitable reading.

But the influence and benefit received from Groves were in this instance reciprocated. Groves continues:

> Shortly after this, he called on me, and asked me if I did not hold war to be unlawful. I replied, "Yes." He then further asked, how I could subscribe that article which declares, "It is lawful for Christian men to take up arms at the command of the civil magistrate." It had, till that moment, never occurred to me. I read it, and replied, "I never would sign it"; and thus ended my connection with the Church of England, as one about to be ordained in her communion (41).

Mr. Groves' conviction that war is utterly unsuitable for a Christian was shared by the whole earlier generation of Brethren. It was a usual thing for army and navy officers to resign their commissions upon conversion among Brethren, a testimony to the power and depth of the work of grace at that period. An instance was Captain F. Lane, R.N., whose daughter, Mrs. W. T. P. Wolston, told me that the same night her father was converted he sent in his resignation. The First Lord of the Admiralty, Earl Spencer, was a personal friend, and viewed the resignation as a hint that he wished for a better post, which was offered, but to no purpose.

This conviction was not based upon the views that lead some others to the same attitude. They did not assert that to kill is essentially immoral, for they recognized that God has ordered capital punishment. Nor did they say that war is *inherently* wrong, for the Scripture shows that God has ordered wars, as one branch of capital punishment and of His government of the world. That killing and wars as conducted by fallen man are often, indeed commonly, wicked does not prove the wider propositions stated, or alter the facts of Divine action as mentioned.

Their attitude flowed from that heart-union with the Lord Jesus Christ which had become their enjoyed portion, as it had been that of God's choicest saints before them. They were in the power of the truth that "God hath called us into the fellowship of His Son, Jesus Christ our Lord" (1 Corinthians 1:9). When the day comes that the Lord shall reign and act as judge and make war, then will they, the servants, also share these offices (Luke 22:24–30; 1 Corinthians 6:2,3; Revelation 2:26–28; 3:21, etc.); but until the Master reigns the servant may not do so (1 Corinthians 4:8). Shall the bride of the Lamb take up office or duty or glory before her Bridegroom? The word "fellowship" means partnership: shall a junior partner act in independence of the senior of the firm?

As yet it is the Father who administers the universe through His angels, while the Lord Jesus acts as Head of His church. As yet Christ is the dispenser of the grace of God, not of His holy wrath; and therefore this is the blessed calling and privilege of His followers. He declared that as a man on earth He had not been appointed a judge or a righter of the injustices of the earth (Luke 12:14). Thus He refused to act in a civil cause; and when men would have constituted Him judge in a criminal case (John 8:1–11), He so convicted the prosecutors that they abandoned the proceedings and the case lapsed. His followers while left on earth are to walk as He walked, follow His steps and example, and do as He did when here (1 John 2:6; 1 Peter 2:21–23; John 13:15). This is the essential mark of discipleship.

This dispensing of the grace of God is by far the harder course. It involved the Lord in hatred, rejection, persecution, and death; and in ten thousand instances it has brought the same portion on His faithful followers. The horrors which men have inflicted upon one another on the battle-field pale before the prolonged terrors and tortures they have inflicted upon the unresisting witnesses to the grace of God in Christ. They are hated because they are not of the world, as He was not of the world. If they acted as being of the world, the world would love its own, as Christ testified (John 17:14; 15: 18–21). The world, including those great organized religious institutions, miscalled Christian Churches, has ever generated its intensest fury against those other-worldly folk, who, with Christ, testify of it that its works are evil. To be flattered and honoured by that world, as is the portion of the successful soldier, is itself to prove that the servant of the Lord Jesus has, in this matter, missed the path of fellowship with his Master, even though in other respects he may maintain his testimony to Christ as Redeemer, as a few soldiers have done, in contrast to the many such who have lost their testimony.

Groves knew that he was not of this world, not in some undefined, non-effective sense, but precisely as Christ was not (John 17:16), and he carried this into practice, which last is where he differs from so many who make the same profession. On the one hand, the ambitions and dignities open to candidates in the sphere of human affairs, including its religious section, had simply no attractions for him, even as they had none for Moses after he had seen in advance the coming glories of the Christ (Hebrews 11). On the other hand, its politics and its quarrels were no affairs of his as a Christian. He could sorrow deeply over its awful state, and would relieve its miseries where possible, as he did with pain and peril amid plague and war in Bagdad; but he acted everywhere as an outsider, a benevolent alien in a foreign land, as much in England as in Persia. To his heart it was no theory or mere doctrine, but a conscious, blessed, practice-compelling experience that God had rescued him out of the sphere of authority of darkness, and had translated him into the kingdom of the Son of His love. That kingdom is as actually existing a policy as is any earthly kingdom. "Our citizenship (the State, the constitution, to which as citizens we belong) is even now in the heavens, for the kingdom of heaven is a present kingdom" (Lightfoot, Philippians 3:20). In modern terms, Groves knew he had been denaturalized and renaturalized (Colossians 1:13). This position was crystallized into a crisp sentence by a teacher of the next generation of Brethren,

Henry Dyer, when he said: As a Christian I do not say "our king," but "the king!"

But if a believer is not in the power of this truth as an actual heart condition, no fine spiritual theory about it, however correct, will rule his practice. If he feels himself as yet to be of the world, he will feel it his duty to commingle in its affairs, and in war among the rest of those affairs; and he may do this as conscientiously, and even as prayerfully, as a David or a Joshua. But this is not the properly *Christian* position or conduct; it belongs to the old covenant, not to the new, to law and justice, not to grace. For one may live physically in this age of grace, yet morally in the age of law; and in the day of Christ each, no doubt, will find his portion correspondingly. This principle may be studied in Romans 2:25–29; 11:13–24; Matthew 7:1,2; James 2:13.

The position of the Brethren was stated with distinctness in J. N. Darby's answer to an inquiry from a French Christian at the time of the Franco-Prussian War of 1870. It is found in volume 2 of his *Letters*, page 130, and reads:

> … It is clear to me that a Christian, free to do as he will, could never be a soldier, unless he were at the very bottom of the scale, and ignorant of the Christian position. It is another thing when one is forced to it. In such a case the question is this: is the conscience so strongly implicated upon the negative side of the question, that one could not be a soldier without violating that which is the rule for conscience—the word of God? In that case we bear the consequences; we must be faithful.
>
> What pains me is the manner in which the idea of one's country has taken possession of the hearts of some brethren. I quite understand that the sentiment of patriotism may be strong in the heart of a man. I do not think that the heart is capable of *affection* toward the whole world. At bottom, human affection must have a centre, which is "I." I can say, "My country," and it is not that of a stranger. I say "My children," "My friend," and it is not a purely selfish "*I*." One would sacrifice one's life— everything (not oneself, or one's honour) for one's country, one's friend. I cannot say, "My world"; there is no appropriation. We appropriate something to ourselves that it may not be ourselves. But God delivers us from the "I"; He makes of God, and of God in Christ, the centre of all; and the Christian, if consistent, declares plainly that he seeks

a country—a better, that is to say, a heavenly country. His affections, his ties, his citizenship, are above. He withdraws into the shade in this world, as outside the vortex which surges there, to engulf and carry everything away. The Lord is a sanctuary.

That a Christian should hesitate whether he ought to obey or not, I understand: I respect his conscience; but that he should allow himself to be carried away by what is called patriotism—that is what is not of heaven. "My kingdom," said Jesus, "is not of this world; if my kingdom were of this world, then would my servants fight." It is the spirit of the world under an honourable and attractive form, but wars come from "lusts that war in your members."

As a man I would have fought obstinately for my country, and would never have given way, God knows; but as a Christian I believe and feel myself to be outside all; these things move me no more. The hand of God is in them; I recognize it; He has ordered all beforehand. I bow my head before that will. If England were to be invaded tomorrow, I should trust in Him. It would be a chastisement upon this people who have never seen war, but I would bend before His will.

Many Christians are labouring in the scene of the war; large sums of money have been sent to them. All this does not attract me. God be praised that so many poor creatures have been relieved; but I would rather see the brethren penetrating the lanes of the city, and seeking the poor where they are found every day. There is far more self-abnegation, more hidden service in such work. We are not of this world, but we are the representatives of Christ in the midst of the world. May God graciously keep His own.

Groves also had been effectively attached to that new Centre. Outside of Its orbit he had no interests: to him to live was Christ. By revelation of Christ as cast out by this world, and now the Man in heaven, he had been brought to the state of heart of Paul Gerhard, the German saint whose lines have been so exquisitely rendered by Mrs. Bevan under the title "Bands of Love. Ruth 1:16,17" (*Hymns of Tersteegen, Suso, and Others*, First Series, 102):

> A homeless Stranger amongst us came
> To this land of death and mourning;
> He walked in a path of sorrow and shame,
> Through insult, and hate, and scorning.

A Man of sorrows, of toil and tears,
An outcast Man and a lonely;
And He looked on me, and through endless years
Him must I love—Him only.

Then from this sad and sorrowful land,
From this land of tears He departed;
But the light of His eyes and the touch of His hand
Had left me broken-hearted.

And I clave to Him as He turned His face
From the land that was mine no longer—
The land I had loved in the ancient days.
Ere I knew the love that was stronger.

And I would abide where He abode,
And follow His steps for ever;
His people my people, His God my God,
In the land beyond the river.

And where He died would I also die,
Far dearer a grave beside Him
Than a kingly place amongst living men,
The place which they denied Him.

Then afar and afar did I follow Him on,
To the land where He was going—
To the depths of glory beyond the sun,
Where the golden fields were glowing—

The golden harvest of endless joy,
The joy He had sown in weeping;
How can I tell the blest employ,
The songs of that glorious reaping!

The recompense sweet, the full reward,
Which the Lord His God has given;
At rest beneath the wings of the Lord,
At home in the courts of heaven.

To which, for our own reflection and stimulus, let us add these further lines:

> "The path of sorrow, and that path alone,
> Leads to the place where sorrow is unknown."

(John 12:24–26; Luke 14:25–27; Acts 14:21,22; Romans 8:17; 2 Timothy 2:11–13; Revelation 20:4).

This was in 1827. He was still preparing for the examination at Dublin for ordination, but this project was abandoned under circumstances to be narrated in a later chapter. He continues:

> Yet ... I was still so far attached to the Church of England, that I went to London, to arrange my going out as a layman, for the Church Missionary Society; but as they would not allow me to celebrate the Lord's Supper, when no other minister was near, it came to nothing (42).

Thus by walking in light already gained from Scripture upon one point, the liberty to break bread without an ordained celebrant, he was kept from walking in darkness upon the greater point of freedom to work in the gospel without ordination itself: and he gained a rich fulfilment of the promise that to him that hath light, and walks in it, shall be given more light, as his next words show.

> My mind was then in great straits; for I saw not yet my liberty of ministry to be from Christ alone, and felt some ordination to be necessary, but hated the thought of being made a sectarian. But, one day the thought was brought to my mind, that ordination of any kind to preach the gospel is no requirement of Scripture. To me it was the removal of a mountain ... From that moment, I have myself never had a doubt of my own liberty in Christ to minister the word; and, in my last visit to Dublin, I mentioned my views to dear Mr. Bellett and others (42, 43).

At the end of 1828 he wrote to a correspondent:

> You ask again, am I exercising the ministry on my own nomination? I trust not, for if I am, the work will come to nought; I trust I exercise it on the nomination of my Lord by His Spirit; if you can point to any other nomination as necessary, or that there are any persons excluded until they are appointed by man, I hope I am willing to weigh the evidence you bring;

and then, with that large charity which allowed a course to others to which he could not himself submit, he added:

> I wish you, however, distinctly to understand, I do not object to ordina-
> tion by men, if it be exercised on principles consistent with Scripture,
> but if they think they confer anything more than their permission to
> preach in their little part of the fold of Christ, I should decline it until
> they shew how they came by that authority from the word of God, and
> what are the scriptural rules and limitations of this authority (48, 49);

which last demand, it would seem, virtually nullifies the earlier con-
cession, being impossible of fulfilment.

The essence of this burning topic, in both its practical and its
theological aspects, can be traced back by the discerning heart to the
rights of Christ and the place of the Word of God, to what, in short,
Groves indicated in these words:

> The tendency to sectarianism, however, is in these provinces much more
> marked than in Bombay or Madras, and this is why I feel so thankful
> the Lord has given me such favour with so many, in endeavouring to
> show them the beauty and glory of being contented with Christ as a
> *Head* and His Word as a *guide* (306, 307).

And again:

> What important principles are these; first, to have Christ as your *only*
> Head; secondly, His Word as your *only* guide (311):

Important principles indeed! So important, so fundamental, so
energetic, that he who practises them thoroughly can never be a
cleric, of any type, in any degree; since the least measure of clerisy
impinges in some measure upon the *solitary* headship of Christ in
the church and the *solitary* authority of the Word of God.

So paralysing, so deadening is the influence of clerisy as to demand
the most complete avoidance and resistance. It is this which, to my
regret, forbids me to take the Supper of the Lord according to the
Church of England form, or in a similarly constituted Church, even
were the clergyman and communicants believers. For so long as it
be held that only an ordained celebrant can consecrate and officiate the most vital of all features of clerisy is maintained, and all the

other elements of priestcraft are allowed implicitly, even by men who repudiate them formally; for to sanction the greater is to sanction the lesser, and clerisy holds the solemnizing of the Supper to be the most exalted of all its functions.

Brought thus far, in living energy of the truth as in Jesus, Groves very naturally soon discerned another important fact concerning true worship, and the rightful place of the Holy Spirit in the church, even

3. THAT THE SPIRIT OF GOD IS THE ONLY LEADER OF SPIRITUAL WORSHIP.

Contrasting external worship by regular forms, whether God-appointed forms as at Jerusalem, or man-appointed ritual as at Gerizim, the Lord declared to the sinful formalist at Sychar's Well the essential nature of true worship: "The true worshippers shall worship the Father in spirit and truth: for such doth the Father seek to be his worshippers. God is spirit [it is the nature of His being]; and they that worship him must worship in spirit and truth" (John 4:23,24). That is, sacred places, postures, acts, and forms of words are now no more recognized by God. Men of former ages worshipped Jehovah as *God*; believers of this age are to know Him as *Father*, and ritual and formalities, however seemly between subjects and their sovereign, are out of place between children and their father. The reverence of children, if it is to be pleasing to the father, must come spontaneously from their hearts, it must be the devotion of a loving spirit, the expression of a true affection, and the most elaborate and beautiful forms cannot take the place of such natural, confiding intercourse.

But how shall man on earth, with no outward perceptions of the invisible God, provoke his heart to *such* acquaintance with God and maintain his spirit in such an exalted intercourse? Or arriving at some measure of fellowship, how shall he rightly express his emotions in holy, acceptable worship? The answer came at Pentecost, in the indwelling and inworking of God himself by His Spirit. The Spirit of God creates and maintains in the believer the knowledge of God as our *Father* in Christ, and draws out the spiritual powers of our being to worship Him as *Father*. And so Paul, in the enjoyment of this ministry of the Spirit, contrasts it with the formalities of

Jewish ritual worship by those living in a fleshly economy only, the outward circumcision. He declares that it is the circumcised *heart*, cut off from its former fleshly condition, that is the essence and secret and necessity of relationship with God; and that they are that true circumcised people who "worship by the Spirit of God, and glory in Christ Jesus, and have no confidence in the flesh" (Philippians 3:3).

Let those whose worship is marked by even the simplest routine ask their own hearts honestly whether that routine does not necessarily, if imperceptibly, dull the intense activity of the spirit in its effort to be inwardly conscious of God. Let those whose ceremony is ornate, lovely, sensuous, search their hearts if they can truly affirm that, in seeking God, they have no confidence in the flesh, in these outward features which gratify the senses, but that they glory in Christ Jesus *alone* in their approach to God. And let them say before God why they have these sensuous features at all if they really have *no* confidence in them. The fact of our present state is, that the external and material retards the activity of our internal and spiritual faculties. If not, why do we instinctively close the eyes when we really set ourselves to seek a heart-consciousness of God? The perfect Man did not need to do this—Jesus "lifted up his eyes" when He spoke to His Father (Mark 6:41; John 17:1).

Groves' mind had no common faculty of analysis in the mental, moral, and spiritual realm, and the following remarks may help to the realization of the true inwardness of ritual. On his journey to Bagdad in 1829 he visited a colony of Moravians, and wrote:

> In observing the external order and regularity, so manifest in the religious exercises of the Moravians, my mind has been strongly impressed with the danger of the soul being deceived by this into an entirely false estimate of its real state. Perhaps the absence of all regularity may be esteemed a greater danger by many; but the absence of that *fixed* regularity might allow the soul, by leaving it free and unshackled, an opportunity of watching its real movements, and might lead it to detect real indifference and coldness, whereas it now flatters itself with the sense of regular and orderly service.
>
> When affection really exists in a family, every child shows its attachment, and thinks on those little personal and individual occasions of so doing, which arise neither all at one time nor in one way, nor for one

thing, nor in the same words. Perhaps, then, as we have in a family some regular expressions of attachment, such as the morning and evening salutation, but the greater part irregular, so, in every Christian society, the points of public control had better be few, and the great majority of cases left free, as every man is disposed in his heart, otherwise you have only a subtle, self-deceiving hypocrisy spreading through your community, appearing like order, but in reality having nothing of real order at all—of that order which consists in unity of hearts, not of bodies, in similar forms. In contending for the importance of forms for the sake of order in public worship, this must never be lost sight of, that the order which attracts the eye of man and that which meets God's approval are very different: take, for the sake of illustration, the case of the best ordered cathedral service, every part of which is regulated to the nicest point of time and order. This looks very imposing to the common observer, but how does it appear to Him who looketh on the heart? First, there are the choristers who keep all in time, but are the annoyance of all about them by their disorderly indifference;—then the congregation, if accustomed to the service, follow the recitative with their voices, led by the ear, whilst their hearts may be occupied with their various objects of interest, whether pleasure or profit; and lastly, there is the spectator, unaccustomed to the service, who considers only the music, but understands not a word of what is said; so that, in fact, if we consider that the only order of any value is that which proceeds from the unity of the hearts of the worshippers, from the truth and spirit of the petitions offered up, it may, perhaps, be affirmed with truth, that, in the sight of God, the most externally disorderly set of jumpers [a class of enthusiasts known at that time, whose behaviour may be inferred from this nickname] that ever met together, may and often have more real unity of spirit than is really existing under all the show and semblance of decency. I do not wish to advocate external disorder, but I am, if possible, more anxious not to be deceived by the existence of external order into the supposition of there being an essential connexion between it and unity of soul in the service of God (60, 61).

But as the Spirit of God is personally the power that inspires real worship, so is He by consequence the leader of such worship when it is collective. To suppose that an additional leader, of human choice and appointment, is necessary is to assert the insufficiency of the Holy Spirit, and is impious, however little this be intended by many. And thus of the exercises of a church taught by an apostle we read: "When ye come together, *each one* hath a psalm, hath a teaching, hath a revelation, hath a tongue, hath an interpretation," and it is shown that two or three persons might exercise either gift on the one occasion (1 Corinthians 14:26–33). These words are unmistakably distinct, and the same is seen when believers gathered at Troas (Acts 20:7–11). It was not the case that Paul alone took part through that whole night. He "dialogued" and "talked with them"; there was interchange of thought; nor is any other type of Christian gathering known to the New Testament.

As clerisy entrenched itself in the church in the early centuries, this right of God the Holy Spirit to lead the worship of the saints was more and more denied to Him, spiritual worship of necessity declined, ritual took its place, the officiating clergy performed all the service, and attained their goal as indispensable mediators between man and God. The rare and meagre attempts made to justify this from Scripture took the form of appeal to the Old Testament, not to the New. This Groves indicated by saying:

> The more I trace the existing evils of the Church of Christ, the more I believe, in my inmost heart, they have originated in the natural worldliness of man seizing on that in the Jewish dispensation which suited his carnal nature, and grafting it into the spiritual dispensation of the Lord of glory (330).

The paralysis that so soon seized the Reformed Churches in the sixteenth century was thus induced. The most terrible proof of this is, that when the princes asked the theologians how they ought to deal with the thousands of believers who would not submit to State ruled churches or to infant baptism, the Reformers replied that Moses had ordered the secular power to stone false prophets and therefore the princes had a duty to punish these "heretics" even unto death! And so was seen the melancholy spectacle that the Reformers and the Reformed princes, but lately escaped from the intolerance and cruelty of the Romish Church, themselves quickly became equally intolerant and cruel, in persecuting dissenting believers. This, rather than the Jesuit counter-reformation, was the true set-back to the work of God at that time: His own people abandoned grace and returned to law as their principle.

It was no wonder that such Churches returned also to legalistic forms and ritual in public worship, or that this rapidly succumbed to death and decay, and became mere lifeless externalism, not spiritual worship. Nor did the Nonconformist bodies, that escaped at cost from the strangle-hold of the State Churches, free themselves fully from the practice of substituting their own self-chosen ministers for the public leadership of the Holy Spirit, and their own modified routine of worship for the movings of the Spirit. Yet all through the centuries, now and then, here and there, God drew hearts back to His Word as the only source of knowledge of His good will, and showed to such, among other things, the true nature of worship, and His Spirit as the only power thereof. The Society of Friends were among such. And at the beginning of the last century Groves was added to this goodly succession.

At the very commencement of those gatherings in Dublin for mutual edification, the believers meeting were not enlightened as to this matter. When in 1829 they met in the house of Francis Hutchinson he "prescribed a certain line of things, as the services of prayer, singing and teaching that should be found amongst us on each day" (*Neatby* 22); and after they had removed to the room in Aungier Street, as Mr. Bellett adds:

> …the settled order of worship which we had in Fitzwilliam Square, gave place gradually … Cronin bears similar testimony—"We felt free up to this time [evidently 1830], *and long afterwards,* to make arrangements among ourselves as to who should distribute the bread, and to take other ministries in the assembly" (*Neatby* 35, 36).

Had this remained permanent it is unlikely that anything further than the personal edification in measure of those concerned would have followed, for there would have been little to distinguish them from other such groups of godly persons that have arisen, served some good spiritual end for a time, and then have either passed away or lapsed into formalism and uselessness. But at the end of 1828 Groves had sown in J. G. Bellett's heart the seeds of truth gathered from the Scriptures, which grew in the souls of him and others, truth that was to set them free in this sphere, and, what was of supreme importance, was to set free the eternal Spirit to fulfil among them His own rightful office as Leader in the assemblies of God.

Bellett has given the following account of the incident. "Walking one day with him [Groves] as we were passing down Lower Pembroke Street [Dublin], he said to me:—'This I doubt not is the mind of God concerning us—we should come together in all simplicity as disciples, not waiting on any pulpit or ministry, but trusting that the Lord would edify us together by ministering as He pleased and saw good from the midst of ourselves.' At the moment he spoke these words, I was assured my soul had got the right idea, and that moment I remember as if it were but yesterday, and could point you out the place. It was the birthday of my mind, dear J____, may I so speak, as a brother," meaning, no doubt, as one who would be known later as of the Brethren (*Neatby* 12).

When a man passes on to even one other man some truth that he has learned from Scripture, it cannot be known what a large harvest will grow. How very careful, therefore, ought we to be to sow in other hearts all truth as we learn it, for seed kept in the barn will not grow, but be useless; and, on the other hand, how very, very careful ought we to be to sow only good seed. When one looks in the Cairo Museum at the recovered specimens of the golden rams or calves worshipped in ancient Egypt, serious thoughts enter the heart. Who first suggested the worship of the golden calf is not known by us. But Aaron and Israel copied it, to the immediate undoing of the people. And after more than four hundred years Jeroboam, the first king of Israel, copied Aaron, using his very words; then every one of the kings of Israel, as the history repeats and repeats, "walked in the sins of Jeroboam"; until at last the ten tribes went into captivity for these iniquities, and are still under the dread judgment. What a fearful harvest from the original suggestion to worship God under the form of a calf.

But it cannot be estimated how rich and gracious a harvest the heavenly Sun of righteousness has caused to grow in His church during the past one hundred years from those words of A. N. Groves. In all parts of the earth today there are very many thousands of Christian gatherings, known as Brethren or not known by this name (it matters nothing), where the Spirit of God has in measure His due place and rights, and where His grace is known in corresponding measure. These are a fruit of his remark quoted, and the spiritual influence upon both the church of God and the world is beyond conception.

After fifty years of uninterrupted fellowship with such assemblies in many lands, of different parties of Brethren and among other Christians, I know the dangers possible to this method of worship; the tediousness of some ministry, wearisome pauses, the weakness of the witness, the lack of edification, the actual and maybe gross disorder in the gatherings. Such manifest evils (except perhaps the second) were, however, in the church at Corinth. My soul owns with deep thankfulness the wisdom of God in preserving to the church Paul's letters to that assembly, with their sombre picture of moral and doctrinal evil, and their clear instruction as to the Divine manner of meeting such fearful conditions. And to meet the fact of unprofitable meetings and ministry no suggestion whatever was made that the control of the gathering should be taken from the Holy Spirit and be vested in some of His servants. How foolish, yea, how profane the suggestion sounds when stated thus plainly. How can one whose eyes have been opened to this trespass upon the rights of the Spirit of God but mourn over the fact itself and deplore its results. That He in His grace grants blessing even when He is wronged does not justify the wrong, nor avoid the loss of blessing inherent in the restraint put upon His working in the saints.

I have mingled also in the worship and church life of such Christians as do not follow the New Testament in these matters. In all that I see of the Lord among them I rejoice unfeignedly; but in such places also there is fearfully tedious ministry, painfully empty and unedifying worship, if worship it be, and disorder. To give an extreme instance, I knew both the pastor and senior elder of a chapel who had such an altercation in a business meeting of the church that the Head of the church intervened in judgment and the elder fell dead as he was speaking. It is with me a deep persuasion, begotten, I think, of experience enough, that the spiritual state and energy of churches which, in spite of all failures, wish and seek to wait upon the Spirit of God is, on the average, *distinctly* higher and richer than anywhere else.

There are particular churches of other types that are in a high spiritual condition: I acknowledge it gladly, and thank God. But if such be examined closely it will be found that it is the degree in which they do in fact yield to the Spirit of God His place that is the secret of their condition, and that the human order and forms really hinder.

It were a worthless task to fight merely for one order of worship as against another: it is of the greatest possible moment to plead for the rights of the Holy Spirit in the church of God, for it is as far as He is free that He can work in power in the church, and, through it, upon the world. My observation is—and I have no shadow of doubt of it—that those assemblies which seek to follow the New Testament in worship and ministry are today by far the strongest of forces for the defence of the gospel and for its propagation. There is reason for the oft-made remark that if you want Christians who know their Bibles, go among the Brethren. There is reason why my late esteemed friend, Frank Cockrem, Secretary of the Open-Air Mission, told me, first, that he had serious difficulty to find the type of gospeller he needed for their faithful work, and secondly, that he scarce knew where to turn for them save to the Open Brethren. There is reason why in sundry places where the denominations cannot longer man village pulpits, the Open Brethren can take them on: they have still a supply of rising preachers, because the Spirit has still some freedom to stir the hearts of younger brethren in the gatherings and in the gospel. It may be that the speaking is sometimes not all it might be as to outward style, and it were well that this be improved; but at least the way of salvation is made clear and plain. And this helpful state will continue just as long as the Spirit of truth is honoured in the assemblies, and no longer. How therefore can one but deplore the tendency to resort to human arrangements for ministry, and protest and warn against it?

It is matter of common knowledge that one well-known teacher among Open Brethren very rarely attends conferences where the ministry is left to the leading of the Spirit. Nor is he the only one thus minded. Again, at certain large annual summer gatherings there was for years a chairman to lead each meeting, and at the outset it was announced by him that the conveners had invited certain brethren to speak, and, while these would be left free among themselves as to the ministry, no one else would be permitted to speak. Occasional attempts by others were promptly suppressed. Thus did the conveners notify the Spirit of God what persons He might or might not use to edify the gatherings. Apostasy is the taking up of a different position to that formerly held. Is, then, such conduct, personal or collective, less than apostasy from what is admitted to be the Scriptural principle and practice? and is it not, therefore, in this matter, apostasy from the Scripture itself?

It is not the preaching of the gospel that is here in view, whether in a hall used by an assembly or elsewhere. The New Testament does not contemplate the church as the sphere of the evangelist, but the world. Nor is it the church corporate that is viewed as spreading the gospel, but every individual Christian. The preacher, therefore, acts as an individual, and is personally responsible and personally free as to the methods he uses: only they should be wholly worthy of (1) the majesty of his Master, (2) the dignity of his subject, and (3) the awful solemnity of the eternal issues.

It is of gatherings of believers that we have written above. Here the Spirit claims in the Word the sole right of leadership. And He alone is competent. The depriving Him of His full rights as leader of worship and ministry is irreverence on the part of those who profess to have acknowledged those rights. It is already causing diminished unction upon gatherings, much more than did the unprofitable ministry it was adopted to prevent, and is inevitably decreasing the supply of Spirit-stirred ministry. And it tends to increase. In a certain magazine for December, 1935, of thirty-one "forthcoming conferences" twenty-seven announced the speakers arranged.

The advance of this evil can be at least retarded if hearers and speakers who revere the Spirit, and value His methods, cease to attend such gatherings, and support those only where He is fully honoured.

It is a sheer necessity to the powers of darkness that the witnessing energy of the church be crippled: for this it is obviously necessary that the working of the Spirit of power in the church be restrained; and one most effective means to this is that He be hindered in His working in the hearts of disciples in the gatherings of saints, they being induced, by one false plea or another, themselves to filch from

Him those rights of which the spirits of error fain would rob Him.

Here surely is a principal reason why churches of believers in all lands so often remain infantile, immature, ineffective, dependent upon some foreigner who, willingly or unwillingly, knowingly or unknowingly, is essentially a cleric, their priest, upon whom public spiritual functions devolve, and without whom, or a similar successor, the testimony quickly dies. "The apostles did not trust their converts, but they trusted the Holy Spirit in their converts." Then why not trust Him wholly, in the leading of worship and the prompting of ministry, as in personal life? For

> They who trust Him wholly
> Find Him wholly true.

An honoured voice from outside of Brethren shall exhort to this. George Bowen of Bombay, writing upon the words "Let all things be done unto edifying" (1 Corinthians 14:26), said:

> On successive Sabbaths, having a definite object in view, we visit various churches. We sit down with the people of God of a certain denomination, hear the sermon that is preached, and observe the worship that is rendered to God. Again, we worship with those of another denomination. We notice many points of difference in their mode of celebrating divine worship and seeking their own edification; but at length we come to a worshipping body whose customs are so fundamentally different from those of the churches previously visited, that the differences among the latter appear to be quite trifling in comparison. In the church that we have now stumbled upon in an out-of-the-way place (in the Epistle to the Corinthians), instead of one man officiating for all, while all sit silent save when they sing or make common responses, and where everything is arranged to exclude as much as possible anything like spontaneousness, we find that when the members come together, "everyone hath a psalm, hath a doctrine [teaching], hath a tongue, hath a revelation, hath an interpretation." One, two, or three speak in an unknown tongue; and another interprets. Prophets speak two or three in succession. If anything is revealed to another that sitteth by, the first holds his tongue. May we not learn from this that the Holy Ghost loves a larger liberty than is accorded by our arrangements? We cleave to them as though they had been imposed by the solemn and unalterable decree of the Great Head of the church: and a proposition to depart from them is

regarded almost as treason against Christ. It is singular, however, that the apostolic church should be completely defunct to us, as regards the force of its example in these matters. There were some great abuses in those early churches; think you they were the greatest conceivable abuses? Is it not possible that the apostle Paul coming into one of our staid and orderly churches would look upon the whole of the decorous and tasteful service as one unmitigated abuse? He would perhaps say, Is the Holy Ghost dead, that you make no provision for his manifestation? Is there no communion of the saints in the assemblies of the saints? (*Daily Meditations*, October 8th).

Bowen wrote thus in Bombay not long after Groves' years in India. Is he another who drank at his fountain? In any case, are not his words true and his questions vital?

And there is another important matter. Each Spirit-taught searcher can discover for himself that the New Testament suggests no other type of Christian gathering. In this respect there is no distinction between a meeting to break the bread and other meetings. The Lord is equally present when two or three meet to pray or to build up each other, and it is *His presence* gives character to the gathering and should regulate it in all particulars. Whenever believers assembled, few or many, the Spirit of God ordered the proceedings, prompting teaching, prophesying, worship, or testimony to the unsaved. No such thing was known as appointing preachers or teachers for particular occasions; nor is it in the least necessary, if only believers come together in dependence of heart upon the Head of the church for gospel testimony as for food for the sheep. I know many assemblies in different countries where no arrangements are made, because the Lord is trusted and honoured, and where the blessed work of the Spirit in converting sinners goes on in power. And this enables the work to continue in periods of persecution, or in regions where travel is uncertain, and no arrangements are possible. It conduces to exercise of heart Christ-ward in all who are present, and hinders that supineness of soul which results from need of exercise of heart being done away by the knowledge that another has been appointed to give the ministry, and that therefore the rest assembled may merely settle down to listen, or to go to sleep in the inner man, and perhaps outwardly.

In answer to the question whether the prompting of ministry by the Spirit admits of prior preparation by the speaker, and the assertion that such preparation dishonours the Spirit, Groves wrote:

> I tell them it is of the same class of errors as those which characterize Popery, see 1 Timothy 4:3; being an attempt to set up a higher standard of holiness than God's, and must end, like theirs, in deeper sin. We as little deny the truth of God's promise, that our bread and water shall be sure, by going to our daily work to earn it, as we do that of the Spirit's help, by studying God's word in dependence on His guidance in order to minister to others. We have no more reason to expect the bread of life to be miraculously supplied to us for feeding others, than we have the natural bread; natural understanding is given us to obtain the one, and spiritual understanding to attain the other; thus Paul's exhortation to Timothy, that in order that his profiting should appear in all things, he should *give* himself to reading, to exhortation, to doctrine [teaching], he should meditate upon those things, and give himself wholly to them (423).

This is just, but it is not the whole matter. In the early churches there were two orders of ministers of the word, prophets and teachers (1 Corinthians 12:29; Ephesians 4:11; Acts 13:1), just as there had been in Israel of old. For the priests were the divinely authorized teachers of the law (Deuteronomy 17:8–13; Malachi 2:7), and were to search into its meaning, to read it publicly to the people (Deuteronomy 31:9–13), explain it to them, and apply it to their practice. This we see Ezra and others doing (Nehemiah 8). Thus also there were "teachers" in the apostolic church, and these were to read the Scriptures publicly and to explain and enforce them: "give heed to reading, to exhortation, to teaching," was a charge laid upon Timothy. There is real need for a revival of this salutary practice of public reading of the Word of God, that is, of considerable portions of it. And so John gave an exhortation and promise concerning his Revelation: "Blessed is he [singular] that readeth [that is, publicly], and they that hear the words of the prophecy, etc." (Revelation 1:3). Yet who endeavours to secure this specific blessing?

Thus in the gatherings of Christians there should be opportunity for those gifted as teachers to exercise their gift; yet not by appointment or pre-arrangement, but ever by the leading of the Spirit.

But the prophet received his message by immediate impulse by the Spirit on the occasion, and for this ministry also there is to be room. Yet it is clear that prophets made themselves well acquainted with the written oracles, even as Zechariah, one of the last of Old Testament times, for example, refers to the messages of all the former prophets (Zechariah 7:7). Prophesying is not a standing up and saying whatever comes into the mind, however odd or extravagant it may be, but requires a holy waiting for the Spirit to impel. And teaching is not the giving forth of a well-prepared exposition, save as the Spirit of God burdens the heart with that theme for that occasion. Happy is the church that has both gifts, and grants freedom, *and gives time enough,* to both.

When it is urged that, while Brethren said that the Spirit of God

...."more or less determined the form of each exercise, whether it were worship, supplication, exposition, or exhortation," but "To what precise extent, however, the ultimate form proceeded from His guidance was left indefinite" (*Neatby* 205).

the answer is that so it is left in Scripture. There is no definition upon this point, but rather an admission that the frailty of the human agent may mingle in the expression of the divine impulse. Hence while prophets spoke, others sitting by were to "discriminate" (1 Corinthians 14:29). But this element of weakness in the human instrument did not alter the *fact* of the activity of the Spirit of God as leader and energizer of the worship and ministry, nor does it justify a complete or partial frustration of His rights in this sphere. That there were utterances verbally inspired, and therefore inerrant, is distinctly asserted (1 Corinthians 2:13; etc.); but even he who makes this claim says to his readers, "judge ye what I say" (1 Corinthians 10:15).

8

The Church of God (3):
Its Government and Discipline

God hath set in the church ... governments. 1 Corinthians 12:28.

Paul ... to all the saints ... at Philippi ... with the overseers and deacons. Philippians 1:1.

The elders I exhort who am a fellow-elder ... tend the flock of God ... exercising the oversight. 1 Peter 5:1-2.

If each man lived a solitary life each would be a law unto himself and could sing:

> I am monarch of all I survey,
> My right there is none to dispute.

But community life brings divergence of views and conflict of interests and creates the need of rulers. Even in heaven there are leaders, archangels as well as angels. And among men God has endowed some by nature with the gift of ruling, and the gift presupposes its exercise, for the good of the community. Hence in the world "the actually existing (*ousai*) authorities have been appointed by God" (Romans 13:1). The same need is found in the spiritual communities, the churches of God; the spiritual endowment for governing spiritually is still granted, and its presence supposes its exercise, for the good of the several churches in which it is given.

This unavoidable problem soon arose in the early communities of Brethren in Dublin and England, especially as the first in England, that at Plymouth, presently became very large. In the earliest days Groves did not contribute to this question because he left for Bagdad in June, 1829, before it had arisen; but ere long his views became decided and were expressed distinctly and emphatically.

171

The New Testament offers no suggestion or instance of the appointment of elders (who were the same class of men as presbyters or bishops, the three terms were equivalent) by any of the eleven apostles, of whom Peter was one. Peter describes himself as simply a "fellow-elder" with brethren who were not apostles. When Paul appointed elders (Acts 14:23) Barnabas acted with him, and Barnabas, though termed an apostle (verse 14) was not one in the sense of the eleven and Paul, as having received an express commission thereto from the Lord himself. The figment of apostolic succession has no basis in the New Testament. It was, therefore, simply as evangelists founding churches that Paul and Barnabas acted.

Elders were not recognized until they had proved, by their life and by service rendered voluntarily, that the Lord had endowed and called them (1 Timothy 3:1–7; Titus 1:5–9). Hence churches after their founding remained of necessity without elders for so long a time as proved needful in different places to discern which men the Lord fitted for oversight. Titus was charged by Paul to act in this matter in Crete; but in other cases, as Corinth and Thessalonica, it was simply left to the saints themselves to discern, and to own by obedience, the hand of the Lord in giving them rulers (1 Corinthians 16:15-16; 1 Thessalonians 5:12-13); and the brethren in question were exhorted to serve in this holy capacity without any question of formal appointment being raised (1 Thessalonians 5:14; 1 Peter 5:1–4). In other instances, as Jerusalem (Acts 15:2, 4, 6, 22) and Philippi (Philippians 1:1), no hint is given as to how in these churches the elders entered upon their position. The same is true as to the elders at Ephesus (Acts 20:17); yet who were the elders was known, for Paul could send for them and declare that the *Holy Spirit* had made them overseers in that flock (verse 28.) This was all that they required of authority.

1. The facts so briefly indicated show firstly, that a church may exist, for a shorter or longer period, without formal rulers, from which it follows that their presence is not of the essence of the church of God.

2. They show, secondly, that the manner of recognition of elders, when given by the Head of the church, was variable, so that

this also is not of the essence of the matter, nor was an apostle or apostolic delegate indispensable.

3. But they show thirdly, that apostolic churches possessed elders as gifts from the Lord, and that it was expected that such would be given and recognized and obeyed in each and every church.

These facts are here mentioned that the reader may bear them in mind, and be thereby helped in considering the development of the matter in the early assemblies of the Brethren and Groves' statements upon the divergencies of opinion and practice that arose.

As to paragraph (1) above, that the matter of government is not primary or of the essence of church fellowship, Groves wrote in 1848:

> There is only one way of union, that of brethren and sisters with their Lord and Father, holding communion together by the one Spirit. These grand principles being admitted, all other things, such as forms of church order, are, I believe, quite subordinate; and whilst not obligatory on any, open to all to be accepted or modified; so that this relationship of the body with one another and their common head and Father be not denied: nor the power of the Spirit hindered. I greatly approve and value a fixed ministry; but will ever protest against an *exclusive one*, and especially that hypocritical *freedom*, which in *words* grants *liberty*, but in *fact* denies it (455).

All such questions therefore, were approached by Groves as being secondary in importance, and such as should not be allowed to disturb the unity of the family or the harmony of the body. But maintaining this, he yet knew their importance and had positive views upon them. In an autocar the engine is primary and wheels are essential; but the subordinate accessories to engine and wheels have much to do with smooth running; and smooth running is greatly to be desired in a church, and godly rule and spiritual ministry have very much to do with this.

Groves' last quoted words as to *fixed* and *exclusive* ministry read very like an intentional reference to what a well-known leader, Mr. G. V. Wigram, had written four years earlier, in 1844 (according to Dr. S. P. Tregelles):

> E.—Do you admit "*a regular ministry?*"

W.—If by a regular ministry you mean a stated ministry (that is, that in every assembly those who are gifted by God to speak to edification will be both limited in number and known to the rest), I do admit it; but if by a regular ministry you mean an exclusive ministry, I dissent. By an *exclusive* ministry I mean the recognizing certain persons as so exclusively holding the place of teachers, as that the use of a real gift by any one else would be irregular. As, for instance, in the Church of England and in most dissenting Chapels, a sermon would be felt to be *irregular* which had been made up by two or three persons really gifted by the Holy Ghost (*Three Letters*, 13, Tregelles).

Dr. Tregelles affirmed from personal knowledge that this principle of ministry obtained at first in Plymouth, Exeter, Bath, and London and other places. By the clear agreement upon this matter of Groves and Wigram (men on some important matters widely opposed), Tregelles' account is confirmed, and it may be accepted that this was the general practice in those first years. There was then no such notion as that every brother had equal right to minister the Word, whether qualified by the Spirit or not. But, on the other hand, it was strenuously maintained that liberty must be given in the gatherings for the Spirit to move whom He would, for how otherwise could it be known what persons He had gifted and called to minister, or how should a continual succession of able ministers of the truth be maintained? These questions remain of the deepest importance for the well-being of the church of God.

But if this liberty be granted how shall abuse of it be restrained? How shall the mouths of vain talkers and deceivers be "muzzled" (*epistomizo*)? (Titus 1:10,11).

In churches or assemblies ordered on worldly principles the plan is to appoint certain preachers or conference speakers, presumed to be profitable talkers, and thus exclude others. This takes the control of ministry of the Word out of the power of the Holy Spirit, and the ultimate spiritual results are what may be expected: a diminution of unction; a drying up of the supply of God-moved ministry; an ever-increasing dependence upon a few speakers, with a corresponding restricting of the range of subjects opened and consequent narrowing of outlook in the general body of the saints; a want of perpetual progress in the understanding of the divine oracles and therefore of the purposes of God. The tendency is for these privileged speakers to obtain a dominating influence in their circle of churches, their views become the virtual creed and practice of their hearers, and inevitably a real sectarian outlook and spirit will and must prevail. It is deeply to be regretted that this method of excluding tedious or undesired ministry has set in so decidedly among some who profess to hold that the guidance of the Spirit in gatherings of Christians is the Divine plan.

But even where this worldly method is followed it has been still found needful to have a higher controlling power. In episcopal spheres, as the Church of England, the diocesan bishop has a duty to deal with unsuitable clergy. In non-episcopal Churches it is a Conference, Synod, or Presbytery that acts. At conferences with arranged speakers the committee selecting these stands in the shadows behind, and usually a chairman is chosen to control the public proceedings. But all such arrangements still include the defect, not to say unbelief and irreverence, of taking away the rights of the Holy Spirit and entrusting them to His servants. Here again He, in His love and pity, goes on blessing to the sheep of Christ, for whose welfare He is on earth, the truth that may be taught; but He cannot avoid the consequences mentioned above of this distrust of Himself and usurpation of His rights.

In the apostolic days the Spirit's liberty was preserved, and no restriction upon ministry in *advance* was practised. Not until men had proved themselves to be habitually vain talkers did the duty or right to stop their mouths arise. The excluding of teaching because certain prominent persons might not like it was thus avoided, and this abuse of power, far more disastrous than vain talking, could not enter. Where leading brethren can get control of the ministry, by gaining the task of inviting speakers, they can, and sometimes they do, quietly exclude any branches of truth unpalatable to themselves, and the sheep are robbed of perhaps the very food or medicine they may need and which the Chief Shepherd would provide were He permitted real control by His Spirit.

Even when men went down from Jerusalem to Antioch and taught the fundamentally false doctrine that salvation depends upon law and ceremonies, there was no immediate or arbitrary prohibition upon them speaking, nor summary exclusion of them from the church; but leaders in the local church earnestly repudiated the doctrine, which was thus openly debated before the assembly. This plan could not but have conduced to general enlightenment and edification (Acts 15). An appeal to the apostles at Jerusalem was then made by the church as a whole and settlement was reached. Ever since the death of the apostles the only way by which their mind upon a matter can be gained is by appeal to their writings, seeking therefrom the teaching of the Spirit of truth who inspired those writings.

Two facts are here found. (1) The local elders and teachers first dealt with those teaching the error; (2) They did this openly in the church, and thus the assembly as a whole had to consider and deal with the matter. There was no power given to Titus as an individual to control or prohibit deceivers or vain talkers: the instruction as to this follows immediately upon the statement that elders must be able to exhort in the healthful teaching and to convict the gainsayers; and one reason why elders must be able to do this is *"for* there are many unruly men, vain talkers and deceivers, specially they of the circumcision, whose mouths must be stopped" (Titus 1:9–11).

It should be further observed how great and glaring and dangerous the abuse was before this power of "muzzling" could be used. The speaker must be "unruly," a man who would not submit to godly rule in the church; also, not merely a "vain talker" but also a "deceiver"; for here are not two classes mentioned, but the three adjectives all apply to the one class of person. An example is given, showing that Paul meant especially those Judaizers who dogged evangelical ministry to undo its blessed effects, and others like to these. The men in view work privately to the subverting of Christian households, and they have an eye to financial profit, "base gain."

It is evident that a young brother, just beginning to seek to help in ministry, however feeble his early attempts may seem in comparison with the weighty expositions of seniors, is not here in view. Let him be encouraged and guided, rather than for bidden. Nor can even the wearisome ramblings of a senior in years be bracketed with those described. These may need to be restrained, but should not be treated with the severity required by the others. Is there no general profit by the exercise of long-suffering by an assembly or a conference? When R. C. Chapman was asked how they were getting on at Barnstaple with a brother who had been a trouble elsewhere, the gracious answer was: He is a valuable brother, a very valuable brother: we did not know our need of patience till he came among us! The first of the great and lamentable divisions that have enfeebled Exclusive Brethren was precipitated (in 1860) by unspiritual discipline against a brother because his ministry was not appreciated.

Yet when restraint must be put upon profitless ministry it is the elders of the church who are responsible to act, and the church as a body is to approve. "Let the prophets speak by two or three, and let the others [assembled] discriminate" (1 Corinthians 14:29).

Considering that the general rule of the church, including the necessary and delicate duty discussed, devolves upon its elders, the subject of eldership, though, as Groves said, subordinate, is of very real importance. The very earliest conditions among Brethren are therefore of interest.

1. As to that first gathering in Dublin in 1829, J. G. Bellett wrote (in a MS. narrative of those early days);

> …the settled order of worship which we had in Fitzwilliam Square gave place gradually. Teaching and exhorting were first made common duties and services, while prayer was restricted under the care of two or three, who were regarded as elders. But gradually all this yielded. In a little time, no appointed or recognized eldership was understood to be in the midst of us, and all service was of a free character, the presence of God through the Spirit being more simply believed and used."

Thus a most blessed fact, the presence of the Spirit, was used both rightly and wrongly: rightly in that worship and ministry were left to His leading, as His Word directs; wrongly in that the proper rule of the assembly by elders, which also His Word directs, was suffered to lapse. The mistake thus innocently made has worked incalculable harm to Brethren assemblies ever since, by allowing, on the one hand, autocratic dictatorship where strong individuals have been present, and democratic disorder elsewhere.

2. But in some other early centres more Scriptural ways obtained. In the first meeting in England, at Plymouth, there was a recognized eldership. Dr. Tregelles' testimony is decisive as to this. He wrote:

> At Plymouth Mr. J. N. Darby requested Mr. Newton to sit where he could conveniently take the oversight of ministry, and that he would hinder that which was manifestly unprofitable and unedifying. Mr. J. N. Darby addressed Mr. Newton by letter, as an *Elder:* I have seen a transcript of such a document made (apparently for circulation here) in the handwriting of Mr. G. V. Wigram; it was written by Mr. J. N. Darby, from Dublin, and it is addressed to *B. Newton, Esq., Elder of the Saints Meeting in Raleigh Street, Plymouth...*" Liberty of ministry was recognized amongst those who possessed any ability from God; but it was considered that ministry which was not to profit—which did not commend itself to the consciences of others—ought to be repressed.
>
> And this was the sense in which the phrase "liberty of ministry" was used... On one occasion Mr. Newton had in the assembly to stop ministry which was manifestly improper, with Mr. J. N. Darby's and Mr. G. V. Wigram's presence and *full concurrence:* a plain proof that they *then* fully objected to unrestrained ministry ... there was restraint, not upon edifying teaching, but upon that which was unedifying; advice and exhortation in *private* were generally resorted to, but *when needful* the case was met in a more public manner... I have had pretty much acquaintance with several localities, and I may specify Exeter and London as places in which it was believed to be right to judge whether ministry was to edification, and to put a stop to that which was considered to be not so. In London this was done *repeatedly*—far oftener, to my knowledge, than ever in Plymouth (*Three Letters* 6, 7, 8, 9).

This makes evident (*a*) that even in those first days, marked by so great grace and power, the difficulty of unsuitable ministry was met; and (*b*) that in that time it was dealt with on the Scriptural principles above stated. The primary liberty of ministry was preserved; action was not taken in advance by notification that this or that subject must not be expounded, as is sometimes improperly done; the offence was dealt with only if and when it was committed; it was dealt with by the elders of the meeting; the general conscience was regarded as to whether ministry was or was not to profit. But this involved that elders were known and recognized in the assemblies of those days.

3. The Church at Bethesda, Bristol, arose independently of the Dublin leaders, except as far as A. N. Groves had influenced personally both Henry Craik and George Müller before they worked in Bristol. It commenced on August 13th, 1832, according to George Müller's statement under that date in his *Narrative,* page 98:

"This evening one brother and four sisters united with brother Craik and me in church-fellowship at Bethesda, *without any rules, desiring only to act as the Lord shall be pleased to give us light through His Word.*"

Both Müller and Craik were early and firmly persuaded that recognized rulers in a church are necessary and Scriptural. To quote what I wrote formerly:

> …they (Müller and Craik) were as necessarily the first rulers of that church as any apostolic evangelists were of churches they founded. But as the fellowship multiplied, and they saw the Spirit qualifying other brethren for oversight, and moving them to addict themselves thereto of their own will (1 Corinthians 16:15; 1 Timothy 3:1), they invited such formally to join them in the eldership, and then announced to the assembly the names of those thus invited, which followed the example of Paul's exhortation regarding Stephanus. Thus there was no *selection of* rulers by the ruled—a principle contrary to the divine order, according to God's mind, since all authority is by delegation from God, the sole Fount of authority, not by conferment from below, from the subjects; but there was *recognition* by the church, with opportunity for stating any valid objection to a brother entering that responsible position. This method has continued, with real advantage to that assembly.
>
> There never was any Scriptural reason why this plan should not have been followed in all other cases when brethren were used of God to commence churches. Following the precedent in Acts 6:3, the church at Bethesda has always itself selected deacons to attend to business matters (*The Local Assembly*, 48).

The views of Mr. Müller and Mr. Craik are set forth in detail by the former in his *Narrative*, pages 279–282. Those who can peruse Henry Craik's valuable, but now rare, *New Testament Church Order,* will be profited. In both, the principles and practice above advocated are advanced. Nor have there ever been wholly lacking other assemblies of Brethren who have followed the earliest practice as above outlined. But before long the view was urged, and became generally dominant, that elders cannot now be formally acknowledged. Two reasons were set forth.

First, that there are now neither apostles nor their delegates, as Titus or Timothy, with authority to appoint such. This may be seen argued in Wm. Kelly's generally helpful book *Six Lectures on the Church of God,* 193 *et seq.*

But the answer to this has been shown above. (*a*) It was not as apostles, but as evangelists founding churches, that Paul and Barnabas acted. (*b*) That elders were raised up by the Holy Spirit, and then acknowledged and obeyed by the churches, without formal appointment, which method is permanently available. Is the Spirit of God in the churches limited and incapable because Paul and Titus are not here? And was it unavoidable that all churches since that first generation must be without this advantage of godly rulers, which was needful for those first churches? Both Scripture and history are against the notion. (*c*) The theory also sets aside apostolic practice as not being for permanent guidance, and thus nullifies those parts of the New Testament in question.

This last point should be carefully noted as a warning. When in those early days in Dublin the eldership at first acknowledged was allowed to lapse, the brethren in question tacitly surrendered their primary and fundamental principle that the Word of God was their only guide and that all that it taught as to the church of God was to be practised. They suffered, in fact, the reasonings of the human mind to lead, at the expense of the guidance of Holy Scripture, and certain portions of the New Testament became for them inoperative. Yet Darby had rightly said to F. W. Newman: "every word [of the New Testament], depend upon it, is from the Spirit, and is for eternal service" (*Neatby,* 47). That this surrender of principle made thus early was made unconsciously will not be doubted; but at this fine-edged junction the train had already left its proper track.

The second ground for not recognizing eldership in the churches was a theory that the church of God is in ruins, and that it is not the way of God ever to restore to its former glory that which has been ruined, but that He gives grace to a Nehemiah how to live and act amidst the ruin and rubbish. This was Mr. Darby's special contribution to ecclesiastical thought. His reasonings may be found in volume 1 of the *Collected Writings.*

In my pamphlet *The Local Assembly* (44) I wrote as follows:

> But *what* is in ruins? The invisible church, composed of all Spirit-baptized persons, is indefectible, it cannot be ruined; against *it* "the gates of Hades shall not prevail." The local assembly may indeed be sadly ruined; but *it* can be restored, as, by the grace of God, has been seen times without number—at Corinth, for example. The only other institution in the question is that agglomeration of sects which is called Christendom. But *that* is unrecognized by the New Testament, is not of God at all, and that *it* is in ruins is no matter for regret. Hence this specious phrase "a day of ruin" does but cover a very misleading fallacy. It was the undefined notion of something universally visible that allowed of the theory that that something was irreparably ruined as to external form. The only visible body known to the New Testament, the local church, *can* be maintained by the grace of the Holy Spirit.

And to this may be added that the argument drawn from the period of the second temple is set aside by the glorious promise made by God when no more than a foundation for that temple had been laid, and when the old men, who remembered Solomon's temple, were dismayed at the insignificance of the proposed restoration; for then God declared, "The latter glory of this house shall be greater than the former, saith Jehovah of hosts" (Haggai 2:3,9). The tabernacle of David is to be restored and its ruins built again (Acts 15:16); why then should not the spiritual house of God be maintained?

As early as 1828 A. N. Groves was writing consistently with that primary principle mentioned.

> As for order, he wrote, if it be God's order, let it stand; but if it be man's order, I must examine whether or not it excludes the essence of Christ's kingdom; for if it does, I remember that word, "Call no man master upon earth; for one is your Master, even Christ, and all ye are brethren."

And this is followed characteristically by emphasis upon the spiritual as compared with the external:

> Be assured, however, for the mystical body of Christ my prayer is, that I may very gladly spend and be spent, even though the more abundantly I love the less I be loved (49).

If this gracious spirit alone had prevailed in the many brethren then beginning to walk in love and according to the Word, when they came in the succeeding years to discuss questions of church order and discipline, the history of the movement then commencing would have been vastly brighter and happier. It will be only as far as we have personally drunk of this spirit, and are pervaded by it, that we shall read with understanding and profit what Groves further wrote upon these subjects.

During the years that the spirit of strife was germinating and budding amongst some in England Groves was in India and not directly involved. But in 1838:

> ...in allusion to a letter from Christians at home, the *Memoir* tells us, who professed they were "seeking for more zeal and practical union," while the course they took gave rise to many divisions, he says:—"They want to understand more of poor Job's feelings (chap. 19:28) when he advised his friends to let him alone, seeing the 'root of the matter' was in him; also the meaning of Romans 15:1–7"; and in allusion to the brethren generally, he says:—"The Lord will own their Scriptural ministry; but if they have not suitable elders to rule, such as Timothy is instructed to select, let them, in earnest, cry to the Lord, that He would do that thing for them. Real subjection to God's will and Word, where there is neither rank, talent, nor any external distinction to uphold the principle of rule, is a grace rarely, very rarely, found. To those who have learnt to answer to all these remarks, 'we are now in the apostasy, and must submit to these disorders,' I answer, the apostasy has nothing to do with our duty in maintaining and exhibiting every ray of light that the Holy Ghost gives, just as to the Jews, even to the fourth verse of the last chapter of Malachi, it is said, 'Remember ye the law of Moses which I commanded unto him in Horeb for all Israel, with the statutes and judgments.' And if this be *really* the Laodicean period of the new dispensation, as I believe it is, I think if the Lord were to speak by another Malachi, before 'the great and terrible day of the Lord,' He would say to us who have 'ears to hear,' not only return in *ministry*, but return in *rule*, and give ear to EVERY WORD that having proceeded out of the mouth of God, stands recorded as *His*" (384, 385).

And then in words before quoted, but which will bear repeating, he puts his finger upon the point above stated, that the surrender of eldership in the assemblies was a surrender of the principle of following Scripture to follow human reasoning, and says:

> Dear Caldecott well says, that the struggle now is between the Word and tradition. It ever has been, it ever was among the Jews, and is among the Gentiles. We take our stand on the Word; and in proportion to our practical inconsistency with it will our testimony be weakened; because people all see when we are *partial* in the law, magnifying the importance of that part of truth by which we are distinguished, and passing by that which is expressed with equal clearness [as the place of rule and eldership, for example], thought not adopted into our system. You will forgive these remarks: indeed I do honour and love these brethren; yet I am jealous over them with a godly jealousy; and as I bear their reproach by sending many friends from India to receive from them the good they may so abundantly get, yet I would say to them, especially in connection with sectarian tendencies, "Remember from whence thou art fallen, and repent, and do the first works." Remember, I only use the word confusion above, as expressive of any order that is *not God's* in spiritual things. Much that may *appear* order in the flesh, supplants the order of the Spirit, whether in rule or in ministry. The Spirit's order is connected ever with His *own gifts,* and these are the credentials to which those led by the Spirit look, and by which they are *guided* (385, 386).

Those who are acquainted with the dismal controversies that shortly raged among Brethren, or even if the earlier discussions in this chapter have alone been grasped, will appreciate the bearing of these remarks, and will note the conviction already formed in the mind of the writer that his loved friends in England had already "fallen" in their testimony, and needed to repent and to return. He saw that in the matter of rule in the house of God they had ceased to walk by the Word, where he and they had at first taken their strong and united stand, and where for himself he was determined still to stand.

History is ever repeating itself. At the Diet of Worms Luther took his stand on the Word—Convince me of error from Scripture and I at once abjure; otherwise I cannot, so help me God! But when the forming and ordering of Christian churches became the practical question the strong man forsook his strong position, became weak, and vastly injured the cause he had truly at heart by agreeing to a course not sanctioned by the Word, the forming of State-controlled church systems.

In the second year after the first division had been consummated, at Plymouth in 1845, Groves wrote:

> I have been thinking much on that striking passage, Romans 12:1, "I beseech you by the mercies of God," etc., and I do pray that my soul may look for its judgment only from the Lord. Where is the love that "thinketh no evil," that "suffereth long and is kind?" It is surely the concision, not the circumcision, that is now at work. May the Lord give you grace to take no part in those unhallowed strifes, but to let your testimony be for Jesus, and the Spirit of Christ, as that which manifests our connexion with Him, not occupying yourself in those comparatively unimportant questions about the external orderings of the assemblies of God's people. [An allegation that clerisy was being established in the assembly at Plymouth was part of the ground of division there at that time.] It is much my desire, if the Lord clears away difficulties, to give up the rest of my short space to an uninterrupted ministry, somewhere, or in some form; but if I were in England, I should, as far as I now see, give any little strength I had to our friends in Bristol or Barnstaple, but especially the former. [This is to be noted, as revealing in which districts he felt the principles dear to his heart were being best maintained.] I have no question but that those whom God has called to minister should wait on their ministry, and give themselves *wholly to it,* if their profiting is to appear in all things. I have also no doubt that this is the way appointed of the Lord for waiting on the Spirit, and in which waiting they are to expect to be taught to choose for the flock the proper pasture, and how to divide it. I cannot discern the slightest difference in the word between what is necessary to help the brethren in one form of ministry in the evening, or at the breaking of bread, although I quite feel that it would be desirable that those brethren who speak to the Church's edification should have opportunity to speak. [This sweeping away of subtle and false distinctions, now widely held, between the meeting for breaking of bread and other gatherings is pregnant and of profound importance. The apostolic churches knew no such distinctions. *Every* gathering was to be led directly by the Spirit, with liberty *for Him* to use those who could speak to edification.] But of this I think I can now feel practically

convinced (as I ever have in theory) that recognized pastors and teachers are *essential* to the good order of all assemblies; and as such required and commanded of God; and though I should not object to unite with those who had them not, if it were the result of the Lord's providence in not giving them any, I should feel quite unable to join *personally* those who rejected them as unnecessary or unscriptural. If the question were put to me (as it often has been) do you consider the Spirit unequal to the task of keeping order in the way we desire to follow? [that is, without recognized rulers and leaders] my reply is simply this, show me that the Lord has promised His Spirit to *this end,* and I at once admit its obligation in the face of all practical or experienced difficulties: but if I see pastorship, eldership, and ministry recognized as a settled fixed service in the Church to this end, I cannot reject God's evidently ordained plan, and set up one of my own, because I think it more spiritual.

And then in reference to Mr. Darby's reasonings above outlined, he continued:

D_____ seems [to feel himself] justified in rejecting all such helps as the way of obtaining proper subordination in the assembly of God's saints, by saying the "Church is in ruins"; this is his *theory;* but neither in the *word,* nor in my own experience or judgment, do I realize that this state of the Church, even though it existed to the full extent he declares, was to be met by the overthrow of God's order, and the substitution of one so exceedingly spiritual (if I may so use the term), as it seemed not good to the Holy Spirit to institute, when all things were comparatively in order (420–422).

Thus against all human theories, however well and earnestly urged, Groves adhered to his primary rule to appeal steadily and only to the Word of God, in the spirit of a former exclamation:

Oh, my brother, let us not put the experience of 1,500 years against the word of God (224).

And upon the important matter of the capacity of believers to judge as to what the prophets might be saying (1 Corinthians 14:29; and 1 John 4:1: "Beloved, believe not every spirit, but prove the spirits, whether they are of God: because many false prophets are gone out into the world"), and of the propriety of speakers submitting to the expressed judgment of a church as to their ministry, he wrote:

It is before the Church at large that the minister of God stands to be judged; and there is no feature more truly characteristic of the early steps of decline into Popery, in the second and third centuries, than removing the Church from the exercise of this their bounden duty. The flock of Christ in whom the Spirit dwells, is as competent now to know whom the Holy Spirit has qualified to be a minister of the word as in the days of the apostles, both by comparing the word ministered with the word written, and by the edification they experience in their own souls: nay, if they are spiritual, they are *bound* to recognize such; yea, their recognition is essential, not to the ministry of the word at all, for that every member holds from the Spirit only, but to any individual's *exercise* of it in any congregation of saints. I feel that a stated recognized ministry is essential to Church propriety and spiritual order (441).

Is it not clear that along these lines, and on them only, there can be found a scriptural and spiritual solution of the problems of unprofitable ministry and disorders in the house of God? But the solution involves (1) that each church shall seek elders from the Head of the church, with, of course, the humble purpose to love, honour, and obey them when given. (2) That the ministry of the word shall be left in *reality* to the control of the Spirit of God. (3) That the elders shall feel their responsibility to the Lord and His people to restrain ministry they and the saints as a body deem unedifying, subject to the guidance of the Word of God in this regard. (4) That every type of gathering of children of God that does not conform to these conditions be considered nonscriptural and be given up, and thus such gatherings only be held as can have the advantage of the leading and authority of the Lord. The presence of some unconverted persons in a gathering of Christians is no warrant for varying the order. Their presence is contemplated in 1 Corinthians 14:23, where the ordering of gatherings of saints is the very subject of the chapter; and it is ministry by several Spirit-led believers that is expected to act upon their conscience.

It is when we go outside of His Word that we are cast on our own poor wisdom and feebleness, and must invent our own devices, or borrow those of the world, to deal with the problems created, and for meeting which naturally there is no guidance in Scripture nor resource in Christ.

> Oh! my brother, let us not put the experience of 1500 years against the word of God; if we believe we shall have what we ask for. Let us remember, that a double-minded man is not to think he shall obtain anything of the Lord (224).

There is another matter connected with the working of the house of God that may be considered.

In 1848 two opposed principles of discipline were followed. By some it was urged that if there was evil teaching in a meeting all belonging to that meeting were defiled thereby, even though they might not know of the evil doctrine, or had even protested against it. Consequently no one coming from that meeting ought to be received to fellowship elsewhere. The whole meeting was interdicted, without discrimination of individuals.

On the other hand, others, notably George Müller, Henry Craik, and their fellow-elders at Bethesda Chapel, Bristol, declined this principle. They refused to sit in judgment upon a church as a whole, or to decide upon affairs in another assembly. They held that the right and duty of a Christian church is limited to dealing with those individuals who present themselves for its fellowship. Is such an individual personally sound in faith and godly in walk? then he is entitled to full Christian fellowship, and is not to be debarred only because in the circle or system where he usually associates there is this or that evil.

It is obvious that it is the latter practice that agrees with the first principle of Brethren, that every godly person, because he has a place in the family of God, is entitled to a place at the family table, and is not to be refused on account of connexion elsewhere with "Christian" systems and practices not of God.

It is equally certain that the church at Corinth was not interdicted though so gross evils, practical and doctrinal, were found in it.

Involved in this matter was the further question whether the churches of God are to be regarded, for disciplinary and adminis-trative purposes, as separate units, or as bound together, in a real, if undefined, federation. The first was accepted by the Bethesda church, and those churches which sided with them at that time, or which have since adopted the principle; the second by the opposite party. In the issue, the former churches have known no widespread divisions, for the reason that things that are not joined together cannot be sundered one from another; but the assemblies that held to the federation principle have known many universal divisions.

Against the implied presumption of a competency to sit in judgment upon a system, church, or person Groves' heart, because of its humility, ever protested. He wrote in 1838:

> I wish you to understand distinctly, that whilst for myself I feel every ray of light given me of God to be a talent I dare not hide, yet I entirely disallow the right *of judging* and rejecting *others*, seeing the Lord has said, "judge nothing before the time," the Lord is at hand, showing by whom, and at what time, judgment shall be administered: and again "who art thou that condemnest another man's servant? To his own master he standeth or falleth, yea, he shall be holden up, for God is able to make him stand." This clearly evinces to my mind God's abhorrence of our judging one another: whilst he as strongly tells us by the apostle to judge *ourselves*, that we may not be judged of the Lord. I see on every side, nothing but a tendency to reverse this order. Men unmercifully and unsparingly judge others, and neglect to judge themselves; they are keen-sighted as eagles to see motes in others' eyes, but perceive not the beams in their own (380).

Groves, of course, did not overlook the duty of the local church to deal with persons within itself, according to Matthew 18:17 and 1 Corinthians 5:12-13. He denied the right and competency to extend judgment beyond that sphere. Upon the matter of the rightness and advantage of each assembly standing distinct from other assemblies, as to outward ordering and discipline, the following, written in 1847, is clear and weighty:

> In THEORY nothing can be more simple and apparently true than that if you are all "baptized into one body," by *one Spirit*, you ought to speak the same thing and be of the same judgment; but in *fact*, nothing is more certain than that, notwithstanding the unity of the body and the unity of the baptism, this is *not*, and never has been the case: we must therefore,

in a multitude of cases, leave every man to be "fully persuaded in his own mind." In smaller matters, this will be easy; in graver, it will be better to form small separate households of faith in love, each preserving their conscience inviolate, than that either party should coerce others into their views and opinions. Uprightness of conscience is essential to all spiritual prosperity, but coercion into some judgment is not. Infinitely better is it for each household of faith to seek to walk in all things well-pleasing to the Lord, than to undertake the management and direction of other households.1 The unity of the national family is not destroyed by each household acting for itself, as long as all act for the welfare of the nation, and within its appointed laws; and even if these are transgressed, every individual cannot take the place of judge, but those to whom it is appointed by the king. If those who judge can show the king's commission for pronouncing sentence upon another man's servant, and calling him to the bar, well; they all *have* the right of passive judgment, namely by withdrawing from him, or from any household of faith, if they think he or it is walking against the will of their Lord, but here I consider their authority ends; and certainly for myself, I could not exercise more; nor should I feel called upon to submit to more, except from the household of faith to which I more immediately belonged; to them I would concede much, and from them be subject to much more. What I mean is this, if all the households of faith in England were to unite in bidding me cease teaching, I should consider their authority nothing, if my conscience stood clear in the matter; but if the household to which I felt myself called to minister were to desire me to cease, I should at once feel it right to do so, notwithstanding any clearness in my own conscience as to their being in error in their judgment. I think the mode of pressing unity adopted by some, is most absurd (441, 442).

Those who are intimately acquainted with the controversies and divisions among Brethren from 1845 onward will perceive what case, and the proceedings taken in it, prompted these remarks. The principles and methods here recommended would have avoided that most sorrowful and scandalous episode in the history of the church of God, and its baleful consequences. As one who has in writing advocated the same principles, having found them in the Word of

---

1. One has written of "the somewhat dreamy and enthusiastic turn of Groves' mind." Does not this paragraph now quoted show rather a very well balanced and practical mind? And it is only one of many evidences of this.

God, I cannot but be struck now to find such a statement of them. And as regards the vital church principles for which the Bethesda church then stood, and for which they suffered not a little, it will be interesting to read Groves' verdict. On his deathbed in Bristol, five years after the controversy, he said:

> I feel perfectly satisfied about the past; and as one in His presence, my heart *has full repose* in ALL the steps taken by the beloved brethren, and I *pray God* they may be *kept* in the *unity* of the *faith*, and *stand fast* in the *liberty* with which *God* has *made* them free; may they ever act as servants, not of man, but of God (509).

The disruption of Brethren began with the strife at Plymouth in 1845, when J. N. Darby attacked B. W. Newton on certain grounds, ecclesiastical and personal. It has been urged that in that very first dispute was revealed the complete lack in the Brethren church system of any means or tribunal for dealing with controversies. The fact rather is that the true and Scriptural means were forsaken and unscriptural measures followed. Mr. Newton should have been arraigned *only* before the Plymouth assembly of which he was a member. This Mr. Darby attempted, but the elders of the church refused to allow the church to be made the battleground. This being so Mr. Darby should have left the matter to the judgment and action of the Lord, seeing that the only competent earthly tribunal was closed to him. But neither his temperament nor his plans allowed this: he pressed the fight forward, and presently his opponent unwisely agreed to an unscriptural course, and a number of brethren from outside the assembly were invited to investigate the matter. This course not being of God led to no settlement, and a later more general gathering was held at Bath. This also, being without the sanction or blessing of the Lord, served only to spread the fire. The strife and estrangement would have remained limited and local had the Scriptural position been respected, that the local assembly is the only body corporate known to the New Testament, and the only human tribunal before which believers may arraign a believer.

The same false step was repeated among Open Brethren in London in 1924, when a brother wrongly charged with holding false doctrine was invited to attend before a company of thirteen brethren selected from outside his assembly, and unwisely did so. Neither he nor that assembly ever recovered from the hurtful effects of those proceedings. Indeed, the assembly soon ceased to exist. Any course which has not divine warrant can work only harm in the church of God.

One phrase above is worth special notice. Groves wrote: "It will be better to form *small* separate households of faith in love." Not a few of the special trials and dangers in the spiritual house of God are a result of assemblies growing too large. The first Christian Church, at Jerusalem, became very great, and soon the Head of the church broke it into a hundred fragments and scattered these abroad.

It is indeed good that church order and gospel service, as much as personal life, shall be conformed as closely as possible to Scripture. But even this will not attain its goal unless the inner spirit of Christians be of God. It is the lack of this that allows truly good men to work untold harm, thinking they do God service. Thus in 1847 Groves wrote:

> In the carriage going to the Fort, Bell was reading some of W.'s papers, the language of which we both consider disgraceful to the writer alone. It is easy to accuse others of being guided by Satan, but how difficult to see that he is urging on our *own spirits*. Whenever it is the Lord's pleasure that I should return, I do most fervently pray that my soul may be filled with Himself and not with those angry questions: what seems *really* wanted is that *true humiliation* of soul before God, which makes the beam in our own eyes visible, and the mote in the eye of another comparatively disregarded. "Who art thou that judgest another man's servant?" often recurs to me, when I read those exaggerated statements; and I often fear that if such a state of things continues, some signal mark of God's displeasure will rest upon it all. For myself I would join no Church permanently that had not some constituted rule. I have seen enough of that plan, of every one doing what is right in his own eyes, and then calling it the Spirit's order, to feel assured it is a delusion; and I consider it far more dishonouring to God than where no pretension is made beyond that of governing according to the best of the spiritual wisdom given us, guided by the Word and Spirit of God, which is always promised to us for asking (420).

In the same year, September 1847, he continued:

I do pray the Lord will keep you from entering into curious questions at home. I believe all those subjects which cause such contention are really as the small dust of the balance in comparison with the preservation of love and harmony in the body. May you be able to seek to establish all in grace; for God has given you a heart to feel the preciousness of His saving power and His forgiving love; and this is the class of truth that draws all hearts personally to Jesus and one another; be content to appear ignorant about many things which others think they know a great deal about, if you may but be permitted to exhibit *Jesus*, precious to *all—His* meekness, *His* tenderness, *His* forbearing pity in the midst of all our weakness and perverseness, dwell upon; and be assured God's Spirit will be with you: the exaltation of Jesus is the saint's proper work and true glory; and be always assured, the tree that is most loaded with God's fruit will bend its head most lowlily towards the ground. In spiritual things humility and faithfulness always accompany each other. May you be rich in the love of the Church of God, for their profit as well as your own peace: but know nothing of Paul or Apollos (439).

In the next year, 1848, he alludes to those who were making strife over different explanations of matters prophetic:

They have need to watch lest the theory of the rule of the Spirit turn into a state of things that dishonours the Spirit. I feel we want a more practical, searching ministry, leaving in a subordinate place dispensational teaching and the antecedent and succeeding circumstances of our Lord's return, especially if mixed with theories, that, as they are taught, may be true or false. What we want is spirituality of mind, subduedness of spirit, an ability to look on another's things rather than our own, and power to manifest our spiritual strength by our ability to bear with weakness in others, rather than by our skill in finding out faults and failings alike in persons as in systems (460, 461).

This further instance of the balance of judgment that marked him is striking in view of the fact that for twenty years his soul had ardently desired and expected the coming of his Lord. And in January 1851 he added:

It seems all but absolute folly for any who hold the *oneness* of the Church and the oneness of the Spirit, which in all ages has been in that Church, to find fault with N.'s expression, that the "germ of the heavenly calling was known to Christians in former days." Had not Palaerius [Italian writer, burnt in Rome 1570] the germ of this knowledge, when he wrote the following passage: "Verily, a man may say, that the Christian hath been nailed to the cross, buried, raised again, and is gone up into heaven, become the child of God, and made partaker of the Godhead." [This last phrase is, of course, theologically an over-statement: "partaker of the divine nature" is the Scriptural phrase, 2 Peter 1:4.] The phraseology at present connected with this doctrine may have been unknown, but, I believe, the heavenly calling of the church, its death to present things, and its living in the risen glory, have been, in all ages, the general doctrine: some of the worst corruptions of the Church of Rome had their rise in a false profession of these very truths. The order of mendicant friars, who renounced all property on the earth, was founded on the idea of their being civilly dead and already associated with the heavenlies. All these theories and professions of *theoretic states* have proved in their issue what a very different thing it is to live in the power of heavenly principles, and to profess and contend about being the only right possessors of them. My earnest prayer is that we may have grace to let go contention, and quietly follow our Master, seeking to adorn the doctrine of God our Saviour in all things. I am sure what we all need is to be humbled for the absence of that close walking with God, *in our souls,* which is the power of the inner man; and I feel all these contentions tend to occupy us with things without ourselves, and beget a judging and censorious spirit (469, 470).

And in the following March, 1851, he adds:

I feel now [in India] a little out of the whirlpool of Church trials, and only hear of the distant rumours of unsubdued distractions; but these the Lord will, in His own time, bring to a close, when we have learnt that judgment of others, and determining accurately on their condition, is not the business of the saint's life, but himself walking humbly with God (470).

In words the last of which have searched and humbled my own heart, he wrote:

No language can do justice to the Lord's exceeding grace! I have often been led earnestly to desire that the freedom from earthly care the Lord has given me may only be used for His glory, so that my disengaged affections might be set more entirely on heavenly realities. As it regards things at home, I can see much grace in the Lord's delaying my return, and it has been important as it respects things temporal here: yet to be of any use in the midst of the most blessed opportunities of service, the soul's living in *holy, happy communion with God is essential: I feel, through life, opportunities are not the things needed by us, but grace to* USE THEM GRACIOUSLY when presented (456).

Throughout the hundred years that have succeeded, the followers of Darby have maintained the resolute antagonism to "Bethesda" which he evoked in 1848. Ninety years later (1938) it was used by them in several European lands as the ground of cutting off whole communities once in their fellowship but now having fellowship with Open Brethren. It may help some honest minds to estimate better the real facts to read these extracts concerning that church the very year that that bitter strife was raised against it.

It was on the 20th March, 1848, that Mr. Groves landed in England, and joined his wife in Bristol, where he had ever experienced more sympathy and fellowship than elsewhere (459).

Of the spiritual state of the church he gave this account, full of a penetrating insight:

Dec. 14th [1848]. There is a great deal of most interesting spiritual work here, and all that is needed is spiritual power to carry it on effectually and happily. I think the allusion to *true Church unity,* in Acts 2:42, is most important. They continued steadfastly in the apostles' *doctrine* and *fellowship,* and in breaking of bread and prayers. Where these unities are, there is *real* fellowship and power, and in the measure in which any one is wanting or defective, the true principles of essential unity are wanting. Much of this true unity may be found here; but what we want is the power of *individual* communion brought to bear on the *collective* communion of the Church (462).

Mr. G. experienced much joy and refreshment, while in Bristol, among the believers who meet for communion at Bethesda and Salem chapels: he minstered among them, and, in watering others, was himself watered. The blessed Lord, however, whose will it was to bring him into the conflicts which seem to be the accompaniments of our present imperfection in knowledge and in grace, made him share with these beloved brethren the sorrow caused by the introduction among them of certain questions, relating to the experience of Christ while on earth, which at this time caused division in *Plymouth*. Mr. Groves shrunk greatly from the controversy, and his feelings with regard to it may be gathered from the following observations, made by him when the matter was first put before him:—

"I always feel the very attempt to subject the one adorable Christ of God to a process of mental analysis, is, in its very operation, desecrating. It has engendered the worst of divisions in the Church, and will, I believe, ever do so; however carefully, however *cautiously* pursued. When I look at Jesus as the Word represents Him, I see one whole of aggregate loveliness, suited to my every necessity, able and willing to love, succour, comfort, bless, redeem, sanctify, and make accepted the vilest and most unworthy: this is all my joy and glory; Jesus, descending, dying, ascending, and returning to bless and take His own, is my all and in all."

In these sentiments, his friends and brethren in Bristol fully participated. Mr. Groves deeply sympathized with them in the trials which came upon them on this occasion; and he was thankful for the opportunity given him of strengthening their hands; though as on a former occasion in India, he had to suffer on behalf of others, the unkind words of many; his soul reposed in the truth as it is in Jesus, and he had the comfort of seeing many blessings spring out of these very circumstances which seemed to threaten the godly quietness and peace of his beloved friends. When writing, in allusion to these events, to Mr. Butler, a deacon of the Church at Bethesda, Mr. Groves says:—

"May the Lord make the assurance of His favour that which compensates for all other trials. The more I contemplate and dwell on the whole of the past in connexion with the course pursued by the people of God in Bethesda, the more I feel I have every reason to praise God that they were allowed to act with the wisdom they did, in so difficult and trying a matter." (463, 464).

On his next visit to England, four years later (1853),

He speaks, as usual, of the joy he had as before at Bethesda and Salem Chapels, where he was strengthened to minister on several occasions, with much profit to others, and blessing to himself (475).

A still nearer view of this church, by one from within, is available, though not much known. Mrs. Anne Evans, afterward of

Brimscombe, Stroud, went to Bristol in 1840. She came from a fashionable London Baptist church, and went to Bethesda with a friend to hear as to the Coming of the Lord. The plain building, the drab dresses of the sisters, the poor singing contrasted unfavourably with the London church; but the ministry of the Word! especially that of Henry Craik!:

> His exposition of Scripture was quite a new feature of worship to me, and it was indeed "marrow and fatness." The meaning of the passage was brought out as I never heard it before, and I found myself feeding truly in green pastures… I never went anywhere else while in Bristol… To me it was like a new conversion… The Bible became a new book to me. The brotherly love shown was such as I had never seen before. The godly and simple lives of even wealthy people, who had moved in the highest society, was such as to carry one back to the days of the Apostles, and I felt this was indeed Christianity of a high type…
>
> … the day after, I took up my abode in No. 6 Orphan House. Then followed five years of happy service among the orphans, during which time I was behind the scenes and saw much of the private life of the Brethren, and can therefore testify to the truly spiritual lives they led; their devotion to service to the Lord, and the unworldliness of their daily private surroundings. Here I saw men and women giving up all and following Jesus in one capacity or another.

Such a church as this, numbering many hundreds of saints, Satan must needs attack, and this he did through J. N. Darby. The writer goes on:

> After this there followed a time of agony, of intense sorrow and upheaval; Bethesda was for a time shattered from end to end. Friendships were broken up;—families were divided—husband from wife, children from parents, business relations were dissolved, health and even reason wrecked.

And the agent of this sorrow and ruin went his way all over the land upon similar deadly work, thinking, one is bound to presume, that he was doing God service. Yet it is good to humble oneself under the mighty hand of God. Faith sees Him where the flesh sees only man. The writer continues:

We sadly needed humbling. We had begun to think too much of ourselves. We had increased rapidly in numbers and even in worldly standing, for many had joined us from the upper classes. Our leading brethren, too, were without any check... All this was more than flesh and blood could stand, so Satan was permitted to come down on us and humble our pride in the dust. At this time of sorrow Mr. George Müller was a grand stay to us; he did not lose his head; he held the reins with a steady hand; and when at last Bethesda emerged from the turmoil she was stronger, freer than ever before. We had increased in numbers. The orphan work, which was to have come to nought, was the "wonder of the world"...

When the great Revival commenced [1859, eleven years after the controversy had commenced] the Open Brethren threw themselves heart and soul into it. It was the reading of G. Müller's book by two young men that led to it...

Another personal testimony as to Bethesda in that time is before me. We have just read how attractive spiritually it proved to a young lady from London. In 1858 a young man moved there. He had been in the assembly at Bath since 1852. He continued in the Bethesda fellowship for sixty-eight years and died at the age of ninety-four, honoured by all. I refer to Mr. E. T. Davies. In a letter to me dated January 12th, 1925, he wrote concerning the strife which was subsiding when he joined the church:

> But the brethren in Bristol went on with their work for the Lord, and while being traduced, the Lord blessed their testimony, adding continually to the number of the saved. When I came to Bristol in 1858 I found a most happy fellowship among them, and the ministry of the Word was in the power of the Holy Spirit. To me, as a young believer it was most refreshing and edifying... My personal experience was as the days of heaven upon earth, so profitable was the ministry of the Word, and the fellowship the happiest.

Thus had this church, organized scripturally under elders and deacons, ridden safely through the long and fierce tornado, and was holding on its course. Here was a community attractive to young men and women, rich in ministry and in grace and in service, blessed of God to saints and sinners, with manifest fulfilment of the word "the church had peace, being builded up; and, walking in the fear of the Lord, and in the comfort of the Holy Spirit, was multiplied" (Acts 9:31).

Yet it was of this church, and at that period, that J. N. Darby wrote in 1867 these stern and, in part, false words (*The Sufferings of Christ*, ed. 2, pp. 9, 10):

> I reject Bethesda as wickedness, as I ever did... The Church is the pillar and ground of the truth. That which is not in principle that, is not the Church at all even in its principle, does not gather with Christ, but scatters. When the blasphemous doctrine of Mr. Newton (one for whom personally I have nothing but kindly feeling, and whom my heart, if pained, only yearns over) came out, Bethesda deliberately sheltered and accredited it. I broke with Bethesda and I reject it still ... it has been untrue to Christ, and no persuasion with the help of God will ever lead me a step nearer to it."

If beloved Exclusive brethren who are still possessed by this spirit, still misled by these assertions, having no means to test them, will ponder the facts just before set out, surely they will feel and see how contrary was the mind of Darby to that of the Lord as to this assembly. While he was cursing it the Lord was blessing it. How far, indeed, did Darby believe his own assertions? Only the year before (1866), when Henry Craik lay dying, he had written to him "calling him his 'dear brother,' and wishing that 'although ecclesiastically separated from him,' he might be blessed with every blessing, as the Lord might see he needed in his present circumstances" (*Neatby*, 172). Yet Craik had been one of the two principals in that deliberate sheltering and accrediting of blasphemy, according to Darby's later and published statement, so that his church was simply "wickedness." Oh, that Darby's *heart* had ever swayed his conduct.

Note 3 in the Appendix reviews the matter of Darby's interview with Müller in July 1849, when he acknowledged that no reason remained for further separation.

9

Groves' Letter to Darby

This letter is of quite unusual importance. Historically, because it is the most authoritative statement of what were the original principles of fellowship of the Brethren, given by him who first suggested them. Next because it indicates the points upon which departure from those principles first arose, and who led the way in that surrender. It is also a statement of the new principles being then substituted, and it gave an all too accurate forecast of whither those principles would lead.

It is also interesting as a revelation of the writer, all the more valuable by having been made unconsciously. It reveals penetrating insight, clear judgment upon the issues, incisive statement, and withal that grace of spirit which suffused him even in controversy.

MILFORD HAVEN,
March 10th, 1836.

MY DEAR D_____,

As the stormy weather threatens a little delay, I am not willing to leave England without a few words in reply to your notes, and a short explanation of some other points that interest me. I have ever regretted having so few opportunities of seeing and conversing with you since my return to England, and thereby explaining many things that might have allowed us to depart on the whole more happily than now, yet I wish you to feel assured that nothing has estranged my heart from you, or lowered my confidence in your being still animated by the same enlarged and generous purposes that once so won and rivetted me; and though I feel you have departed from those principles by which you once hoped to have effected them, and are in principle returning to the city from whence you departed, still my soul so reposes in the truth of your heart to God that I feel it needs but a step or two more to advance and you will see all the evils of the systems from which you profess to be separated, to spring up among yourselves. You will not discover this so much from the workings of your own soul, as by the spirit of those who have been nurtured up from the beginning in the system they are taught to feel the only tolerable one; that not having been led like you, and some of those earliest connected with you, through deep experimental suffering and sorrow, they are little acquainted with the real truth that may exist amidst inconceivable darkness: there will be little pity and little sympathy with such, and your union daily becoming one of doctrine and opinion more than life and love, your government will become—unseen perhaps, and unexpressed, yet—one wherein, overwhelmingly, is felt the authority of *men;* you will be known more by what you witness *against* than what you witness for, and practically this will prove that you witness against all but yourselves, as certainly as the Walkerites or Glassites: your Shibboleth may be different, but it will be as *real.* It has been asserted, as I found from your dear brother W_____ and others, that I have changed my principles: all I can say is, that as far as I know what those principles were, in which I gloried on first discovering them in the Word of God, I now glory in them ten times more since I have experienced their applicability to all the various and perplexing circumstances of the present state of the church; allowing you to give every individual, and collection of individuals, the standing *God* gives them, without identifying yourselves with any of their evils. I ever understood our principle of union to be the possession of the common life or common blood of the family of God (for the life is in the blood); these were our early thoughts, and are my most matured ones. The transition your little bodies have undergone, in no longer standing forth the witnesses for the glorious and simple *truth,* so much as standing forth witnesses against all that they judge error, have lowered them in my apprehension from heaven to earth in their position of witnesses. What I mean is this, that then, all our thoughts were conversant about how we might *ourselves* most effectually manifest forth that life we had received by Jesus (knowing that that alone could be as the Shepherd's voice to the living children), and where we might find that life in others; and when we were persuaded we had found it, bidding them, on the Divine claim of this common life (whether their thoughts on other matters were narrow or enlarged), to come and share with us, in the fellowship of the common Spirit, in the worship of our common head; and as Christ had received them so would we to the glory of God the Father; and farther, that we were free, within the limits of the truth, to share with them in *part*, though we could not in *all*, their services. In fact, as we received them for the life, we would not *reject* them for their systems, or refuse to recognize any *part* of their systems, because we disallowed much. Trusting, that if this inter-communion could be established, to effect all we desire, by being upheld by God in walking in the light, as the Christ-like means of witnessing against any darkness that might be in them, according to the rule of the Lord; John 3:19: "This is the condemnation, that light is come into the world, and men loved darkness rather than light because their deeds were evil, neither will they come to the light lest their deeds should be reproved." A more difficult ministry of witness, than a preaching one of words, or separating one of persons, yet possessing a *much more* mighty power over the hearts of others, and a much more influential one in blessing; and which, dear brother, I know no heart more ready to acknowledge than your own. The moment the witnessing for the common life as our *bond* gives place to a witnessing *against* errors by separation of persons and preaching (errors allowably compatible with the common life), every individual, or society of individuals, first comes before the mind as those who might need witnessing against, and all their conduct and principles have first to be examined and approved before they can be received; and the position which this occupying the seat of judgment will place you in will be this: the most narrow-minded and bigoted will rule, because his conscience cannot and will not give way, and therefore the more enlarged heart must yield. It is into this position, dear D_____, I feel some little flocks are fast tending, if they have not already attained it, making *light* not *life* the measure of communion. But I am told by our beloved brethren, C. and H., that if I give up this position of witnessing *against evil* in this PECULIAR WAY OF SEPARATION from the systems in which any *measure* of it is mixed up, I make our position one of simple unpardonable schism, because we might join some of the many other systems. I cannot be supposed, of course, to know fully *their* grounds of acting, but I thought I knew *yours*, at least your *original* ones. Was not the principle we laid down as to separation from all existing bodies at the outset, this: that we felt ourselves bound to separate from all individuals and systems, *so far* as they required us to do what our consciences would not allow, or restrained us from doing what our consciences required, and no further? and were we not as free to join and act with any individual, or body of individuals, as they were free *not* to require us to do what our consciences did *not* allow, or prevent our doing what they did? and in this freedom did we not feel brethren should *not* force liberty on those who were bound, nor withhold freedom from those who were free?

Did we not feel constrained to follow the apostolic rule of *not judging other men's consciences,* as to liberty, by our own; remembering it is written, "Let *not* him that eateth despise him that eateth not; and let not him which eateth not, judge him that eateth; seeing that God hath received" both the one and the other? Now it is one of these two grounds; their preventing me from, or demanding from me, other than the Lord demands, that divides me in a *measure* from every system; as my *own proper* duty to God, rather than as witnessing against THEIR evils. As any system is in its provision narrower or wider than the truth, I either stop short, or go beyond its provisions, but I would INFINITELY RATHER BEAR *with all their evils,* than SEPARATE from THEIR GOOD. These were the *then* principles of our separation and intercommunion; we had resolved never to try to *get men to act* in UNIFORMITY *further than* they FELT IN UNIFORMITY; neither by frowns, nor smiles; and this for one simple reason, that we saw no authority given us from God thus to act; nor did our experience lead us to feel it the best means at all of promoting their blessing or our common aim of a *perfect spiritual uniformity* of judgment; whilst to ourselves it afforded a *ready* OUTLET to the PROPENSITIES of the FLESH, under the appearance of spiritual authority and zeal for the truth. But in all these matters, we desired that our way might be bright as the light, and our words drop noiselessly as the dew, and if, at the last, they remained "otherwise minded," we would seek of

God, that even He should reveal it unto them. There is something at present so like building what you destroyed; as if when weak you can be liberal and large, but when helpen with a little strength, the *true* spirit of sectarianism begins to bud; that being *"one of us,"* has become a stronger bond than oneness in the power of the life of God in the soul. I know it is said (dear Lady Powerscourt told me so), that so long as any terms were kept with the Church of England, by mixing up in *any* measure with their ministrations, when there was nothing to offend your conscience, they bore your testimony most patiently, but after your entire rejection of them, they pursued you with undeviating resentment, and this was brought to prove that the then position was wrong, and the present right. But all I see in this is, that whilst you occupied the place of only witnessing against those things which the divine life within themselves recognized as evil, and separating from them ONLY SO FAR as they separated from Christ, you established them as judges of themselves, and of themselves they were condemned; and at the same time you conciliated their heavenly affections, by allowing all that really was of the Lord, and sharing in it, though the system itself in which you found these golden grains, you could not away with. But the moment your position and your language implied a perfect separation, alike from the evil and the good, and a rejection of them, in consequence of their system, without discrimination, you no longer had their consciences with you, but they felt that though only a brother in a Father's house, you exercised more than a Father's power, without a Father's heart of mercy, and they, therefore, appealed from you to your common Head, both in behalf of themselves and their systems. There is no truth more established in my own mind than this: that to occupy the position of the maximum of power, in witnessing to the consciences of others, you must stand before their unbiassed judgment as evidently *wishing* to allow in them *more* than their own consciences allow, rather than less, proving that your heart of love is more alive to find a covering for faults, than your eagle eye of light to discover them. I send you this letter as we were the first to act on these principles, rather than to H_____ and C_____, whose faith and love I do so truly desire to follow. They have written to me two very long and kind letters, which I purpose more effectually and fully to answer, by meeting the positions contained in them, in a little tract, which I hope to prepare on the voyage, and finally, to publish.

I particularly regret not meeting you at Bristol, as I had much to say to you relative to Rhenius, and other things connected with India, for my heart would naturally seek sympathy and fellowship with you and those dear brethren with whom I have no dividing thoughts relative to the great bearings of truth, or the truths themselves, in which lie the power and peace of the Gospel,—neither in the objects or principles of ministry do I differ;—my difference with you is only as to the manner in which you maintain your position of witnessing for the good against the evil. I feel no one ever expects me, when an acknowledged *visitor* in the house of another, to be answerable for the ordering of that house, or as thereby *approving* it—they would naturally come to the house in which I had control, and where the acts were looked upon as *mine,* to form such a judgment; and even in such a case, if I was but *one* among many in the government, no honest mind would make *me* responsible for faults, against which, in my place and according to my power, I protested; because I submitted to those acts in others, rather than forego a *greater* good, or incur a greater evil. If it is said man cannot discriminate, nor feel the *force* of my witness, unless I separate, not by heart and life, but by contiguity of person, altogether from all kinds of false systems, my answer is, that He, whose place it is to judge, and to whom we are called to approve our hearts, can, and to *Him,* in this matter, I am content to stand or fall.

Some will not have me hold communion with the Scotts, because their views are not satisfactory about the Lord's Supper; others with you, because of your views about baptism; others with the Church of England, because of her thoughts about ministry. On my principles, I receive them all; but on the principle of witnessing against evil, I should reject them all. I feel them all, in their several particulars, sinning against the mind and heart of Christ, and letting in, in principle, the most tremendous disorders, and it is not for me to measure the comparative sin of one kind of disobedience against another. I make use of my fellowship in the Spirit, to enjoy the common *life* together, and witness for that, as an opportunity to set before them those little particulars into which, notwithstanding all their grace and faithfulness, their godliness and honesty—they have fallen. Nor shall I ever feel separation from the good for the sake of the evil, to be my way of witnessing against it, till I see infinitely clearer than I do now, that it is *God's*. I naturally unite fixedly with those in whom I see and feel most of the life and power of God. But I am as free to visit other churches, where I see much of disorder, as to visit the houses of my friends, though they govern them not as I could wish; and, as I have said, I should feel it equally unreasonable and unkind, for any brother to judge me for it, though I leave him in perfect liberty to judge himself. You must not, however, dear brother, think, from anything I have said, that I shall not write freely and fully to you, relative to things in India, feeling assured in my own heart, that your enlarged and generous spirit, so richly taught of the Lord, will one day burst again those bands which narrower minds than yours have encircled you with, and come forth again, rather anxious to advance ALL the living members of the living Head into the stature of men, than to be encircled by any little bodies, however numerous, that own you for their founder. I honour, love, and respect your position in the Church of God; but the deep conviction I have that your spiritual power was incalculably greater when you walked in the midst of the various congregations of the Lord's people, manifesting forth the life and the power of the gospel, than now, is such that I cannot but write the above as a proof of my love and confidence that your mind is above considering who these remarks came from, rather than what truth there may be in them.

Yours very affectionately in the gospel,

(Signed) A. N. GROVES.

Mr. Neatby's comment as follows is worth repeating:

> The closing words of the letter have a great moral beauty. They are also valuable as showing that an observer of no common shrewdness recognized in Darby a moral elevation such as many in the present day are unable to conceive that he possessed… Whether we agree with Groves or with Darby, or differ from both, it will be hard to deny that this

letter is marked by no ordinary combination of faithfulness, delicacy, and large-hearted wisdom (*History*, 63, 64).

It has been shown above that Mr. Darby's writings and actions later than this letter confirm its statements as to the original principles of Brethren; and this is further very distinctly endorsed by the remarks of Lady Powerscourt mentioned, that a changed attitude had been shown by persons in the Church of England consequent upon a change of attitude by some Brethren towards them, this new attitude being a reversal of that originally taken.

Note to second edition.—While this edition is in the press I have, for the first time, read original copies of the principal printed letters and pamphlets issued in 1848 and 1849 upon the Bethesda controversy then raging. They include statements by Darby, Wigram, Alexander, and Dorman against Bethesda, and, on the other side, by Groves, Congleton, Robert Howard, R. Nelson and "Vindex." As far as I know, nothing else of importance to the historian was issued at that period. Nothing in these contemporary discussions calls for modification of what is written in this book or in my paper *The Local Assembly.*

10

The Evangelist:
His Call, Training, Leading

I thank him that enabled me, even Christ Jesus our lord, for that he counted me faithful, appointing me to service. 1 Timothy 1:12.

God separated me … and called me … to reveal his Son in me, that I might preach him among the Gentiles. Galatians 1:15,16.

1. THE CALL.

That may surely be said of A. N. Groves which the Lord said of Saul of Tarsus: "He is a chosen vessel unto Me, to bear My name … for I will show him how many things he must suffer for My name's sake" (Acts 9:15, 16). And the call of God in pursuance of that choice was heard by him early in life.

Frederick Stanley Arnot as a boy played with the sons of David Livingstone and heard the home letters of the great missionary explorer. In those days of his childhood (if memory serves, I think he said in his seventh year) his heart said, If I grow to be a man I must follow in the work of this good man: and it proved the call of God. It was thus with Groves. He began his autobiographical notes by saying:

> When I was between thirteen and fourteen, I used to attend Fulham Church with the school to which I was sent.

He adds, what has been before quoted, that he used to read novels in church under cover of his Prayer Book, and he continues:

> …it was during this state of open rebellion against God, and while walking in open defiance of His holy will, that the first permanent impression was made on my mind relative to missions. It was after a sermon

207

preached by John Owen. I recollect the thought arising in my dark soul, "Surely it would be a worthy object to die for, to go to India, to win but one idolater from hopeless death to life and peace" (23, 24).

In 1833 he referred again to this, when writing from India:

More than twenty years ago [it was twenty four or five years], when I was a school boy, attending Mr. Owen's preaching at Fulham, India (I know not how or why) occupied my wishes, for I knew not Christ (242).

Amidst all the spiritual conflicts and pressure, as well as the outward trials, it is a secret strength to the heart to be thus sure of the definite call of God to serve in the gospel. Nor should any go out to the battlefield until it is a conviction that the Lord has sent, and not the mere feelings of the natural heart, nor the appeals or urgings of men. Had David left his sheep and gone to the camp of Israel out of a boyish curiosity or youthful love of adventure, he might never have returned alive, or only in disgrace; but he was definitely commanded to go by the only person, his father, entitled to send him, and God was with him to give safety and victory. Too many have run to the dark places of the earth, drawn by kindly motives, or sent by mission boards perhaps, but without the King's commission, only to mourn later over a true sphere either missed or forsaken, and to be a sorrow to fellow-workers and a hindrance to the Spirit of truth.

But let us take heart of grace. God is always doing greater things than we know at the time. In a remote hamlet in Devonshire I was the only witness of the conversion of the ruffian of the district, a man of perhaps fifty years. He remained after a gospel meeting for conversation, and commenced by saying: "I have been a very wicked man; I have committed every crime a man can commit except murder, and I've been near to that more than once." Answering my question as to what had at last awakened him, he said it was a hymn sung the night before. It was Watts' "Alas, and did my Saviour bleed?" He said, "I went through the battle of Abu Klea, in the Sudan war." He had served twenty-one years in the army, and had finished his education in sin. That battle was twenty-six years before the time of his conversion. He went on: "After the battle, as we lay on the desert sand, a young lad was bleeding to death at my side, and as he died he sang that hymn. I was already the blackguard of my regiment, and it made no impression on me. I never heard the hymn again until last night, and as it was sung I saw again that dying boy, and it was too much for me, and I had to go out of the meeting to hide my feelings. I went home and said to my wife, We must change our lives, and that's what I came for tonight." And that night the Lord changed not only his life but him, thus suddenly making fruitful the seed sown a quarter of a century before. How little John Owen or that unknown soldier knew what God was doing.

Let us keep on with our testimony; whether writing letters, as Livingstone; or preaching our regular sermon, as John Owen; or singing our Saviour's praise with our last breath, as the dying lad on the desert sand: let us keep on with our testimony, usual or unusual: "In the morning sow thy seed, and in the evening withhold not thy hand; for thou knowest not which shall prosper, whether this or that, or whether they both shall be alike good" (Ecclesiastes 11:6). We are called to work in faith, not only to live and to walk by faith; the faith that is at all times sure, and therefore in due time sees, that our labour is not, cannot be, vain, being wrought in fellowship with the Lord (1 Corinthians 15:58).

2. The Training.

But after the master mechanic has selected the piece of metal there is much to be done upon it before it can be the fine-tempered, keen-edged tool, or the delicate instrument, he will use. If some have left home or business for gospel service without a call thereto from God, others, chosen of Him for this work, have gone before His hour had come or themselves were fitted for the intended tasks.

A deep sense of the need of perishing men is very needful for a winner of souls; and Groves that day in church was made to feel that the idolater was faced by "hopeless death," nor did he ever lose that keen sense of the fearful state and need of men "having no hope and without God in the world" (Ephesians 2:12). He believed earnestly, with all the power of his tender nature, that men are lost, literally lost, are "children of wrath," and the doctrine of the non-eternity of punishment for the wicked he termed "that pernicious teaching," and said:

I tell them it is the gospel of Satan, to give the unconverted comfort in continuing in a damned state; soothing them by the hope of getting out of it in the end (456, 457).

And these were not the callous words of an arm-chair controversialist, but of a man who literally gave *all*, money, strength, time, love, life in its entirety, to the endeavour to save some from the doom of sin.

But such a living sense of the need of men must not hurry even the chosen of the Lord out into the work before the very hour appointed of the Lord, for that is the only best hour. The need of the human race was just as dire before the Babe was born in Bethlehem as then or since; but God waited four millenniums; and not until the "fulness of the time came," not until the "consummation of the ages" did He send forth His Son (Galatians 4:4; Hebrews 9:26). And Israel groaned under the lash all the forty years while Moses was being trained as a prince in Pharaoh's palace, but God did not move for their deliverance; and then when Moses, stirred in soul, himself moved for their help, God said No! and sent him to the deserts for another forty years; and Israel must still toil and groan. But in the consummation of that age, when Moses and Israel, Egypt and the Amorites, were all alike ripe and ready, then God sent His servant and saved His people. Wesley goes forth to save the Red Indians to discover in the task that he himself is not saved.

Thus Groves, early impressed with the need of men and drawn to wish to serve them, must be himself first converted, as we have before observed, and then must have the valuable personal training gained in preparation for his professional life and in the pursuit of it. The mental and moral discipline of trade or profession is invaluable for the worker in the gospel. Is there anything more unsuitable or harmful than the way in which young men, especially of the upper classes, are taken from educational spheres, sent to theological halls, where they are largely secluded from their fellow-creatures, and sheltered from the rough and tumble of this very real human life, and, thus lacking oft-times first-hand insight into men and affairs, are ordained as clergy or ministers, or sent forth as "missionaries"?

Knowledge of books is valuable, but personal acquaintance with all sorts of men and all sorts of matters is invaluable. There is a very common and quite understandable feeling in men of the world that "ordained" men are *not* men of the world in the sense in which they ought to be, though too often they are so in the sense in which the follower of Christ ought not to be.

So for fourteen years Groves must gain the discipline of character afforded by the ordinary duties of life, professional and family; he shall be allowed to prosper almost phenomenally, and to taste the sweets and learn the perils of prosperity; shall discover the weakness of his own heart; shall learn to wait in quietness; to pray away obstacles to the fulfilling of the Divine call to service; to gain the mind of God from His holy Word, upon the church of God and the work of the gospel; and shall discover that suffering with Christ yields a sweeter joy than any other that can be known in this life. The reverses in his father's fortune taught him to face adversity; his own prosperity enabled him to learn the blessedness of sacrifice.

> The early religious impression soon wore away, yet I never was free from recurring convictions, and I recollect from a hundred little circumstances too minute to mention, that these thoughts still dwelt in my heart, though buried under a load of ignorance and love of sin (24).

This might have continued to the ruin of his life but that the bitter disappointment of being refused his cousin by her father sent him to Christ for comfort and salvation. He says:

> ...these new views about the religion of Christ strengthened my almost extinguished thought of being a missionary. It was some consolation to feel that a life which was become useless to myself, might yet bless others (26).

Thus a little quickened he then, like Moses, endeavoured to make his own arrangements for doing this good work. But the mercy and wisdom of God frustrated it.

> I then, after consulting these good men [two godly ministers in Plymouth], in perfect good faith, *gave myself to the Lord and missionary work abroad,* and though I for many years turned back, I ever felt myself a renegade, in fact, like Jonah, shut up in the belly

of the whale. I wrote to the present Bishop of Lichfield and Coventry; he was then Dean of Wells; and he wrote me a kind letter and referred me to Mr. _____ of the Church Missionary Society. To him I also wrote, offering my services to the Society, and received an encouraging and kind answer. I then instantly began to prepare for my future work (26).

But God, who had foreseen something better for him, and through him for the whole work of spreading the gospel in the nineteenth century, blocked this self-chosen and very usual scheme. He suddenly found that he could have his cousin, and he says:

> When the communication was made to me, I did just like Joshua with respect to the Gibeonites—accept what came, I am sure of the Lord, but without consulting Him. We were soon married, before I was twenty-two; and in the joy of possessing one who had so truly loved me, and after five years of trial, I for a moment quite forgot all my promises to the Lord and His work abroad; but this could not last long (26).

And then follows one of those acute and just discriminations which his mind so clearly made, and the statements of which make his *Memoir* such profitable reading:

> I do not think I was wrong in marrying my dearest Mary, for I had fully felt we were married in the sight of God years before; but I did a right thing in a wrong spirit. I ought to have asked Him (my Lord), and told Him my difficulties, and He would, I know, have eased my way, and still have let me have all I sought (26).

There followed a period which he deplored as having been brought upon himself, but which nevertheless was very needful and very useful as part of the preparation he and his wife needed, and is thus a cause of thanksgiving to our all-wise God, who turns our weakness to His glory in the perfecting of us and of His plans for us. He continues:

> After we were married, and the first joy of surmounted difficulties had passed away, our religious judgments could not long remain uncontrasted, and I soon powerfully felt they were awfully different, either from her having gone back through sorrow, or from my having gone forward, or partly perhaps from both. But it now became the *settled bent*

of her life to root out my desire to go out as a missionary, and to reduce me to the same state of religious feeling as herself ... We were greatly prospering in the world, her family were delighted and happy, and these things embraced all she ever knew or thought of happiness; but *it was not so with me; I had given myself to the Lord,* and to a work that I had not fulfilled, and there seemed nothing but daily increasing difficulties. We were prospering more and more, so that renunciation became doubly difficult, and by six years' opposition [it was then 1822] her mind had settled down into a fixed resistance, and her only care was (besides making me happy in every way which love and watchful care could devise) to provide for the dear little ones. Often did I, with every earthly thing that man could desire, feel most miserable. I had a wife who loved me, dear little children, and a most lucrative profession, yet I had not the Lord's presence as in days past, and therefore I was miserable (27).

In how many instances it has been as here, that opposition to one responding to the call to gospel service has come from those most loved, wife, husband, parents. But let no one violently beat down the obstacle or break open a door of escape. Groves was not yet spiritually equipped. He had many lessons to learn before he should be "complete, furnished completely unto every good work" that "God had afore prepared that [he] should walk in" (2 Timothy 3:17; Ephesians 2:10). God's providential machinery neither needs nor will bear forcing; it runs smoothly, each part falling into its place and serving its purpose at the exact moment. To force it may mean irreparable damage (Psalm 78:17–31; 106:13–15).

One of the perils of earthly felicity is that it acts as an opiate, dulling the senses to things heavenly. It is a silken cord that binds powerfully to the earth. Christ's freedman must be taught to say from the heart:

> "We thank Thee, too, that all our joys
>   Are touched with pain;
> That shadows fall on brightest hours,
>   That thorns remain;
> So that earth's bliss may be our guide,
>   And not our chain."

It is through being deprived of that which is good, right, natural, indeed at first necessary, that the childlike heart learns to be weaned from earth, and to say

> Jehovah, my heart is not haughty, nor mine eyes lofty;
>> Neither do I walk in great matters,
>> Or in things too wonderful for me.
>> Surely I have stilled and quieted my soul;
>> Like a weaned child with his mother,
>> Like a weaned child is my soul within me.

But brought to this state of humility, childlikeness, stillness, like the infant when the first fretful cryings for its mother's breast have subsided, and it has learned to wait for stronger food, the heart then relies on God and waits for Him, and can add:

> O Israel, hope in Jehovah
> From this time forth and for evermore (Psalm 31);

for to hope in God becomes the permanent habit of the mind, with the vast enrichment this brings. Six years is no long time to learn this lesson, so indispensable to one who would serve God and man, more especially in such work as lay before A. N. Groves.

It was consequent upon this period of deep soul exercise that he began to see in the light of God things that before he had judged by natural judgment. This of itself was a mental revolution that comparatively few experience, or are even willing to experience. Yet without it Groves would have remained but a sincere yet mediocre Christian. Now he was brought to say, in words before quoted:

> my great desire has been to cast myself on the word of God, that every judgment of my soul, concerning all things, may be right, by being, in all, the mind of God (43).

The first matter on which his judgment was now reversed was, that not general literature but the Book of God is the source of the divine knowledge and heavenly influence required for spiritual service. Of this mention has been already made.

Then followed the adoption of those thoroughly unworldly principles regarding property, of which he spoke as the commencement

> ...of that great work of stripping off from our united hearts the thick clog with which we had been cumbering ourselves so many years (28).

It is truly nothing less than a heaven-sent illumination and conviction that can persuade the heart of man that possessions are a "thick clog," a cumbrance, of which he is well rid. Yet not only sins, but "weights" must be stripped off if the heavenly athlete is to run the race so as to win the prize (Hebrews 12:1). But oh, how eagerly and subtly our heart persuades itself that *our* possessions do not hinder *us*, however it may be with others.

And now God began the task, insuperable to any but Himself, of changing his wife, so as to make her shortly the staunch and utterly reliable helpmeet that he would need in the special service and severe strain that should come upon him. And because so many others wait to see such a change in some one dear to them, who is a hindrance in the path to the whole will of God, space shall be given to his account of this change in Mrs. Groves. It illustrates his previous words that God was about to show "that nothing is too hard for Him" (28).

His wife was first brought to agree that a tenth of their income should be given to the Lord.

> It then became the question, *who* should give it and how. Personally I could not, from my engagements, and therefore she consented to go and distribute it, as opportunities presented themselves (28).

It is well to notice the definite blessing that resulted from this personal service, blessing that in no way could have been gained had the money been given to others to be used among the poor. The narrative continues:

> Besides the poor in our own parish, Mary Walker, in the college near the cathedral [Exeter], was one about whom she became most deeply interested; she was in every way a sufferer; she had a bad husband, great poverty, and a most agonizing, *slow mortification of the feet* and hands, to contend with, yet faith, and love, and praise mounted over all. Her intercourse with this poor saint soon taught dearest M_____ there was something in religion of which she *knew* nothing, a sustaining power

of which she *felt* nothing. Her mind became deeply affected under the trials of her own soul, and her bodily health soon gave way; yet, from the dread lest the idea of *missionary labour* should rise in my mind again, she gave me not the least hint of what was passing within. She took to her bed, told me she felt she was dying, and gave me directions what to do in the event of her death. I was almost distracted, yet knew not where to look but to the Lord for her. After some weeks she again recovered a little, and went out again among the poor, but, as she often used to say to me afterwards, feeling that hell was yawning for her (28).

Oh, how little does one know what is passing in the soul of another! "Who among men knoweth the things of a man, save the spirit of the man, which is in him?" (1 Corinthians 2:11). Truly it is only "the heart knoweth its own bitterness" (Proverbs 14:10). Here were husband and wife, loving each other dearly, yet each carrying a secret load of grief, known only to each and to God; and no doubt friends and acquaintances deeming them both singularly fortunate in each other and in their circumstances. How keen-sighted, how quick-scented (Isaiah 11:3, mar.) do we need to be so as to detect such oppressed hearts, if so be that we may find grace to relieve them. Yet oft it is that whom the Lord will specially use He takes out into a desert, a deserted place, where no other is, but the inner heart is in terrible loneliness, looking for a comforter but finding none; until God Himself draws near in a nearness not before known, Himself comforts with heavenly sweetness, and presently the soul comes up out of the wilderness leaning upon her Beloved, and from that sacred, solitary interview and onward is other than she ever was before.

> O Love, in Whom alone is love's repose,
> Grant me to welcome thorn as well as rose,
> Great are Thy mercies: Thou dost never tire
> Of making roses bloom upon the briar. (A. C.)

Such an hour was at hand for Mary Groves, but as yet she felt

...that hell was yawning for her; she felt, adds her husband, that she was keeping me back, *yet so fixed and determined was her opposition*, that, *long after she got light and peace it remained* (29).

How glorious an endowment is the human will! What a firm hand it is on the helm of life's bark once it is informed and harmonized with the perfect will of God. But how terrible and dangerous a faculty when it is no more than *self-will*, and steers in blindness, through dark and turbulent waters, towards disaster. Yet how patient and skilful is God to subdue and rectify our stubborn will, as He was about to show in this life. Mr. Groves continues:

> But on those days, when there was service at the penitentiary, she was accustomed to go and hear Mr. Marriott, and one day he expounded the concluding verses of 1 Corinthians 1, "God hath chosen the weak things," etc. This was the first thing that gave her a ray of hope, for she said, "If this be the plan of God's government, then there is hope that He may, for *His* NAME'S SAKE, *glorify Himself* IN ME, the vilest, the most worthless of His creatures"; but yet she dreaded so much the *reviving my missionary hopes,* that she still buried all these thoughts; but on the next Tuesday or Friday, we were invited to dearest B_____'s, and Mr. Marriott expounded the same chapter, and the Holy Ghost seemed to say to her, "That's for you, poor troubled soul, take it and go in peace." Her soul was overwhelmed, she returned and told me all her heart, and from that day, the Lord began to let light shine into our dwelling, the days of our mourning were ended, as we thought, and the days became too short to tell of the Lord's goodness, and think of our happiness (29).

Thus did God forge another link, a spiritual, between these two hearts so long one in things earthly, but not yet in the things heavenly. Here is another point to be deeply considered. For union in spiritual life and labours hearts must be united by *spiritual* bonds; not merely by natural affection however pure and strong, but by a joint spiritual perception of the will of God and a joint inward delight in doing it. Just as he waited patiently for his wife to join him with unreserved conviction and devotion in the matter of dedicating their entire means to the Lord, so was he wisely waiting, and praying, for willingness, free and unconstrained, in her as to going afar with the gospel.

"I did not yet feel able to *touch the subject of missions,"* he says, but he gently drew his wife further as to their means, and led her on, as we have seen, to the dedication of a fourth of their income; and presently she joyfully consecrated the whole; and thus were they further at one, and a mighty forward step had been taken, and an altogether higher platform reached from which to view life for God.

Yet even now he wisely took no step of his own to expedite progress. But God showed that He is still the One who "worketh for him that waiteth for Him" (Isaiah 64:4). His narrative continues:

> I had never yet spoken to M. about missions, yet, seeing the Lord had done so much, I saw no reason to doubt He could do all that remained (31).

Nor was this confidence disappointed, for just then Bishop Chase, of Ohio, was brought to him, as we have before read, and

> He asked me if I would go out to B_____, and spend Sunday with him. During Sunday, he conversed much with me on going out with him, and all my hopes of going and my ardour revived; and I thought that it was of the Lord, and would appear more easy as a first step, than going to the south of India, where my heart was first set (31).

Thus he had not yet learned to distinguish between the reasonings of his own mind and the true leadings of the Lord, as he afterwards became skilled in doing. It was of God that he met this devoted servant of Christ, for thereby his fervour was renewed; but the thought to go with him to America was not of God, which shows the urgent need of three things: (1) of carefully weighing and re-weighing proposals which may at first commend themselves to the mind, but really only on natural grounds, such as that the step would be easier than some other step; (2) of remembering that a truly good man may not have the mind of the Lord as to *me*. And in truth not a few, it is to be feared, have gone to a sphere of service under strong pressure from a devoted worker, but without the commission of the Lord to that sphere; and (3) the need and wisdom of leaving all practical arrangements *really* at the disposal of the Lord, so that He can shut doors, as well as open them, and our heart be as deeply satisfied with the shutting as with the opening.

Thy way is perfect; only let that way
Be clear before my feet from day to day:
And hold my heart contented, hushed, and still;
Far, far from me be choices of my will.

By those fond choices I have been beguiled
But now I would be as a weaned child.
Thou art my portion, saith my soul to Thee:
Oh what a portion is my God to me. (A. C.).

The story continues:

On Monday, he came in and lunched with us, and when we were sitting at table, he said, turning to my two dear little boys, "Well, my little men, will you go to Ohio? There are plenty of peaches in Ohio." I turned round to poor M., and said, "Well, dear, will you go?" It was too soon; her heart could not bear it: she burst into a flood of tears and said, "I expected this would come out of your visit yesterday, and, therefore, was so reluctant you should go." I replied. "Well, my love, I have waited now ten years, and whatever burdens of soul or body I have brought on myself, I will not bring them on you, you had no share in them, nor will I urge you" (31, 32).

There he left the matter and waited still; nor is there any hint that waiting was now a tax upon his spirit. He knew that God was working, and he could doubtless say with both restfulness yet longing, "Let *Thy* work *appear* unto Thy servant" (Psalm 90:16). And God rewarded his faith and patience, and Himself did in his wife's heart what yet was needed. He goes on:

Thus it continued about four months, when one day she came to me and said, "Well, N., you may write to Bishop Chase, and say we will come" (32).

And thus the stubbornness was at length subdued, the strife of ten years ended in victory for her Lord against herself, and from that time self no more weighed in her calculations. Oh, blessed freedom! Oh, gracious, patient, persevering, triumphant Saviour! And now Mary Groves knew what a later writer meant by the lines—

> Force me to render up my sword
> And I shall conqueror be!

and could have sung Moule's words:

> My glorious Victor, Prince divine,
> Clasp these surrendered hands in Thine;
> Henceforth my will is all thine own,
> Glad vassal of a Saviour's throne.

For now she was as the vassal knight, kneeling before his overlord, who gripped his outstretched hands as a sign of supreme control, and to whose sovereign disposal the vassal formally renounced his present dignities and estates, receiving them again with such increased honours as the sovereign saw fit.

3. HINDRANCES AND LEANINGS.

But though the citadel was won, and her will and her life were henceforth wholly the Lord's, it remained to save these two from taking an unappointed path. The car may belong to the driver, but he must steer it. It cannot be left to a career of its own, not without disaster. Ohio was not to be their sphere, and the Lord kept them from it.

> I wrote, he says, and waited long for an answer, and at length, when none came, I concluded all that had passed in England amounted to nothing, and I gave up the thought (32).

And now another step was taken in good faith which yet was not in the line of the path of God for them, but which nevertheless He in grace first overruled for good and later thwarted. When they had given up the thought of Ohio his wife said:

> "Well, N., now you had better write again to the Church Missionary Society, and say we are ready to go anywhere" (32).

The Society accepted his offer and begged him to change from India to Persia.

> Mr. Bickersteth came down, and, in our dining-parlour at [Exeter], I related to him my circumstances. I told him I had offered myself to the Society ten years ago; and that my whole desire was to do the Lord's

will, and the greatest good to the Church at large, but more especially to that object to whose interest I had pledged myself—the *cause of missions.* "*But* this," I said, "may be done in two ways, *first, by giving one's means, secondly, by personal exertions.* In the *first* point of view, I have an increasing professional income, and this year have received nearly £1,500, and dear Mrs. G., on the death of her father, will most probably have £10,000 or £12,000 more, the whole of which, with my present income, will, of course, vanish, the moment we take the contemplated step" (32).[1]

But Mr. Bickersteth was used of God to negative such a consideration and to keep the bark on its true course.

[His] answer was, "If you are called of the Lord to the work, *money cannot* be set against it; it is men whom the Lord sends, and He stands in need of men more than money" (32).

[Would God that all leaders of missions today remembered this. Money would then figure less in their reports and appeals, and the sometimes not unjustified reproach be removed that it is the first matter in mind.] Groves goes on:

I thought his judgment a wise and holy one, and I do to this day. He added, "if you could give to the work as many thousands as you could hundreds, still, I would say, Go:"—for we had told him, if we remained, we intended simply living on a minimum, and devoting all besides to God (32).

This point settled they now faced the momentous hour when the matter must cease to be private and be announced openly; the bridge must be burned, their Rubicon be crossed.

Hitherto, all our way had been together, and much in the retirement of our own souls with God; the sacrifices we had made were properly *our own,* and the loving reception of our most gracious Lord, even of the least, and His quick return of blessing, prepared us, by the experience of His love, to bear the loss of much beside, when we were called upon so to act as to involve the happiness of others, peculiarly dear to us (32, 33).

---

1. Here is another instance that Groves' mind was thoroughly practical. However enthusiastically he carried out a plan, he weighed well the practical considerations involved.

The opposition of their relatives has been before described, and how he promised his uncle and father-in-law not to leave England till a loan of £1,000 made to his father, not himself, had been repaid by him. This obstacle greatly tried his spirit. He wrote:

> *Here again* my hands were tied; I felt it, after I had done it, but the promise was made; and purely from love, I knew he would exact the fulfilment of it. I now saw many years of trouble before me again, for, from the moment it was known I proposed leaving, my income decreased… This, and many arrangements I had to make for others before I left, set me almost as far as ever from the hope of leaving, except that dear M. was on my side (33).

And thus appeared an early fruit and large reward for the wise patience he had shown in waiting for the Lord to grant to him the free and full concurrence of his wife, for now she was not against but for him,

> …and by so much as she had hindered me in the first years of our marriage, by so much the more did she now encourage me, and kept up my heart, which was almost bowed down. For months, I was in such a state that I ate every mouthful of food with disrelish; but the Lord comforted her, in making her my comfort; and it was said of her at last, that she was worse than I; and indeed she was just so much the better, as she appeared to the natural eye worse (33, 34).

We have read before how that, his heart having been exercised by this delay, the trial was in a few months removed by the sudden death of Mrs. Groves' father. It was with them as with Abraham and his sacrifice of his son—they expected to lose Mrs. Groves' inheritance, and in their hearts had renounced it, but the sacrifice was not required of them. It may be presumed that it was God's way of providing the large expense of the more than one year after he gave up his profession, before they left for Bagdad, as well as of the preparations for that journey. At any rate, I find no hint that others shared in these expenses. Had they done so, Groves' grateful heart would surely have prompted him to say as much. But he did not take with him from England enough to complete the journey, for before they were through South Russia he wrote in his *Journal*, on November 11th, 1829:

> I have been thinking much today of the Lord's goodness to us. I have calculated that the money we brought from England would not have carried us through our journey, had not the Lord helped us on the road by the hands of dear friends who never knew that such help would be desirable to us (69).

Now one year in England, at the house of a friend of means, and the preparations for the journey, though these were heavy, could scarcely have consumed £10,000. One can only presume that much was given away in England.

He was now free for what *he* had in mind but far from free for what his God had in mind for him. He had long contemplated ordination as a clergyman, until Mr. Hake's question as to the Article upon the Christian and war turned him wholly from that purpose. But for the abandonment of this purpose God had prepared him by a quite distinct providence, one to which he often afterward referred. With the view of taking orders he had been going over to Dublin University; but, as he tells us, shortly before Mr. Hake spoke to him,

> …my connection with Dublin was broken off in a most remarkable way, just when it had answered the purpose of breaking down the high church feelings which I had carried there. Mr. T. of Calcutta, asked me, "Why are you wasting your time in going through college if you intend going to the east?" My reply was, that if I returned disabled, I should be able to minister in England; and here the matter ended.

Thus did he reveal that he was not yet on the high spiritual plane to which he was to rise, but that merely natural reasonings still in measure ruled him. But his wife, so long far behind him, had now advanced beyond him.

> As we walked home, Mary said, "Don't you think there is great force in Mr. T.'s question?" I said, "I thought there was; but not so great as to prevent my going that time; for I had got my examination ready: and, moreover, if I did not go that term, then the last three would be as nothing; and it would look so unsettled to break off my course suddenly. It would, moreover, give additional pain to those whom we had already

so deeply tried; and as I had my money laid by for the journey, I determined to go this time, and then I need not go again for nine months; and I thought this would allow me ample time to consider." She did not concur, but thought the reasons savouring more of this world than the next. However, I had made up my mind, and went to take my place on Saturday, to go on Monday morning (41).

But while man proposes, God disposes. When we do not discern His path by spiritual perception, then He knows how graciously to wall us about that we cannot go forth (Lamentations 3:7). With this intention and arrangement for Monday morning he went to rest Saturday night, but

> On Sunday morning, he recounts, about three o'clock, we were awoke by the noise of something falling… On proceeding into the dining-room, I found the candles lit, as they had been left the preceding evening, and my little drawers broken open, all my papers scattered about the room, and my money gone. As I was returning upstairs, I met dearest M. in the hall, and said, "Well, my love, the thieves have been here, and taken all the money." "And now," she said, "you won't go to Dublin." "No," I replied, "that I won't,"—and we spent one of the happiest Sundays I ever recollect, in thinking on the Lord's goodness, in so caring for us as to stop our way up, when He does not wish us to go (41, 42).

When a soul has been brought to this stage, that it is grateful that God frustrates its cherished designs, it is at last well fitted to face in peace those circumstances, never long absent from service in the gospel in the hard places of the battle-field, which we call reverses, disappointments, delays, and also those keenest of all tests to faith, the times when we seem forsaken by friends and forgotten by our God. And bitter indeed is the lot of one who betakes himself to such dangerous posts without having been thus prepared and fortified in heart by a deep conviction of the perfection of all the ways of the Lord.

This perfection in the providence of God was seen in the detail that in the cabinet ransacked by the thieves

> …there were *two* packets of money, one containing £40 for the Irish trip, and *one*, £16, in another drawer, for taxes; the former was *taken,* the other left. This circumstance was often noticed as most remarkable by Mr. Groves.

It was now only needful that his heart be liberated from the whole bondage to ecclesiasticism that stood in the way of that full liberty to minister the word, by direct empowerment from the Head of the church, into which he was to lead so many others. We have seen how the Lord effected this. The Church Missionary Society would not permit him as a layman to celebrate the Lord's Supper. This led him on to the truth that no ordination of men is required by one whom Christ himself has commissioned, and from that moment he had no further doubts of his liberty in Christ to minister the word of truth (42, 43).

> I stood in the way before thee,
> In the way thou wouldst have gone;
> For this is the mark of My chosen,
> That they shall be Mine alone.

11

The Pioneer: Groves in Bagdad 1829–1833

From London to Bagdad today is a simple matter; by air a few days; by rail, ship, and motor not more than ten or twelve days, or a fortnight at most. It well illustrates the extraordinary external changes that a hundred years have seen that it took Groves six months. Leaving England on June 12th, 1829, the party reached Bagdad on December 6th. The journey then lay by sailing vessel to St. Petersburg and thence by the immense overland route across Russia, through the Caucasus, Kurdistan, and the Mesopotamian valley. It was a long, toilsome, and, in places, dangerous journey, especially for those with no former experience of such travel; and the responsibility of a large party put no small strain on Mr. Groves as the leader. He had with him his wife, two boys, and John Kitto, their tutor, also a Mrs. Taylor, the wife of the British Resident in Bagdad, and her party.

The journey was deeply interesting, if in measure adventuresome, and marked throughout by those providential interpositions by which a faithful God comforts hearts which endure hardness as good soldiers of Jesus Christ.

Groves was now thirty-four years of age; not a newly-converted novice, but a matured and well-seasoned man. It is only rarely that *the Lord* sends out any other sort of disciple. Paul had been serving Christ from eight to ten years, and Barnabas longer, before they were sent forth of the Holy Spirit on their special service afar (Acts 13).

The frame of mind in which he entered this path, under circumstances so utterly changed from the regularity and comfort of the past, and the anticipations he had as to the future, are worthy of study by others facing such a step. He wrote from the ship:

After many years of reflection about the work of a missionary, I am now actually on my way. Home has been left, friends who were as one's own soul have been parted from, and we shall soon now have everything new to seek; but still the hand of the Lord is strong upon us all enabling us to hope in His mercy, and believe in His promises. I never had very strong expectations of what we were to do being *manifestly* very great, but that we shall answer a purpose in God's plans I have no doubt. My source of enjoyment and happiness, therefore, for the future, I expect to arise much more out of the realization of Christ in my own soul to be my Christ, than from anything in my external prospects. Elijah fully fulfilled God's purpose; yet he does not appear to have made more than one convert (Elisha) to the Lord his God, though there were some he knew not who had not bowed the knee to Baal. Nor did Noah make one convert; yet he fulfilled the Lord's purpose in his preaching; so before the Lord comes again, "as in the days of Noah," we shall, I expect, have to stretch forth our hands without many regarding; but let it be our concern, that we do, as individuals and as a mission, preach Christ faithfully, and love Him truly. May the Lord, of His great mercy, keep among us the spirit of love and brotherly union; this is a very earnest prayer of mine, for it is so lovely to see brethren dwell together in unity (53).

It was well, indeed, as Bagdad quickly proved, that his training for service had been in the hands of His foreseeing Master, not in those of the most prudent of his brethren, and in the stern school of daily life, not in the seclusion of a training home or college. An unusually able and very devoted Jewish brother told me that, though he had taken the full courses in two of the best-known missionary training colleges of the United States, he found in the sphere to which he went in Europe that he had not gained a *spiritual* knowledge of the Bible, in spite of all the instruction received. Thus his spiritual equipment had to be acquired on the battle-field, which is dangerous for the person and for the war.

Groves was to find Bagdad a veritable desert, where all circumstances would drain the energies of the soul and supply nothing. Yet he came forth from the furnace fresh and unscorched, because in advance he counted upon Christ, realized in his own soul's experience as his source of happiness. Thus had Paul, though in the terribly irksome position of being chained day and night to a pagan soldier, written: "Rejoice in the *Lord at all* times; again I say, Rejoice" (Philippians 4:4).

To meet the severer tests it may prove insufficient to rejoice only that Christ died for my sins: we need also to know Christ as our indwelling life, ceaselessly energizing the soul with His own inexhaustible vitality; so that His energies of faith, peace, love, joy, courage and indomitable hopefulness may be infused into our weak heart and we thus "live by the faith of the Son of God" (Galatians 2:20). It was Paul's secret, and Groves' secret; may it be ours by faith, more and more, that we too may be able, with quiet confidence, to say: "I can do all things in Him that strengtheneth me" (Philippians 4:13).

It was well, too, that Groves had learned from the Word of God that success is not to be measured firstly by any outward standard, but by fidelity to the present will of God. In the fact, marvellous results have come from his incentive and example in gospel work; but, as regards the more than three years of hardship and suffering in Bagdad, from that he appears to have seen few results, perhaps only one unquestionable convert. Yet looking back, after that long season of strain and sorrow was past, he still could go on in strength and assurance, undaunted by difficulties; and could say:

> It may be said, you have not succeeded; I say, that is begging the question. *If we have done the Lord's will we have succeeded;* the angels that went to Sodom succeeded, as well as Jonah who went to Nineveh, though the former destroyed, the latter preserved the city (225).

Thus encouraged in the Lord, though not by results that were then visible, he refused to abandon missionary work, as some suggested, but was "steadfast, unmovable, always abounding in the work of the Lord." And the outcome has abundantly justified him. Happy is the sower whose seed germinates quickly, as seed does in the hot and moist lands in the tropics; but blessed is he who can cast it abroad in the faith that he will find it after many days. It has been said truly, that if one succeeds without suffering, it is because another has suffered before him; and if one suffers without succeeding, it is that another may succeed after him.

Nor must Groves' prayer for brotherly union within the party pass unremarked; for when dissension arises between workers, they must either part, as did Barnabas and Paul, or the work withers at its roots. But spiritual union is spiritual strength.

In view of the passing of Mesopotamia under British influence in recent times, it is interesting to learn from Groves that there was a general wish for this in 1830. He writes that,

> ...although the Pasha does not directly tax them high, yet from a bunch of grapes to a barrel of gunpowder, he has the skimming of the cream, and leaves the milk to his subjects to do with as they can. And hearing, as they now universally do, that our government in India is mild and equitable, most of them would gladly exchange their present condition, and be subject to the British Government (98).

The fraud in rulers and ruled was that which has prevailed from time immemorial in lands not influenced by the truth and laws of God, and which can only be lessened by the light of the gospel and the power of the Spirit of truth. Groves found the state of the people "very, very bad." But he knew, from the example of Christ and the apostles, as well as the direct precepts of the New Testament, that it was no part of his commission as a disciple to attack directly these public conditions. He writes:

> I never felt more powerfully than now the joy of having nothing to do with these things; so that let men govern as they will, I feel my path is to live in subjection to the powers that be, and to exhort others to the same, even though it be such oppressive despotism as this. We have to show them by this, that our kingdom is not of this world, and that these are not things about which we contend. But our life being hid where no storms can assail, "with Christ in God"—and our wealth being where no moth or rust doth corrupt, we leave those who are of this world to manage its concerns as they list, and we submit to them in everything as far as a good conscience will admit (99).

The church is "called into the fellowship of God's Son" (1 Corinthians 1:9), and when He takes His great power and reigns, she will reign with Him, and the saints shall judge the world and also angels (1 Corinthians 6:2-3). But this is yet future for Him and therefore for His people: "We *shall* judge the world," says Paul to the Corinthians, and reproaches them that they had come "to reign without us" (1 Corinthians 4:8). The Roman Church misapplies this truth, as all others, and perverts it to its own aggrandisement. It claims the present enjoyment of Christ's sovereignty, and refuses the present sharing of His rejection by the world. Political Protestantism does essentially the same; and all other attempts by Christians, however sincerely meant, to improve the world by participating in its public affairs are of the same character. That Groves' attitude conforms to the New Testament requires only fair comparison of the two to see. Our Lord and Example, and His apostles, took the same attitude. John 17; Romans 13:1; Peter 2:13–17 are plain. A key word of Christian conduct today is "subjection," in every walk in life; only in the Kingdom age will it be changed to "sovereignty." It is no part of the God-given duty of the church to tame the wild beasts of Daniel 7, and the attempt is vain.

Groves was not singular in this position. It was the general view and practice of his associates in those days. Their hearts had been brought into actual, effective fellowship with Christ Jesus as rejected by the world, as still despised by men, but as received up into the glory of God. They dwelled in heart where He is, viewed these matters from the standpoint of that throne, and deferred all interference with matters governmental until their Lord shall intervene in them at His return to the earth.

They knew their part to be to walk on earth as He had walked when here, in this as in every other respect.

In Bagdad Mr. Groves determined to learn Arabic as the language used by the majority. In this he succeeded, and to the end of his days it was his habit to converse in that language with a very faithful servant, Hannai, a native of Mosul, whom God gave to him in his time of severe trial in Bagdad and who continued with him to the end of his life. Of the language he wrote:

> I daily feel more assured that the colloquial use of the language is the very instrument of an evangelist's labours. And let such a missionary feel infinitely happier to hear it said he speaks very low Arabic, but that everybody understands him, than very pure, but which is unintelligible, except to the Mullahs [Moslem religious teachers]. If he speak not in a very mixed dialect of Turkish, Persian, and Arabic, he will not be understood here; there is, however, an immense preponderance of Arabic over the others (181).

This was a judgment formed by experience. He had written earlier:

> I believe I have many times mentioned the deep-rooted opposition which exists among the clergy and literary men in the East to having any thing translated into the vulgar dialect: they are worse than the literati of Europe used to be with their Latin, many among whom but lately came to see that it was no disgrace to communicate their ideas in a vernacular tongue: as the common sense of mankind has triumphed over the literary pride of the learned in Europe, so may babes one day overthrow the pride of these orientals. I obtained the other day, for the little girls, a translation of one of Carus Wilson's little stories into the vulgar Armenian of this place. The contrast between the effect produced by reading this in an intelligible language, and their usual lessons, was most striking: in the latter there is of necessity a perfect indifference; but on reading this they begged and entreated they might have it to carry home, which is promised them for next week. Of this I had no doubt before; but the experiment has been most gratifying and encouraging (119).

Here is the spirit of the pioneer, ready to make an experiment for which he had no precedent, but only a conviction of the soundness of it. Of course, the wisdom of the method is now widely conceded, yet not universally. And was not there something deeper than literary pride in the opposition of the learned to knowledge being generally accessible? Knowledge is power. Among an illiterate people the man who can read and write commands respect, influence, and a monetary value beyond others. It was in the interests of their caste that the scribes, and also the clergy, kept the rest illiterate. Clerics were more venerated by the masses, and were more indispensable, spiritually and secularly, when they alone read and wrote. To the superstitious their religious services seemed the more divine for being rendered in an unintelligible language. "The prophet of the great smoky mountain" was an object of awe to the savage tribe. And for the rendering of this alleged necessary help to the soul the clergy were indispensable, and loved to have it so.

And another thought. In England it is compulsory that the services of the Established Church be read and sung in English. But what is the object and effect of the common practice of intoning?

Happening to be showing a Continental friend around Westminster Abbey I heard the intoned service. I know English, yet there was only one sentence I could make out, the Gloria, and that only because I knew from its frequent repetition in its place what it was. Thus is the same end reached as if the service were in Latin. But Christ spoke, and the Apostles spoke and wrote, in the vernaculars. The New Testament is everyday Greek: a sufficient precedent.

An English worker in Syria, known to me, had attained the very summit of success in this matter of language when a native, speaking in English(!), said: "Miss F. talks Turkish like a Turkey."

The first active service that opened to Groves was an Armenian school. He had no such estimate of educational work as a gospel agency as many have. Of his journey through Russia his biographer says:

> He did not then agree with the efforts some would have made to educate the lower classes: his mind seemed to be absorbed in the one thought of evangelizing: "Education," he observes, "is one thing, which may or may not be a blessing; the knowledge of God's Word is another: to forward the one, separated from the other, I would not put forth my little finger; to the latter, all my strength. The one leads to pride, rebellion, infidelity, and discontent; the other is at least a check where it operates no further; but where it does you obtain a valuable subject" (58, 59).

Yet he was ready to follow providential leadings, and his *Journal* of 1831 says:

> Then, as to our work; when we left England, schools entered not into our plan; but when we arrived here, the Lord so completely put the school of the Armenians into our hands, that on consultation both dearest Mary, myself, and Mr. Pfander thought that the Lord's children and saints must take the work the Lord gives, particularly as there appeared no immediate prospect of other work (164).

A visit to Alexander Duff's schools in India further modified his opinion, and in 1834 he wrote from India:

My interest in boarding schools is very much increasing; not because I think it was the way in which the Apostles propagated Christianity,[1] but because I see the Lord now blessing it. I think direct preaching to the natives a much higher and more noble work; and one the aim after which my whole heart feels the overwhelming importance of; but if the *aim,* in truth, be Christ's honour, persons are often blessed of the Lord, to effect, though with labour, what, in the days of the Spirit's energy, was done by a single sentence brought home and sealed (326, 327).

And some years later, at his station at Chittoor, there were schools for boys and girls.

It is evident that he ever looked on this agency as strictly secondary, and it is to be regretted that many have not kept it so. It can never be a substitute for direct evangelistic preaching. There is a constant tendency for it to cease to be a means of contact with the people, to increase in size, and to develop in complexity and in the standard of education, till it becomes an end in itself, and an ever-increasing tax upon workers, time, and money.

There is, moreover, a general policy of governments as to education. In the first stage they welcome mission schools or even insist on missionaries including such in their agencies. But this is when they have no schools of their own. They even lay the snare of giving money grants to such schools, thereby gaining a hold and control. In the second stage, governments become competitors, by creating their own educational system. And finally, by a steady levelling up of the obligatory curriculum and standards, they make the agency such a burden on missions as to cause it to be either no longer possible or of no spiritual value. And if the missions resolve still to hold the field they become mere educationalists, serving only temporal ends, not eternal, and their schools even degenerate into being disseminating centres of higher criticism, evolution, and other popular soul-poisons.

In times of war, tumult, persecution—conditions that will again prevail as the age ends—this form of activity becomes impracticable. It should never be considered more than a temporary expedient,

---

1. It was not. The apostles left all such useful works to be developed by those who were converted and were not *"separated* unto the gospel."

however long it may be possible to continue it in an area. And while it lasts, the truly godly worker will endorse in practice Groves' remark:

> Our schoolmaster has come to a full understanding of the principles on which we intend to conduct the school, *to have nothing that is contrary to God's word admitted*, and I think he very fully and heartily enters into this plan (92, 93).

And then he glances at a question at which some have stumbled, the expectation of the parents to have a voice in the conduct of the school; in seeking to meet which desire, for fear of losing the children, some have compromised Christian principle and nullified the spiritual value of the work.

> But he [the schoolmaster] informs us that the parents of many of the children are dissatisfied with our superseding the church prayers, called the Shanakirke, by the New Testament, and ask, "Who are these people? Are they wiser than our bishops and ancient fathers, that we should reject what they introduced?" This is what we must expect. But we can, with a quiet heart, leave all to the Lord to order as He will. That the schoolmaster is truly on our side I feel very thankful, and I hope we have the hearts of many of the children (93).

There is a deadly peril to which school work is liable, and to which I have known some workers succumb. Visiting one large mission school for Jewish children I enquired if they saw any of these converted to Christ, and the answer was that they did not seek definite conversions, for, were such known, the rest of the pupils would be at once withdrawn! In this event, as one can understand, the annual report and statistics would make poor reading, and funds would fall off, for fear of which conversions were not even desired.

It was my privilege to hear the first address in London of Mr. D. E. Hoste after he had succeeded Hudson Taylor as Director of the China Inland Mission. Upon this subject he said: "We do not wish to be obscurantists: but we ask your prayers that we [the C.I.M.] may be kept from the idea that it is our business to educate China."

Let God be greatly praised for the many children that have been brought to Christ in mission schools, and for good indirect results also. My impression, from observation in many lands, is that this is mainly through the humbler type of schools in undeveloped regions. As regards higher education I am deeply convinced that far richer spiritual results would have followed had the time, strength, and devotion been expended in direct evangelistic labour.

Groves' remark above is noteworthy, that it is only "with labour" that by this agency is achieved what, by the Spirit's energy in the spoken witness, has often been accomplished by a single sentence. To preach the gospel "in [the power of] the Holy Spirit sent forth from heaven" (1 Peter 1:12) is the apostolic method, and where this is done indirect agencies are not much used.

But the school at Bagdad did not continue long. In addition to the perpetual difficulties created by general public disorder, within sixteen months of their arrival the plague attacked the city, and while this was raging the river flooded and demolished 7,000 houses and destroyed 15,000 persons. The horrors and dangers of those months baffle description, and Mr. Groves' narratives are heart-rending.

When these miseries were subsiding the city was besieged, with the view of deposing the Pasha, and not till this was accomplished did order again prevail. Of the total population of some 80,000, about two thirds perished, and one of these was Mrs. Groves. Her death by plague was followed by that of a baby girl given to them in Bagdad. Thus the husband and father was doubly bereaved, and left with his two boys, and their tutor Kitto, who was entirely deaf. A heart of stone could not read the *Journal* of those days and not melt. Of course, provisions became very scarce and dear, including water, and the survivors endured semi-starvation. Naturally at such a time robbery and violence abounded. Mr. Groves himself was attacked by the plague, but only slightly; and then by September (the plague entered at the end of March, 1831) he had typhus fever.

Well indeed it was that he had not come to such times before having been disciplined in spirit and taught to know his God. As it was, the *Journal* abounds with trust and praise, and breathes perfect peace and unfeigned assertions of the perfection of God's ways. The following extracts will glorify God:

> April 13 [1831]. O, what a blessed portion is ours, to have the God of Israel and his unchangeable promises for our sure and abiding place

of rest—our little sanctuary unto which we may always resort! Yea, in the secret of His pavilion He will hide us (126).

The peace he enjoyed was thus noticed by Kitto:

"I am sure Mr. Groves feels no personal anxiety on the subject; and I endeavour to get the same feeling, that we shall be safe, or if we are visited by the pestilence or sword it will be for some wise and useful purpose. He thinks it would be a poor return for the protection we received during our long and perilous journey were we to distrust that care by which we have been hitherto preserved" (126).

April 26. But for the presence of the Lord in our dwelling as its light and joy, what a place would this be to be alone in now; but with Him, even this is better than the garden of Eden. These are invaluable situations for the experience of God's loving, distinguishing care, and here we realize our pilgrim state much better than in the quiet of England, with all its apparent external security (132, 133).

April 27. For ourselves personally, the Lord has allowed us great peace and assured confidence in His loving care, and in the truth of His promise, that our bread and our water shall be sure; but certainly nothing but the service of such a Lord as He is would keep me in the scenes which these countries do exhibit (135).

April 28. News more and more disastrous. The inundation has swept away 7,000 houses from one end of the city to the other, burying the sick, the dying, and the dead, with many of those in health, in one common grave (135) … it requires great confidence in God's love, and much experience of it, for the soul to remain in peace, stayed on Him, in a land of such changes, without even one of our own nation near us, without means of escape in any direction; surrounded with the most desolating plague and destructive flood, with scenes of misery forced upon the attention which harrow up the feelings, and to which you can administer no relief. Even in this scene, however, the Lord has kept us of His infinite mercy in personal quiet and peace, trusting under the shadow of His Almighty wing, and has enabled us daily to offer up to His holy name praise for suffering us to assemble in undiminished numbers, when tens of thousands have been falling around us (137).

An opportunity had offered to leave the city with a caravan that was to cross the desert to Damascus and Aleppo, but Groves could not feel at liberty to abandon the place to which he believed his Master had brought him. The sequel justified this. For nearly three weeks the caravan was surrounded by the inundation. Some were drowned, many died by plague, and the rest had to return. Groves comments that

> …in this instance at least we *see* great reason to bless God for keeping us back. Yea, the Lord will instruct us and teach us the way in which we should go, and will guide us with His eye; this is our confidence and comfort; and in such a time of unheard of perplexity as this, what a source of abiding peace. *We feel it well to know our God in such circumstances as ours* (139).

On May 7th he wrote:

> This is an anxious evening. Dear Mary is taken ill—nothing that would at any other time alarm me, but now a very little creates anxiety; yet her heart is reposing on her Lord with perfect peace, and waiting His will … To nature it seems fearful to think of the plague entering our dwelling; in our present situation, nothing but the Lord's especial love could sustain the soul in the contemplation of a young family left in such a land, at such a time, and in such circumstances; but we feel we came under the shadow of the Almighty's wing, and we know that His pavilion will be our sanctuary, let His gracious providence prescribe what it may. On His love, therefore, we cast ourselves with all our personal interests (144).

> May 8th. The Lord has this day manifested that the attack of my dear wife is the plague, and of a very dangerous and malignant kind, so that our hearts are prostrate in the Lord's hands. As I think the infection can only have come through me, I have little hope of escaping, unless by the Lord's special intervention. It is indeed an awful moment—the prospect of leaving a little family in such a country at such a time. Yet, my dearest wife's faith triumphs over these circumstances, and she sweetly said to me today, "The difference between a child of God and a worldling is not in death, but in the hope the one has in Jesus, while the other is without hope and without God in the world." She says, "I marvel at the Lord's dealings, but not more than at my own peace in such circumstances" (144, 145).

May 12th, writing two days before her death, but as if she were already gone, he said:

> Though the Lord has taken away the desire of my eyes, as it were with a stroke, and left me a few hours to cry unto Him in the midst of deep, deep waters, yet these visions of His love have so revived me, that my whole soul is brought to acquiesce in His holy and fatherly arrangements with respect to her who was once the joy, the help, and the companion of all in which I was engaged… It never entered my heart that I was to be left alone, as far as earth is concerned, most alone. Those friends for whom this journal is alone designed, know how much she was to me, and deservedly so: this, however, the Lord saw had its great, great dangers too, and in His infinite mercy to us both, may have ripened her so rapidly … and left me here to serve and praise (151).

And the day of her death found his empty, stricken heart still blessing his God for His mercies. He says:

> May 14th [1831]. I cannot help exceedingly blessing my heavenly Father, however these calamities (for to nature they are such, though not to the heirs of glory) may end, that He has allowed me to continue in health so long as to see everything done I could have desired and infinitely more than I could have expected for her whom I had so much reason to love (153).

Upon this event Kitto remarks:

> When I compared my own fretful and repining acquiescence in my own losses with the faith, patience, and confidence with which a man of such warm and affectionate feelings was enabled to support a much heavier loss, my spirit felt rebuked before his, and profited too, I hope (154).

The next day only he felt the dread disease attack himself, and knowing how probable it was that his own end was near, he wrote:

> Should these be my last lines in this journal, I desire to ascribe all praise to the sovereign grace and unspeakable love of my heavenly Father, who from the foundation of the world set His eye of redeeming love on me in the person of His dear and well-beloved Son. I bless God for all the way He has led me; and vile and wretched sinner as I feel I am—unworthily as I have in all my life served Him—yet I feel He has translated the affections of my inmost soul from earth to heaven, from the creature to

Himself. As to the dear, dear, helpless children, I have committed them to His love, with the full assurance that if He transplants me from hence to Himself, to join the partner of my earthly history, He will provide for them much, yea, very much better than I, or ten thousand fathers could do. To His love and promises, then, in Christ Jesus, I leave them; and strange and wonderful as His dealings appear, He has made my soul to acquiesce in them. To all the family of the redeemed of the Lord, especially those I know, I entreat you to let your conversation be as it becometh the gospel of Christ; always abound in His most holy work, for you know your labour is not in vain in the Lord. Be as those who wait for their Lord with your lamps trimmed, for shortly He who shall come will come, and will not tarry. My soul embraces those I especially know with all its powers, and desires for them that Christ may exceedingly be glorified in them and by them, amen, and amen (155, 156).

Was a more moving dying testament ever penned? Thus does the crushed olive yield its oil and the beaten incense its fragrance. Yet he did not then die, but lived further to declare the praises of the Lord. But as is usual, the sterner tests came as the days and weeks went by and his loss and loneliness pressed more heavily on the heart as realities than they had done as prospects. Thus five days after his wife's death he wrote:

This has been a heavy day with my poor heart, so slow a scholar am I under my dear Master's teaching. Yet I feel He will fill me with His own most blessed presence, and then I shall be able to bear easily all other bereavements. How strange it is that feeling should rule with so much more power than principle over the happiness of the soul, even when the spirit imparts strength to direct the conduct aright. The feelings seize on the slightest recollection; and oh, what fuel have they when everything in the minutest daily circumstances, everything in the events passing around us, at once comes directly on the heart and presses upon it; and when there is not a soul near, not only not to supply all that is lost, but not even a portion of it; and yet notwithstanding all this that now weighs on me, I feel the Lord Himself will be yet more to me than all I have lost. I feel I have been skimming too much on the surface of Christianity instead of being clothed with Christ. O! what a child am I in the life of faith, but I feel the Lord has my poor soul in His training, and though the discipline may seem severe, it is only the severity of uncompromising love (158, 159).

And the next day he adds:

O how easy it is to kiss our dear and loving Father's hand when He turns bright providences towards us! How easy, then, it is to praise! but I feel my dearest Teacher is teaching me the hardest lesson, to kiss the hand that wounds, to bless the hand that pours out sorrow, and to submit with all my soul, though I see not a ray of light... Through much tribulation we must enter into the kingdom; therefore, blessed Lord, prepare me for Thy service. I am a poor, inexperienced soldier; clothe me with the whole armour of God, that my soul may praise in the darkest day (159).

From this period we will take but one more passage, one of peculiar value and beauty. On June 7th he wrote:

The more I contemplate the circumstances in which I have of late been placed, the more I see of the trials and anxieties of the missionary life, and of the mysteriousness of God's dealings, the more I feel overwhelmed with the importance of the soul having a deep sense of the love of God in Christ, before it ventures upon such an undertaking. Our dear Father very often, in love, explains to us His reasons; at other times, He gives no account of His matters; in the one case to excite love and confidence, in the other to exercise faith. It does seem to me, that no doctrines but those of the sovereign grace of God, and His love entertained towards the soul before the foundation of the world, and the revelation by the Holy Ghost of the love and fellowship of Christ, and through Him with the Father, so that we have thereby our life hid with Him where no evil can reach us, can happily sustain the soul. There is something so filthy, so worthless in all our services, when events render it probable to the soul that it will soon appear before God, that the new creature cannot endure the deformity and defilement, and turns away its distressed sight to the love of the Lord, and the garment He has provided without spot, or wrinkle, or any such thing. The experience of my dear, dear Mary on this head was most striking. She often said to me, "They often talked to me, and I often read of the happiness of religion, but I can truly say I never knew what misery was till I was concerned about religion, and endeavoured to frame my life according to its rules,—the manifest, powerless inadequacy of my efforts to attain my standard, left me always farther removed from hope and peace than when I never knew or thought of the likeness of Christ as a thing to be aimed after; and it was not till the Holy Ghost was pleased of His infinite mercy to reveal the love of my heavenly Father in Christ as existing in *Himself* before all ages, contemplating me with pity, and purposing to save me by His grace, and to conform me to the image of Him whom my soul loves, that I really had peace, or confidence, or strength. And if in any measure I have been able to walk on with joy in the ways of the Lord, it has been from the manifestation of *His* love, and not from the abstract sense of what is right, nor from the fear of punishment." This was the theme of her daily praise—the love and graciousness of her Lord; and I can set my seal, though with a comparatively feeble impression, to the same truths, that the sense of the love of Christ is the high road to walk according to the law of Christ (167, 168).

Of a heart that thus, by loving, abides in the love of God this will ever be true, "Blessed are they that dwell in Thy house: They will be still praising Thee" (Psalm 84:4).

During those most terrible weeks communications from the outer world were, of course, interrupted, and he wrote on May 27th:

Oh my heart longs for Christian communion—someone to whom I can talk of Jesus and His ways, and with whom I may take counsel; yet it now seems as though many months must elapse before our dear friends can come from Aleppo; but the Lord knows what is best, and to Him we leave all our cares and the providing for all our necessities;

and the next day he adds:

I have also had intelligence today that my dear brothers and sisters had been two months ago on the point of setting off from Aleppo; but whether they received news of the plague and returned, or are waiting at Anah, I know not, but I greatly need them—yet still the Lord knows best how much I need them, and when (163, 164).

Not the least bitter drop in the cup had been to know that fellow-workers were on the way, but could not get beyond Aleppo in northern Syria.

A year after Groves left England a party of seven started to join him. It consisted of Cronin (who had just become a widower), his mother and sister, Parnell, Newman,[1] Hamilton (an Irish Brother) and Cronin's infant daughter. The party was detained for fifteen months at Aleppo.

---

1.   The afterward celebrated Oxford professor, Francis William Newman, brother of the Cardinal.

There Parnell married Miss Cronin, and lost her almost immediately by death. Hamilton returned to England, and scarcely had the little company at last succeeded in reaching Bagdad, in the early summer of 1832 when Mrs. Cronin also died (*Neatby* 67).

In the September following, Newman, with Kitto, returned to England, partly to enlist additional missionaries. Groves, as we shall see later, left for India in May, 1833, and never returned to Bagdad. Cronin and Parnell, with Groves' sons, remained in Bagdad for a considerable time, but as there was no prospect of a permanent work being established, the effort was finally abandoned, and Parnell and Cronin returned to England. Neatby adds:

> It is an interesting fact that Wigram was only prevented at the last moment from joining this missionary band. That we thus get a list of almost all the names of men who had taken a leading part in the move-ment before 1830 is a striking proof, not only of the fervour of the zeal of the first Brethren, and of their readiness to stake everything on principles of action that may now appear to us rather visionary, but also of their superiority to any ambition to found a new sect. To follow Groves to Bagdad, on a mission that must be deemed singularly unpromising, was the prevailing passion in Dublin. If the little group there that furnished most of the makers of Brethrenism had the weakness of Quixotism, at least they had its strength and nobleness (67).

I quote these remarks only to notice their testimony to the enthusiasm to spread the gospel of the early Brethren. If only this had continued the dominant work of all, the later strife and divisions might perchance never have arisen. 1 Corinthians 15:58 is the medicine for the disease mentioned in chapter 1:11.

Of the life of that group of remarkable men in Bagdad one scene of deepest import may be given, carrying a lesson deeply needed in many mission stations I have visited. Henry Groves, the eldest son, writes:

> The savour of those early prayer meetings every morning, and of our Friday meetings for fasting and prayer and for the reading of the word, even now live in my memory as the recollection of holy things that appear the more sacred from the apostolic character which they seemed to assume, bearing witness that the Spirit of the day of Pentecost was with the Church in very deed (218).

And Groves himself writes:

> Nothing can exceed the happiness of our union; the love of Christ is so simple, yet so true a bond. We have a most happy meeting for fasting, prayer and searching God's word every Friday, which refreshes us from the secularity of our other occupations (222).

This practice of prayer, with fasting, Groves continued in India. Under date February 9th, 1834, he wrote:

> I have had today a season of sweet enjoyment in my Lord. I had set it apart as a day of holy remembrance of those I love, that by fasting and prayer I might have an opportunity of bringing them and their circumstances all distinctly before the Lord; for the numbers are now so increasing that I feel it essential to do so (280).

It is melancholy that that happy union was afterward broken. How cruel is ecclesiastical strife, that it can murder ruthlessly even the love of God and heavenly union in the breasts of brethren. What can more brand it as of the devil, the first and arch-murderer! In 1849 Cronin debarred Groves his house on the ground of second Epistle of John 10, thus, as Groves wrote, concluding "an unbroken intimacy and friendship of twenty-five years." Yet though

> The wheels of God grind slowly
> They grind, exceeding small;
> And though His judgments tarry,
> Yet they come at last to all;

and after thirty years, in 1879, good Dr. Cronin (another friend of my father) received the fulfilment of the Lord's words: "With what measure ye mete, it shall be measured unto you" (Matthew 7:2). He was himself cut off from fellowship by his party of Exclusives.

Of the rest of that missionary band only Newman need now be noticed, for doing which I have a reason. Neatby writes that at

> ...the very beginning of his [J. N. Darby's] career, he brought into almost servile subjection the mind of one of the most remarkable men of the nineteenth century. This was Francis William Newman, the younger brother by four or five years of the more celebrated (not, I think, the abler) J. H. Newman, the Cardinal. He took a double first at Oxford,

became Fellow of Balliol, and was afterwards Professor of Latin at University College, London, and finally Professor of Political Economy at Oxford; and his writings cover an even wider range than these achievements might have led us to expect. Fifty years ago [about 1850] he was a recognized leader of a phase of strongly theistic free thought, and it was chiefly his books that gave rise to that brilliant polemic, Henry Rogers' *Eclipse of Faith* (*History* 45).

Darby also wrote a polemical work against his views, entitled *The Irrationalism of Infidelity*. He did much to poison the thought of his generation, but it is not as widely known as it ought to be that in his old age he recovered his faith in Christ. I learned this from the Rev. Frederick Glanville, vicar of St. Matthew's Church, Kingsdown, Bristol, in whose parish I then lived and with whom I was friendly. We met one day at Weston-super-Mare, where Professor Newman ended his days, and chatted about him. Mr. Glanville narrated an incident that illustrated the versatility of his mind. He told a friend that he had had a three-weeks' holiday. Being asked where he had gone, he said he had not been anywhere, but finding he had an Ojibbeway Grammar he had amused himself translating *Hiawatha* into Ojibbeway. This is a Red Indian language.

Mr. Glanville said that his father had been an intimate friend of the Professor and had assured him that the latter in his later years returned to the faith of his early manhood. Hoping for confirmation of this I did not mention it for a long while; but some years after, meeting in Oxford an elderly lady long resident there I repeated what Mr. Glanville had said. She was Mrs. Mozley, whose husband was son of the celebrated Oxford Canon and Lecturer. She replied that she had no doubt it was true, for her husband, on returning from Professor Newman's funeral, had told her that it had been stated over his grave, by his request, that he died trusting for salvation to the precious blood of Christ. The Lord be praised for His recovering grace; but, alas, for the baneful influence exerted during the eclipse of his faith.

There is a reflection pertinent to such a case, and of importance: the most pronounced, prolonged repudiation of the faith, and public opposition thereto, is not sufficient proof that the opposer never was a true believer. The evidence of genuine faith in Christ, and hearty devotion to Him, of Newman's early years was ample; and as Butler long since said, if a fact is once established by adequate proof, no amount of negative evidence can overthrow it. This bears directly upon the right application of those passages of the New Testament which deal with the backsliding, moral and intellectual, of persons treated in these passages as believers. Backsliding, open and prolonged, is not adequate proof that a man is not a child of God.

I shall be pardoned for adding the following remarks as to visits to Aleppo. Being on the Lebanon mountains in December, 1927, I sought from the Lord leave to gratify three desires; one to visit the famous ruins at Baalbek, another to see the upper Syrian country, and the third to go to Aleppo.

It is interesting how early in life God begins to work out a purpose. This has been remarked upon above in the cases of Groves and Arnot. In my young boyhood I saw among my father's books one with a plate of the great columns at Baalbek, and in my heart I felt how wonderful it would be to go and see such a place. I have no doubt that this was the seed which grew into an interest in ancient sites, which, in the outworking of the providences of God, I have been permitted to develop, so far as to visit several, to some little advancement in understanding His book, so thoroughly oriental and ancient on its human side.

On this occasion I saw over Baalbek, and spent the night at a great hotel, being the only guest, as it was midwinter, save for a Syrian engineer working on the great highroad the French were then constructing. There were also present the proprietor of the hotel and his son-in-law, owner of an hotel in Damascus. It was bitterly cold, Baalbek being some 4,000 feet up. It was a summer resort of the Roman emperors. We sat by an apology for a stove, and I learned by questioning that the elderly Syrian proprietor, though a Maronite by religion (an ancient church affiliated for some time now to the Roman Catholic Church) was, in a simple, elementary degree, looking to Christ as his own Saviour. Thank God, that there are such souls in such gloom-pervaded spiritual systems.

I then asked the son-in-law what he knew of God and he told me this story:

When I was only engaged (he said) I kept a room in this hotel that I might have a place whenever I came to see my fiancee. After Turkey entered the Great War [1914–1918] an enemy of my father-in-law here, wishing to harm him, wrote him a letter which was wholly a lie, to the effect that he was happy to inform him that, on account of the great services he had rendered to the Allies, if they won the war the British intended to reward him in such and such ways. The letter being opened by the military, as the writer knew it would be, they at once visited him. But he was too old and respected a resident to be really suspected. However, in searching the hotel they found in my room a book against the Young Turk Party, then in power. I was at once arrested in Damascus and interrogated. I could only protest that I never had taken part in politics, was not a member of any secret societies, that the book had been sent to me from Egypt, but I had never even read it. I was not believed, and a court-martial condemned me to be shot.

I was then taken from the house, where I had been confined, and placed in a dungeon in the castle. A terrible despair seized my soul in the darkness, and I considered if there was any way by which I could take my life, but no plan opened. But that night, in this fearful situation and state of mind, God brought to my heart two texts from the Bible, by which I was comforted, and came to know Him in reality.

Just at this time a dear friend of mine called at my hotel to enquire for me, and learned from my servant my position. He was the editor of the principal Damascus newspaper, and, as the Government were using it to disseminate official news, he had access to Jemal Pasha, then ruling Syria. To him he at once went, and appealed for my release, assuring the Pasha, from long acquaintance with me, that I was unquestionably innocent. The Pasha rang up the president of the court and ordered my release in two hours, which was done.

This was his story, told here in bare outline; and as I listened my heart glowed though my body was chill, and I felt I had gained by my visit far, far more than a sight of the ruins of Roman emperors and their temples. I had seen how the King of kings restores a ruined human temple and makes it a house where He is praised. What a record there is on high of marvels that God is ever working in secret for His own eternal glory. His dealings in this case exemplify the general principle that He brings us into severe trials to serve spiritual ends, and these being reached it is simple for Him to deliver out of the difficulties, however great.

Before dawn I left Baalbek in snow and darkness for Aleppo. The journey would take me through the whole tableland of Upper Syria, which I wished to see; as much of it, as far indeed as the Euphrates, is part of the Promised Land, and was included in the conquests of David and the dominions of Solomon, and will again be held by Israel under Christ, their Messiah (Deuteronomy 1:7; Joshua 1:4; 1 Chronicles 18:3ff; 2 Chronicles 9:26; Ezekiel 48:1). It is a vast grain country, and one does not wonder that the great empires, ancient and modern, have coveted it. And it is the natural highway from Asia to Africa, down which Abraham passed, Aleppo being probably already there.

About midday French soldiers in my third class compartment suddenly commenced shouting out of the windows and firing their rifles. It was to attract the engine-driver and stop the train. We were at a district where the line runs on the edge of the eastern deserts, and several Druse prisoners had sprung from the train in motion (a hint as to its speed) and had fled over the deserts. We had to wait two hours while they were rounded up, which allowed me to converse as to salvation with a young British official from Iraq. It meant also that we reached Aleppo after dark instead of by daylight.

It was a city of 400,000 people: 300,000 Moslems, 40,000 Jews and as many Armenians, with a further mixture of races. From the lights I saw that the station was a good way from the city. I did not know a single person; it was unlikely that I should happen on any one speaking English, and I had to find my way to the one hotel of which I had heard where English would be spoken. Naturally this would be the most expensive hotel, as it catered for wealthy tourists, and I had no more money than might suffice for one night. But I knew the God of A. N. Groves, and my heart was quiet in the assurance that I was in His path for me.

As I reached the platform barrier, to pass out into the darkness, I heard a foreign voice calling my name repeatedly. I was thankful, though I cannot say surprised. My heart, by happy experiences, had ceased to be surprised that "the God who doeth wonders" should do wonders (Psalm 77:14). If we walk with Him wonders become frequent, all wrought out of regard to the Son of His love, whose name is Wonderful. This angel of the Lord's deliverance was a beloved Armenian brother, Matossian by name, teacher of English in an American school. He took me to his house, bowed with eastern courtesy, and said: "My home is yours." It appeared that an Armenian brother I had met on the Lebanon learned that I was going to Aleppo, and had asked his brother-in-law to meet and to care for me. My ignorance of this kind thought allowed an enriching exercise of faith and of experience of God's peace and provision. Thus is faith more blessed than sight, and it can sing truly:

> "So on I go, not knowing;
> I would not if I might:
> I'd *rather* walk in the dark with God,
> Than go alone in the light;
> I'd *rather* walk with Him by faith
> Than go alone by sight."

But what had drawn my heart to this distant city? It was simply the knowledge that, nearly a hundred years before, those brethren who have been mentioned had stayed there on their journey to Bagdad. As far as I knew no one from their Christian circle had since visited the city, and I recognized a secret persistent impulse in my heart that I must do so. In fact, after my purpose to go was known, I learned from an English lady who had lived north of Aleppo (Miss Frearson, now of the Armenian Orphanage at Shemlan, Lebanon) that that intrepid pilgrim, J. H. Dutton, had once toured in Armenia (burdened forsooth with a bulky model of the Tabernacle) and had been in Aleppo. But no lasting result attended.

As I lay that first night on the floor of the reception room of my new friend, I found I had developed influenza, caught no doubt at Baalbek. It is an old and frequent visitor, but that attack was violent and with complications. But the loving-kindness of these friends was sweet to my soul, and I am sure to His heart who said: "Inasmuch as ye have done it unto one of these least, ye have done it unto me." When I could get about I made the acquaintance of several English-speaking Armenian Christians, and enquired as to the city, especially its religious state. But Aleppo too lies high, perhaps 1,500 feet up, on a vast plateau, and its winter climate is bleak. I could not risk a relapse of the illness, and after some days I returned to Palestine, using the money that had not been spent at the hotel, and having a three days' wearying and adventurous journey by cars.

In the June 1928 following, my indulgent Master gratified another desire, and allowed me to return to England over the high lands of Asia Minor. The train passes in sight of Tarsus, where Paul was born; climbs the wild mountain pass he must have traversed, a formidable and dangerous matter then; stops awhile at Iconium (still called Konieh); and enables the traveller, on the way to Constantinople, to observe the general features of the mountainous Galatian region, where the apostle saw so much suffering for the gospel, but also such triumphs.

This journey starts from Aleppo, so I must needs pass a second time through Syria and that city. My friend, Mr. J. W. Clapham of New Zealand, whom God had much used in the gospel in Palestine, asked if he might accompany me on this second trip, as he had a desire to serve in those parts, and I knew the journey and had some friends in Aleppo. I left him in that city, where he stayed for a time and taught to some the way of God more perfectly. His later visits have been used of God to commence there a witness to New Testament principles, concerning the church of God, as well as in Antioch, not far away—the Antioch of Acts 11:19, 26.

When some day A. N. Groves and his fellow-sufferers get to know that their seemingly fruitless toils have inspired others a century later, will they not feel afresh that their labour was not vain in the Lord, and renew to Him their praises?

And yet—as I ponder this heroic and pathetic period of Groves' life, a question will not be silenced, though happily I have not to answer it, indeed am not competent to do so. Was Bagdad ever part of God's own plan for His beloved servant? It developed his acquaintance with his God, with the advantage this was in later service; it gave some knowledge of the gospel to many, and salvation to at least one, who in turn served God well, and probably to others not known to us as yet; it was an inspiration to many in devotion to Christ and the gospel. That God turned all to good is certain; and yet—and yet? It is possible to go by a longer route than God intended.

When, as a boy of fourteen, God first impelled him towards the blessed work of saving benighted souls in distant places, it was INDIA that was pressed upon his attention, and for some twelve years INDIA alone continued to draw him, until the Church Missionary Society begged him to change to Persia, "Mr. Bickersteth telling him, they had for *years* endeavoured, but without success, to obtain a missionary" for Bagdad (50). Was this of God, as part of His way of taking him to India, or was it of man? I cannot say; and the question is raised only to press on such as have indubitably heard the call of God, as well as, and even more, upon those who advise such, to be as assured of the place to which God has called as of the call itself. It is clear that even in Bagdad India was still in his thoughts, for on May 21st, 1831, he wrote:

> Should India be your field of labour, whether it be finally ours or not, it will be most important, etc. (170).

About the year 1901, in the course of a regular ministry I was then exercising, I gave my first address and appeal as to gospel work abroad. The text was the latter part of 1 John 2:2: "but also for the whole world." A young man named Fred Curtis, and his wife, went home that Sunday morning to find that each had heard the call. In due time Barbados was clearly indicated as the sphere. But elder and well-informed brethren considered that there was greater need in Demerara, and persuaded them to change their purpose and go there. I said little, but was not satisfied. On the voyage Mrs. Curtis was taken so ill that the ship's doctor declined the responsibility of her going beyond the first port of call, and they were put ashore at Barbados. The long and fruitful service, continued till death, showed that God had had His own blessed way.

Without presuming to determine as to others, let each be very careful and assured as to his own path. God had called Anthony Norris Groves to India, and to India He now led him.

12

India

Depart: for I will send thee forth far hence. Acts 22:21.

Today [1938] the well-to-do take a winter holiday tour in India, with a journey of less than three weeks from London. In 1833 it was no pleasure trip. Leaving Bagdad on May 21st, detained at Bushire by the illness of a companion, it was July before Groves reached Bombay. In the next year a sea journey from Calcutta to Madras occupied him thirty-seven days. Today it would demand only four or five days. And his further voyages, from Madras to Scotland and back, via the Cape, each consumed three months.

It was little wonder that in those days missionaries going to India formed no definite expectation of seeing England again. And even now some go forth armed with the same mind. A Jesuit leader in India said to a friend of mine, visiting that land, that their men go out with no idea of ever leaving, but your people, said he, come and go like tourists. There is another side to this question. Health enters into it, and, for men of God, there is the matter of distinct Divine leadings. But the Jesuit touched a tender spot, indicating a real danger. The one to whom he spoke inquired of some as to their visits to England, and was answered that if they did not go every few years they would be forgotten and funds would fail. But has God no money or food or clothes but in England? In many out-of-the-way places I have learned that Omnipotence has servants everywhere, and secret stores in unsuspected spots.

In July, 1833, Groves reached India, and, save for two visits to England, and the third during which he died, to India he gave the remaining twenty years of his life. At this late date it will be more profitable to gather up some of the important lessons to be learned from the *Memoir* than to recount details of his tours and labours.

1. HIS SPIRIT AND ATTITUDE TO OTHER WORKERS.

He maintained in India the principle already reviewed, of enjoying fellowship with all that is of God, though found in association with that of which he disapproved. Before leaving Bagdad he had written as to his objects in going to India, that

> One very especial one is to become united more truly in heart with all the missionary band there, and show that, notwithstanding all differences, we are one in Christ; sympathizing in their sorrows and rejoicing in their prosperity (226).

On account of truths for which he stood he had not a little opposition to endure, but he met it with a love and grace that commended him to many who differed, and without being himself soured thereby; so that after fourteen years he could still write:

> I often bless God for enabling me to feel I belong to all that belong to Him, and that I have no call that makes it imperative on me to separate from any household of faith, because of evils that may exist among those in whom the Lord dwells and walks; neither have I any prohibition against forming part of any such household, where my own soul is edified; so that I never feel I separate from one because I unite with another. If I am hindered from intimacy with many, it is because they have, of their own will, annexed terms that I cannot comply with. I believe they do it conscientiously, though, I think, wrongly; but I feel no heart-division from them on this account. I rejoice in all the Lord's goodness has vouchsafed to them, and show my love and oneness with them, as fully and as often as I can, publicly and privately owning all the congregations of the faithful in the land, "but none of their system" (446).

that is, he owned every individual believer, and every separate congregation as such, for such are a Divine institution; but he did not own any of their inter-church systems or arrangements.

Thus minded he could be thankful for any testimony to Christ, however feeble it seemed. He deplored the spiritual and moral state of the Syrian Christians in Malabar,

> ...resisting every effort for their spiritual good, and loving darkness rather than light... Their leaders, like those of the fallen churches I have seen, are blind leaders of the blind (245);

but, animated with the generous and sincere love noted, he could add:

> Yet after all, as to the weakest and worst of the works I see, I would infinitely rather they remained and were added to than discontinued (247).

There can be no question that it was this very attitude and spirit that led many to consider those principles and practices that he alone in India at that time advocated, and by the acceptance of which they were led into a fuller conformity to the mind of Christ in life and service.

2. Human Systems in Church Life and in Gospel Labour.

But Groves' generous heart did not blind his mind. He had been enlightened by the Spirit of God through the Word of God, and he could not but see that corruption and weakness, not health and power, were the result of human arrangements in the things of God. Always graciously, but equally plainly he spoke upon these topics, seeking to exercise the heart and conscience of others, stirring them to submission to the Word of God in these spheres of worship and service. His utterances are a fine blend of love and frankness.

> The more I see of the dear C.'s, the more I love them. Has not your heart deep sympathy with that character of piety one meets with in spiritual members of the Church of England? I acknowledge the system to be wrong, very wrong, yet my heart finds great repose in those fair pearls which lie within, what seems to me, so naughty a shell (297). I feel assured that all attempts to increase the *exclusive* spirit of the Church of England will do injury. My heart has this repose, that the truth shall prevail; and my determination is more than ever fixed, to stand and try what, in the name of the God of truth alone, one poor wretched ransomed sinner can do to mitigate the evil which I fear will arise. I was told I was the greatest enemy the Church of England ever had in India, because no one could help loving my spirit, and thus the evil sank tenfold deeper; but, indeed, I do not wish to injure, but to help her, by taking from her all her false confidences (314). The dear old bishop [Corrie] is dead, and was buried yesterday. A man with a kinder, sweeter spirit you could not have, and he was untarnished by his elevation. We went to his funeral. I loved him much, and wish I could feel the system with

which he was connected right, but I cannot. Every day my heart is more and more convinced we must stand by the truth the Lord has revealed to us, and for which the Lord has made us responsible to Himself and to the Church (365). Never was there a time when it is more important than now [1833] to make every effort that they do not rivet on this land the evils of ecclesiastical dominion, viz., the pride and earthliness under which the established churches in Europe have groaned. When in civil things we obey them beyond the bounds, as it is thought, of human sufferance, patiently and meekly, let us stand up for the Church's liberty, and not be again brought under the yoke of bondage (253). Today I have been much struck with the stress the apostle, in his epistle to the Galatians, lays on his commission not being in any measure human; and that the way in which the apostles were led to give him and Barnabas the right hand of fellowship was, that they *saw the grace* that was given to them. Perhaps you may think I am proud in not submitting to human authority, but of this, indeed, my heart does not accuse me: in all civil matters I will *willingly* be subject, but the *liberty* of the church is *not mine to yield* (244, 245).

It was on this principle that Spurgeon, contending earnestly for the faith, answered the cry that we must be charitable. The truth, said he, is not our property, but God's, and he who is charitable with another person's property is a thief.

The advantage of being independent of all human organizations Groves had appreciated in his early days in Bagdad, saying:

I feel I am happy in having no system to support, in moving among either professing Christians or Mahometans: to the one, a person so situated can truly say, I do not desire to bring you over to any church, but to the simple truth of God's Word, and to the others, We wish you to read the New Testament that you may learn to judge of God's truth, not by what you see in the churches around you, but by the Word of God itself (69).

The importance of this last point lies in the sorrowful fact that the lives of most of the members of the great Churches are as corrupt as the lives of the Moslems around them, and the latter see no moral reason why they need become "Christians." Entering a large Moslem village in Egypt we asked the question, Are there any Christians here? The answer was Yes; and we were guided to the only "Christian" they knew, the depraved Greek trader who, in defiance of one of the very few salutary rules of their religion, sold to them intoxicants. It is commonly the same whether the Church be Roman, Greek, Coptic, Nestorian, Syrian, or another. And it is with such utterly degenerate systems that leading opinion in the Church of England labours to effect reunion, systems in which the high ecclesiastics are often as vile as the masses! Can one touch pitch and not be blackened? Surely a child of God should not abide in such connexions!

Groves wrote further In 1834:

> Never was there a more important moment than the present for India; up to this time everything in the Church has been as free as our hearts could wish. Persons have been converted, either by reading God's Word, or through one another, and have drank the living waters whenever they could find them full and clear; but now the Church of England is seeking to extend its power, and the Independents and Methodists are seeking to enclose their little flocks. My object in India is two-fold: to try to check the operation of these exclusive systems, by showing in the Christian Church they are not necessary for all that is *holy* and *moral;* and to try and impress upon every member of Christ's body that he has some ministry given him for the body's edification, and instead of depressing, encouraging each one to come forward and serve the Lord. I have it much at heart, should the Lord spare me, to form a Church on these principles; and my earnest desire is to remodel the whole plan of Missionary operations, so as to bring them to the simple standard of God's Word (285, 286).

This last remark is to be noted. It was not only church systems, but mission organizations that Groves saw to be not according to Scripture. He was grateful for all that he saw of God in the workers themselves and their work, but he was very sure that the systems and societies were human and a hindrance. The blessing of God attended the work in spite of, not because of, these arrangements. It is so still. Of this, at least, I have no manner of doubt, that where workers in the gospel have a real active confidence in the Lord for all needful directions and all needful temporal support they have no need of a society behind them. In 1831 Groves wrote in Bagdad upon this matter with the same sincere and generous sympathy as upon church systems:

I do not desire for one moment to set myself in opposition to those blessed institutions whose labours roused us from our lethargy [the C.M.S., L.M.S., B.M.S., and other societies had been at work before this]; but this I may say, that I do not think their plan is the best, or the only good one. Notwithstanding, I desire to bless God for them, and co-operate with them whenever I can (118).

But while rejoicing as far as he possibly could, he was certain that essentially the system of societies was harmful. His words in 1834 have been already given:

From my arrival in Bombay to the day I reached Jaffna [six months], I had been continually hoping to find missionary institutions carried on with that simplicity which, I think, so highly becomes us, but I have been deeply disappointed. Wherever I have been, the system of the world and its character of influence have been adopted, instead of the moral power of the self-denial of the gospel. I trust the Lord has allowed my coming here to be of some little use in eradicating this baneful system . . . [and] I long to see some one mission carried on in unison with the principles I feel to be right (274).

And of certain brethren, whose connexion with a society was terminating, he wrote in 1836:

I trust they will show that Societies are not *needed to carry on* very extensive missionary work, any more than to begin it (363).

As early as 1831, before any others had joined in his course and work, he wrote from Bagdad to one who was hoping to serve abroad:

Should India be your field of labour, whether it finally be ours or not, it will be most important that we establish a full and free communication between each other, not only for comfort, but for instruction and union; that, at least, those who think there can be no union or unity of action without systems of man's devising, may see that the cultivation of the spirit of brotherly love, with perfect liberty and freedom of action, would attain it much better (170).

In view of these his considered convictions as to societies, and of the fact that a century of operations by his successors have justified these convictions on a literally worldwide scale, could it be anything less than deep sorrow to the heart of Groves did he know that, among those who profess to work on his lines, there have arisen organizations with names and associations almost indistinguishable from the ordinary "mission" or "society"?

As such societies were not needed in his day, they cannot be needed now; as surely as they exerted a "baneful" influence then, so they do today.

It is a fact to which I can bear personal, unequivocal testimony that in all spheres, heathen, Moslem, Jewish, Catholic, the very terms "mission" and "missionary" have become a definite and immediate hindrance to the reaching of men. They regard the names as indicating an attack on their own religion, and are prejudiced, rendered wary, and often immediately hostile.

3. CHRISTIAN INFLUENCE.

In 1827 he had written:

> …how consolatory it is to feel that holiness is the only influence in the Church of God worthy the ambition of a child of God, and that that influence is as much within the reach of a bed-ridden member of the family, as of those who are flourishing in the zenith of their popularity: and that the prayers of the holy bedew the Church with as many blessings as the labours of the active, if prayers are all that the providence and fatherly dispensations of the most High allow them to offer (44, 45).

And of seven years later, when he was nearing Calcutta, we read:

> "May the Lord so help me," he adds, with his usual panting after holiness, "that I may leave it holier than I enter it; I mean not as to my standing in Christ, but in conformity to His blessed will; that the fruits, which I hoped were preparing in the yet unopened bud in time of winter, may blossom in this time of spring, and come to perfection in some distant summer" (283).

With his clarified vision in things spiritual he saw distinctly that far other and baser springs of influence than holiness of life were largely relied on in Christian service; such as social position, money, learning, a fine style of living, and, among subject races, national prestige. It was abundantly evident to him that Christ and His apostles deliberately forswore all such means of influence. When the Son of

God descended to this earth to create and to spread the Good News, He "emptied Himself," "became poor," and graciously accepted all that abasement and discomfort which poverty involves. It was thus with the apostles. Pertinent is that story of Thomas Aquinas, and pungent his answer, that when the Pope had showed to him the treasures of the Vatican, and had said, You see, brother Thomas, that we cannot now say with St. Peter, "Silver and gold have I none"; and neither, said he, can you now say with St. Peter, "Rise up and walk!"

Spiritual and heavenly influence wanes in the measure that outward and earthly influences are employed; they create an atmosphere that chokes it. God will not give His glory to another. All human influence is tarnished by human sin and weakness: sin and holiness cannot combine and co-operate; link weakness to energy, and the latter is limited by the former, the chain being no stronger than its weakest link. Therefore Paul, though learned and able in high degree, discarded the use of these intellectual influences, of purpose hid his knowledge of all subjects but Christ, and preached Him in the guise most offensive to the cultured Corinthian taste, as crucified; and he adopted intentionally a plain, unrhetorical style of speech; that the power of the Spirit of God might be the solitary influence exerted (1 Corinthians 2:1–4).

It was these considerations that led Groves, as has been above noticed, to relinquish the study of general literature and depend upon deep, spiritual acquaintance with the heavenly oracles, and also caused him to renounce wealth and embrace poverty. It is not that wisdom and wealth are inherently sinful, for God is infinitely wiser and richer than all; nor that position is wicked, for He is the Most High: it is simply that these things are unsuitable to the existing conditions of earth and to the ends to be served, are rather a very real hindrance thereto. Money attracts the poor for earthly reasons; prestige impresses the socially humble, though there be no submission of the will to God; and thus the carnal become adherents to the religion of their superiors, and even genuine converts are made into dependants of their instructors, instead of becoming Christ's freemen.

It was because Groves saw clearly that organized church systems and missionary societies worked surely in this harmful direction of dependence upon false influences, that he could not but oppose the systems, though he loved many in them. He was certain that the effect upon disciples and their witness was baneful. In reference to his tract on Christian Influence, and to the subject itself, he wrote:

I do feel so sure that we have lost our true power by decking ourselves out, and prosecuting our plans, according to the spirit and principles of the world, whereas I am *sure* we ought to stand in *contrast* with it at *every point* (229). During my stay at Bombay [1833], I ventured to suggest to some of the missionaries privately, that certain expensive and apparently self-indulgent habits might be avoided, but all resisted the idea. If even good and devoted servants of God are deceived as to what constitutes their true influence in the Church of Christ, namely, *being like Christ,* can we be surprised that the world at large go altogether wrong? The more I think of the *principles of Christ's Kingdom,* as revealed in His Word, and witnessed to inwardly by the Spirit; the more I reflect on the character of our Lord's life on earth; the more I feel sure we cannot, *if we desire to know God's will,* be deceived as to the general course we ought to pursue, nor in what our true power consists, which really is in being *earthen vessels* (230). There is a strong tendency among Christians at Bombay to simplify the missionary plan, but there appeared little or no apprehension that the conformity to the world, which they allow lowers the missionary's spiritual power, lowers theirs also (231). By our union with the world, we have altogether lost that testimony of God being on our side, which Rahab speaks of to the spies (Joshua 2:9–11), the "fear of us" being put into the hearts of our *enemies,* because God is among us. (See also Judges 7:14, and a number of similar passages.) He has now no faithful witness in us; we have sown the ground with mixed seed, and are everywhere ploughing with an ox and an ass, which the Lord abhors, and how can we be blessed? Who now fears the church because God is in the midst of her? She is now just feared in proportion to her wealth and riches, numbers, and power, as the political unions are. How strong we should be if we felt as the two spies did (Joshua 2:24); but we have sown to the wind, and are reaping the whirlwind (235, 236). For my own part, I do not feel a doubt that the union of church and state, and ecclesiastical establishments on carnal principles, are the hot-bed of all those corruptions into which many are plunged at this day; yet the very persons who condemn the fruit nourish the root and water it with every care (248).

And in 1834 he wrote:

> I have just read a letter from a Mrs. Ward, of the Burmah Mission, which deeply interests me: it is written in a fine devoted spirit; she says—
>
> When we went out we were treated with a great deal of respect by all kinds of natives, but it was the kind of respect that the poor pay the rich, rather than the respect which is felt for eminent piety. And when I tried to impress the minds of the native sisters with the importance of modesty, cleanliness, etc., they would say, that they should very much like to live as we did, if they had money enough to do so. Thus I felt deeply the necessity of trying to exert a *different kind of influence*, or of trying in some way to be an example to the native Christians. And our reformed plans have not been without a beneficial result. The Christians now think, and what is of more consequence we *feel*, we are consistent (278).

"Reformed plans"—the mere sound of the words would send a shiver down the spine of many a mission secretary and committee man, and would make the blood run cold of many a missionary. What heroic courage was displayed by John Woolman, the eighteenth century Quaker, when he toured the settlements of Friends in the United States to persuade them voluntarily to set free their slaves. Scarcely less courageous was Groves in broaching to missionaries the curtailing of self-indulgences. And he discerned that it is "those who act under societies are in so many ways fettered" (280), and hence his decided rejection of that plan of working.

In an oriental city of half a million souls I was the guest of a dear man of God, the head there of a large and elaborately organized mission. He narrated that for years they had their schools, meeting places, and workers' houses scattered about the city, often in inconvenient and unpleasant circumstances. So one of their number was commissioned to go to their home base and raise a loan of £20,000 at 5 percent interest. With this was purchased a fine central site on a main shopping street, and a commodious block of premises was erected. It comprised school rooms, a large auditorium, a book shop, and capacious and healthy flats for workers; and it was expected that from the rents of handsome shops on the street, and of upper flats to be let, as well as by hire of the auditorium for meetings, they would repay the loan and interest in twenty years, and also save the many rents of former premises. In addition, the whole work was now centralized, with all the reduced toil and added convenience for the workers.

I said to my esteemed friend that it was a most excellent business scheme, with only one drawback—the spiritual. I reminded him that he had just before been deploring the fact that converts gained from Islam almost uniformly looked to the mission to support them, instead of developing personal faith in God. I asked was that not natural, virtually inevitable? Their mind worked thus: These foreigners have invited me to change my religion; it has cost me everything to do so, and I am beggared: but they are rich—look at these great premises!—so, of course, they will look after me! The same conditions are working the same spiritual evil in a hundred places where far less money is involved.

The godly influence on his century of George Müller's faith and witness is acknowledged by all spiritual persons. That influence was based upon exactly the principles that Groves advocated. He has given in detail the reasons which prevented him and Henry Craik from co-operating with the missions, societies, and institutions of their time and for commencing a new work, "The Scriptural Knowledge Institution." These reasons may be read in full in the first volume of his *Narrative*, pages 109–112. They are:

1. That the end proposed by those societies was the gradual betterment of the world, till all men were converted; to which they could not subscribe, as not being a Scriptural expectation.

2. The connexion of such societies with the world, unconverted persons being often members upon payment of a subscription, and members for life if the amount subscribed were large, even though perhaps living an evil life.

3. The practice of *asking* the *unconverted* for money.

4. That the committee members managing the society could be "manifestly unconverted persons, if not open enemies to the truth; and this is suffered, because they are rich, or of influence, as it is called."

5. "It is a most common thing to endeavour to obtain for patrons and presidents of these societies, and for chairmen at the public meetings, persons of rank or wealth, to attract the public. Never once have I known a case of a POOR, but very devoted, wise, and experienced servant of Christ being invited to fill the chair at such public meetings. Surely, the Galilean fishermen, who were apostles, or our Lord Himself, who was called the carpenter, would not have been called to this office, according to these principles."

6. The contraction of debts by societies, which is "contrary to the spirit and to the letter of the New Testament" (Romans 13:8).

A hundred years ago these were bold words and deeds—pioneers must needs be courageous, independent of human opinion. But the testimony of such men of faith was made widely effective by the Spirit of God, and in due time various missionary societies were formed which sought to eliminate the more glaring of the evils specified. For this God is to be praised. But why maintain at all the plan of society organization, seeing that the subtler of the spiritual evils cannot be avoided? Is not the one vital reason the financial? And would not this consideration lose the more part of its weight were another point upon which Groves laid much stress adopted? This point is:

4. DESCENDING TO THE LEVEL OF THE PEOPLE.

On the overland journey in 1829 he met at Shushee (modern Shusha) five German brethren, working among Armenians and Mohammedans, of whom he wrote:

The brotherly love of the missionaries has provided us with a resting place during our stay with themselves, to our great comfort, for they are truly dear brethren, and from communion with them I have derived the greatest joy and satisfaction. That perfect unity of sentiment which subsists between us as to the importance of laying aside every thing of this world's greatness, and descending to the level of the people, is most grateful to me; and this is not the sentiment of one of these dear brethren, but of all. They have now the best house in Shushee, and although nothing can be more plain, simple, and frugal than the interior arrangements, still the exterior is striking, where everything else is so despicable and mean as in this town. The consequence is, that the people continually taunt them with having renounced the world, and yet living in so grand a house, and for saying that a little room a few feet square would do for them. All these five disciples feel the point of this, and wish to be free from the burden (67).

It will be well to observe again that Groves' education upon such matters as these had not to commence when he arrived in the foreign field, as is the case with so many, to their great embarrassment. He was already informed of the mind of Christ from His Word and example, and already imbued with the strong spirit of Christ so as to follow that example.

In India he was shocked to find that the hateful spirit of caste persisted among followers of Christ, professed and real, and pained that many missionaries were equally widely separated from the people they were there to reach. In January 1834 he wrote:

> I have had with me today one of the Christians of this place, the chief man among those who are standing up for caste; and he says plainly that he does not care what Christ or the Apostles did, he never will eat with Pariahs nor receive the Lord's Supper with them, nor after them, but only before them, neither would those of his views receive it after their ministers. I have just been with Mr. S., the chaplain, and he says there is no hope but in beginning again. In this I think he is quite right (268).

It was such a fresh start that Groves was sent of God to make, and it is certain that since his time some real advance in this matter has been made, and many devoted servants of the Lord have followed and are following Groves as he followed Christ. How urgent the need was of a nobler spirit and practice may be seen from this incident of only a few weeks later than the former:

> I met with a curious illustration of the prevailing feelings of missionaries. Immediately after my bearers had put down my palanquin at the end of the station, another handsome palanquin came and was put down. I found from the bearers that it belonged to a Padre, and I was getting out to see him, when I met him on his way to my palanquin. During a short conversation, I found he was a converted Jew, sent out principally by Mr. J. E., of Edinburgh: he was on his way to Cochin, the place where more Jews reside than in any other part of India. During our conversation I said that if he would really stamp upon the minds of his brethren the

impress of a soul alive in Christ, he must go and live among them at Jews' Town. He instantly replied, this was the very thing he would not do; for he was convinced by experience, that nothing was to be done with the Jews, without keeping them at a distance, and not making yourself too cheap, and keeping a certain degree of external respectability. If those who teach take such views of the source of power in Christianity, can we be surprised that the taught are led wrong? (282).

If this odious spirit had been completely exorcized from the breasts of Christians and workers in the gospel it would be a pleasure to omit such a miserable picture; but I have heard a most devoted worker from the southern States speak similarly of the negroes; I am told that the same unchristlike attitude is maintained by many white Christians toward the black believers in South Africa; and I know that in other lands also there are not wanting missionaries and Christian residents of the same kind.

With such persons and such conduct frequently meeting him it was no wonder that a man such as Groves should say:

The farther I go, the more I am convinced that the missionary labour of India, as carried on by Europeans, is altogether *above the natives;* nor do I see how any abiding impression can possibly be made, till they mix with them in a way that is not now attempted. When I think of this subject of caste, in connexion with the humiliation of the Son of God, I see in it something most unseemly, most peculiarly unlike Christ. If He who is one with the Father in glory emptied Himself, and was sent in the likeness of sinful flesh, and became the friend of publicans and sinners, that He might raise them, it is truly hateful that one worm should refuse to eat with, or touch another worm, lest he become polluted. How strikingly the Lord's revelation to Peter reproves it all, "what God hath cleansed that call thou not common" Acts 10:15 (271, 272).

This was but a restatement of convictions before expressed thus:

What a comforting thought to the saints who suffer in this dispensation is Philippians 1:29, to feel that it is a gift and *favour.* How *slow* we are to learn really to suffer, and to be *abased* with our dear Lord (Philippians 2:3–10). However, I think we are generally much more able to take up cheerfully any measure of bodily or mental trial than that which degrades us before the world. To see that our *abasement is our glory,* and *our weakness our strength,* requires extraordinary faith: wherever I go, I perceive the evil influence of contrary principles. I am persuaded that not following our Lord, and going down among the people we wish to serve, destroys all our real power; by remaining above them, we have power, but it is earthly. O that the Lord would raise up some to show us the way (252).

Honest soul that he was, he was prepared to be the answer to his own prayer. In 1830 he had written in Bagdad:

…whatever plans are proposed for these countries, let them have *as little* of the world and *as much of Christ in them* as possible; and whatever there be, let it be without pretension or parade (80).

In 1834 in India he wrote:

I have not ceased from seriously conversing with my dear brother and sister [his hosts], on the subject of personal self-denial, and the lessening the appearance we make before the heathen, pointing out, that all influence derived from such things is purely worldly, and such as the Lord cannot bless (274) …the deep subject of interest with me is the uprooting the whole class of feelings connected with the natives, that missionaries may do by them as the Lord did by the publicans and harlots. However the Lord may dispose of you, let this be your firm abiding purpose, to share in the humiliations of the gospel (275)… I have long felt there are *two kinds* of self-denial that we, as missionaries, need great grace to carry out fully. The first is, *personal,* touching all that is connected with the honour of this poor body, whether in food, raiment, or in the appendages of external respectability; the other is the self-denial involved in really coming down to the natives (277).

And shortly he deals with the application of these views to himself:

I think I very clearly see that whatever others may do, believing as I do that *self-denial,* or rather the spirit of love from which it flows, is *essential to our individual and collective prosperity,* and hoping by the Lord's gracious help to get a *body of men like-minded* to work with me, I must *first act* myself; for I could not desire any brother to live more *simply than I did.* In all these cases I feel it infinitely better to say, *"let us,"* than *"do you";* and yet I feel assured, without inconceivable crucifixion of self, the work that is to be done in these lands cannot be accomplished; for the material you have to work on is so very low, that close and real contact, so as to leave a lively impression, involves an abasement so great, that none yet have had the heart to attempt it. To be generous with a thousand pounds a year is one thing, with a hundred another, with ten another; but if we expect self-denial or a generous self-sacrifice from these poor people, whose subsistence is of the barest and most precarious kind, we who have dearer views and brighter hopes must lead the way. It must be some who, like us, are free to act thus; those who act under societies are in so many ways fettered (279, 280).

And then he gives a picture as sweet as one formerly drawn was ugly:

I am here staying with a Colonel F., a single-hearted, devoted man in his attachment to his Lord. He has just been telling me of a Roman Catholic Bishop who lately paid him a visit, an humble, simple man, a Frenchman, who would not leave his people, but went out under the trees, where they were, and sat on his little mat, saying, they would be unhappy if he remained all the day away from them at Colonel F.'s house. O, may we be willing to learn these lessons, even from a Roman Catholic! Surely they will rise up against us in the great day if we disregard the glorious light given to us. What is the use of God's word to us, if it be not a lamp to our feet and a light to our path? (281).

In the light of that Word he endeavoured to walk. Naturally his journal says but little of his own self-denial as he sought to practise what he preached.

At the severe privations endured in Bagdad with peace and joy we have glanced, as also at the picture of him travelling with a young Arab, who

...is with me by night as well as by day, for our dormitories are very simply managed; the little carpet I sit on by day serves as my bed at night, and a cloak covers me. *I cannot tell you how comfortable it is to be independent of everything but the sunshine of the Lord's countenance* (238).

And another passing glimpse is given thus:

I am now solitary in a native boat, among a strange people, whose language I do not understand. However, the Lord is here, and His presence comforts all hearts and smooths all difficulties to those who trust in Him (298, 299).

And another is afforded by this description of the palanquin, the covered chair carried by bearers, formerly much used in India:

> There is something very simple in the house afforded by a palanquin; it is at once your library, your sitting-room, your bed, though only six feet long, two and a half wide, and two and a half high (261).

Truly very simple: but let imagination try to conceive the other side of living much in such simplicity in a land of burning heat.

Our Lord occasionally went to the houses of the rich, now of a respectable Pharisee, now of a disreputable tax-gatherer; but He moved usually among the poor. Paul sometimes was guest of a brother who could be the host of the whole church (Romans 16:23), or of one who owned a slave and was of some position (Philemon); but commonly his surroundings involved hardship. Both conditions therefore are allowable in Christians, or the apostle would not have shared the one or submitted to the other; but more blessed is he who condescends most to the condition of those whose spiritual good he seeks. The treasurer of such a city as Corinth (Romans 16:23) must from duty have lived in a style in some relation to his office, but the spirit of Christ working in him would tend ever to a reducing of his establishment to fellowship with his poorer brethren.

It would be striking were a collection made of the number of mighty men of God who have learned the lesson Groves advocated and practised. There is a real connexion between self-deprivation and spiritual unction. Wesley said that God commonly retrenches the superfluities of our souls in the same measure that we do those of our bodies. Groves' early associates, men of unusual spiritual vigour, were one with him in this matter. Mr. Parnell, with £1,200 a year, at one time lived in a house with a rent of £12 a year. J. N. Darby was habitually most abstemious, though comfortably provided. George Müller lived most simply, though sometimes gifts sent for personal use gave him a large income. Robert C. Chapman was a man of social position and means. He said that he knew at his conversion that pride would be his besetting sin. So he went to the town in which he used to drive his carriage and pair, with coachman and footman, and took a workman's house in a back street. And he added quaintly: "My pride never got over it." Let this be pondered by such as long for real deliverance from spiritual slaveries.

It has been my privilege sometimes to share the houses of the very few well-to-do friends I have felt happy to cultivate, and by their love to gain some renewal after life under other conditions. But on many long journeys in many lands, lasting up to two years and more at a time, I have commonly shared the humblest of homes and barest of fare with the poor, often for weeks and months together; and I am very sure that it is in such circumstances that my fellowship of heart with Jesus of Nazareth is sweetest, that my soul best flourishes, and that most grace and effect attends the ministry of the truth. My heart enters deeply into these further words of Groves, with which I shall leave this subject:

> How wonderful the connexion between the humiliation of the minister, as the *instrument* by which God's Spirit works, and the life of those ministered to (2 Corinthians 4:7–12). O, how little my soul knows of bearing about in the body the dying of the Lord Jesus, how then should His holy, heavenly life be manifested! What would I give to know more what it is to die daily! (243).

There is one other vital factor in Christian life, growth, and service upon which Groves had decided views, which may be considered with profit. It is:

5. PERSONAL DEPENDENCE UPON GOD.

It is to be greatly deplored how incompletely Protestants in general have ever carried out the fundamental principles of the Reformation. The two chief of these were, that the Holy Scriptures are the only standard of faith and rule of conduct, and that the believer has direct relations with God through Jesus Christ by faith. These principles were applied to the primary matter of the salvation of the individual from his doom and the setting him in a justified standing by faith. For this blessed end every mediator was swept away save Jesus, the Son of God, and every sacrifice save His redeeming death; but here virtually the application ceased. For the purpose of the corporate life of believers in the church of God, with its order and worship, and, in the matter of spreading the gospel (especially in the last one hundred and fifty years), the principles were abandoned in favour of human schemes and methods.

This failure as it regards the church will be examined in Chapter 14. Here the subject is treated as it concerns gospel witness. Perhaps the most vital objection that Groves had against the plan of societies for the spread of the gospel was that the evangelist was thereby kept, at least in large measure, from that direct dependence upon the Lord Himself which is indispensable to the richest life in his own soul and in his spiritual children. He saw clearly that thereby the worker was impoverished and the churches gathered were stunted.

In such utterly vital matters as guidance in service, and temporal support therein, he was Christ's freeman, completely dependent upon Him direct, and completely free to carry out His wishes, unfettered by restriction from others, save as he might feel it of the Lord to co-operate with them.

That these features marked the earthly service of the Son of Man does not need proving. "Mine hour is not yet come," on the one hand, and "The hour is come," on the other hand, are sentences that proclaim His immediate contact with God for restraint and for action. Such phrases would read strangely in a report by a missionary to his committee upon his carrying out or not carrying out their instructions.

The authority given by Christ to the apostles did not give them lordship over the churches (2 Corinthians 1:24), nor had elders such a right (1 Peter 5:3). Paul had no control over the movements of Apollos (1 Corinthians 16:12); the latter was free. And Paul distinctly shows that the relation between himself and a younger man such as Timothy was that of father and son, not that of master and servant: "as a child serveth a father so he served with me in furtherance of the gospel" (Philippians 2:22); Timothy was a "fellow-worker" (Romans 6:21), not a *junior* worker; his service and obedience were free, not obligatory, were those of love and reverence.

Is it not the case that other methods have been followed, partly because it is the modern westerner's way of doing things—he must organize? Partly, because workers have not faith to trust in their heavenly Father to feed and to clothe them, or in their divine Lord to guide and to use them? Partly from a reluctance to suffer privation and danger as a good soldier? And partly from a sincere desire of other loving hearts to save workers from hardship? Yet such salvation is inconceivable loss; for to be saved from the need of direct faith in God is to forfeit that inward, ever-deepening intercourse with Him which is the essential source of vitality of spirit, which gives confidence to face dark days, and courage to attack unknown positions when the Captain calls.

The modern organized method is the poorest of preparations for forward movements into the unknown, or for seasons, such as war, when communications break down. And the regularity and sufficiency of supplies removes the evangelist from the level of the infinite majority of his converts in their daily needs and trials, and induces them to become dependent on him rather than on God, so that their faith does not grow exceedingly or their love to one another abound, because they all look to the "missionary." If anyone will consider the matter narrowly he may see that the poverty of Paul completely avoided these and similar spiritual perils, and worked to exactly the opposite conditions. It was a chief element in the rapid growth of independent, permanent churches.

By the teaching of the Holy Spirit Groves had been brought down to the deepest principles of action. As his paper *Christian Devotedness* shows, a hesitancy to trust God practically he regarded as a slur upon the fatherliness of God. To this he often recurred. In 1833 he wrote:

> Much enquiry has arisen here in consequence of a sermon I preached, on the neglect of the due consideration of the fatherly character of God, one of the peculiar prerogatives of which is, that He should provide for His children as He likes; and that they shall never seek even the shadow of independence of Him, the desire for which was the first great sin of Satan. One of the sweetest proofs of our return to God as dear children is that we have learnt to rest on Him with *unlimited rest*, and do not care for those things on which the hearts of the Gentiles are set (259). The more I dwell on the first chapter of Malachi, the more I am persuaded that in ceasing to realize the fatherly character of God, we fall into all those sins of which God accuses His people: we provide for ourselves

instead of leaving our Father to provide for us; we will not in any wise serve Him for nought; we look on Him as a master who is to pay his servants their hire, rather than as a father, all whose inheritance we are to share (268).

A passage written towards the end of his life opens up another of the deeper reasons for the affairs of the child being at the disposal of the father. Out of the ripe experience of twenty-five years he wrote in 1851:

> When God's time is come, it is wonderful how difficulties remove: the high places sink and the low places rise, and the way becomes a plain. Those to whom it is given to know this is not their rest, and that, having food and raiment, they must be content, are made to feel the reason why so many of the family of God are in trial is, that, as a *state*, it most leads to dependence on God. The moment a man feels adequate to his own wants, his tendency is always to self-reliance, and in order to destroy this, the Lord comes in and breaks his pleasant vessels (469).

Both Scripture and experience having taught him the sweetness and value of this dependence directly upon God in all things, he longed that fellow-workers and fellow-believers everywhere should share it with him. He saw the vital importance of it for the native church, and he wrote thus in 1840:

> Those who know the natives will, I am sure, feel with me, that this plan of missions, whereby the native himself is thrown *on God*, is calculated to develop that *individuality of character*, the absence of which has been so deeply deplored, and the remedy for which has so seldom been sought. The native naturally loves a provision and ease, and thereby he is kept in dependence on the creature: the European, on the other hand, loves to keep the native in subjection, and himself in the place of rule. But it must be obvious to all, if the native churches be not strengthened by learning to lean on the Lord instead of man, the political changes of an hour may sweep away the present form of things, so far as it depends on Europeans, and leave not a trace behind (393).

The present universal unrest of the nations, and, as to India, its present political independence, makes this obviously practical outlook more urgent than when these words were penned. And with the object of strengthening in others the desired dependence upon God

Groves would not allow others to depend on himself, or his own heart on others. As early as 1828 he had written:

> For myself, I wish no man living to show the least regard for my opinion for any other reason than its being the same as the mind of God, and I wish myself, and all others to think, that it is at our peril we reject the poorest member of Christ's body who speaks according to that mind; it will be the same sin as rejecting Christ (47).

His testimony has been already given to his satisfaction, that those with whom he acted in the earliest years (1831) did not claim submission from him nor did he desire it from them. Similarly, in the words of his widow, we read that

> It was a peculiar feature in Mr. Groves' character that he *cheerfully* gave up his most *valued* fellow-labourers if they felt the Lord had led them to another sphere of service… He liked all with him to feel themselves the *Lord's servants,* and was careful not to obstruct their way in carrying out any new plan of labour (371).

And he expressed a real concern of his heart when he wrote:

> I find daily that men would rather suffer any measure of bondage in the things of religion than dwell in individual responsibility before God for every action, thought, and affection (364).

Nor were these sentiments limited to European brethren. He knew that the church of God, according to the mind of God, is properly an universal society, in which distinctions of race, colour, country simply do not exist. Therefore its principles and rules are of equal application to all its members everywhere. Hence he rejoiced unfeignedly when two Indian brethren, Aroolappen and Andrew, as well as an English brother, set forth in 1839 or 1840 to serve in the gospel on these principles. Of the first named, he said:

> That dear young native, by name Aroolappen, who went from us some months since, has, amidst many discouragements and many allurements, remained faithful to his purpose. He has determined to commence his labours in a populous neighbourhood, near the Pitney Hills, in the Madura district, a little south of Trichinopoly; and he has the prospect of being joined by a native brother, who is prepared to go forth to build,

with the spade in the one hand and the sword in the other—the way in which the wall will, I believe, be built in these troublous times (392). The late visit of Aroolappen to his family in Tinnevelly has led to the discussion of these principles among the immense body of labourers there; and though he has not taken up his residence among them, he is sufficiently near for them to observe both himself and the principles upon which he is acting. Indeed we would commend these early buddings of the Spirit's power—for we trust they are such—to your very fervent prayers, that our brethren may be carried on in the spirit of real humility and dependence upon God (393). I assure you we all feel that, had we seen no other fruit of our labour than these two or three brethren, acting on these principles of service, we should have said, truly our labour has not been in vain in the Lord. I think, therefore, we may consider that, under God, our residence in India has been the means of setting up this mode of ministry among the native Christians and the heathen, and our continuance will be, I trust, by the grace of God, the means of establishing and extending it (392).

Nor was this confidence disappointed. The assembly of believers that Aroolappen commenced continues to this day. Of him Mr. Neatby wrote in his *History* (72):

> …a very vigorous and extensive work, substantially on the lines of the Brethren, sprang up in the north of Tinnevelly, under the leadership of a disciple of his [Groves] named Aroolappen. This really remarkable Christian, who displayed from early days an energy of faith not unworthy of his teacher, is not claimed as a convert of Groves … Groves seems first to have met him in Tinnevelly at the end of 1833, and their close friendship remained uninterrupted for twenty years, and was then only severed by death. The present missions of the Open Brethren, not only in Tinnevelly but also in Travancore, are, as I understand, to be affiliated to Aroolappen, and through him to Groves.

How well worth while it is to expend love and labour upon one young man.

It was, of course, of the essence of the matter that such as these should have a personal working faith in God as to their temporal needs, and Groves rejoiced unfeignedly to see in these brethren such a confidence in their heavenly Father, and reliance upon His promises and power. He himself suffered hardship with the gospel and could justly encourage them to do so; he knew the faithfulness of God, and could strengthen their faith. Especially of Aroolappen he wrote with thanksgiving:

> Dear Aroolappen has declined any *form* of salary, because the people, he says, would not cease to tell him that he preached because he was hired. When he left me, I wished to settle something on him monthly, as a remuneration for his labour in translating for us, but, unlike a native, he refused any stipulated sum (392).

This reproach, "he preaches because he is hired," is exactly what is said in every land against salaried preachers. I have heard it many times in England. "He gets his living by his job, as I do by mine," has been said to me by commercial men. Such *men feel* that it ought not so to be in the realm of the spiritual and it is a very real and honest cause of stumbling to them.

In some spheres where Groves' principles are professed, European workers pay salaries to native workers, thus effectually preventing that stalwart faith and direct dependence upon God which are so indispensable, and keeping their brethren in subjection to themselves, by directing their activities. And what shall it be in the end thereof, when this outside support and direction fail? What but a sad exhibition of immaturity and inefficiency, save in the few who, by the grace of God, when flung into the water will learn to swim, though with effort and danger. And where is the consistency of an Englishman who professes it is on principle that he refuses a salary and control, inflicting both on his Indian brother or sister?

To the heart of A. N. Groves this reversion to the way of the world, and departure from the path of faith, could not but be a grief; and if he had the mind of Christ in this matter, then must the heart of Christ also share this grief. Oh, it is hard to be distrusted, hard to the heart of God even more than to the heart of man.

NOTE

The following particulars concerning J. C. Aroolappen and his work are worth recording. His grandson, when about twenty-eight years of age, was converted through Mr. A. Young of Mount Zion, Tinnevelly.

Under date 29th March, 1920, he wrote as follows to Mrs. Young:

> My grandfather, Mr. J. C. Arulappam, who was with Mr. Groves, was born at Ukkiramankottah, Tinnevelly Talq. He left Ukkiramankottah and started for mission work in his fifteenth year. He was born in the year 1810. He had been in his mission tour to Arcot, Sittoor, and other districts. From there he came down to this valley [Christianpettah, Wartrop] which was then uncivilized and unchristianized. He started work in this valley in the year 1840 and established Christianpettah and its church within two years, say in the year, 1842.[1] He died in the year 1867, March 14th. He was then 57 years old. His last word was Hebrews 13:7, etc., and 2 Timothy 4:7,8.
>
> He had congregations in all these villages shown below and had churches in those places. He made visits to those places and worked among them, with some catechists [preachers]. He had teachers for all those villages. He used to invite all those Christians for general meeting yearly, twice to Christianpettah, and had very nice meetings on those days. His catechists' names are Mr. Matthew, Mr. Mark, Mr. Simeon, and Mr. Mariyan."

The names of thirty villages follow, and the writer continues:

> Of these 30 only three were not handed over to C.M.S., or rather did not wish to go to C.M.S., Padupatti, Annikaripatti, and Christianpettah. My uncle, Mr. J. C. T. Arulappam handed them over to the C.M.S. seven or eight years after the death of the old Mr. J. C. Arulappam...
>
> There was also a boarding school at Christianpettah, and a printing office during the time of old Mr. J. C. A.

These details show how varied, zealous, and effective Aroolappen's service was, and how owned of God. That his son should have diverted so large a part of the churches from the New Testament lines on which his father had worked shows that spirituality does not run in the blood any more than when Samuel's sons walked not in his ways. It is sad, but not new. Paul's churches were being turned aside even while he was yet alive (Galatians 1:6; 2 Timothy 1:15). Of the three churches that continued on the original lines all remained faithful until 1934, when Annikaripatti was seduced through sheer

---

1. Pettah=village. He founded a village of Christians, and an assembly of the type he had learned from Mr. Groves to be Scriptural.

deception by the Roman Catholics. The other two being adjacent had merged into one assembly, and have continued faithful until now. Throughout the seventy-two years from the death of Aroolappen in 1867 the only foreign residents were a Mr. Berger of Holland for a short time only, and Mr. Young (from whom these particulars come) from 1903 to 1910, though the latter has visited the brethren at intervals. The father of the writer of the above letter was a sincere Christian and held the work together for many years.

In 1925 Mr. H. Handley Bird, well known in India for long service in the gospel, wrote of a then visit to Christianpettah as follows:

> ...the meeting continues to grow with no European control, presence or money. It is this fact, almost unique in India, that brought me down for their three days' annual meetings, and we have had a good time. There is no paid teacher among them. From the first, Arulappam firmly refused to receive payment for service in the gospel. Two trained lads are supported to teach their two primary schools; and for their support, and the repairs to buildings, the church has one yearly offering (it was yesterday), when they bring sacks (or handfuls) of grain, an egg, or a basket of eggs, vegetables, goats, fowls by the score, calves, etc., and the girls bring babies' garments, fancy bags, etc. Much is sold at once to the village merchants. It was all very quaint and Indian but was carried through with a good deal of heart exercise on the part of many of these very poor folk. My mind went back to Bezaleel and Aholiab snowed under by the devotion of Israel, just saved from the wrath at the intercession of Moses.

These facts show that the Divine principles for gospel service and church life which Groves taught to Aroolappen have been followed with success in rural India. That there are not far more instances may be attributed mainly to the fact that they have not been given a thorough trial more often than has been the case. I know by observation that they have succeeded and are succeeding among the poor, illiterate, and superstitious rural populations of other countries.

Mr. Young tells me that Aroolappen was preaching with A. N. Groves in Trichinopoly, when Brahmins reproached him for preaching for pay from the European. He translated the remark to Groves, and said from that day he would take no salary. He had done so before, having been connected with the C.M.S. It is such faith in God that is necessary if such a work of God is to be seen as he afterwards did; and that faith will not be produced so long as the native preacher and church are kept subordinate to the foreigner and dependent upon him.

An abundance of original and contemporary material having come providentially into my hands, I prepared an account of this servant of God, as announced at the end of this book.

13

The Outcome

The little one shall become a thousand. Isaiah 60:22.

When Groves and his wife left all to follow the Lamb whithersoever He might go, it was with the expectation

> ...that many may be led by this weak effort of faith in us to take steps they might not otherwise venture upon (118);

and after two years he wrote that he had from the first been convinced

> ...that the result to the church of God would be greater than our remaining quietly at home,

and that

> ...many had been led to act with more decision, and some to pursue measures which possibly might not otherwise have been undertaken (164).

By the perpetual energy of the Spirit of power the impulses thus set in motion have never subsided. Apart from that Divine energy they must have ceased, for the manner of life in question has no natural inducements to lead to it or advantages to maintain it, but much to retard and to quench it. Nothing less than a ceaseless Divine impulse could have caused to arise a ceaseless succession of men and women impelled to go from all that nature holds dear to a life that offers nothing of outward attractiveness in the way of prestige or comfort.

This consideration bears on the right estimate that should be formed of the whole movement that Groves initiated, which is known now as The Brethren. "The baptism of John—was it from heaven or of men?" was a question that nonplussed those asked, and opposite opinions have been formed upon the same point touching the Brethren.

To one able student of the movement, the Brethren have acted on but a "narrow stage"; their principle that Scripture only should rule was

> …an experiment in the hands of eminent men, [and their ideas upon the church of God were] an ecclesiastical experiment [that] must fall unregretted (*Neatby* 3, 183).

But to another unusually keen outside observer already quoted, Robert Govett, in its first days it was the mightiest movement of the Spirit of God since Pentecost.

I write from an inside point of view. I was born, born again, reared, and commenced Christian service in the innermost circle of Mr. Darby's devotees, and continued there till about my twenty-second year. And it is simply honest to thank God heartily for much that thus accrued to me. For over fifty years I have moved somewhat extensively among Open Brethren. My break with the Exclusives was upon the question of liberty to minister elsewhere than in their circle. While moving mainly among Open Brethren, I have never been wholly out of touch with God's people of other persuasions. Exercising what judgment is made possible by this three-fold contact, with both branches of Brethren and with others, I can but support Govett's estimate, though not adopting his superlative adjective. I feel myself incompetent to say which of all the workings of the Spirit through eighteen centuries may have been the mightiest; but that this movement was and is from Him I cannot question.

Every student of the Brethren movement is under the greatest obligation to Mr. Blair Neatby's *History;* but whilst his collection and survey of facts is indispensable, his opinion upon the facts may, of course, be questioned. I take this central paragraph from the dividing epoch after the great cleavage of the original movement in 1848:

> From this time our attention will be mainly focussed upon Darbyism; partly from the necessity of the case, since the Open Brethren—as those that refused to abide by Darby's decree came generally to be called—are in the proverbially happy condition of scarcely having a history; partly

because Darbyism has been by far the most powerful and typical phase of the whole movement, and Open Brethrenism is best dealt with as a species of modified Darbyism (184, 185).

Here are three statements to which I demur.

1. *That Brethren have occupied a "narrow stage."* Is this a correct description seeing that meetings of Brethren are literally universal? There can be but few regions of the earth where representatives are not found. And their influence upon the general spiritual life of the century has been incalculable. If allowable when the *History* was written in 1901, which I doubt, it may be doubly questioned today.

2 *That Open Brethren have scarcely a history.* That they have no such tumultuous history as Darbyism does not warrant the statement. John Richard Green did no small service to historical study by giving a history of the English *people*, instead of, as is common to too many histories, an account mainly of kings and their wars. An account of the river Nile were very inaccurate that dwelled mainly on its cataracts and neglected its long, placid stream that fructifies vast inhabited stretches.

3. *That Darbyism is a phase of the Brethren movement.* If this present study is accurate it shows that Darbyism was a turning from and reversal of the most vital principles of the Movement rather than a continuance of it—

(*a*) The first such principle was the reception of *all* godly persons, in disregard of every consideration but their personal faith in Christ and upright walk. While Exclusives may admit this principle in theory, they from the first cancelled it in practice, by automatically rejecting all Open Brethren for refusing Mr. Darby's principle of discipline, despite personal purity of faith and piety of practice. Mr. Neatby's statement to this effect is painfully accurate. Referring to Mr. Darby's 1848 circular from Leeds against Bethesda, Bristol, he says:

On Darby's own showing he had now receded indefinitely far from the only platform where, as he once held, "the fulness of blessing" could be found—a "meeting … framed to embrace all the children of God in the full basis of the Kingdom of the Son." No ingenuity in proving that Müller and Craik had made themselves obnoxious to the "discipline of the house of God" could get rid of the plain fact that two Christian leaders, whom all their fellow Christians were at liberty to honour "for their work's sake," were to be cut off with their whole flock from the Table of the Lord on ecclesiastical grounds. Leeds gave the lie direct to Dublin as pointedly as ever Geneva gave it to Rome; and this is equally clear whether we agree with Leeds or Dublin, or with neither (164).

(*b*) This involved the introduction of a plan of church life and discipline foreign to the original Movement, even that the assemblies collectively form a body corporate, and have an inter-assembly discipline to be enforced universally. This was a reversal of the former plan of dealing locally with each individual.

(*c*) This in turn came to involve a denial in practice, if not in theory, of the liberty of the individual to enjoy Christian co-operation outside the meetings, and thus further destroyed personal liberty, and also that manner of testimony to the real unity in Christ of all the children of God which was the original Divine purpose of the Movement.

(*d*) The belief and practice that churches should have recognized local elders was renounced, and indeed held to be unscriptural, and there was substituted the method of all the male members of an assembly meeting to discuss its affairs, and, in London at least, a central oversight meeting to rule all the assemblies in that huge area. Neither of these expedients is to be found in Scripture, nor was found at first among Brethren.

It would seem that of the more important of the principles and practice that at first characterized the Brethren Darbyism retained only the liberty of worship and ministry.

A powerful leader heads a wide revolt in a kingdom, and establishes an order of things which rejects almost all the chief features of the old order. How could it be just to describe the after history of the revolters as the history of the original and still continuing kingdom? Even were it so that thereafter the kingdom remained smaller than the new power, and that it bore on its institutions traces of the influence of the revolution; and were it, moreover, the case that henceforth it should be "in the proverbially happy condition of scarcely having a history," whilst the revolted area became notorious for recurring strife and bloodshed, yet could no one be justified in regarding them as one empire and the original kingdom as a modified form of the revolt.

The true treatment of such a situation would be to consider to what extent in the course of time the old kingdom recovered from the shock, maintained its position, laws, and type of life, recovered vitality, extended its borders, and perchance had the joy to receive back former subjects and territory. I am persuaded that if these tests be applied to the history of Brethren it would be seen that it is the Open Brethren meetings that are entitled to regard themselves as the continuation of the original movement. Testimonies to this from some who knew the first days are in the Appendix.

Let us examine the features above indicated.

I *AND* 2.

By the mercy of God all sections known as Brethren have been preserved from David's folly of compiling statistics. No figures are available. It was doubtless true that in 1848 Mr. Darby carried a majority of the meetings with him. Yet the smaller number held on their way, influenced in measure by his forceful, assertive teachings and actions, but preserving their independence of life and practice. They recovered from the shock of the disruption forced upon them, and showed ere long that it was they who had inherited in goodly measure the burning zeal of Groves to reach with the good news the unreached millions, and to establish among them assemblies of believers on the principles he had taught. They became, and are to-day, a missionary force second to none in vigour and diffusion. There are at this day literally many thousands of such churches in almost all lands, among almost all races. And is it not to their credit, rather than reproach, that the work goes on so unostentatiously that they seem to be "without a history?" In truth the history of heroism, self-denial, and answering Divine unction and working, would be hard to equal were it, could it be, told. To this missionary activity Mr. Neatby did, indeed, bear ungrudging testimony, but he seems to have missed its bearing on the larger issue here discussed.

As has been said, figures happily cannot be given, but I very much doubt whether the whole number of Exclusives, of all parties, in all lands, equals those of this universal extension God has graciously granted to the Open assemblies.

And it may be worth remarking that with many observers, one reason, generally unrecognized, for a mistaken estimate of this situation, is the Englishman's habit of thinking of the English-speaking world as almost the whole earth. Exclusivism has not reached far outside this partial world; save in Germany, Switzerland and Egypt chiefly; Open Brethren activities are worldwide, which must be taken into account in a just estimate of the power and influence God has exerted on the lines of the original movement.

3. DARBYISM AND THE ORIGINAL PRINCIPLES.

(*a*) As to the reception of all believers. It is the case that in some areas this is more or less restricted by an insistence that believers must leave a denomination or mission before being received, or occasionally there may be an insistence upon baptism by immersion before reception. But this is by no means general, or wide enough to characterize the Open Brethren as a whole. I have tested the point in a good many places where I was not known, and have never been refused a place at the Lord's table. Nor have even those brethren whose principles of reception are thus narrow ever required my acceptance of their practice as a condition of receiving me. As a general fact the first principle of reception is maintained.

(*b*) The principle of administrative and disciplinary action is that each assembly is responsible directly to the Lord, and is not necessarily bound by the acts of another assembly. Of course, in practice the act of one assembly in discipline would be respected by another assembly, but as a matter of caution rather than of obligation. Nor have I ever known a brother to be refused fellowship because of a liberal relationship with

Christians in other spheres, or because of even marked differences in the interpretation of Scripture upon such topics as prophecy, the public ministry of women, or the like. Where objection might be made to diverse views being taught publicly, I believe no suggestion that the person should be debarred the Table of the Lord would be made. At least, I have never heard of it being done.

(c)   It is in the lack of recognized eldership that Mr. Darby's views have mostly influenced the church life of Open Brethren. Yet in reality there are a considerable number of assemblies where such leaders are found, and many more where they are virtually, though not formally, known.

The general situation appears to be that the original principles survived, that those holding them kept their feet amidst the storms, addressed themselves strenuously to the evangelization of the lost, and have been very extensively prospered of God, in His great grace. And in the course of years it has been their joy to welcome many who followed, or were brought up in, Exclusive principles. And, indeed, I am glad to be assured that at least one whole body, still known as Exclusives, have, of later years, returned in practice to the first principle of reception, and will receive to the Table an Open Brother known to be godly even as they will such a member of the Church of England, and without requiring either to dissever himself. And I have myself, though well known as a public advocate of Open principles, been welcomed to the Lord's Supper by prominent men in other circles of Exclusives, out of England. If this change of spirit and attitude makes progress it will be greatly to the joy of the heart of the Lord who died that all His people might be one.

Of the present day dangers attacking Open Brethren I have written on previous occasions, and shall say somewhat in the following chapter. But it is due to the glory of God, and for encouraging others to follow the teachings of the Word that Groves rediscovered, as well as his life of self-sacrifice, to indicate and to emphasize what a marvellous harvest, in extent and richness, has grown from the seeds of truth he sowed and the influence his character and toils exerted.

In his measure he was a grain of wheat that fell into the ground and died, and by dying yielded much fruit. Would God that this spirit might master fully every Christian. What an untold harvest would then ripen for the heavenly garner.

Finally, let it be said that the success or failure of the Brethren in the carrying out of these principles is not the major issue. Suppose that their failure had been more complete than any suggest, the vital question would remain—Are these principles the mind of the Lord for His church? Are they revealed as such in His Word? If they are, then, though all before us had failed, it abides our duty and blessedness to attempt to walk by them. The duty is inevadable. And it is an interesting and happy fact that today, as a century ago, simple godly souls are taught to discern these truths in the New Testament and to practise them, without knowing that others before them had so done. A few years ago I came upon such a group in a Continental capital, and they are to be found in widely sundered regions. If these principles are not in the New Testament how do honest hearts thus find them there? But as they are in the Word, how is the obligation to walk by them avoided by the majority who are called by the Name? The next chapter will show.

14

Development, Expediency, Tradition

Why do thy disciples transgress the tradition of the elders? Matthew 15:2.

And he answered and said unto them, why do ye also transgress the commandment of God because of your tradition? Matthew 15:3.

Ye have made void the word of God because of your tradition. Matthew 15:6.

Ye leave the commandment of God, and hold fast the tradition of men. Mark 7:8.

Full well do ye reject the commandment of God, that ye may keep your tradition... Mark 7:9.

Making void the word of God by your tradition, which ye have delivered. Mark 7:13.

Idolatry, the worship and service of the creature rather than the Creator, was instituted in Babylon soon after the flood. With the dispersion of the peoples it spread thence to all lands (Jeremiah 51:7; Revelation 17:4), and all systems of idolatry show its distinctive features. The student may pursue this subject in detail in Alexander Hislop's *The Two Babylons*, the first six chapters.

With the changes of climate, circumstances, and consequent racial characteristics each people developed this primal false religion to suit its peculiar conditions. This took place under demon inspiration and priestly direction; the primary idea being to pervert the races to the worship of Satan and his rebel angels, and the chief secondary principle being to rivet on the masses the fetters of priestcraft and enslave them, to the aggrandizement of the priestly order. Thus the process of "development" entered.

To serve the ends in view every device and deception that cunning craftiness could invent was adopted. Demons and priests literally lay in wait to deceive, and no device was too deceitful or despicable. 2 Corinthians 11:3 is illuminating. The words *exapatao*, to deceive thoroughly, *panourgia*, every kind of work, and the former word in 1 Timothy 2:14, mean in idiomatic English that Satan stops at nothing, but stoops to anything, thoroughly to hoodwink mankind. Whatever seemed likely to serve the purpose was used. The end was held to justify the means. This was expediency facilitating development, the adaptation of religion to the changing times and conditions.

If any suspicion or rebellion may have arisen in any minds as to these priestly manoeuvres it soon subsided. The lusts of fallen men, both sensual and aesthetic and philosophical, were all gratified in the scheme; the system of religion became firmly established and the national habit, till at last scarce a voice questioned its propriety or its rights. And in any heathen land today Babylonianism is still evident, still dominant, and if the infinite majority of its slaves be asked why they do this or that they simply reply, "Our fathers have always done it!" Thus the expedient became the traditional.

Development, expediency, tradition, mother, daughter, granddaughter, this is the triune goddess that has deluded, degraded, enslaved mankind. But her rise and supremacy involved inevitably the rejection of that clear light as to the true God that all men possessed after the flood, to the fulness and sufficiency of which illumination the utterances of five men found in the book of Job bear ample witness. This process of deliberate rejection of the Creator is outlined in the first chapter of Romans.

When God called Israel to be His peculiar portion among the idolatrous nations He flooded them individually and nationally with the light which the peoples had rejected, and taught them how to walk by that light in the detailed relationships of daily life. He gave them the ten thousand precepts of His good law, which if a man do, he shall live by them. They had the added advantage over earlier times that God's Word was written down, thus giving them a permanent record to which to refer, and the means of checking, detecting, and rejecting those teachings of demons by which other races were deceived.

At first Israel succumbed to the gross side of things and reverted to outward idolatries, with the sensualities that always accompany. But the severe national chastisement in Babylon, at the hands of idolaters at their headquarters, cured them nationally of this outward apostasy, and they returned, as to their guiding principle, to the observance of the law of God through Moses.

When their own true and living God visited them personally, as Jesus of Nazareth, He found them, indeed, engaged in the prescribed outward forms of His worship, but perceived that in heart they had really lapsed to the worship of that same triune goddess that ruled the rest of mankind. His law had directed that a man should dedicate unto God a portion of his income, and out of the rest he should, among other things, honour his father and his mother, by caring for them in temporal necessities. But in the interests of the greedy priesthood, the first precept had been "developed," and made to mean that a man was free to devote to the temple all that portion of his goods by which his parents might have benefited. The higher dedication, as it was deemed to be, was held to make void the lower, for, to be sure, the greater includes the less. It was a device to enrich the priest-ruled coffers; it was "development" aided by an "expedient" at the direction of the leaders.

If any consciences doubted and protested they did not prevail. In the course of time it became an established custom, a tradition of the elders, and only one among plenty of such expedients: "many such like things ye do." Development, expediency, tradition dominated. But here also wholly at the expense of making void the Word of God.

The outward form and aspect of the churches of the apostolic age bore no resemblance to those of the mighty Confederation, the foundations of which were being laid quietly in the second and third centuries, and the gorgeous superstructure of which was commenced in the time of Constantine, and became the "Holy Catholic Church." The former was a humble, pure-minded virgin espoused to Christ (2 Corinthians 11:2); the latter was (and is) a splendid, brazen-faced harlot (Revelation 17).

The agency that effected the change is shown in the third verse of the former passage: "I fear, lest by any means, as the serpent beguiled Eve in his craftiness, your thoughts should be corrupted from the simplicity and the purity that is toward Christ." The virgin's thoughts were led to dwell upon, and then to dote upon, another lover, a beguiler, the world and its god. It was the identical power that perverted the world after the flood.

The processes of the outward changes resulting from this inward depravity may be studied in the Bampton and Hibbert Lectures of Dr. Edwin Hatch, Reader in Ecclesiastical History, in the University of Oxford, a quite unimpeachable witness. In the former (*The Organization of the Early Christian Churches*) he shows that the outer form of that Catholic Church was taken over from the pagan Roman Empire; and in the latter (*The Influence of Greek Ideas and Philosophy upon the Christian Churches*) that its most powerful inward conceptions were borrowed from pagan philosophy. Or see Bryce's *The Holy Roman Empire*, 10–13.

If it be asked how, then, does this vast ecclesiastical corporation seek to justify its claim to be the Christian church, its answer in all centuries is this same plea of "development." After elaborating his historic facts to show how dissimilar the Catholic Church system is to the original apostolic churches, Dr. Hatch himself stultifies the moral effect of his demonstration by falling back on the notion that no doubt all worked out as Providence intended. So Providence intended the virgin to develop into the harlot, and Itself superintended the degradation! In the fifteenth century a Papal representative explained that as the temple followed the tabernacle, and was much more ornate, so the beauty and glory of the church in his time had followed its apostolic meanness! Whoever would see this subtle perversion fully employed may do so in Cardinal Newman's jesuitical book on the Development of Doctrine. This reasoning it was that led him to Rome.

All this profound and complete change by "development" was, of course, for the same end as in paganism and Judaism, the imposing of the yoke of priestcraft upon the masses. And for this purpose every kind of expedient was again adopted.

Ere the last apostle was gone Diotrephes, coveting pre-eminence, found the apostolic rule of the equal right of every believer to a place in the Christian circle to be in the way of his ambition to govern. He therefore found it expedient to shut out some, and restricted the circle to whom he pleased (3 John 9, 10).

Others like him followed; the supremacy of the "bishop" was asserted and pressed; the inferiority of the unofficial part of the community was declared, with their consequent need of such supervision by superiors. Federation was introduced, organization multiplied, rules and regulations were imposed and enforced; and in due time little was left that resembled apostolic days. Preachers were paid salaries by the higher authorities, and were by them located to places, without liberty to move, save by permission. All these, and similar disastrous changes, were introduced by bishops and councils as expedients to serve episcopal supremacy.

At last this great system of churches was sufficiently strong for the State to deem it expedient and politic to make terms with it; whereupon Constantine offered to appoint it the official religion, and the bishops deemed it expedient to embrace gladly so favourable a proposal. In due time, by the adoption of other skilful expedients and manoeuvres, the chief bishop, he of Rome, was able to assert himself as no longer the ally of the State, but the Lord and Master of all States.

In due time these expedients became the permanent practice, the tradition of the church, and to justify them appeal is made to tradition. The Roman branch of that great corporation finds tradition particularly useful, and boldly claims that the hierarchy is the depository of an unwritten apostolic tradition which warrants these changes; which means that, while by their labours, sufferings, and writings the apostles changed pagan harlots into Christian virgins, by their oral tradition they provided means for changing back the virgin into the harlot! And if today the average Romanist be asked why he observes this and that religious custom he will answer that "the Church" has always so done. Similarly, as we have read from Mr. Groves, the Armenian Church people were demanding concerning himself, and the replacing in his school in Bagdad of church prayers by the New Testament:

> Who are these people? Are they wiser than our bishops and ancient fathers, that we should reject what they introduced? (93).

In his personal narrative *With Christ in Soviet Russia* (185), Mr. V. P. Martzinkovski shows the same feature in the Greek Orthodox Church. Discussing baptism with him a bishop admitted that the New Testament demands personal faith before baptism: "Yes, you are correct" he admitted. "But here's where you make a mistake: you don't take into consideration the fact that the Church possesses the fulness of the Spirit, and that it later on changed this order, in accordance with the demands of the times, and began to demand baptism first and then faith." The proper reply was given:

> But your Lordship, the Church is subject unto Christ (Ephesians 5:24). Is it possible therefore that it has a right to change anything governed by Christ's commandment?

And later the ecclesiastic illustrated that their hold upon the masses is their real guiding aim by saying: "If we abolished the baptism of infants, the people would forsake us."

It was thus in a conversation I had with a friendly Roman Catholic priest: I quoted Scripture; he always replied, "Our Church teaches so and so." In this matter Rome is consistent. Knowing that many of her characteristic features cannot be justified by the Scriptures, she ranks tradition above Scripture. Her confession of faith includes these declarations:

"I most steadfastly admit and embrace apostolical and ecclesiastical traditions, and all other observances and constitutions of the same church"; and then, with a noteworthy weakening of the terms used, there follows: "I also admit the Holy Scriptures"; which, however, is immediately limited by the words, "according to that sense which our Holy Mother the Church has held, and does hold, to which it belongs to judge of the true sense and interpretation of the Scriptures"; and finally, the admission of the Scriptures is stultified by the clause, "neither will I take and interpret them otherwise than according to the unanimous consent of the fathers." In his *Fifty Years in the Church of Rome,* Chiniquy devotes a whole chapter (XVI) to this last clause, to which he had sworn allegiance as a priest. He enlarges upon the fact that the fathers are unanimous upon practically no point of theology or church practice, so that in result neither Roman priests nor people can interpret Scripture at all, and therefore seldom concern themselves with the Book, but rely on tradition.

But expediency leads to this elsewhere than in the Roman system. Addressing the Pilgrim Fathers in 1620, less than a century after the Reformation, John Robinson, the great Puritan, said:

> I cannot sufficiently bewail the condition of the Reformed churches, who are come to a period [= a full stop] in religion, and will go at present no further than the instruments of their reformation. The Lutherans cannot be drawn to go beyond what Luther saw; whatever part of His will our good God has revealed to Calvin, they will rather die than embrace it. And the Calvinists, you see, stick fast where they were left by that great man of God, who yet saw not all things. This is a misery much to be lamented,

The great Reformers had surrendered the principle of carrying out the Word of God to follow what seemed to them best suited to the times; they crystallized their beliefs into creeds (a human expedient for perpetuating them, instead of relying upon the divine vitality of truth), and their ecclesiastical views into rubrics and regulations, another expedient for making them enforceable and their followers "most steadfastly embrace" these deposits as firmly as the Romanist his oral tradition. Thus the Word of God is virtually deprived of supremacy, and in matters ecclesiastical is nullified almost as often by Protestant tradition as by Roman.

The Church of England exhibits this. By Article VI it gives to the Word of God its true place as the sole source of the knowledge of how to be saved; but by Article XX it denies to the Scriptures their true place as the sole authority in church life and order, by declaring that "the Church hath power to decree rites and ceremonies." In practice, in that communion, the record of what the Church has hitherto ordained, as recorded in the Book of Common Prayer, is the fountain of authority for the law-abiding and the battle-ground of the lawless. In the debates on the Revised Prayer Book it was startling how very few speakers and writers paid any regard to the Word of God, or even mentioned it. And it is a persistent effort of the "Catholic" section to set up the testimony of the fathers of the first few centuries as the court of appeal, which is much the same as the Roman position, only that Rome lays stress on an alleged oral—that is, unwritten—apostolic and patristic tradition.

The Church of England does indeed make the reservation that nothing may be ordained which shall be contrary to Scripture. This is the position of the many who argue that this or that is not *un*scriptural, and therefore is allowable. One shrinks from this. It makes a big gap in the hedge. It is far safer to be limited by positive Scriptural warrant than to claim latitude for what is not plainly forbidden. On that line a good Scriptural case could be made out for allowing polygamy, slavery, and the Christian slaughtering his fellows in war, for none of these is positively prohibited.

The Nonconformist bodies at first went to Scripture alone as ground for seceding from the Church of England, but shortly they, too, formulated creeds and constitutions, rules and regulations; and it is by these, much more than by the Word, their descendants settle questions and are fettered.

In large measure the same feature obtains with missionary societies. Their constitution and rules prevent the individual member from unrestricted appeal to, and obedience to, the Word of God. The conceptions and directions of men, the founders or present directors of the society, must carry the day in practice. Hence individuals who feel bound to follow the Word alone find they must leave their society.

In all of these cases, to a greater or lesser degree, that obtains which Christ rebuked, even that the Word of God is made of none effect by men's traditions; and every tradition of what men, even the best of men, have thought and ordered is essentially an expedient, a device for serving this or that end. As A. N. Groves so acutely discerned: "The struggle now is between the Word and tradition. It ever has been, it ever was among the Jews, and is among the Gentiles" (385). Oh, that all beloved brethren would declare resolutely with him, and would go forth to practise it, "We take our stand upon the Word," giving heed to his further words, "and in proportion to our practical inconsistency with it will our testimony be weakened." Their practice might not reach perfection, but their principle would be perfect; and in the raging storms which the faithful must yet face they will find a rock beneath their feet, a perpetual light upon the path, and a preserving peace in the heart.

A. N. Groves is not quoted to set up him, or others of his time and circle, as any authority by which we are bound. That would be to follow yet another tradition. He is quoted because hitherto it has been believed among Brethren that his principle as to the *solitary* authority of Scripture is the principle which Scripture itself lays down as to itself. I do not quote him because he was right, though I am sure he was; but so that each may be compelled to decide whether he was right, and whether he himself will adopt the same principle.

Tradition is an expedient of the lawless heart of man (which is native to us each) to enable it to follow the plan it approves, instead of the will of God, which it ever finds exacting. The only possible escape from this rebellion lies in entire submission of heart and ways to what God has written in His Word. Eternally true are Luther's words to Erasmus (*Bondage of the Will*, 52, 53):

> The Word of God and the traditions of men are opposed to each other with an implacable discord, no other than that with which God and Satan oppose each other; and the one undoes the works and subverts the dogmas of the other, like two kings laying waste each other's kingdom.

Thus the history of nineteen Christian centuries assures us whither this road of expediency leads, and shows that of all devices for corrupting the church of God none has been equal to this in the service of Satan. It also shows distinctly that the most terrible of historic features, religious persecution in the name of Christ, whether by Roman, Greek, or Protestant churches, has been, as it still is, mainly the attempt of expediency to crush out the appeal to the Word of God, an attempt as the Word shows, to be made in the future yet more fiercely and universally than ever in the past (Revelation 17:6; Luke 21:12). In the last analysis, and in the present moral application of it (though by no means excluding a literal meaning, present and future), the urgent cry: "Come forth, My people out of the midst of Babylon," means forsake expediency, for that is the most essential, permanent characteristic of mystic Babylon.

Another interesting feature may be noticed here. In the book of Revelation the harlot Babylon of Chapter 17 has been pictured earlier by the name Jezebel (chap. 2:20). Jezebel, the queen of Israel (1 Kings 16:31; chapt. 21), was a fearfully typical representative of the Babylonish religion and its effects. It is to be observed that historically "Jezebel" became so vast and powerful that she filled the whole horizon, and the true church of God, driven oft-times by her to the dens and caves of the mountains, seemed quite insignificant, even as Elijah and the hidden remnant seemed in the days that Jezebel ruled Israel. And this is how most church histories treat the Middle Ages. The doings of "Jezebel" occupy most space in those histories. But "Jezebel" is not the church in Thyatira; Christendom is not Christianity. From the point of view of God and His Word, "Jezebel" is only in the church, not the church, and is one day to be destroyed out of it (Revelation 2:22,23). Her history of cruelties and harlotries is not the history of the Church of God. God's viewpoint has been adopted most accurately in Mr. E. H. Broadbent's fascinating study in church history mentioned, *The Pilgrim Church*, in which the history of the true church is traced through this whole age, and the effects upon her of "Jezebel's" tyranny and depravity are shown.

Now it was in connexion with developments beginning among Brethren that Groves, as early as 1838, that is, within ten years of the commencement of such meetings, declared the issue to be between the Word of God and tradition. What did he mean? What did he see?

He was dealing with the assertions, then first appearing, that the church of God is in an apostate and ruined state, one that it is not possible to restore, and that in consequence the original method of government and order in a Christian assembly cannot be followed, but that, as a result, other ways of securing order must be adopted.

Very plainly this was simply an application of the doctrine of *Development:* the times and conditions have changed; the original practice is impossible. What then can be done? Clearly only what seems most *expedient* under the altered circumstances. And that which was thus determined by the weight and prestige of one or two great leaders became the established practice, and for a hundred years has become *tradition.* And the practical effect was, and is, to restrict authority to a few (more or less) powerful personalities; and, as has been mentioned, in one circle where tradition has thus ruled there is a dangerous approximation towards a priesthood.

One of these expedients was the theory that all the assemblies in some given civic area form one church and should be ruled by a central oversight. The beginning of this can be traced to the very year in which Groves wrote as above. On October 6th, 1838, G. V. Wigram wrote thus to J. N. Darby:

> There is a matter exercising the minds of some of us at this present time in which you may be (and in some sense certainly are) concerned. The question I refer to is, *How are meetings for communion of saints in these parts to be regulated?* Would it be for the glory of the Lord and the increase of testimony to have *one central meeting,* the common responsibility of all within reach, and *as many meetings subordinate* to it as grace might vouchsafe? or to hold it to be better to allow *the meetings to grow up as they may without connexion and dependent upon the energy of individuals only . . . ? (Neatby,* 60).

Thus the issue was distinctly faced between the apostolic plan of each assembly being directly dependent upon the Head of the church or a grouping of assemblies under a human central control. It is as noticeable as regrettable that the writer makes no appeal to Scripture to settle this truly momentous issue. It is simply a question of which course will be the "better." That is to say, the Word of God ceased to be the only authority and expediency was given a hearing. Alas, alas, that expediency carried the day. Upon this important issue the Word of God was made void and tradition has ruled. Thus here again development, expediency, and tradition perverted what God had at the time commenced.

There is reason for thinking that this theory as to the gatherings in a great city originated in early days, and was maintained for increasing the authority of the metropolitan bishops; and that out of it developed the obnoxious practice of the reservation of the sacramental elements for use away from the congregation (See Hatch, *Organization*, 196).

The unspirituality, the mechanical nature of the scheme is easily seen. Woolwich and Islington are some eight miles distant, on opposite sides of the Thames; Woolwich and Plumstead adjoin; but because the two former happened to be in the civil administrative area called London, the believers in those assemblies formed one church, whereas because Plumstead happened (at least formerly) to be just outside that arbitrary area the saints there were not of that church and were not directly subject to the decrees of the Central Oversight. And, of course, with every change in the civic area outside assemblies automatically become part of that church and subordinate to the Oversight, as immediately as the district incorporated becomes part of London and subject to the London County Council.

Here, as surely as in other religious circles, practical surrender of the authority of Scripture, and the following of expediency, proved disastrous. For in so vast a city but a few could attend such a meeting, and control passed into a few hands; and of these, a still smaller number of earnest, determined men were the real masters of all the London meetings. And since London is the centre of the English-speaking world, decisions reached there carried almost universal authority, and this Central Oversight became a ready instrument for worldwide despotism and worldwide division. It was also small wonder, human nature being what it is, that it has not been unknown for keen competition to arise as to what party should gain most influence on that Oversight, producing some regrettable incidents.

For many years my beloved father was lessee of the room where this Central Oversight met. In 1921 we spoke together of its practical working. He said: "Since I have been shut away in this room the past twelve months with my Bible, I have seen that the whole thing was a mistake." I suggested that the plan must have been attended with decided inconveniences. How, for example, could the brethren at Finsbury Park, on the far north, form a right judgment as to a case of discipline at Greenwich, miles away on the south? He replied: "Exactly; and what I have come to see is that the brethren at Finsbury Park could not 'put away from among themselves' a person who never had been amongst them."

How obvious! Why then did so very many acute and sincere minds fail to discern this at the beginning? Why, indeed, if it were not that the appeal to expediency at once operates to blind the mind as to Scripture. The effect of this was seen distinctly in 1860 when one of the meetings in London excommunicated a brother. Another meeting enquired, "What sin or sins, according to Scripture, of an excommunicable character" the brother had committed? The answer was terribly significant of the surrender of the primary principle of Brethren, that only the Word of God must rule. It was, that the sins were "of a character not needing to be determined by Scripture" (*Neatby*, 224). Here again is the false position as to Holy Scripture to which development, expediency, and tradition always lead.

Was not this deceptive doctrine of development Satan's wile for that thorough hoodwinking of our first mother Eve? The suggestion was: By a certain act you can *develop* into something more splendid than you are: you shall become as the *elohim* (angels), who are greater than you in power and glory. Therefore it is *expedient* that you take that step! And this unholy ambition and conduct has been the *tradition* of her seed ever since, inducing that "vain manner of life handed down from [=tradition of] your fathers," to redeem us from which the Lamb of God shed His precious blood (1 Peter 1:18,19). Shall then the redeemed return to live by this principle? In Eden, and for evermore, the course can be followed only in disregard of God's plain command.

—oOo—

But I must be as faithful with my beloved Open brethren, who graciously grant me fellowship, as with my beloved Exclusive brethren, who conscientiously refuse me it.

It were strangely unlike our subtle foe if he failed to beset Open brethren with this wile which has so well served his fell designs from Eden and onward.

The number of features, and their nature, found today among Open brethren which are not apostolic is portentous.

As to church order, Darby's theory that elders cannot now be formally recognized carried the day, and few Exclusive or Open assemblies have scriptural government, which is lamentable.

In some large centres a committee of active brethren from Open assemblies in the area meets to discuss common matters and activities. A central committee may easily stiffen into a Central Oversight. In one case this name has been employed, showing that the danger is real and present.

As to ministry, save at the Table on Sunday morning little ministry is today left to the Holy Spirit to provide, for either ordinary or special gatherings. Saints come together looking to man, not the Lord, and if some attractive speaker be not present, little is expected, and therefore little is received. Especially in large centres is this true, for such commonly lead the way in declension. Both assemblies and preachers are usually booked far ahead, a year being quite common. This is purely mechanical, void of Divine guidance, and is a cause of spiritual poverty.

The leading brother in an assembly was speaking of the poor state of that church. I remarked: It looks as if you need the Lord to send you a Timothy or a Titus to stay among you a few months and set in order what is wanting. He agreed that this would be a great help. Yes, I said, and if the Lord were to send you such an one next week, what could you do with him, for I suppose all your meetings are arranged for six months ahead? And so it was.

Aiding this deterioration are various "Classes" of different names, all training the young in programmed meetings, instead of emphasizing the lordship of Christ in His House and the living ministry and direct control of the Spirit.

In gospel service the centralizing process is at work by there being central organizations to represent the widespread activities of workers from these Islands, with its lists of these workers and its central fund for aiding them. In this connexion there are also *pro forma* "missions"; Christian Missions to Many Lands, The Godavari Delta Mission, The Garanganze Evangelical Mission.

Then there are various property trusts, for holding assembly and other premises in different lands, which acquire with ownership the right, and indeed the legal duty, to watch the actions of the assemblies, their tenants.

These and similar changes I discussed at length in 1925 in my book *Departure*, and I shall not here repeat this discussion in detail. That book helped many to discern the drift and to follow the Scriptures. But those most responsible for the changes were unaffected and have pursued their course with resolution. Thus, between that year and 1935, one of the property trusts doubled the number of the halls it owns in England, advancing from thirty-one to sixty-one in ten years. Again, on the agenda for the meeting of elder brethren held at Central Hall, London, October, 1935, the fifth item read: "The importance that mission properties be vested as far as possible in The Stewards Company Limited, or a suitable substitute." And the determination to maintain a central fund, as contrasted with the New Testament way of gifts being sent direct, was shown in 1933, when many brethren, not responsible for the fund, signed a printed circular urging that more gifts be sent to it.

These features have persisted and it may again become a duty to discuss them openly, but in this place some general features only will be indicated.

1. Lists of workers, central funds, general property trusts, and the like are *not of faith*. They are the very arrangements that men of no faith at all in God can and do work efficiently, for they demand for their success no more than good human judgment and worldly prudence.

In the early days of Brethren, faith was a powerful characteristic. Men of learning and ability ceased to rely on their own gifts and arrangements for ministry, and came together to trust the Holy Spirit for ministry. Men of means devoted fortunes to the work of God and trusted Him to meet their daily needs. This was finely apostolic.

One of these kept open house for the people of God, looking to

Him to send supplies. Sweet, and encouraging to the faith of many, were the experiences of His love and care. Now the method is Holiday Homes run by Limited Companies, firstly as a business venture, and the faith element—well, not prominent.

This waning of vital working faith is evidenced on a large scale. In another land, at the first pressure from the State, a vast community of Brethren formed themselves into a union, the essential rule of which is that nothing shall be tolerated therein contrary to the will of the government. No one pretends that such a union is according to the New Testament; indeed it involves at least twelve features contrary thereto; and it is manifest that to make the will of man the test of what shall be done or taught in the assemblies of God is to surrender unto Caesar that which is God's. Our nonconformist forefathers freely shed their blood rather than concede this right to rulers. It is the negation of religious freedom.

I understand that the workers from the British Isles in a province in the Far East have lately yielded similarly to official pressure. The churches of a land in S.E. Europe have lately (1947) done the same.

Or again, this want of faith is seen in methods often taken for equipping a worker leaving for abroad. Formerly it was an individual matter, and the worker had to wait much on his divine Master, and by so waiting gained faith, patience, and at last assurance that his way had been opened by God. Quite often today elder brethren virtually decide whether he shall go, send out a begging letter, and the matter is arranged with much less real faith and deep testings of heart in the worker himself.

Or yet again, begging letters are widely circulated by post appealing for funds to build a hall here or there, or for some other object. If there were no list of meetings this could not well happen.

So general are these things that in 1929 a well-known magazine had an editorial headed "Are We Leaving Faith Lines?" The next year a further article appeared to the same effect, and in 1931 a third discussion emphasized the same question.

Christians who have never seen in the New Testament the line of direct faith in God as to service, may go on in such ways, walking with a good conscience by what light they have, and will be owned of

God; but the seriousness arises, when, as recently, a missionary who has known the path of faith for long years fails in faith, and gets elder brethren to issue an appeal on his behalf; or when a leader in missionary activities in this land admits, as one did to me, that the path of faith is no doubt the better way, but yet he lends active encouragement to the spiritually poorer method, which can only help into gospel work men not spiritually equipped for it. For "whatsoever is not of faith is sin"; it is impossible without it to be well-pleasing to God; and indeed it were better for them not to have known the way of faith than, after knowing it to turn back from the holy commandment delivered unto us.

2. A second vital feature is that such measures and methods are *not according to Scripture.* No one pleads the Word of God as ground for them. It is in consequence of this that they are not of faith, for faith must have God's warrant for a course. It comes by hearing His Word. Men may make up their mind to get certain money for certain ends, but they cannot have faith that the Bank of England will supply it unless they hold the word of the Bank to that effect. They may or may not have resources enough for their scheme, but the resources of the Bank are not behind them if they have not its promises. God is not behind what His Word does not sanction, and painful experience will yet prove this, indeed is now proving it in spiritual weakness and poverty.

Thus the Word of God is treated as neither final, binding, nor sufficient. A present instance of this is as follows. A wealthy man left a large sum in trust for the furtherance of evangelistic work in his county. I happened to be near and attended, as an interested observer, a meeting of brethren from all over the county to arrange for the use of the tents and Bible carriages for the approaching summer. It was there decided which evangelists should be secured, if free, where the tent should be located, and so forth.

An able and worthy brother was asked after the meeting where he thought such a gathering as had just been held could be fitted into the Acts of the Apostles to arrange for the gospel labours of Paul and Barnabas, Timothy and Titus? He replied at once that of course it could not be done. Thus, without intention and without reflection, the New Testament as guide is superseded, the principle of individual responsibility to the Lord alone for service is set aside, and a tendency to centralize and to control is set in motion. God in grace will bless the preaching of His message, but this present good will not avoid the ultimate and injurious effects of following our own ways instead of the ways in which Christ, and the apostles He personally trained, did His work.

Here I do no more than remark upon the dangers to the faith and freedom of the evangelist who works under a trust with a fund to which he can look for temporal support. In this case the trustees are not spending the monies as steadily as possible in increased gospel efforts, but have invested much of the capital and use the income. Thus again faith as to the future is set aside, and with it the plain instructions given by the Lord to His first evangelists that treasure is *not* to be laid up on earth.

It is sorrowful thus to see faith waning and the Word of God virtually abandoned as rule and guide. The danger to the soul is alarming. When two brethren were pressed in 1928 that central property trusts are not apostolic, they replied: "If they [workers and others abroad] find it of service in the spread of the gospel, it seems to us mere trifling to quarrel with it because there was no such thing in apostolic days." Thus what any man deems expedient is sufficient warrant, and the very appeal to apostolic precedent, which once for Brethren settled all questions, has for these writers sunk to "mere trifling." And in 1939 a well-known leader wrote to me that these questions here in view are "comparative trivialities."

But waning of faith and practical surrender of the Scriptures are NOT trivialities: rather are they sure precursors of the day when over our feverish activities God will write ICHABOD, the glory is departed; they are solemn assurance that whatever is not built upon the rock of obedience to His words will collapse into ruins when His judgments burst as a tempest.

The comparatively secure and orderly Victorian era will not be seen again in our days. General sifting and testing has set in for the people of God. More and more widely are governments enforcing restrictions against real spiritual activities. Movement of money too is less and less free, making dependence upon supplies from afar ever more precarious. A great war breaks down human schemes and dependence. The call is thus urgent for a greater, more energetic, and direct trust in God, yet all too widely faith is weaker, not stronger. Every measure, every method that weakens it is so far from being a triviality that it prepares for ultimate collapse and disaster.

At the last it will be found that only men of apostolic faith following apostolic methods will hold on their way in the work of the gospel. Hard times suit faith and faith suits them. And all these so kindly intended endeavours to make the path easy, in short to intervene between the servant and his Master, are deeply injurious, however well meant. It is sheer necessity that the Lord shall have the *real* control of His agents and affairs; and this will work out today, as ever before, in individualism in service as against collectivism, both in the worker and in his relations with those who co-operate with him by prayer or by gifts.

The Lord's methods of life and service were designed in troubled times and for such times. They are perfectly adapted thereto, and no others are so. But they demand faith in God and direct obedience to His words. What can be more sadly significant of a changed attitude toward Holy Scripture than when a leading ministering brother wrote to me lately in justification of his virtual resolve to attend no more "open" conferences, and said he "presumed" that in the gatherings of the saints at Philippi, Paul, Silas, Luke, and Timothy did not wait for the leading of the Spirit but arranged among themselves who should speak, and probably under the direction of Paul!

The Word can mean just what we please if we give this free play to the imagination. I answered that I preferred to think that at Philippi, Paul acted according to the instructions as to ministry that he gave later to the Corinthian church (chap. 14), and which he there declared to be binding on all churches (verse 33), the essence of which instructions was the supremacy and sufficiency of the Holy Spirit in the assemblies.

3. It being not disputed that the human methods in question are not of faith or found in the Word, how do their advocates attempt to justify them? Some modern attempts may be cited.

(*a*) In April 1928 a missionary magazine wrote plainly against any duty to adhere to apostolic methods on the ground that "the missionary finds himself in circumstances very different from those disclosed in the New Testament," and added that "The methods of the Apostle Paul were the then methods of the Spirit of God, but there would be no missions to the heathen today had those methods remained unchanged."

(*b*) In 1929 in a certain mission field a document was issued to justify its "mission," which advanced two fundamental propositions. It said:

Let it be stated with emphasis, the New Testament does *not* give us a pattern for the details of assembly or evangelistic procedure but rather massive principles, gracious precepts, and certain precedents, which abundantly suffice for those who being led by the Spirit of God are sons of God;

and then, what is an evident corollary:

Expediency is a New Testament principle, not less valued because so much abused.

(*c*) In December, 1930, a well-known periodical published a letter urging the same argument.

(*d*) The next year a third magazine set it forth again.

(*e*) In 1937 the leader in that other land who arranged the compromise with the State, and formed the union mentioned, printed at length the same argument, that the New Testament gives no pattern for the church and we are at liberty to arrange as we think best. When in 1938 I pointed out to him and others that this implies that the New Testament is no longer our guide or authority, he replied that we have the Holy Spirit for this.

(*f*) In 1938 one of the writers of the sentences quoted in the paragraph above issued a booklet which said:

Perhaps the novelty of certain methods may fill us with concern, but unless there is a clear departure from Scriptural principles and apostolic practice, the fact that it was not done in this particular way when we were young is not conclusive that it may not be God's way today. There were some things that were novelties in our fathers' days, but they adopted them in the fear of the Lord. Principles abide unchanged but methods have perforce to change. The same bait will not do for all fish nor for all seasons, but the object remains the same—to catch fish. There are limits, no doubt, and we need never go to the world for instruction in the ways of the Lord, but Scripture leaves room for spiritual intelligence, to be exercised in constant dependence by prayer on the present guidance of the Spirit, and there is plenty of room for all our spiritual desires to find scope within the limits of the revealed will of God.

Here are the same assertions as before. 1. Principles abide but methods must perforce change. 2. Scripture sanctions the use of our own "spiritual intelligence," which is essentially the same as doing what we think expedient. 3. We have the present guidance of the Spirit, may safely vary from the ways the apostles worked, and find plenty of room for our own "spiritual desires."

As to point 1, we say that the methods here opposed *are* a "clear departure from Scriptural principles and apostolic practice," and from the former because from the latter. For example: the choosing beforehand our own speakers for a gathering of Christians is different in principle, not in practice only, from waiting upon the Spirit to prompt ministry at the time; and *it is* just that going to the world for instruction which the writer deprecates. Thus also the principle of the direct control of the Lord over His servants is infringed by the method of missionaries paying and controlling native evangelists.

As to point 2, expediency, the second quotation given above claims that expediency is a New Testament principle. According to this there is no New Testament pattern that we have duty to follow, but the New Testament itself gives us liberty to do as we think expedient in the eternally momentous business of saving men from perdition and of erecting a house where the Lord God may dwell. Moses had the advantage of a complete pattern, as did David and Solomon also;

but we are not under the law, argues the document, so that does not apply to the vastly more difficult matter of building a spiritual and eternal house. In this, each workman is left to do what he may deem expedient. If we were told this concerning a house of brick and timber we should think it incredible. Does an expert railway signal engineer leave his workmen to erect a system of signals, for the safeguarding of human life, as they consider expedient, guided only by "massive principles, precepts, and certain precedents?" Nor can it be shown that it was because it was the dispensation of law that so complete details were given of the tabernacle and the temple, and no liberty of variation, no room for expediency, was allowed. Was it not rather the Divine care that the type should be minutely perfect? And does it not thus afford to the spiritual mind today a wealth of detailed instruction as to the building and the ordering of the spiritual house of God?

Moreover, when these principles, precepts, and precedents, which it is admitted the Word does contain, are scrutinized as a whole, it will be found that they do compose together a pattern quite complete for all God's house. *But only for those who have eyes to see it.* And here is the true crux of the question. In the office of the engineer there will be drawings and specifications which offer complete and detailed patterns for a complicated set of signals. To *him* they are a pattern, but very probably to others they would not be.

Also, all through the centuries there have been believers who have used the Word as a pattern, and today some are thankful to be in their succession. As to the fact of there being a pattern it is nothing to the point that it has not been always understood by each and all in exactly the same sense. Workmen may thus vary as to the exact meaning of their patterns, but the pattern is there, which is the first point now before us. And it is worth remarking how much *agreement* there has been between truly humble souls heartily willing to follow the Word.

Perhaps a personal testimony may be allowed and be found helpful. For more than fifty-five years I have been concerned, actively and incessantly, in gospel and pastoral labours, among both the poor and the well-to-do, the cultured and the unlettered. In perhaps twenty different lands, from Norway to India and Burma, I have been privileged to share the toils of beloved fellow-labourers, and thus, in the providence of God, to gain some acquaintance with work among Buddhists, heathen, Moslems, Jews, Catholics, both Roman and Greek, Copts, Armenians, Protestants, infidels, theosophists, spiritists, and other modern cults. If I do not know the work among any one of these as thoroughly as some who have been confined to one or other of these spheres, for the present purpose I have the advantage of breadth of observation. It has followed of necessity that no small variety of problems, spiritual and practical, individual and collective, evangelistic and connected with the church of God, have been faced. And to the honour of the Scriptures I can but testify that, so far, not one question has been referred to the Word of God but that the guidance needed has been found there. If there is no detailed pattern there, how does any one see it there? If it is there, how is it some do *not* see it? Is it possible that our weak heart may not wish to see it, so as to feel free to do what we think expedient? I am afraid of my own heart.

It is not necessary to the present purpose to enquire what *Scripture* means by expediency; but it must be urged that our duty is to please God in everything, and this our natural mind is by no manner of means able to do (Romans 8:6–8). Therefore Divine instruction as to what is expedient is simply indispensable, and for this instruction where shall we turn save to the Scriptures? So that Scriptural expediency is not a licence for us to act according to our own thoughts, but it casts us back on Scripture to be thereby illuminated by the Spirit of truth. Our primary and ceaseless need, and our chief means of safety, is that poverty of spirit which our Lord blessed, and which Newton's lines describe perfectly:

> Quiet, Lord, my froward heart,
>   Make me teachable and mild,
> Upright, simple, free from art;
>   Make me as a little child.
> From distrust and envy free,
>   Pleased with all that pleases Thee.

As a little child relies
  On a care beyond his own;
Knows he's neither great nor wise,
  Fears to stir a step alone,
Let me thus with Thee abide,
  As my Father, Guard, and Guide.

I had once to deal with an elderly lady of social standing, demon driven, and an infatuate of the false Messiah of the Agapemone. She told me of an evidently good conversion when young, and of how precious the Bible was to her soul for many years, until one day she heard in her heart a voice say: "My child, you have done well to follow My Word, but now I myself am come to dwell in you, and you will not need the Book longer, for I myself will teach you." This she accepted, and the issue was as stated. In principle wherein does this differ from the reasoning that, being sons of God, having God within by the Spirit, we do not need the letter or the pattern as Moses did? Moreover, the argument forgets that Moses had the Spirit of God, as God said: "I will take of the spirit which is upon thee, and will put it upon them" (Numbers 22:17). This was a special enduement to capacitate for special service in God's House, Israel. Yet they needed the pattern and the Word.

And this further reflection is important, that, like every scriptural principle, expediency can be safely applied only within the limits of its scriptural application, and this does not extend to the sphere of church matters. It is upon the very topics of the detailed ordering of the house of God that the Word says: "If any man thinketh himself to be a prophet or spiritual, let him take knowledge of the things which I write unto you that they are *the commandments of the Lord*" (1 Corinthians 14:37). The commandment of the Lord is not something that we are left free to follow or to forsake as we think expedient.

And as to gospel work, take as a supposed test case, that Timothy, say, had argued thus: Paul sanctions expediency, therefore I may adopt diametrically opposite methods to his in gospel efforts. Paul founds only churches; I will organize a "mission" formed of workers foreign to this part, which shall supervise the whole of this "field."

Paul is often persecuted by rulers: I will establish formal friendly relations with them on the basis of their own rules and requirements. Paul teaches that all racial distinctions are utterly abolished in Christ; I too will *teach* this, but in practice I will form a close fellowship of workers, one for Jews, another for Romans, another for Greeks, another for half-castes like myself, Timothy. Paul trusts God to support him through the saints, or he labours with his hands; and he expects and encourages us who labour with him to do the same. I indeed shall be pleased for the saints to support me, though I will not take a fixed salary, for it might curtail my own independence; but I will hire local evangelists at a salary, and then I can control their service. In general, I will meet the changing times as seems to me expedient, especially as I consider my circumstances to differ from those of Paul.

It may be profitable to conjecture how, confronted with such use of his words, Paul would have thought, spoken, and *acted*.

We turn now to point 3, the doctrine that we may dispense with obedience to Scripture because we have the Spirit to guide.

In Israel God chose Moses and Aaron as His special messengers to and rulers of His people, but we read that certain men said unto them: "Ye take too much upon you, seeing all the congregation are holy, and Jehovah is among them" (Numbers 16:3). But the Lord did not allow that the fact of His presence with all His people was reason for rejecting His appointed messengers. Will any of the brethren who use this argument before us look Paul in the face and say: We do not propose to follow your example or adhere to your instructions, Paul. We find them confused and unsuitable to our times, and, then, we too have the Spirit to guide us.

We shall here give proof of how dire an influence this very reasoning exerted upon J. N. Darby at the time he divided the Brethren into camps in 1848 and ruined their united witness.

In 1902 Mr. W. H. Cole wrote his *Reminiscences of the Plymouth Meeting of "Brethren."* He united with that assembly in the year 1843, while the early harmony still prevailed, and he was there through the troubled period that followed. His account is practically unknown, yet is so deeply interesting that we give it in full in the Appendix. It is one of the extremely few original documents now accessible recording that period, and ought not to be lost. Speaking of Darby's determination that the whole church at Bethesda, Bristol, should be cut off from communion, and of his visit to Plymouth to secure that end there, Mr. Cole says (page 10);

> I asked him what spiritual [this is probably a misprint for *scriptural*] authority there was for cutting off a whole assembly of God's people. He replied to the effect "I grant there is none. But if some godly men meet together to seek the guidance of the Holy Spirit, they may expect that guidance, although there be no scripture whatever for the course they consider they have been led to take." (Is not that the dogma that the followers of his discipline have taken as their rule ever since? They would have division then; they have reaped divisions in abundance since.)

How solemn is this, how full of warning. If Mr. Darby had restricted his actions to what the Word of God positively sanctions, his whole devastating campaign would never have occurred, and the blessed testimony to unity that God was then raising would not have been ruined. But though he knew clearly that the vital element of his discipline, the cutting off of assemblies as such, was not Scriptural, he fell back upon this most dangerous plea that the Spirit will guide the prayerful apart from the Word. A quotation from his writings to be made shortly will show that he had already acted upon this fatal principle in an earlier controversy in Geneva in 1843, when he divided an assembly there, also on grounds ecclesiastical.

And the fallacy of the reasoning is apparent; for other equally godly men prayed together over the same questions, yet reached exactly contrary conclusions.

Exactly the same reasoning serves the Liberal Catholics of the Church of England. Summarizing a statement signed by twenty of their leaders *The Times* (January 20th, 1939) says:

> They believe that the Holy Spirit is always guiding the Church into all truth and therefore that there has been development of doctrine; and they say: "We find it hard to resist the conclusion that 'infallibility' is discredited." The truth of the Gospel must be established not by appeals to the formularies of the "undivided Church," but by free discussion which accepts the principles of scientific criticism.

Here indeed are grapes sour enough from the degenerate vine of this principle: schism in the Church of God; "development" of doctrine; infallibility discredited; scientific criticism in religion accepted as a guide.

Now the leading of the Holy Spirit is indeed a blessed and practical reality, yet this argument has been employed by different persons as warrant for the most contradictory or unspiritual conduct. There are three spirits that may prompt action: the spirit of the man; a wicked demonic spirit (1 Timothy 4:1), often speaking as an angel of light (2 Corinthians 11:14); and the Holy Spirit. Against the two former the Christian must be ever on his guard. His own spirit may becloud his judgment, as when fear of man, of persecution, prompts him to avoid the cross and to seek reasons for taking some easier way. Against deceiving spirits we are most expressly warned (1 John 4:1–6). How then may the disciple be sure that it is the Holy Spirit alone that guides him? There are two main tests: (1) In any matter upon which God has spoken in His Word the Spirit will guide by the Word; (2) in any event the Spirit will never lead contrary to the Word but ever in harmony with it.

In all matters concerning which God had spoken through Moses it would have been irreverent for the priests or people to have met to pray and expect some special guidance of the Spirit of God. God had declared His will and they had only to obey His Word. But on special occasions as to which the Word did not speak special guidance was given (1 Kings 12:21–24; etc., etc.). The next chapter (1 Kings 13) gives a solemn example of the seriousness of disregarding a message of God already given and following a supposed special direction. The prophet from Judah had received a distinct command from the Lord, but he disregarded it in favour of an alleged special communication, and lost his life by so doing.

It would have been equally vain and irreverent for the Corinthians to have waited for some guidance of the Spirit upon any matters upon which the Lord had spoken by Paul, either when he was with them or by his letters. They had but to obey the word, and if they were spiritual they would obey it (1 Corinthians 14:37). But as to whether Asia or Bithynia was the sphere of service at a given time the Word of God said nothing, and then special guidance by the Spirit was afforded (Acts 16:6–8).

So undeniable is this that those who wish to walk their own way and work on new lines are compelled to begin by denying that the New Testament contains any pattern for church life and evangelistic service, or, if a pattern is there, that it is obligatory. Yet the Word of God *does* speak about the order of the house of God. Parts of it are written expressly that men might know how to behave in that house (1 Timothy 3:14,15), and in this very letter the question of the government of the house by elders is set forth. Therefore the needed guidance upon these matters will be given through the Word. *If it be* so that the Word leaves any details indefinite, then we may leave those details indefinite, and follow the Word in so doing. But this is wholly different to making definite arrangements which are utterly unknown to the Word and which in important matters are actually contrary to the Word. To *this* the Holy Spirit will never lead, for He will never contradict His own instructions.

The Scripture gives its own ruling upon this matter, and it held good in both Old Testament times and New. One of the most richly inspired of the prophets cried: "To the law and to the testimony! If they speak not according to this word, surely there is no morning for them," that is, they shall remain and wander in the darkness of night (Isaiah 8:19–21). And John the apostle declares: "He that knoweth God *heareth us;* he who is not of God heareth us not" (1 John 4:6). And writing upon this very matter of church order, in some of its aspects, Paul says: "If any man thinketh himself to be a prophet, or spiritual, let him take knowledge of the things which I write unto you that they are the *commandments of the Lord*" (1 Corinthians 14:37,38), to which he at once adds the same warning that Isaiah gave as to wilful ignorance involving darkness, saying: "If any man is ignorant, let him be ignorant."

Thus do writers inspired by the Spirit direct to utterances He has already given as the test of guidance. And this was the habit of the Son of God himself on earth as He moved, taught, and worked by the Spirit: He too appealed constantly to what was written in Holy

Scripture. Yet that Book had been written from four to fifteen hundreds of years before He came, but He did not think the changes of those long centuries called for any other course than to fulfil what was written in the eternal Book of God. But the argument now discussed implies that what is therein written is neither sufficient, final, nor binding, and it substitutes for the Word a principle of conduct variable and destructive, and which leads quickly to results definitely contrary to the Word.

To return to the document now before us (See p. 305), it faces a question certain to be raised. Referring to its advocacy of expediency it said: "'But,' some will say, 'where will this lead us?' That is not the courageous language of faith. There is no occasion for alarm. The Holy Scriptures and their Author are all sufficient for the humble believer who is Christ's freeman, and yet is under law to Christ." Here again the question rises as to what need there can be of following what seems to one's own mind expedient if the Scriptures are all sufficient? and how can one who is under law to Christ be at liberty to forsake His Word and do as he thinks best?

But we know well whither expediency has led. It has led to the Fall, to paganism, to Judaism, to Catholicism, to Lutheranism, to Darbyism. At Worms Luther bravely announced his fundamental, anti-Roman principle that the Word of God was his only rule, and that he must obey it: "I can do no other, so help me God." Shortly he came to see clearly that the apostolic plan was the separateness as to organization of each local church of believers, but he turned therefrom and consented to a State church, as did Zwingli, Calvin, and the English Reformers. Thus, principally, was the great Reformation crippled by its parents.

Luther's reason for the disobedience was pure expediency. He said:

> The right kind of evangelical order cannot be exhibited among all sorts of people, but those who are seriously determined to be Christians, and confess the gospel with hand and mouth, must enrol themselves by name and meet apart, in one house, for prayer, for reading, to baptize, to take the sacrament, and exercise other Christian works. With such order

it would be possible for those who did not behave in a Christian manner to be known, reproved, restored, or excluded, according to the rule of Christ (Matthew 18:5)... But I cannot yet order and establish such an assembly, for I have not yet the right people for it. If, however, it should come about that I must do it, and am driven to it, I will willingly do my part. In the meantime I will call, excite, preach, help, forward it, until the Christians take the Word so in earnest that they will themselves find how to do it, and continue in it... (*The Pilgrim Church* 148)

Yet it is certain that Luther must have known more than enough real and spiritual Christians to have made a commencement had he been willing to follow the New Testament, instead of deeming it expedient to act otherwise.

Alongside of this let there be put this argument by a well-known missionary among Brethren in support of his proposal in 1925, that there should be created a body quite unknown to the apostles, a "field council." He wrote:

Firstly, any step that makes for a substantial transference of responsibility and action from the European missionary to the local churches at this advanced period in the history of the field [the work in that sphere had been in progress for over eighty years] is a move in the right direction. [But, he reasons, on account of the immature state of the churches such transfer must be made very cautiously, for] Unfortunately we are not dealing with Spirit-filled assemblies, sensitive and quick to respond to the Spirit's leading, but with unspiritual bodies in which strongly fleshly passions lie slumbering, quickly incited to fierce activity, as has recently been proved in the comparatively small and unimportant matter of the ... school.

It is evident that if this work had followed on Mr. Groves' lines the believers would have been no more dependent upon or subordinate to the Europeans than Aroolappen ever was on Mr. Groves, and the situation here acknowledged would not have arisen.

He continued:

Secondly, many of the churches to be served by the Council are not churches in the New Testament sense. Void of proper elders, destitute of the gifts of the Spirit for assembly functioning, *they must be cared for from outside* until such time as growth develops the requisite gifts and eldership, and to talk here of the independence of the individual assembly is meaningless and absurd—it is the independence of Master James of other folk to care and provide for him! We are not here dealing with theory, but with hard fact, as we turn to the conditions and needs of the ... field.

This means that the New Testament pattern is clear (which should be noted, as the writer was one of the signatories to the later document of 1929, which stated that there is no New Testament pattern to follow), but the believers are not yet equal to following it, so some human methods must be adopted in hope that they will thereby be helped to become so. A vain hope. The reasoning is identical with that of Luther. In his case expediency led to the Lutheran system: in this it would have led to another non-scriptural institution, had the proposal not been negatived through the opposition of some who sought to follow the New Testament.

How contrary is all this to Groves' conception of how New Testament churches can be fostered, and to the testimony given by the fact that the church built up by Aroolappen, on the lines he learned from Mr. Groves, prospered in very real measure. Which was the apostolic method there is no doubt. Are we really to believe that the ways that the Son of God taught to the apostles are not feasible, and we must produce better expedients?

The apostles successfully followed those methods under conditions as bad as any land can offer. Dr. Howson (*St. Paul*, chap. 6) tells us that the Lycaonians were "illiterate idolaters," a "rude and unsophisticated people," marked by the "wild fanaticism of a rustic credulity," bound by "mythology and superstition," "proverbially fickle and faithless." I thought afresh of those strenuous labours when in 1928 I passed over that now mostly desolate tableland of Asia Minor, and stood awhile in the streets of Konieh (Iconium). Ought we not to take courage and to step out on the faith that the same God will do the same work if we walk closely with Him? I write only with deep sympathy with my brethren in their vast difficulties, and as a sharer of their weakness; but I do find it impossible to accept their reasoning and yet to retain faith in the risen Lord and in His Word, or to think it conceivable that expedients of my own devising will produce the desired results if apostolic methods fail in this. And in point of fact, neither have the latter failed where they have been thoroughly tried, nor have the human ways succeeded in producing apostolic results. All over the world the result of these ways has been disappointing as regards the speedy upbuilding of self-supporting churches.

So expediency has led to Romanism and to scarcely less corrupt Protestantism, Lutheran and other. It was the argument of the English Bishops in urging their late Revised Prayer Book. The twentieth century, it was asserted, differs so much from the sixteenth that it is expedient to alter the forms and declarations of public worship to suit better the public mind. This is Laodiceanism, the wishes of the people ruling, which is ever mere expediency.

Giving his reasons against elders being formally recognized by a church Mr. Darby, in the controversy in Geneva in 1843 as before mentioned, asserted that

> Obedience and not the imitation of the apostles is our duty. . . . I only doubt whether it be God's will that you should do what the apostles did; and I say that God has left for faithful Christians directions sufficient for the state of things in which the Church now is. To follow these directions is more truly to obey, than *if* we should set about imitating the apostles; and the Spirit of God is ever with us to strengthen us in this way of true obedience . . . people forget the want of power, when they think it possible to follow the apostles, because they have their writings. *(Collected Writings,* Ecclesiastical 1: 225, 226, 284).

But why so, seeing that the same almighty Spirit who empowered the first Christians is with His servants still? Also, it ignores that whenever He has since worked in power He has done so along His own originally chosen lines. The fallacy of Mr. Darby's reasoning began in his major premiss, that there ever was a corporate visible *system* of Christianity. The outcome was that the assemblies that followed him were left without rule by recognized elders, and developed into the very thing that Mr. Darby said had been ruined beyond power or right to restore, even a corporate universal ecclesiastical system. It was natural; for if they were not to follow the writings of the apostles what could they follow except what seemed to their own judgment (which meant, to Mr. Darby's judgment) to be the best? This is expediency, however disguised or denied.

But observe the practical similarity of Mr. Darby's reasoning and that first above quoted. The former said there was an apostolic system, but it is not intended to be our pattern; the other says, there never was a pattern. The assertions appear divergent in form, but their result in practice is identical. And both, inconsistently yet honestly, affirm the sufficiency of the Lord and the Scriptures, yet inevitably follow human judgment when action is to be taken.

But our document argues strenuously that our position is legal in spirit, genders bondage of soul, and that we are not under Moses, but are sons, and at liberty from detailed restrictions. Yet it is strange that it was held and followed by the men who more than others in our times led the people of God out of legal bondage into the liberty of the gospel. But it is in the very epistle (Galatians) wherein this status and freedom are most fully taught that the sons of God are most solemnly warned that to *this* law, as beneficial as inexorable, they are perpetually subject, that "whatsoever a man soweth that shall he also reap"; and it is in pursuance of this inevadable principle that they who turn from the method of life marked by obedience to the voice of God's servant, and by trust, and who walk (carry on their affairs) by light of their own kindling, shall know assuredly the fulfilment of the word "This shall ye have at My hand, ye shall lie down in sorrow" (Galatians 6:7; Isaiah 50:10,11). Let the sorrow of so many godly workers over the stunted growth, the arrested development, of both converts and churches (of which the above quoted statements are a sample) testify to the unsuitability of human plans and the fixity of the law cited.

It was further urged that the objection to the doctrine of expediency is not "the courageous language of faith." But it is at least the cautious language of humble reverence for the Word of God. Now "faith cometh by hearing, and hearing by the word of Christ," and only thus (Romans 10:17); nor is it possible to act in faith unless assured that the Word of Christ is in favour of the course in view. In the nature of things this is impossible when the action proposed is avowedly not a following of anything in the Word, but a mere decision of the human judgment, even if it be of a consensus of human judgment, as of a committee or a council. Hence the spiritual accuracy of Mr. Groves' remark quoted, that whenever he could follow Scripture literally he felt easy as to the act, but where he could not, or fancied he could not, he felt weak in proportion to his distance from it.

And this matter of vital faith in God brings us again to the true spiritual inwardness, the real heart of these questions. Some may feel impatient about so much discussion of methods, thinking these to be of little consequence so long as right ends are kept in view. Let such possess their souls in patience, and reflect awhile that the corrupting of the church was brought about very largely by changes of method.

The original method of government was always by more than one elder in each assembly. This was changed to the plan of a single bishop. At first there was no election of elders, only a definite acknowledgment by the believers of such as the Lord had raised up. This gave way to election of bishops, and later to their appointment by the civil power. The mode of baptism was altered in such wise as made possible the perverting of the practice and the doctrine. The manner of observing the Supper of the Lord was first changed, and then false doctrine was easily attached to it. And so on, until Christendom and Christianity had little resemblance. Satan was acute enough to discern this to be the safest and surest mode of destroying the effective testimony of the church.

It is thus still. In this land hundreds of evangelical churches have been quietly transformed into ritualistic churches by stealthy changes in the method of doing apparently the same thing, the observance of the Lord's Supper, for example.

And in the matter chiefly before us, methods of gospel and pastoral service, an innermost reason of the Lord's choice of the methods He instituted is that they both require and foster vital, continuous, working faith in Himself as the ever-present Director and Energizer and Supporter of His servants and their service, as well as of the churches of believers they, by the Spirit, gather through the gospel.

And by faith we do not mean only as to temporal supplies, though this is a constant realm for faith; but we mean a fixed confidence in the Lord concerning *all* matters spiritual, especially in gospel service and in the church, as well as in affairs personal; such a faith in the wisdom and power and final success of the Lord that the servant will follow His methods, reckoning with the Son of God that it is better to work with God even if one must seemingly fail and labour for naught (Isaiah 49:4).

And because faith is the proper, morally indispensable quality in man to enable God to grant His approval those methods which develop actual faith in us, and in the converts, are the only right and blessed methods. To hinder faith becomes, therefore, a most necessary aim of the Devil, and among other of his snares this is one of the most effective, that he induces us to adopt methods which falsely promise good results though they do not demand vital faith, such as counts upon God only in all things at all times.

There is undoubtedly a real power in oratory and rhetoric; but Paul abjured it, for it did not consist with real faith in the necessity for and sufficiency of the convincing energy of the Spirit of truth (1 Corinthians 2:4). Would that all preachers followed him in this.

There is a real power in organization: in magazines which make workers and their needs known to benevolent hearts; in lists of workers which give information about them; in large funds announcing their income and distribution. No one questions that such methods have power to serve certain ends; but they do not demand a persistent, energetic, direct faith in a living God. Men of the world can and do employ them for *their* ends. Their *tendency* necessarily is to draw away the heart from God toward themselves; at first with an attention divided between Him and them, and at last to interpose between the soul and Him. That some workers do not wholly succumb to this does not alter that this is their natural tendency. Here is a basic reason why some oppose all such methods; here is reason enough why the Lord never adopted them. From these methods men like Groves and Müller deliberately turned, so as to give to the disbelieving world and an unbelieving church a fresh proof of the reality and faithfulness of God and the power and sufficiency of faith and prayer.

It is an unvarying, yea, unalterable rule in the kingdom of God that "according to your faith" it shall be unto you. But the hired evangelist looks to the missionary who pays him, and the sixth of Matthew has little preciousness to his soul. Were he called to look daily to God for food and clothing it would be to him a far, far sweeter thought that God is a father caring for him in these items. The very birds and flowers would be dearer to him, and would speak to his heart. This would develop closer fellowship with the Lord, would enrich his experience, and then his ministry and testimony; and so his example and instruction would encourage in others, both saints and sinners, a like faith in his prayer-hearing God. This has been shown ten thousand times in all centuries and all countries; it cannot be served by the method of hiring at a wage for spiritual work; and thus is seen in this one matter alone that the question of method is of the very highest importance. And what is true here applies to all other questions of method.

Thus are we witnessing a decided weakening of faith in God, with a setting aside of His Word, and now an unblushing advocating of this false and fatal doctrine of development and expediency. How can one watch this without the deepest concern and misgiving? Unless the Lord shall change many hearts they will find themselves shortly descending rapidly a slippery slope, until the testimony committed to Brethren having been ruined by them will be taken away from them, even though they be heard boasting that they are rich and increased with goods. Yet always the Lord will reserve to Himself a little flock; but they will be a people afflicted and poor, and being this they will trust in His name. Happy are they who choose His reproach among these.

Viewing the Brethren movement as a whole, Exclusivism early gave up the original testimony on its ecclesiastical side, in the matter of church order, reception, and discipline, and did this under the influence of development and expediency. Now Open Brethren are largely giving up the testimony on its practical side, in matters indicated, and are justifying this by development and expediency.

No doubt many meetings continue on the old lines, but these are mostly the smaller and remoter assemblies; and not a few workers also do so. Being unorganized, continuing simple and lowly, they remain largely unnoticed, save by heaven. But all too generally, under influences and along lines indicated, the present generation of Open Brethren has grown up accustomed to the newer ways of church life and gospel service. These have already become traditional, and the Word of God is made of none effect upon the matters in question. The many only ask whether this or that promises to be *useful*; whether it is *scriptural*, and so of the Holy Spirit, is scarcely asked. Thus does expediency rule.

—oOo—

If the present ventilating of these matters issues in less reliance on central funds, and the further resumption of the less regular but apostolic method of gifts going direct to workers; if it results in beloved friends who have adopted human schemes and methods and principles finding themselves without sufficient funds to support their organizations, or for the hiring of native helpers, and so on, so that these methods collapse, and they be brought back thus to the path of undivided trust, of immediate transactions with their faithful God, it shall be productive of true spiritual prosperity for their own souls, and thus in their service. And the Searcher of hearts knows that this is all that I, for my part, seek by this discussion. And one most happy result will be to eliminate almost entirely the dreadful danger of putting through one's own undertakings without these being in the plan of God, merely because one can get by one's own schemes money for them. I have seen this work untold harm and sorrow in many a life and career, and sometimes on a colossal scale in "missions." To be saved from it, by the Lord Himself having the actual control of supplies, is a priceless boon.

I know this path well after nearly fifty years of its trials and sweetness. I have watched at close quarters beloved children of God in the paths of denominational and organized missions; and thanking God heartily for all that is of Himself in them (and it is often very much), I yet am deeply persuaded that as far as their methods are unapostolic they are thereby impoverished in soul. Nor have I ever seen that the blessing which has attended their service (often, thank God, great) has been upon those of their methods which are of human invention, such as organization and its accompaniments.

Humbly, I trust, as being not worthy to be in His service at all, I bear testimony that the Lord's ways are verily ways of pleasantness and *all* His paths are peace. I have watched apostolic methods of evangelizing and of church life succeed, as of old, in too many lands to be persuaded that they are unsuited to any one land.

I am one example that a worker avowedly disconnected from any and every list and fund can be sent of God on extensive travel through unknown lands, and be provided, when it may so please God, with sustenance and funds without resort to England; finding as a fact that the Lord has servants and supplies everywhere, and finding also that it may sometimes please God, for the exercise and development of one's soul, that keener and longer need be known in this land of wealth than in lands of general poverty. The Lord loves to do things differently from anyone else, that the soul may say with comfort, "This is the finger of God," and may adore. Blessed, thrice blessed are all who put their trust undividedly in Him. May He bring back to this path of faith, and therefore of literal obedience to His words, any who have been allured from it. Even if He hurl a Jonah into a truly disagreeable and precarious position, it is only for a time, and that he may afterward value the more the dry ground upon which to do God's work in God's way.

A widely informed brother, not meeting in the assemblies, wrote to me to the effect that Brethrenism has "lapsed," and that history affords no instance of a movement that had so lapsed having been quickened generally. The latter is the case, which is a deeply solemn warning. I replied that I do not consider that the meetings known as Open Brethren have yet lapsed, and I pointed to their persevering service in the gospel. But should the principles now opposed ever find general acceptance with the assemblies, then Brethrenism would indeed have lapsed, having abandoned its primary divine and energizing principle. To preserve from this calamity to the whole church and cause of God is well worth every effort.

It need scarcely be added that the matters of method here discussed do not in themselves involve any question of Christian fellowship, private or in the assemblies. We are to receive with joy all who love our Lord Jesus with a love incorruptible, honouring the supreme fact about them, their personal relation to Christ, in spite of their denominational and society connexions. We are to rejoice sincerely in all that is of Christ in them and in their labours. I have visited such in spheres many; as A. N. Groves, for example, used to do, as I am sure Paul would do, yea, as the blessed Lord Himself does. But this does not deter from the duty, to them and to the work of God, as well as to all fellow-believers, of opposing in love whatever in their ways is not of Christ, and most especially the principles here reviewed, which have proved so thoroughly vicious in their age-long results.

15

Various Topics

If in anything ye are otherwise minded, even this shall God reveal unto you. Philippians 3:15.

I exhort Euodia, and I exhort Syntyche, to be of the same mind in the Lord. Philippians 4:2.

The first of these passages recognizes the fact of diversity of opinion upon sundry matters, and directs us to God as able to reveal truth and to unify judgment. The second exhorts to personal concord. At the very first these two principles ruled among Brethren. Upon matters not vital to the faith they allowed freedom of opinion and utterance, yet dwelled together in unity by the power of divine love, and in this harmony Groves' influence was a steady factor.

1. Baptism.

One such matter was the ordinance of baptism. In the course of his emancipation from the Church of England he had been baptized as a believer in 1829. His biographer mentions this and states his frame of heart upon the matter. We read:

> Mr. Groves had recently been baptized in Exeter, a circumstance which naturally became the topic of conversation, it being noticed in the newspaper, as having produced a great sensation. He mentioned, incidentally, that it quite humbled him when, the day after, a Baptist minister crossed the street to salute him as a brother. The writer said, "Of course, you must be a Baptist now you are baptized." He replied, "No! I desire to follow all in those things in which they follow Christ; but I would not by joining one party, cut myself off from others." Then taking up the ring on which his keys hung, he said, "If these keys were to hold by one another, all would go if one fell; but as each of them is attached to this strong ring, so should we take hold of Christ, not of any of the systems of men, and

then we shall be safe and united; we should keep together, not because of any human system, but because Jesus is *one* (36).

That he accepted what was involved in baptism for a churchman of some public standing shows his clear sense that it was a Scriptural obligation upon a believer, and that he judged the baptizing of infants to be a nullity; but equally he refused to elevate the ordinance to a place the Word of God does not give it, by making it a term of Christian communion. Christ is this, not His ordinances.

In 1833 he wrote:

Mr. D. urged me years ago not to preach on baptism, saying, I should thereby become a sectarian; as well might our dear brother H. have been told not to publish his tract against war, lest he should be identified with the Society of Friends. Surely, if we are not free to follow all, where they follow Christ and His will, we have only changed one kind of bondage for another. I do not think we ought to propose to be modelled *unlike* every sect, but simply to be like Christ; let us neither seek nor fear a name. I wish rather to have from every sect what every sect may have from Christ (231).

Thus he not only himself obeyed the Lord in this matter, but he preached upon baptism. And he rejoiced when others saw and obeyed this teaching of Scripture. In Bagdad in 1830 he wrote:

My dear friend and brother P_____ and his wife have been baptized too; to see this conformity to Christ's mind is very delightful, and how wonderful, so strong a current of prejudice is there against this simple, intelligible, and blessed ordinance (106).

In 1833 he stated his conviction that personal obedience is essential to the validity of baptism. He said:

Do you not think that Romans 6:3-4 shows why the form of immersion in baptism was chosen, being the fittest to shadow forth our death and resurrection with Christ? I lay no great stress on *forms*, but I love the *spirit of obedience*. The loveliest part of a *child's* character, and the most marred by the fall, is simple, *unquestioning* obedience, and *willing dependence*. O, indeed, we would be as gods, even after all our sad experience! May we *be willing* to *sit* at our dear Lord's feet, and learn of Him, for He was meek and lowly in heart; then, and not *till then*, we shall find *rest to our souls* (233).

This fact of the *voluntariness* of baptism is of first importance. Unintelligent, involuntary, or constrained acts do not fall under the term "reasonable" or "spiritual" service (Romans 12:1). The recognition of this led to my own baptism as an adult. In general, those who followed Mr. Darby accepted his particular view that the children of believers should be immersed on the responsibility of their parents; not indeed unto regeneration or salvation, but to bring them, as is alleged, into a supposed position of privilege, as contrasted with the world. There were some notable exceptions, such as G. V. Wigram and William Kelly, but my father was one of the multitude that followed J. N. Darby in this as in many other matters. So we, his children, were immersed when quite young. I, the eldest but one, was perhaps nine years. Now I had been already brought to simple, lasting faith in Christ as my Saviour, and was a believer when baptized. But the reason for this event I did not in the least understand. It was not explained to us at all; it was something our father wished, which in truth was reason enough for our minds, had we thought about it. But in about my nineteenth year I noticed that the Lord was baptized so emphatically by His own will that He insisted upon it against the will of the baptizer, and also that it was by his own request that the eunuch was baptized by Philip. I resolved to secure this vital element in my own case, and was again immersed. But like Groves, I did not thereby become a Baptist, I simply became obedient as regards this ordinance, and proved it, in his words, "simple, intelligible, and blessed."

That leading followers of Darby such as those named, and those they in turn influenced, were practisers of the immersion of believers, shows that in their circles also baptism was not made a test of fellowship. Practically all Open Brethren, like Groves, George Müller, and others, have been practisers of believers' baptism, but have welcomed readily to fellowship Exclusives and other Christians otherwise minded. The reception of wholly unbaptized persons would be contrary to all Scripture precedent, but the toleration of different modes of baptism follows from the primary principle that life in Christ, not light upon the will of God, is the ground of communion.

They who exclude believers on the ground of non-immersion, from lack of light as to the mind of God, are under obligation to show that it is an excommunicable sin according to the New Testament. They must virtually rank it with the moral abominations detailed in 1 Corinthians 5, as demanding exclusion. Of course it is a different case if a person admits the duty to be immersed, because it is the will of the Lord, but perversely refuses obedience. For the honour of Christ as Lord, and for his own soul's welfare, neither this nor any other intentional disobedience should be condoned.

Writing from Germany in 1843 George Müller gave a clear testimony to the early practice by saying:

> When we took our position here [Stuttgart] of receiving all who love our Lord Jesus, irrespective of their agreeing with us in all points, one brother came among us who had been always refused by the Baptist Church here because he was not baptized. After this brother had been about six weeks among us, he himself desired baptism (*Narrative*, vol. 1, 556).

This further passage from Groves is well worth quoting and noting. In 1834 he wrote:

> I wish to know on what authority baptism is called the seal of the Christian covenant, as circumcision was of the Jewish. I see not a word about covenant in connexion with baptism. It seems to me, from Scripture, nothing more than a profession of faith in that triune Jehovah, by whose acts of grace and truth the soul has been brought from death unto life. And if baptism be a sign of the covenant of what covenant was John's baptism a sign? Of this I am quite certain, the weakest reasoner, by the same principle on which the Independents establish infant baptism, could justify national communion, without reference to believers or unbelievers: for if they argue that our infants should be baptized because the Jewish infants were to be circumcized, why should not our infants partake of the Lord's Supper as theirs did of the Passover? Again I would say, if baptism be the sign of a *covenant*, of what nature is the covenant? Between whom is it made? and what is its ultimate object? I see not in the New Testament the slightest allusion to a covenant in connection with baptism. No, believers' baptism and believers' communion hang together; and if you allow baptism to the unbelieving, then follows

communion with the same, worldly Christianity, and every other evil. But, in this, the Independents are happily inconsistent (320).

But would he be able to add the final general statement to-day? It is certainly the fact that Scripture suggests no connexion between baptism and any covenant. Yet is there a relationship not always remarked between circumcision and baptism. The former was appointed by God to follow natural birth and all males born naturally from Abraham are included in its duty and advantages; the latter is appointed by the Lord to follow spiritual birth, the new birth by faith in Him, and all, male and female, so born from above are under the obligation and privileges thereof. This effectually excludes from baptism all not yet born of God. And as circumcision did not effect natural birth, neither does baptism effect spiritual birth; but as each born naturally was to be circumcized, so each born spiritually ought to be baptized; yet the one was involuntary, the other must be voluntary.

In 1909 or 1910, on the Nilgiri Hills, South India, I witnessed the baptism of V. D. David ("Tamil" David). He had been a mighty evangelist among the people of that part of India; had later fallen fearfully, and been a sorrow and reproach; was presently restored, and again used in some distinct measure. Such is the grace and power of our Lord. At his baptism he gave in English this account of matters. He had been converted through the Church Missionary Society workers in Ceylon; had been appointed an evangelist, with a salary as usual: had come to see from the Scripture that the Lord expected him to be immersed as a believer. But, he said, I knew that if I took this step I must lose my post and my salary as a worker with the Church of England. I fought the Lord on this point, and it was the real beginning of my backsliding! Now after many years of sin and shame, this Jonah was brought back to the very duty from which he had run away into the deep, dark sea. How much less would have been the cost, how much greater the gain, to him and to the testimony, had he walked in the light when it was first received. Nor can one fail to see in this case a red light as to the perilous rock that a salary is to the servant of Christ in the gospel.

2. THE PERSONAL EXAMPLE AND TEACHING OF CHRIST.

In 1833 Groves wrote:

> I do not think our Lord is looked on in Scripture as the second Adam
> in relation to His *humanity simply*, but as the *Spiritual Head* of a *Spiri-*
> *tual family*, in contradistinction to the natural head of a natural family.
> He puts Himself into the circumstances of the *bond-slaves* of death to
> lead them to the kingdom of light. I enter with my whole heart into
> the practical use you make of the Lord's life and character: surely it is
> the great book for our education in divine knowledge; and it is because
> we have been so disposed to look off this blessed manifestation of God
> to wretched sinners like ourselves, that we have sunk; and we can only
> rise by going back to that feeling, that the character and person of Jesus
> alone are to be traced and followed after in reading God's word (262).

But while Christ under various guises—promise, prophecy, type,
or history—is the Subject of the whole Word, it is clear that His
person and character as man are most clearly and fully set forth in
the Gospels, and so, with his mind on this theme, Groves wrote, ten
days later, that

> I have this morning been reading two or three times Matthew 5, and
> really, the more I read, the more I feel our incalculable lowness, not only
> of attainment, but of aim: we do not even strive after those great and
> glorious things that seem promised so clearly to faith, and which are
> pressed upon us in order that we may be perfect as our Father which is in
> heaven is perfect. There is in this chapter a depth of humiliation, a reality
> of self-denial, an extent of forbearance, that the poor weak heart stands
> appalled before, and how hard to manifest the love it commands (264).

It is clear that he was as far removed as possible from that teaching, already being diligently spread and insisted upon, that the Gospels are mainly "Jewish" in character, not Christian, that the Sermon
on the Mount is for the practice of an imagined remnant of Jews of
the time of Antichrist who will have believed on Jesus as their Messiah, or, alternatively, gives the laws for the millennial kingdom—in
short, as in no case binding for Christians. This view of the Gospels is essential to that whole scheme of prophetic interpretation of
which it forms part, and differences as to which were, for sheer lack

of Christian love, and by reason of intolerance of spirit, already preparing rapidly for the disruption of Brethren, when other questions should afford overt occasion.

It is solemn to reflect that intolerance on both sides of this question of interpretation was a chief factor in so greatly injuring the testimony of unity committed to those early Brethren. At the first it was not so. In 1839 or 1840, one wrote:

> An anti-millenarian, however he may be regarded as mistaken in judgment, may be a valued brother in the Lord, and abide in full communion with these Christians. I know there are such amongst them, as well as others who have as yet no decided judgment upon this doctrine; and when a Christian desires to join them in communion, he is never questioned as to his views upon the subject... (*Collected Tracts,* 3 5).

It is bitter to have to confess that more animosity has been shown between "tribulationists" and "pre-tribulationists" than between "millenarians" and "anti-millenarians." To this day, no doubt, one who did not see the doctrine of a millennial kingdom would be more readily received by some Brethren than would one who held the opposite view upon the other point. Yet the latter is not so serious a disturbance of interpretation as is the former. One rejoices to think that this ill-balanced feud is slowly dying. May it be soon dead and buried.

The question of the application of the Gospels to Christian character and conduct is of deepest practical import. The Lord told the apostles that He had given them an example, that they in turn should do as He had done to them (John 13:15), and it was the conviction of one who heard those words spoken that Christ had left us an example that we should follow His steps (1 Peter 2:21). Now we have no means of learning what steps the Lord took under such and such circumstances save by acquaintance with the Gospels, but in them we can watch Him under all the varied conditions of life: as youth and as man, at home and in society, in temple and synagogue, at a wedding and a funeral, among poor and rich, religious and profane, Jews and Gentiles, the learned and the ignorant, the moral and the immoral.

Moreover, it was their Master's final charge that *whatsoever* He had taught to the apostles they were to instruct other disciples to observe (Matthew 28:20). This comprehensive, duplicated "all things whatsoever" included of necessity the whole of Christ's teachings, from the Sermon on the Mount and onward. And that the apostles so understood is plain from the fact that the practical instructions to disciples given in their letters contain so very many quotations from or allusions to the sayings of their Lord. There are not less than ten or a dozen such from the Sermon on the Mount. And this feature is as distinct in the writings of Paul as in those of the others; indeed, it is Paul who says to converted Gentiles: "Ye ought to remember the words of the Lord Jesus," and then he quotes a saying of Christ not elsewhere found, showing that everything known to have come from His lips ought to be remembered by us as a guide to conduct (Acts 20:35).

It has been a most serious injury to character and practice that the theory mentioned has contributed to a neglect of the Gospels, by providing a plausible excuse for not facing the exacting demands our Lord makes upon His followers. That which tends to laxity of practice can never be sound exegesis. And that this theory does so tend is clear, for it was already bearing such fruit from the commencement, as these words of Groves prove. On November 10th, 1837, he wrote:

> At Arcot, Gundert found every effort had been made to cast doubts into the minds of men relative to my soundness in the faith, especially because I consider *Christ's life* and *words* our *only rule of life;* but this evil speaking has less and less effect; so many have heard me now here that they practically reject the accusation, though they may understand too little to disprove it verbally; but I feel such peace in leaving my cause with the Lord (378).

Thus ignorance or malice was employing a most common device of bigotry, the asserting to be fundamental to the faith a teaching which is not so, with the view to defame the character as a teacher of an excellent servant of God whose ministry was disliked, and to hinder his influence. Surely to each that makes this nefarious attempt Christ, with sorrow and sternness, would say again: "Get thee behind me, Satan!"

The estimate of the Gospels Groves held, and such constant meditation upon them as he gave, has the supreme value and effect that it sets before the soul the *real* Christ, not a person more or less of our own imagining; and thus becomes possible in us that work of the Spirit described as being transfigured into the image of the Lord, as the mirror takes on the glory of the sun when exposed to its light (2 Corinthians 3:18). Groves had thus beheld the beauty of the Lord, and longed to be like Him in heart and ways. It is excellent to cherish the hope of being outwardly like Him in glory hereafter; but this hope, so wonderful, so surpassing, requires a firm basis. What right have *I* to take it to *myself,* and to entertain such a marvellous expectation? The practical answer is that "Christ *in* you is the hope of glory" (Colossians 1:27). Now as to his Galatian children, ten years after their conversion Paul was deeply distressed because Christ was *not* formed in them (Galatians 4:19). It is one thing to have believed savingly that Christ died *for me,* it is another thing so to have received Him inwardly that His moral character, His dispositions, affections, powers are being reproduced in *my heart.* And Groves, having seen in the Gospels this moral magnificence of his Lord, longed exceedingly to partake of it in reality and power. This he expresses thus:

> I often fear lest the soul should be more disquieted about the want of external conformity to Christ than internal; you know I feel them to be parts of one whole, and that I would desire the one to follow the other, as simply and naturally as cause and effect: the heart dwelling in the one and the life following, without carefulness, in the other; for I think external conformity, unsupported by a deep divinely wrought spiritual conformity within, would be very likely to lead to pride (298).

And again:

> Indeed, I do long for *entire* conformity to Christ, as that which alone can satisfy God; for in Him alone is the Father "well-pleased"; He is the manifestation of what *God* is, and what God loves (344).

He mourned the general lack of earnest desire for this, saying:

> I think you will agree with me that personal religion is generally at a very low ebb among us; that *deep* holiness, that following after Christ in all the beauty and purity of His beautiful and perfect character (291).

For himself this was an insatiable craving, and the following passage describes the inseparable connexion he saw between inward fellowship with Christ and outward service to Him:

> I feel tonight such a delightful sense of my heart being melted under the glorious vision of a Saviour's love. It makes the *least* sin of the heart bitter, and my soul pants after an unrestrained union with Him, in all its affections, and in all His work.
>
> Do you sometimes think, as I do, that it needs great spirituality of mind, and very true apprehensions of the ground of the salvation there is in Christ, to bear the superstructure of a devoted service? I cannot tell you how insignificant all service appears to me that partakes of the mere bustle of man. I would not have a faculty unconsecrated or unemployed for my dear, dear Lord, but I would have it only shown forth as the breathings of a secret love, not thought upon, yet *experienced* and shining forth in every faculty the Lord hath bestowed. I mean all activity of body and plans of service are secondary to deep acquaintance with, and living in Jesus. As perhaps you may not understand me, I would say again, that I would not cease to serve; (nay, not a hoof should be left unconsecrated) but that this service should arise from my loving and delighting in the will of Him (whose will was His Father's), and panting after, as my *proper glory and happiness, an entire conformity* to Him in all *things,* who was the brightness of His Father's glory and the express image of His person (336, 337).

If this object, entire conformity to the Lord Jesus, had been with other leading Brethren of that time the absorbing passion it was with A. N. Groves, the bitter, calamitous conflicts that were shortly to cripple their testimony would not have been known. But when these developed, and brethren wrote harsh and false things against their brethren, they lost the right to teach the truth of inward, heart holiness, and that portion of the testimony of the kingdom of God was taken from them, as a body, and given to others who should bring forth the fruits of it. Present justification and future redemption have been taught among Brethren with unsurpassed clearness and fulness, but heart holiness has been a comparatively unstressed theme. This can be rectified so soon as teachers "pant after an unrestrained union with the Lord" in all affections and all work; and this will follow a closer, steadier view of His personal charms; which, in turn, will be greatly aided by a hearty acceptance of His words and works as directly applicable to ourselves, instead of neglecting them as "Jewish."

How salutary must have been that practice of regular public reading of the Gospels in Christian assemblies which Justin Martyr tells us obtained in his time in the second century. (First *Apology,* c. 67. See Westcott, *Introduction to Study of the Gospels,* 418, note 2.)

From this inward conformity of affection and judgment to the Lord powerful effects flow not otherwise to be produced. The blessed, superior state of soul to which Groves thus attained is seen in these sentences from the year 1837:

> Those especial principles that take glory from the creature and put it upon Christ will never find acceptance with men; and even in the Church, they will meet, I fear, but a cold reception.
>
> My heart has perfect repose in the thought of being rejected. I only trust I shall always be able to bear it in meekness; neither in proud disdain turning from and scorning those who thus act, nor in self-vindication retaliating; but accepting all simply as that path in which we are to have fellowship with Jesus, who was so misunderstood, and whose principles were so little appreciated even by His apostles and brethren. It is so valuable a school to learn in; the one in which the more you love, the less you are loved, and still not to faint or be weary. At times my heart is very sick at the aspect of things, such divisions, such jealousies, such evil surmisings; but then I think, thus it was with Jesus; if I am called a teacher of blasphemy, so was He; if I am called a sabbath-breaker, so was He; if my authority to teach was questioned, so was His; though it was the wisdom of His Father; if He was rejected by His own people, so are we; if I am accused of betraying the city of Zion into the hands of her enemies, because I would turn out those who occupy the temple as thieves, to buy and sell in it, so was Jesus: He was accused of betraying His nation to the Romans, or of so acting that they would come and take it away if He were allowed to continue: should we then be surprised, that if He was called Beelzebub His household should share the same fate?
>
> I feel it so important to strengthen those foundations which rest on Jesus, though I weaken those which rest on man. It is not a popular ministry, but God has given me lessons, both to learn and to teach, whether willingly or not, that destroy all thoughts of personal ambition, and in my inmost soul I accept it of the Lord's hand, as most right and necessary for me (376, 377).

It is instructive that in those years the Lord Jesus led other hearts to embrace these truths and to walk in them; and what powerful men of God they became! R. C. Chapman was one such and George Müller another. Of the year 1829 the latter wrote:

> ...it pleased the Lord to lead me to see a higher standard of devotedness than I had seen before. He led me, in a measure, to see what is my true glory in this world, even to be despised, and to be poor and mean with Christ. I saw then, in a measure, though I have seen it more fully since, that it ill becomes the servant to seek to be rich, and great, and honoured in that world where his Lord was poor, and mean, and despised (*Narrative*, 48).

And he also insisted strongly that the Sermon on the Mount is for Christians and is to be acted out literally (*Narrative* 66; 586–592). Like Groves and Wesley he considered the command "Lay not up for yourselves treasures on earth" to mean just what it says; and clearly only he who accepts the duty can consistently enjoy the accompanying comfort that "your heavenly Father knoweth" your need as to earthly things.

In this path Groves, by heart communion with Christ, gained the indwelling of Christ in his heart, and experienced deeply, what is open indeed to all yet reached by few, even the fulfilment of that exceeding great and precious promise, "Take my yoke upon you and learn of Me; for I am meek, and lowly in heart: and ye shall find rest unto your souls" (Matthew 11:29). To him to be yoked with the Lord Jesus as despised and rejected of men only proved that the yoke fits easily and so makes the heavy burden light and easy to be borne. Paul had found it so in his day. His prolonged and, to nature, insupportable trials he declared to be but a "light affliction" and momentary (2 Corinthians 4:17). He used the same word for "light" as his Lord had used, thus giving his Amen to Christ's statement. Each who thus will join himself to the tribe of Issachar, and, as a strong ass, will bow his shoulder to bear, and become willingly a servant under taskwork, shall find that his resting place is good and the land pleasant (Genesis 49:14-15).

And this present enjoyment of God is a true, if limited, foretaste of perfect communion hereafter, in anticipation of which consummation Groves penned this ecstatic exclamation:

O, what glorious liberty we are heirs to, as children of God, one day to love the Eternal Father, Son and Spirit, with unalloyed affections, when our whole nature shall be again on the side of God, and not a place left for the enemy to put his foot to harass the heir of Glory (116).

3. The Coming of the Lord.

At the same time that the meeting in Dublin began which proved the commencement of the Brethren there developed a keen interest in unfulfilled prophecy. But it is important to observe that this was at first unconnected with the Dublin gatherings.

Mr. Neatby's facts are interesting and pertinent, but seem to bear against his inferences from them. He tells us (38, 39) that meetings to study prophetic scriptures "were established in 1827 at Aldbury Park, Surrey, the seat of the well-known Henry Drummond. At these meetings Edward Irving took part, and to Aldbury Irvingism traces its rise." This first fact entirely dissociates the inception of such studies from Aungier Street, Dublin, and its church principles. Lady Powerscourt (known in the family to this day as "the good Lady Powerscourt," as I was told by the late Dowager Viscountess Powerscourt) attended those meetings at Aldbury, and called such at her house near Bray, County Wicklow, Ireland. Until 1833 the rector of the parish presided, which shows it was not a "Brethren" gathering. Thus five years after Groves' suggestions as to liberty of ministry had given form to the meetings of Brethren, there was a chairman at the prophetic gatherings at Powerscourt House, who "called on each to speak in turn on a given subject," and Irvingites were present. It is clear that the distinctive principles of Brethren did not rule at those gatherings. Nor have I seen evidence that Groves ever attended them.

I understand that the principles which gave form to Brethren meetings were: 1. That all children of God should be welcomed to Christian fellowship, without reference to differences of opinion, expressly including, as we have seen, differences upon prophetic subjects; 2. That the Lord's Supper could be enjoyed without the presence of an ordained minister; 3. That human ordination is no requirement of Scripture for the ministry of the gospel; 4. That the worship and ministry of the house of God should be led directly by the Spirit of God; 5. That Christian service is the individual responsibility of the Lord's servant, subject, when in the church, to the general approval of the assembly.

The outer form of Brethrenism was influenced later in two different directions: 1. By opposite views upon the recognition of elders or the refusal of it, and 2. By the regarding each assembly as a distinct church unit or by considering all assemblies as one body corporate. But at the very first the two former conceptions were held, not the two latter.

Now it is surely evident that no one of these formative principles and practices is in the least affected by views upon unfulfilled prophecy. They were discovered and put into practice without any reference to the latter subject, and, as to the first and most distinctive of them all, in definite disregard of what views a Christian might hold upon such topics, or whether he had any views at all upon them. It is also the fact that even after acute differences as to prophecy had developed all parties continued for a time to practise the same principles of fellowship and worship. Darby and many held that the church of God would escape the days of the end; Newton, Tregelles, George Müller, and others believed the church will go through that period; R. C. Chapman, Groves, and Lady Powerscourt thought that not all believers will share in the first resurrection and the millennial kingdom; yet all parties long walked by the same church principles.

Therefore, with the most earnest desire to arrive at the actual facts, I am entirely at a loss to know how Mr. Neatby's concluding words can be justified, that

> Brethrenism is the child of the study of unfulfilled prophecy, and of the expectation of the immediate return of the Saviour ... it is clear now that Brethrenism took shape in part under the influence of a delusion, and that that delusion left its traces, more or less deeply, on most of the distinctive features of the system *(History, 339, ed. 2)*.

I beg to offer myself as witness that prophetic opinions and church principles have no necessary connexion. Reared a Darbyite I held his views on prophecy. Through a long and steady process my views on such matters have been very greatly changed, but I hold more firmly than ever the original principles of the first Brethren as to church order, worship, and service. Others could give similar testimony. This point is well worth establishing. At the very first the combined power of Scripture principle as to fellowship, divine love, and sound judgment assured healthy toleration of differences upon prophetic interpretation, and during that early period marked progress was made in the understanding of the future as revealed in the Word of God.

But once complete systems of interpretation had been formulated advance in knowledge ceased, and for ninety years no progress has been made by Brethren. Whoever has studied B. W. Newton's *Thoughts on the Apocalypse,* on the one side, and William Kelly's *Revelation,* on the other side, will learn but little from later books on either side, as far as I know.

And when, after a time, crystallizing of head opinion was followed by a waning of heart affection, the hope which was at first a power for unity and holiness became a subject of strife and unholiness, and intolerance crushed love and paralyzed progress.

What is needed is a Spirit-infused revival of the eagerness to learn and the liberty to speak of those first days, instead of the tacit assumptions that all is known, that this or that scheme is perfect and must not be revised, that our particular views are of the essence of the faith, that the inexhaustible Word of truth has been, on these subjects, exhausted.[1]

It seems somewhat harsh to describe the "expectation of the immediate return of the Saviour" as a "delusion," yet obviously that expectation was mistaken. The students of prophecy of a century ago were pioneering. Now pioneers may gain a good general idea of new country, but their work will need correcting and enlarging by later more accurate and detailed surveys. What would be thought of the pioneer, or his friends, who strenuously resisted revision of his drawings or descriptions, and wished to drive out of the geographical societies those who advocated or attempted it?

---

1. My paper "The Rights of the Holy Spirit in the House of God" is a call for this earlier liberty of ministry. G. H. L.

When Dr. Daly, the rector who presided at the early meetings at Lady Powerscourt's, issued in 1838 her *Letters and Papers* he wrote in his Preface:

> I should certainly not do what some persons, whom I esteem, have done—publish the sentiments of another, though at the same time considering them erroneous on the fundamental principles of the Gospel; but I would publish the sentiments of another on the future prospects of the Church, though in those sentiments I thought the writer was mistaken; because I consider the first subject to be vital, and that error on it is essentially dangerous; while I do not think so of the other subject. I consider the whole Church of Christ to be much in the dark with regard to prophecy, and more or less in error concerning it; and that the best way to correct the error, and attain more light, is to encourage free discussion upon it. In order to reach the end, it is essential not to mistake as to the way. It is not equally essential to form correct anticipations as to what shall be found at the end. Those who are on the way shall reach the end, and then all their mistakes concerning it shall be corrected.

Only pride will say that these remarks are now no more applicable. The little children of God will still ask questions, and will still enter into the fuller knowledge of the Kingdom of the heavens. That is a bad state which Wesley said had been reached by some he met, that, marked by sundry excellent qualities, yet most unfortunately they knew everything and therefore learned nothing.

The following remarks by Lady Powerscourt, from the year 1833, illustrate the freedom there was, in those early days of the study of prophecy, to express views not popular, as well as the practical use made of the study.

> I should be glad to know what you think concerning reigning with Christ. Do you think it is for all, or only for the martyrs? I have been thinking a good deal upon the subject of late. It seems to me that the reason why it belongs to this dispensation to reign with Him, is because this is the dispensation of martyrdom; the fast days of His church, because of the absence of her bridegroom. Rest at any time seems a mere accident. "Sheep appointed to the slaughter"; the "off-scouring of all things"; "bearing about the body of the Lord Jesus"; "always delivered unto death";—this is the character of those promised days of tribulation. It is still the hour of temptation (Acts 1:4,5; Luke 22:28)… It does not

seem to me to signify so much what the trial is, as the coming out of it saying, "Lord, thou knowest that I love thee." I conceive we are all given opportunity of this martyrdom. It seems distinguished from the suffering that we have in common with the world, in that it is a suffering for principle, a trial of faith, a voluntary preference of suffering in the flesh, to denying Christ in *any wise*. It is a denying ourselves, taking up our cross daily—a cutting off a right hand, a plucking out a right eye, rather than offend. Oh! how many secret martyrdoms are thus endured, unknown to man, but precious to God! Now, I do believe, there never was a time when this doctrine (the connexion between reigning and suffering) would bear less to be overlooked, or required more to be brought forward; for truly, there is such a thing as refusing martyrdom, even as much as if we were to turn from the stake. I speak from experience. The Lord wants proofs not words... I believe there is such a thing as even the believer's being so allured, so led captive by things of sense, as for even the mighty argument to be overpowered: "If ye love me, keep my commandments"; and that many Christians, under the conviction that their souls cannot be lost, *live* in the indulgence of unlawful gratifications, rather than go through the torture of the whole heart being drawn and quartered. But, surely, if the millennial reign of Christ be a particular reward to Him for his sufferings, as "Son of Man," "Son of David," distinct from the everlasting glory, those only who have partaken with Him shall reign with Him. Do tell me what you think of this? For it seems to me, that though there are now many saved Christians, there are but few reigning ones... Do not think from this that I would make light of the all-prevailing principle of *Love*, and wish to go back to rewards. No. "Get the heart, and you have got the man." Love "makes drudgery divine." Love cannot help itself, it outruns and leaves law far behind... Love will stop at nothing; it takes up its cross and travels after its object over every mountain and hill of difficulty. But I mean that all arguments the Lord has used are needful; so dead often is even love, in sleep from continued lullabies of the flesh, and opiates from the devil. What poor, empty creatures we are! (*Letters of Viscountess Powerscourt.* Letter 4, pages 143–147).

Mr. Chapman's view mentioned (held by others also), that not all believers will rise in the first resurrection, follows from the thought that not all will reign; because it is clear from Revelation 20:4,6, that all who then rise will reign.

Groves was one of those early students of the Word who imbibed the view that the coming again of Christ was then just at hand. When the headlight of an approaching car suddenly flashes upon the eye it seems to be nearer than it may really be. Thus it was with the truth that the Lord will return personally to this earth. In this matter Groves is both a warning and yet an example; the former, in calling us to be cautious in reading into current events proofs that the advent is just at hand; the latter, in showing how the blessed hope should stimulate holiness and zeal. But it must be observed that this stimulus is felt at least as much by believers who do not entertain any notion that the coming is just upon us. The sane, healthy, purifying attitude was exemplified by Robert C. Chapman upon being told that one was saying that the Lord might come at any moment. He answered: Well, Brother Hake, I am ready; but it is not in the Bible."

The matter itself will not be here discussed at length, but one quotation will state the vital point. Francis W. Newman wrote of those very early years thus:

> My study of the New Testament at this time had made it impossible for me to overlook that the apostles held it to be a duty of all disciples to expect a near and sudden destruction of the earth by fire, and constantly to be expecting the *return of the Lord from heaven* (*Neatby*, 40).

If the apostles did so expect and teach, then obviously upon this theme they were not Divinely taught. But let one single fact be fairly faced. Peter had a distinct and positive assurance by the Lord that he would live to be old and would die a violent death, and in *this* expectation he lived. And the rest of the brethren knew of this assured prospect of Peter (John 21:18,23; 2 Peter 1:13–15). There is no possible reconciling of these two opposed ideas. They resolutely exclude each other, and the latter denies the former; the apostles did not and could not expect the return of Christ so long, at least, as Peter was alive. Nor could Paul, when in custody in Jerusalem, have expected the immediate return of the Lord, for that Lord himself stood by him one night and told him plainly he "*must* bear witness at Rome also" (Acts 23:11). Paul therefore knew by Divine intimation that neither would the Lord come, nor would he die, until after he had witnessed at Rome. Did the second element contribute to his quietness of heart amongst the perils of the voyage to Rome?

But though Groves was mistaken upon the *fact* we can profit by his remarks as to the *truth:* for that the Lord will come is *true,* though the belief that He would come without lapse of time was not fact. In view of the approach of the plague to Bagdad he wrote:

> Our Mullah is dreadfully depressed today at the prospect of the cholera and the plague coming here, and he said to me, he thought the end of the world must be near because of these wars and pestilences (108).

Exactly so did Luther, four centuries ago, misread the dire events of that period. He wrote to Nicolas Housmann, 14th October, 1526:

> You are right in saying the world is going to ruin. But I only hope the day of the coming of the Great God is approaching, for we hear only of fires, murders, and fury over all (*Letters of Martin Luther*, 153).

Wars, famines, pestilences, earthquakes, wickedness abounding will, indeed, be precursors of the end of the age; but only when they come in conjunction with the presence of Antichrist, and the unparalleled persecution of the saints of his day, and with the following disturbances in sun, moon, and stars, will they become *indubitable* proofs that the Lord is near. Rightly to read signs is not a child's affair. Many wise men have here proved foolish. How easy it is to read into our own immediate circumstances more than they really indicate, especially if they are terrible, this remark of Groves may show: with Bagdad half-ruined and half depopulated he wrote:

> It seems to me that this seat of Mohammedan glory, and of its proudest recollections, has received its death-warrant from the hand of the Lord (134).

Yet it survived, revived, and is today the modern capital of a new kingdom, with a population six or seven times as large as when Groves wrote of its death-warrant having been signed.

But Groves could make a good practical use of a mistaken notion. Speaking of famine, plague, and pestilence he said:

Surely these are among the signs of the times; but the Lord's command to us is, "Let not your hearts be troubled" (111).

And speaking of international affairs in Europe he wrote:

...surely these are signs of the times that may make the most sceptical enquire. O, how joyful a thought it is that the Lord is at hand, and our pilgrimage nearly ending! (122).

Yet his own journey was to last for twenty years more, and these pages are written eighty-six years after his death.

He affords another instance of how difficult it is to forecast the future from the happenings of the present. He wrote in 1831:

Surely every principle of dissolution is operating in the midst of the Ottoman and Persian empires. Plagues, earthquakes, and civil wars, all mark that the day of the Lord's coming is at hand; and this is our hope; on this our eyes and hearts rest as the time of repose, when all these trials shall cease, and the saints shall possess the kingdom (128).

Here is the same proper use of the great hope commingled with misapprehension of immediate circumstances. It was thus that some time later Grattan Guinness wrote positively on the same topic of the speedy downfall of the Turkish State, and used the idea as part of the basis for his most positively asserted but now disproved calculation that the end of the age must undoubtedly come in 1934!

What Mr. Neatby well emphasized in 1901 is, by the grace of God, still the fact, that

...in all this preoccupation with the study of unfulfilled prophecy the Brethren never in any single instance fell into the snare of "fixing dates." They strongly opposed all the ill-starred attempts of the kind that many of their fellow-students have made (*History,* 39).

And this they still do.

In the hour of nature's keenest grief, when he was left amid the horrors of Bagdad after burying his wife, Groves proved the solid support and rich comfort of the hope of the gospel. He said

This has been a day of trials and tears. The visions of the night were filled with her I have lost, and the day has been spent in weeping over her [his infant], I am soon, very soon, to lose; but this is only nature; my soul rests happily in my Lord. I had given up a little for His dear service; but He knew where the heart's reserves were, and has put His hand on them; yet, blessed hope that gilds these darkest days—the day of the Lord is at hand, when we shall meet to part no more. O, may my heart live with this blessed prospect ever before it, and labour each day for the Lord, as though it were to be the waking vision of the morning's dawn. My heart is very sad to think how profitless a servant I have been; but I do purpose, the Lord enabling me, to be more diligent, more devoted in future (186, 187).

Solace in sorrow, stimulus in service are two rich results of the hope of the Lord's return and its attendant events. Probably some have deserved Spurgeon's playful reproof, Ye men of Plymouth, why stand ye gazing up into heaven? This same Jesus shall so come in like manner as He went: *get on with your work!* But this has not been general, and certainly the opposite was the fact with Groves and the early Brethren; few have exceeded them in zeal in the gospel, nor is it generally otherwise today.

From the dread danger of eternal destruction we are not saved by hope but by faith, faith that rests upon a past event, the work perfected on the cross. But from the depressing power of the present we are saved by hope, by the confident expectation of events to come in the future; for hope is faith applied to the future as guaranteed by the promises of God. So with the indescribable horrors of Bagdad around him, pressing upon the natural senses, Groves' soul dwelled in the future. Like his father Abraham, he saw Christ's day and was glad, and exclaimed:

O, what a day the day of the marriage supper of the Lamb will be; may our hearts be waiting for it with holy expectation … and I would call upon you, and all my dear friends, brethren, and sisters in Christ, to rejoice with me at the prospect of that blessed day which is dawning upon us, when we shall see our Beloved as He is, and dwell with Him for ever, when our vile bodies will be changed and made like unto His glorious body, when the whole number of His elect family will be completed, and we shall reign with Him in glory (212).

And again, from India, in 1833:

O, let us praise His name together for His marvellous works towards us! Let us now dry up our tears; the day of the Lord is at hand; and oh, may our souls give Him a hearty welcome, to go out to meet Him, with our lamps full of odoriferous oil, scented with perfumes of love. Let us not cease to exhort one another, and so much the more as we see the day approaching (251).

On the way to England for his first visit he wrote this striking testimony to the power and value of the hope of the coming of the Lord in the deep waters that cross life's pathway.

> O, how many bitter hours I have passed since I last saw my native shores; hours gilded but by one hope, the glorious appearing of our God and Saviour; in other hours, lesser joys and lower hopes have dispelled the heart's sadness: but in the great waterfloods, when billows roll over the soul, that hope alone remains firm and sure, and unchangeably the same (353).

Nor was Groves the first or the last to prove in the tempest that this "hope we have as an anchor of the soul, both sure and steadfast," steadying the heart in the storm by attaching it firmly to that which is within the veil, to the things heavenly and immovable.

The following remarks are suggestive:

> I have been thinking that the wise virgins slumbering, having oil with their lamps, are our brethren in the church of Christ who will slumber on till the time of their Lord's approach, and who, though overtaken thus slumbering, will go in, having in their hearts the true oil of gladness that fits them for the feast, love to their Lord. It comforts me much to think so; for indeed I see among many who do not as yet receive this truth, such a tender love to Jesus, such a real desire for His honour, and something so meek and lowly in their walk, that I dare not doubt the Lord's love is set upon them; and it may be, that those who are awake and give the cry that awakes these true yet slumbering saints, are the very, very few, who, in *heart and soul* receive this precious truth, and who are appointed to watch for the Church, as the Bethlehemite shepherds their flocks, when the Lord first came. For while the number of those who theoretically believe the coming of our blessed Lord is daily increasing, the number of those who really are hastening unto that glorious day, with a confiding and preparing faith, is very small (292).

Show me, O Lord, in Thy mercy, to which of these two classes *I* belong! Or am I, though truly a virgin, one who may miss the feast by being foolish?

And these further words, upon the first resurrection, are also worthy of consideration. They suggest that this man of a single eye was looking in the same direction as his friend, R. C. Chapman, upon this theme. The late Joseph Sladen, who died at an advanced age in 1930, was for very many years in touch with Open Brethren. He was son-in-law to the Earl of Cavan, who also had been associated with them for a great while until his death in 1887. In 1917 the former wrote to me that,

> The late Anthony Norris Groves, one of the first Brethren, saw that the resurrection from among the dead which Paul was endeavouring to attain, was the first resurrection mentioned in Revelation 20:6.

The following extracts confirm this.

> I have had a happy day, and one in which the Lord has, I believe, helped me to set forth the glories of the first resurrection. I think I have found today some light on Philippians 3:10,15. I think that the glory of the resurrection from among the dead is the prize of the high calling of God in Christ Jesus… (296). O, may He bless you, and increase your spiritual treasures. Press on towards the prize set before you in Jesus, that you may attain to the resurrection from among the dead (304). O, I long to know more of the power of the resurrection of Jesus, and the fellowship of His suffering! May the Lord guide me to know these deep things more, being made "conformable to His death" (317). It is my joy to believe that there is a holy, pleasant company, walking even now as risen saints, whom the Lord will own as His peculiar treasure in the day of His manifestation… Our desire is to walk worthy of the redeemed saints in glory, the companions and friends of Jesus (378).

To which desire the devout heart will surely say: "Let us therefore, as many as are full grown, be thus minded" (Philippians 3:15).

16

Heavenly Wisdom

The words of a wise man's mouth are gracious. Ecclesiastes 10:12.

[IF desired, the following thirty-one extracts, with the connected scriptures, may be used as a daily reading for one month.]

1. REPROACH FOR CHRIST.

Matthew 5:11-12; Hebrews 11:24–27; 1 Peter 4:9.

Oh my dear friend! this is a wicked and foolish world, and the only good thing that can be said of it since God has ceased to bless it is, that it is the thorny way by which His servants approach His presence. Against those reproachful epithets which I see you are destined to enjoy, because you bear the image and superscription of your risen Lord, I send you the following infallible antidote, to all who have eyes to see it and hearts to believe it: "If ye be reproached for the name of Christ, happy are ye; for the Spirit of glory and of God resteth upon you." I pray God to write this consolation so deeply upon your heart that you may be enabled to *rejoice* in tribulation, when it rests on you for your Master's honoured name. (8).

2. OUTWARD CRUCIFIXION.

Matthew 16: 24–27; Luke 14:25–35; Galatians 6:14–16.

What a mercy it is to us to have the world, with its honours, its pleasures and its hopes, crucified with Christ; how it takes away the edge from the enemy's weapons; when he thinks to make a deadly thrust at us, he finds he can only touch that which we have ceased to value, because we have a better inheritance; one incorruptible, undefiled, and that fadeth not away (8, 9). I do so deeply realize the importance, to those whom God calls to pass through trials, of setting their hearts with all diligence to make a sanctified use of *all* the *little* events that happen; for if this be neglected, the heart, by imperceptible yet sure degrees, departs farther and farther from God (418).

3. INWARD CRUCIFIXION.

Galatians 2:19–20; Romans 6:6,11; 8:12–14.

I feel daily how very much more easy it is to overcome our attachment to external things than the waywardness of internal affections and tempers. I earnestly pray for freedom from this horrid bondage, that I may exalt and glorify my Saviour in all things (9). It is the setting the *heart* to *crucify self* in *every form* that makes all events subservient to blessing instead of grief; and I feel sure, where this is really undertaken in the fear of God, and simply to *please Him*, and because He would have us so live, we shall find a peace of soul, in nearness to Him, which flows out of this purpose, and abundantly compensates for every sorrow and self-denial. To feel ourselves the Lord's free-born children in the way of holiness1 is a most privileged place, amidst all the bondage of earth's cares (418).

4. AFFLICTION.

Hebrews 12:1–13; James 1:2–4; 1 Peter 2:18–25; 4:1-2.

The school of affliction is that in which the Spirit of God most effectually teaches; when, apparently without rudder and compass, you are obliged to keep the eye fixed on the star of Bethlehem and guide the frail bark fearlessly, though all be dark beside. May God strengthen you to bear all and much more for His sake, who bore the contradiction of sinners against Himself; who, when He was reviled, reviled not again; when He suffered, He threatened not; but

---

1   Neatby wrote of this phrase: "It is worth while to record this sentiment. The peculiar genius of Christianity has not often received a more striking expression" (History, 220),

committed Himself to Him who judgeth righteously. In this let us follow His ever blessed example, which, with all its trials, is so full of comfort, because the Holy Spirit dwells with those who walk thus (9).

5. CONSISTENCY.

Psalm 119:6,128; Luke 1:6; John 19:28–30.

In looking within me, and around me, how much I am struck with the want of and yet the value of consistency; how much we are all disposed to make some one or two points, that run more naturally into the constituted habitude of our hearts and affections, stand for others to which we bend with more difficulty but which are no less the rule which God has laid down. I feel it necessary very earnestly to pray against this caricature of Christianity being the exhibition which my life presents; and that all who name the name of Christ may have a beautiful symmetry in all parts of their Christian character, so that they may neither cause the enemies of the Lord to triumph, nor the weak among the flock to stumble (15, 16).

6. TRIFLES.

1 Corinthians 10:31; 11:1; Colossians 3:17; 1 Peter 3:3-4.

Everyone bore witness to the power with which Mr. Groves pleaded for devotedness to Christ. One of the young people who at this time had assembled around him to ask his counsel was questioning him as to what she might safely give up or keep. He seemed unable, at first, to realize that it was simply certain externals, such as dress, or anything so trifling, which perplexed this young Christian. He replied, with his usual energy: "Oh, of all *such* things I should say, 'The daughter of Zion hath despised thee'." This answer was never forgotten, and often helped the individual to whom it was spoken, and others with her, to count all such things "but loss, for the excellency of the knowledge of Christ" (35, 36).

7. Righteous judgment.

John 7:24; 8:15-16; Matthew 7:1-2; Romans 14:4; 1 Corinthians 4:1–5.

The sense Mr. Groves had of the unity of God's family, from the beginning of his Christian course, guided him in his judgment of others; and helped him to dwell in love, and seek ever the peace and prosperity of those he felt belonged to Christ. He thought it important, as a means of judging righteously, to seek to look at *everything* as the Lord looks upon it, and not as men speak or judge. Though not himself connected with any society, he could not bear sweeping condemnations of religious institutions, believing they had answered important ends, and were, in many cases, owned of God (36).

8. Union with all Saints.

1 Corinthians 3; Psalm 16:3.

If you mean that I do not *exclusively* join you, it is quite true, feeling this spirit of exclusiveness to be of the very essence of schism, which the apostle so strongly reproves in the Corinthians. I therefore know no distinction, but am ready to break the bread and drink the cup of holy joy with all who love the Lord and will not lightly speak evil of His name. I feel every saint to be a holy person because Christ dwells in him and manifests Himself where he worships; and though his faults be as many as the hairs of his head, my duty still is, with my Lord, to join him as a member of the mystical body, and to hold communion and fellowship with him in any work of the Lord in which he may be engaged (48). In our intercourse with Christians, we must remember there is often very little light where there is much grace: in these cases, a *little* knowledge wonderfully warms and sanctifies the heart, and this is the end of all truth (299).

9. Two Leading Objects.

Luke 24:45–49; John 10:14–16; 11:51-52; 12:32-33.

The two great objects of the Church in the latter days, independent of growing up herself into the stature of the fulness of Christ, seem to me to be the publication of the testimony of Jesus in all lands, and the calling out the sheep of Christ who may be imprisoned in all the Babylonish systems that are in the world. In both these, may the Lord of His infinite mercy grant success! (91).

10. GLORYING IN WEAKNESS.

2 Corinthians 4:7–14; 12:7–10.

Oh, how consoling it is, under an overwhelming sense of powerless insufficiency to one's work, to know that God has chosen to put the most precious gift in earthern vessels, that the excellency of the power may be of God and not of man; so that we may glory in our very weakness and ignorance, and natural insufficiency, knowing that the Lord's strength is made perfect in this very weakness. Dear and blessed Lord, make every one of us willing to be nothing, that Thou mayest in all things be glorified (91).

11. HARMONY IN DOCTRINE AND WALK.

Ephesians 4:1–3, 17–24; 2 Peter 1:1–11.

The path God's children may have to take when they are determined, in the name of the Lord, not to give the name of God's truth to anything merely human, knowing that it is a vain thing to teach for doctrines the commandments of men, is so naturally offensive, that our zeal for the truth should lead us to pray for such especial graces of the Spirit as may prevent any unloveliness in our walk from hindering the Lord's dear children in coming to and drinking of that well-spring in Christ by which we have been so refreshed and invigorated (104).

12. SUBJECTION TO CHRIST.

Psalm 45:10-11; Luke 6:46–49; 1 Corinthians 9:21.

Whilst we profess, my very dear friends, absolute freedom from man's control in the things relating to God, we only acknowledge in a ten-fold degree the absoluteness of our subjection to the whole mind and will of Christ in all things. As He is our *life*, which is hid with Him in God, so let Him be our way and our *truth*, both in doctrine and conversation [manner of living]. How many, from the neglect of this lovely union, have almost forgotten to care about adorning the doctrine of God their Saviour in all things. Let us, my dear brethren and sisters, pray that we may be united in all the will of Christ. This is a basis not for time only but for eternity, and for that glorious day especially, when the Lord shall come to be glorified in His saints, and admired in all them that believe (104, 105).

13. The End of the Age—its Character

1 Timothy 4:1–3; 2 Timothy 3.

Things are in preparation for the knowledge of God's holy Word being extended, and thus one great object of missionary labour is in the way of attainment. But still, while I feel assured of there being some choice fruit from here and there a fruitful bough, I at the same time feel no less assured that the great harvest will be of wickedness, and that the pestilence of infidelity is the great spreading evil to be expected, not the spreading of millennial blessedness. As it was in the days of Noah, so do I believe it will be at the coming of the Son of Man; and as it was in the days of Lot, the great mass of mankind will be taunting the church with: "Where is the promise of His coming?" which shews plainly enough that this will be a doctrine of the Church in the latter days, or how should it be reviled? so that our Lord, in contemplating the general apostasy, said: "When the Son of Man cometh, shall He find faith on the earth?" O then, how happy is it to be among those who love His appearing, who long for the termination of that dispensation which has witnessed the humiliation of the Church under the world, and for the rise of that glorious kingdom which shall not be dissolved, and into which no sighing or sorrow can enter (109).

14. GOD IS FAITHFUL.

Joshua 21:45; 1 Corinthians 10:13; Hebrews 13:5-6.

The Lord has been better than all our fears and all our hopes. The more we have proved Him, the more we have found Him to be faithful and gracious, and that not one of the good things that He has promised to faith has been wanting; but His love has abounded far beyond our faith, yea, and it will yet abound more and more. Let us then encourage one another to prove Him more, that we may have deeper experience of His faithfulness (110).

15. FAITH AND SUBMISSION IN SORROW.

1 Peter 5:5–11.

O, my poor heart flutters like a bird when it contemplates the extent of its bereavement as a husband, a father, a missionary! O, what have I not lost! Dear Lord, sustain my poor weak faith. Thy gracious visits sometimes comfort my soul; yet my days move heavily on; but the Lord, who redeemeth the souls of His servants, has declared that none of those who trust in Him shall be desolate. Lord, I believe, help Thou mine unbelief. I do indeed desire with my whole soul to cast myself into the ocean of Thy love, and never to let Satan have one advantage over me, by instilling into my heart hard thoughts of Thy ways. Surely we expect trials, and if so, and Thou sendest one other than we expected, should it surprise us when we see but a point in the circle of Thy providence, and Thou seest the end from the beginning? (161).

16. THE EFFECT OF LOVE.

Titus 2:11–3:8.

O, what a blessed passage is that in Romans 5, "If, when we were enemies, we were reconciled to God by the death of His Son, much *more* being reconciled we shall be saved by His life." Yet the more I feel of this assurance of such unmerited love, the more hateful sin appears in all its shapes, and the more my soul desires entire devotedness to the whole will of God, and conformity to my gracious Lord (187).

17. PREPARATION FOR SERVICE.

1 Timothy 4:15-16.

This day has taught me that if I would not be entirely miserable, I must give up my whole time, and soul, and thought to my Lord; for if I look off Him, I feel bordering on a gulf, the depth of which I cannot fathom. O, may the Holy, blessed Spirit give me such views of the graciousness and exceeding riches of my Lord, that I may really feel, in having Him, I have all things! He alone is the same yesterday, today, and for ever. All created things, the nearest, the dearest, the most beloved, in the moment of greatest need and greatest felicity, elude the grasp and flee away; but He abides always. I desire, therefore, the Lord enabling me, to give myself to preparation for my future labours more diligently than I have ever yet done; that though desolate on earth, I may hold the freest and sweetest communion with heaven; for, of all preparation, I feel the greatest, the most needful to be that of the heart; in order to the constant sensible entertainment of Christ, from whose nearness all the faculties derive the sap and the fruit-bearing strength (190).

18. GOD'S WAYS.

Psalm 77:19-20; Romans 11:33–36.

It appears to me probable that most important openings may be afforded by these [political] changes to our operations in these quarters; but I have seen such things these last twelve months [in Bagdad], that my soul rests only upon God, to see how He will move. His ways are so deep, so out of sight, that what we think likely, He, in a month, brings to nothing, and yet in His own good time will bring the most wonderful and unexpected things to pass (207).

19. Joy in Hardship.

Matthew 5:10–12; Colossians 1:24; Philippians 3:10–11.

Amidst these tempests, I sometimes think 'tis hard to live. Yet, my dear friend, it is sweet to live hardly for Jesus. After all my sufferings and all my sorrows, my heart is not discouraged (208).

20. The Worker's Deepest Trials.

2 Corinthians 1:8-9; 2:12-13; 7:5; Matthew 26:38.

We have much to rejoice us here [Bagdad] and much to try us. . . . Ah, may you, my brother, by the power of the Holy Ghost, live much in Christ, that your joy may be in Him, as well as your fruitfulness from Him; there is nothing else will stand the stormy seas of these lands. Your deep trials as a missionary will be in your own soul, and for this there will be no remedy but having faith in your Physician and living near Him (226).

21. Personal Attachment to Christ.

John 21:15–19; Philippians 1:21; 2 Corinthians 5:15.

Is it not a sweet fruit of unconditional salvation that it has taught the soul to *esteem God's will concerning all things to be right?* Imperfect obedience to the Divine will can only be, I conceive, the fruit of *imperfect love.* Does not our dear Lord say, "he that hath my commandments and keepeth them, he it is that loveth me?" *How He* kept His Father's, all agree; why then should we doubt in what sense we are to *endeavour* to keep His? Our Lord says He told them these things that *His joy* might remain in them, and that their *joy* might be FULL. But in the way most people seem to look at service and obedience, it could only be a burden and source of sorrow. How true it is in natural love that labour loses its character when the object is beloved. I feel what we want is PERSONAL ATTACHMENT to our dear Lord, and all thoughts of trouble in His service would fly like the mists upon the mountain tops before the rising sun (234, 235).

22. THE SPIRIT OF OUR SERVICE.

Ephesians 4:23; Philippians 4:23; Malachi 2:15.

The Lord grant us grace to do right things in a right spirit (254).

23. RETIREMENT.

Luke 5:16; John 6:15; Acts 20:13.

I have today a quiet room in a quiet bungalow in the midst of the jungle. You do not know how sweet the rest is to one harassed by being continually in public, or, I rather should say, with others. For many months I have hardly known, save in the night watches, when others were asleep, that no eye saw me save His that never slumbers. The bustle and excitement to which I have been continually exposed in India have often had power to expel thoughts that pained me, but they have never brought peace to my soul or power to suffer meekly or patiently. There is more strength acquired, *if Jesus be with us,* to the soul by tears in *retirement,* than by any transitory joy, free from outward excitement (261).

24. SELF INJURY.

Proverbs 14:14; Jeremiah 2:12-13.

As I move among Christians, the thought often strikes me how exceedingly they mar their own peace. Husbands and wives, brothers and sisters, are continually ruining each other's happiness about things that are not worth a second thought; and though you can *put your finger* upon the diseased spot in the soul from whence *the discord arises,* those whom you love and wish to make happy will not see it. O, how much must the whole Church grieve our dear, and gracious, and most long-suffering Lord! (264).

25. LOVE TO CHRIST.

John 14:20–24; 16:27; Matthew 22:34–40; Luke 22:28–32.

Has your heart ever been exercised by the consideration of our want of *personal love* to Christ? Mine has for many months; and the other day I was led to feel how manifest was the difference between our affections for human objects and divine. I have often felt that there were many things unlovely, unchristian, ungrateful to the Lord, contrary to His will, and to that holy allegiance that I owe Him, and therefore I did not do them, knowing that *I* could not be happy whilst living in any measure of estrangement from Him; but as it regards a beloved human object, there might be many things unlovely, unchristian, ungrateful, inconsistent with love, but my inmost soul feels that it is not any one, nor all of these reasons put together, that prevent my wounding him, but simply an *ever-present consciousness* that to give *him* pain would *give me deeper,* merely because I love him. Now why is it not so with the Lord? Why in the one case do we *reason up* to obedience, and in the other *obey by an intuitive impulse* independently *of reasoning altogether?* Do you not think the difference real? I think my own heart tells me so most constantly. I do most anxiously desire to feel for my dear Lord those quick promptings of love, whereby I might be prevented ever wounding Him, from *feeling myself the pain, not from reasoning at* all about its unfitness. My desire is to feel for Him with more *acuteness* than for the *most loved earthly treasure,* even the sweetest and dearest saint. I feel there is something in love so hallowing; it kills that hateful self-ishness which twines round all that is human. Even in nature's love, in all the varied relations of husband and wife, parents and children, etc., it is the sweetest relic of the fall even if it ascends not up to God (288, 289).

26. SATISFIED IF CHRIST BE GLORIFIED.

John 4:34; 5:23; Philippians 1:20.

Never did I feel more than now that I needed a single eye and a guileless soul before God. I see so many rocks in my course, yet it shall be the object of my most earnest prayers to have my soul *so satisfied*, if *Christ* be *but glorified*, that I think not, nor care, by whom or where; and to have my heart so affected towards every saint, that my joy in him, or her, shall not be in proportion to my own delight in them derived from personal intercourse, but in seeing each one in the place the Lord would have him (290).

27. Purposes of Affliction.

2 Corinthians 12:9; Ezekiel 20:35; Song of Songs 8:5.

When I think how deeply the Lord has tried me, not only by every variety of affliction, personal and domestic, but by alienating the hearts of those most precious to me from our work, I stand amazed at what God means. Sometimes it seems it can only be to stretch the heart strings to the utmost, to show what the most weak and fool-ish can bear, without fainting, when *He* sustains by the dew of His blessings, by the manifestation of His favour, by whispering: "Fear not, thou worm Jacob." O, how soothing it is to the soul to have Jesus as our refuge, and to be able to commit our way to Him in faith! (313). The Lord is most gracious in showing me that the manifesta-tions of Himself, seen in the choicest of His saints, are dimmed and obscured by the medium through which they shine, in order that the *Lord alone may stand* revealed the *true light* of life, and love of His people. I have been greatly blessed through the trials of the last many months. My whole happiness now consists in not looking for a *moment* aside from the *Lord*, as the giver of every good: and this knowledge, coupled with a clear, abiding sense of His love, as desir-ous and waiting to give all that, if I knew my true happiness, I could desire, enables me to look a little faithfully into the *inner man* (327).

28. Heart Fellowship Limited.

Psalm 69:20; Matthew 7:14; Philippians 2:20-21; 2 Timothy 1:15–18; 4:16–18.

I believe when I left England I had little tendency to trust man in the things of God, nor have I more now. There are a few with whom the soul has communion in the secret things of the king-dom, those *hidden* enjoyments that flow directly from Jesus. I do wonder at the conversation of professing Christians when they meet together. With the world it may be different; but among themselves, you would expect that out of the abundance of the heart the mouth would speak (341). Really when I see how many weaknesses and prejudices the apostles had to bear with in their early converts, I am quite reconciled to bear the same in the converts of India. It would be too happy a state to have all enlightened, simple, zealous, and loving. Happy indeed must we be, in this disjointed world, if we find a few with whose thoughts we can find fellowship in the spirit: I believe I have, and ever shall have, some, and I expect not many. How few the apostles seem to have had like-minded, and can we hope for more in these degenerate days? Indeed, I look for fewer, but, with these, a compensating extent and intensity of holy, happy fellowship (350).

29. THE RIGHT WAY IN THE WILDERNESS.

Psalm 107:7; Deuteronomy 8:2–6; John 8:12.

How sweet an example Ezra is, in passing through the wilderness to the promised land, with all his encumbrances of gold, silver, children, and women (Ezra 8:22-23). Surely we might learn *much* from his example. I would that our faith in God were more lively as respects His fatherly character, as a God whose hand is upon all those for good who seek Him, and against those who forsake Him. It was so wise, Ezra's not seeking the shortest or the easiest way, but the *right* way for the little ones, and for all their substance. Unbelief might have pleaded David's application to Hiram as an excuse for asking help of the king, and also that there was no express prohibition against it; but Ezra's eye was single, and he saw how to find the right way, even by committing all to God, who then directed his path (381).

30. HOLINESS OF HEART.

Ezekiel 36:25–27; Ephesians 3:14–21; Philippians 2: 12–16; 1 Peter 3:3-4.

How blessed it is to feel that the Lord's ascension has secured us the *indwelling* of God's Holy Spirit for ever, to teach us to pray and to assist us in our necessities. I think there is far too little realization of the truth "it is God which worketh in you both to will and to do of [to work for] his good pleasure," and "without [severed from] me ye can do nothing." I should often be in despair but for the faith and feeling I have, that the Spirit's internal workings are *effectual* to make me long for and love what *naturally* I could not desire. To one who knows the natural hardness and insensibility of the human heart, how blessed it is to feel the Spirit abiding within, to breathe life into all their palsied affections, and to concentrate them in God (427). I think that unity and *intimacy* of relationship are conveyed by all these words, so that we may feel that He (the Lord Jesus) is *with* us when we want external help; in us when we want internal help; and *among i*s when we want collective help; in fact, that our own Jesus is all and in all. The *point* of importance to believers is, that *nothing* can be rightly or acceptably done that *He does* not *work* in and among us; but no external regulations that we adopt in our different meetings can prove that our souls are in this state (428). I was much struck this morning with the Lord's declaration that He would put wisdom into the hearts of *all* who were employed about the tabernacle; though there was only *one* Bezaleel, yet each had especial wisdom given for his own work; how much more, in the spiritual building, do we need the Lord's guidance and Spirit for the right ordering of everything. *If we are to do all to the glory of God we must do all by the Spirit of God* (457).

31. CHRIST IS ALL.

Colossians 3:10-11; 1 Corinthians 1:30-31.

I always feel the very attempt to subject the one adorable Christ of God to a process of mental analysis is, in its very operation, desecrating. It has engendered the worst of divisions in the church, and will, I believe, ever do so; however carefully, however *cautiously* pursued. When I look at Jesus as the Word represents Him, I see one whole of aggregate loveliness, suited to my every necessity, able and willing to love, succour, comfort, bless, redeem, sanctify, and make accepted the vilest and most unworthy: this is all my joy and glory; Jesus, descending, dying, ascending, and returning to bless and take His own, is my all and in all (464).

17

Failure and its Lessons

Psalms 51:12-13; 139:23-24

How greatly God is to be praised that His faithful Word records the failures of even the great among His servants. Thereby do their histories comfort us their weaker brethren, without excusing their or our failings; and, too, we may learn not to pass judgment on those we see to fail, even as we dare not judge the men of God mentioned in His Word. If it is in this humble spirit that we consider the following circumstances in Mr. Groves' life we may be profited, even as we are by the histories of Scripture.

Finding his testimony in Madras greatly hindered, he removed in 1837 to the town of Chittoor, ninety-six miles distant. In Madras he had been able to support all the missionary party by his own services as a dentist, but

> ...employment was greatly needed for the native converts, who, by embracing Christianity, lost their means of support. Besides the direct example of the Apostle, in combining manual labour with work among the heathen, Mr. Groves often alluded to an observation of a Mohammedan "Mullah" at Bagdad which had evidently confirmed his judgment in this question. This man had said, "I know you are a devoted man, and give much away, but I know not what your motives are, or what the extent of your riches. If I saw persons labouring from day to day, and giving the fruit of their labour to the poor or to missions, I should then see they were making sacrifices for God (371).

In 1837 the subject of a self-supporting mission was much in Mr. Groves' mind, and at Chittoor circumstances seemed to favour such an enterprise. Land was acquired and a small farm commenced, which helped to support his household and many poor children. In 1841 cultivation of silk was commenced, land being rented. He put forth great energy, expended much time, showed great skill, and seemed to be prospered in the undertaking. His motives were unselfish and excellent, as this extract will show:

> I cannot tell you what encouragement I feel it to be to labour in the hope we shall have to give to further the Lord's work. The Bowdens have lost nearly all those who used to contribute to their support, but the Lord still provides: my desire is to pay all their expenses, should the Lord prosper me (398).

But this the Lord did not do. Disease shortly destroyed the silk-worms, and the enterprise had to be abandoned; and later transactions in the shipment of sugar, which promised at first to recoup the losses on the silk industry, involved only heavier losses, owing to depression of markets. He was thus involved in prolonged trials which embittered his later years and cast a severe gloom over his spirit for a long period. This last was probably in part temperamental, for he was of an ardent disposition, capable, as a quotation given earlier shows, of exalted enjoyment, and therefore of corresponding depression.

The spiritual benefits wrought in him by the wisdom of God his Father are abundantly evident in his journals, letters, and ministry of the period. Two extracts will suffice to illustrate this. At the height of the trials he said:

> God can unravel the most intricate paths; can make the crooked straight. O, there is a softness in God's touch, which gives a help no man can minister! God sees *where* the *sore* is and lays His hand on the *very place*, whereas man only AGGRAVATES the wound. You can do, in connexion with God, what you *cannot do*, or pass through, with men; and what *pains* does God take to encourage our trust in Him, constraining us to pour out our hearts before Him, and to find *Him* a refuge. Yes! "unto the upright there ariseth light in the darkness," be the cloud never so dense, the way never so perplexed, there will always be something in the midst of it which will reveal a Father's love, a *Father's* care; there will be ever a *bow* in the cloud. In the midst of midnight darkness, the believer knows that "light *is* sown for the righteous"; therefore he occupies himself, not with forebodings as to how things will turn out, but rests on the promise of God, and, above all, on His *purpose* in afflicting us, even to make us "partakers of His holiness"; and he stays himself on his God (401).

How richly this divine and adequate purpose was fulfilled, though Groves himself knew not that his face thus shone, is shown by the testimony of another, at the close of the ten years of this trial, in connexion with a visit to the Nilgiri Hills.

> The first day he came up, he was so wretchedly out of spirits at not having received your letters, etc., and doubtless many other things pressed on him. It was Sunday, and his speaking was with *such power!* quite that *of former years,* when I first heard him at Chittoor; quite strengthening and refreshing; it spoke to the *hearts of all,* and all were edified. Since he has come up he is in better spirits, and great grace is upon him. He has had many trials, and is a bruised reed. I never saw such humility in any one. Really to hear him speak, you would think he was quite useless in the Church, whereas no one is so beloved by all. Even the world can bring no reproach against him; so kind, tender, and considerate to all, except when the truth of his Master is concerned, and then he is *bold and earnest* in commending it…
>
> I dare say you hear of his state from himself—the blank, as he calls of it, of his ten years at Chittoor; indeed, I do not like to hear him speak of it, he feels it so acutely; and I do not think it *right,* because he was the means of bringing many to Jesus, and a witness for the Lord in his consistent walk (437).

Let other bruised reeds hold up the head! Let the gold be content in the crucible; the fire shall but make it lustrous.

The only one who could disclose the inwardness of this affliction, his widow, graciously did so, though it must have been painful to herself. Of the early days when the silk industry was developing she wrote:

> …the object he had so near his heart appeared in a fair way of being accomplished, and nothing but funds seemed wanting to carry out his project, when there came from an unexpected quarter the unsolicited offer of a loan of thirty thousand rupees [I suppose then £3,000]. This was regarded by himself, his wife, and brother-in-law, as an indication of the mind of God in this matter; and, on the strength of present appearances, as of old with regard to the Gibeonites, an agreement was entered upon, and neither party had a misgiving as to its being the *very step needed* to put the whole undertaking at Chittoor on a remunerative footing, for carrying out the work of God. This first departure from the

way of faith was, in the providence of God, followed by most bitter circumstances (397).

In the issue Mr. Groves paid considerably more by way of interest than the original loan. It will be well to say at once that the whole sum was finally repaid, and the whole undertaking concluded honourably. If I presume aright, this was brought about by the second Mrs. Groves being of the same sterling quality as his first wife. At least, this is what seems suggested by these words of hers in the year 1853:

> It is interesting to dwell here on the full answer given to his prayers, in obtaining what his faith *looked* for;—even the entire relief from all temporal anxieties, which was brought about at this period. Mrs. Baynes' death [*Mrs. Groves' mother*] made a great alteration in his circumstances, and things connected with his affairs in India were about this time happily settled (486).

"Whoso findeth *a wife*, findeth *a* good thing, and obtaineth favour from Jehovah," for a "worthy woman is *a crown* to her husband"—in the highest respect she completes his dignity, as the crown does the attire of the king (Proverbs 18:22; 12:4).

In no sense passing judgment, but only enquiring, and for the sake of spiritual profit, we may note the following features of these circumstances.

1.   The removal to Chittoor seems to have been induced by reason of difficulties encountered in Madras. Might it have been better to have overcome these by steadfast prayer? In the spiritual realm the line of least resistance is often not the best.

2.   No distinct divine guidance to Chittoor is detailed or suggested. He learned that there was no missionary there; but the same fact was true of a thousand other places.

3.   By this change he ceased to become an itinerant preacher and took up settled work. He speaks of his "station," as a thousand other missionaries do. It is a deplorable word, though extremely accurate, and deplorable because accurate. To be stationary is the contradiction of Christ's key word of command, Go! Groves had heard that

command and had interpreted it rightly. In 1831 he spoke of "my future duties as an itinerating missionary" (190).

In 1834, in India, his mind was still so set. He wrote:

> I yet look forward to having him [Mokayel, a young Syrian] for a travelling companion over many a weary mile in Egypt, Syria, Arabia, and Mesopotamia (279).

And in the same year he adds:

> B. quite agrees with me ... the missionaries ought to go from place to place, preaching the gospel, and only become stationary when they have gathered a church; and rather than remain so, if called to the office of an evangelist, they should do as the apostle did, set some over the church and go on (308, 309).

And just before this he had written:

> I have been greatly exercised relative to the best way of bringing forward the native ministers of Christ in these countries, and I have finally rested on our dear Lord's plan; that is, to get from two to twelve, and to go about constantly with them, eating what they eat, and sleeping where they sleep, and labouring, whether in a Choultry at night, or by the way, to impress on their souls a living exhibition of Jesus (280).

A truly arduous life, yet as truly the way of Christ and of the apostles He trained, and one that has never failed of its harvest. For itinerant evangelizing is always and everywhere owned of God in due season to conversions. It was the apostolic method. But it has been the almost general practice of denominational and "society" organizations to establish *resident* workers, and it is the equally general lament in all such spheres that indigenous, self-supporting, self-governing, self-propagating churches are alarmingly rare, even when converts are gained. In apostolic days they were not rare but the rule, for the groups of believers were shortly cast directly upon the Lord, and were made to stand, for the Lord was able to hold them up, whereas the resident missionary is not able to do this. He was never intended to do so by the Lord, though he is by his society. God knows the innate tendency of the human heart to lean on man rather than on Himself, so His method was that the evangelist should shortly pass on, and Christ be all in all to His people. It is greatly to be regretted that many who went forth to work on Groves' lines have too much followed his Chittoor example, not his earlier practice, and have settled down and become "station," and too largely stationary, workers. That Groves' *family* had to live somewhere is obvious; that the *evangelist* should cease itinerating was a very doubtful step.

4.   He was lured into this by the prospect of forming an industrial self-supporting mission enterprise. That his motives were utterly unselfish we know. He was seeking a solution of the practical and very real problem of support for both workers and converts. But did he not fail to observe a very plain distinction as to the practice of the apostles? Paul toiled hard at his trade to support himself and his travelling companions (Acts 20:34, etc.); but he did this only when necessary, and never in such manner as to become tied to any place and thus be hindered from moving on immediately, at the call of the Lord or by the compulsion of persecution. And, in any case, the apostles and first evangelists never undertook personally the support of converts, the educating of the illiterate or young, or the solution of any such difficulties. These matters were at least as constant and urgent as now, amongst Jews and pagans; but the apostles initiated no industrial or institutional enterprises, but left all such problems to the converts.

What they did was to inculcate and encourage true love to one another, so that those who had enough should share it with those who lacked. And testimony is abundant that this sufficed them. Groves had himself advocated and argued this in his paper *Christian Devotedness;* but now he turned to solve for others difficulties intended by God to cast them upon His own grace and faithfulness, and to be the occasion for developing faith in His children and brotherly love. Has not the plan of missionary-provided schemes of support largely frustrated these essential ends, caused converts to be "hangers on" rather than themselves supporters of the weak, and also been a terrible inducement to the making of insincere professions of faith?

5.   His biographer speaks of the acceptance of the loan proffered as a "departure from the way of faith." It necessarily was that. It was accepting help by a method incompatible with direct faith in God,

being nowhere sanctioned by His instructions or examples for His business of the gospel. It thus became a self-imposed burden, and under it there could be no comfort from the promise, "Cast that which *He* hath given thee upon Jehovah, and he will sustain thee" (Psalm 55:22). It was blessedly true that the Lord graciously helped through all the consequent trials, but Groves had to feel the pressure of the burden, until he almost despaired as he toiled under the weight.

Nor did it occur to him that his kindly purpose to meet all the expenses of other workers, out of the proceeds of his own labours, could only result in imperilling their faith by diverting it to himself. Of his friend Rhenius in Tinnevelly he had written, in 1838:

> ...he is reduced to a fortnight's provision of bread, but has in hand a good stock of faith and trust. I am daily more and more resolved to share my last crust with the brethren at Tinnevelly (389).

How much safer and more soul-enriching it was for Rhenius to be so placed, and for Groves to contemplate reaching his "last crust," and sharing *that,* than to contemplate a sufficiency for all from secular toils. He had forgotten his own reason against laying up in store, that *poverty* and *dependence* are truly blessed conditions, which the carnal mind, indeed, strives to its utmost to avert, but which the child of the heavenly Father should covet.

6.   And there is one thing more, of the last and deepest importance, and which points to a most deadly danger from all such enterprises, educational, medical, industrial. It is that they greatly tend to absorb time and energy to the exhaustion of the vital spiritual force of the soul, not to say of mind and body. I am not left to suppose this may have been so with Groves. It is plainly stated for the warning of readers of the *Memoir,* by his own words, and by his widow. How much more valuable is a faithful biography than a eulogy! We read:

> The following exposition, given at this time, has evident reference to his own circumstances, which he was disposed always to attribute to having been too much engrossed with the external affairs of the mission, which had hindered his enjoying his usual hours of retirement and communion with God:—

Hosea 12:6. The reason the Scriptures so abound with declarations of God's love and pity for His people, and His desire they should return to Him, is that the heart once gone astray has much difficulty in getting back again. We have all need to be on our guard that we do not, like Judah, go astray; and if we do, we must hear Him say, "Turn thou to thy God." We generally find the principles of return are *exactly* opposite to those which caused our turning away from God; thus the prophet says, "Wait on thy God *continually,*" and the beginning of departure is found in only waiting upon God *occasionally.* There is something in the heart which tells us if we are really in *fellowship* with God; the soul that has tasted it cannot be mocked by an apparent return. One cause of going astray is the preferring something to God's worship, even as Israel followed Baalim. Often are we beguiled into worldly things with an idea that we can make them *subservient* to God's glory; but the things we have thought would bend, as a bow, to shoot arrows against the enemies of God, become the means of piercing us through with many sorrows, and leading us away from God. Nothing requires more spiritual discernment than to *detect* the snares of the enemy; they are often so covered over as to appear the leadings of God (403, 404).

Groves did not remember in 1841 what he had written in 1829, on the journey to Bagdad. At Sarepta, a colony of Moravians, he had marked a plain instance of this danger of the spiritual succumbing to the secular in industrial mission work. He said:

All missionary character is now lost here; they are a simple colony of artificers who, for the sake of the preservation of *this* character, have relinquished that of the missionary. I see here the great evil of having anything mercantile connected with missionaries, unless as a simple accident of support, and not as an essential part of the constitution. Mr. N. the Moravian pastor at Sarepta said, a missionary, if prevented from preaching the truth or exercising his ministry, might take up his hat and say, *"Bonjour, Messieurs"* [Good day, gentlemen], and walk off. But a colony, he added, is *"une autre chose"* [another matter], your hands are tied. However, the missionaries might go on as long as they could, and when the alternative came of leaving, or restricting their ministry, those who preferred gain would stay, and those who preferred Christ would go (59).

It might well exercise the consciences of some missionaries as to how far the trading in crochet, and other handiwork of converts, has passed beyond its primary end of helping the converts to live and become, in degree, mercantile, a means of gain to the foreign workers; and how far this has induced in the latter a subtle spiritual deterioration in faith and a good conscience.

Our strongest point needs perpetual guarding as much as our weakest, or, as the adage truly says, we fail at our strongest point. Moses had become the meekest of men, but Israel angered his spirit and he spake unadvisedly with his lips (Numbers 12:3; Psalm 106:33). Groves had been a man of faith in and communion with God beyond most, yet he suffered the outer life to overbalance the inner. Is not this a voice to tens of thousands of us, his brothers and sisters? A most devoted servant of God asked my thought as to taking up a further godly enterprise. I answered, Do it, if you are fully satisfied that you will have adequate time to pray over every detail of it continually.

And perhaps Groves' ardent temperament, so fertile and valuable an asset as it was, proved a weakness. With engaging frankness he has told how, when he suddenly found he could have his beloved Mary, he promptly embraced the opportunity without adequately, or at all, "asking counsel at the mouth of the Lord," or he might not have acted so hurriedly. His biographer, as above quoted, makes, as to this present failure, the same comparison to Joshua and the Gibeonites. The nobler, not only the lower, of our natural powers must be held in restraint and subjected ever to the guidance of God. The offer of the loan was assumed to be of God because it so exactly coincided with the position to which their own honestly devised schemes had brought them just then, and they were carried forward by impulsive, uncorrected considerations. When the south wind blows softly, the sailor thinks he has gained his purpose, and sails out of the narrow, incommodious port into—the *tempest!* (Acts 27:13) The man (Paul) who was in close touch with God proved wiser than the men of greater natural experience and skill. By the dark days of the tempest Groves learned yet more deeply to do as the prophet said, and wait on God *continually*. It will be our wisdom to learn the lesson from the prophet, and thus avoid such an experience.

—oOo—

Now as I went on my journey I came to a stretch of the King's highway named Temperance, which, after the older dialect of these parts, signifieth Self-Control. Here there brancheth off from the highway a by-road that in very ancient times was called Montanism, after one Montanus, an earnest man who busied himself making this by-road because he deemed the King's highway hereabouts to want some of those more striking features that its first stretches displayed, and he thought to supply them in this his by-road. However, for long periods after his time it was not much used; yet of late the same ideas as to the highway have seized again upon some minds (as, indeed, hath somewhat unaccountably happened from time to time), and a goodly number of very sincere people have frequented it. Some of these, seeing that the ancient name of Montanism was now archaic and uncouth, indeed to most folk unintelligible, and, moreover from age almost illegible, have renamed the by-road "Pentecostalism," though in truth it is not quite so old as this name would signify.

Now I observed loitering about its entrance a number of persons, light and airy of form, who at first glance appeared attractive enough, until one looked steadily into their eyes, which then showed as shifty and cruel. These busied themselves by drawing the attention of pilgrims, very politely, and with persuasive words of wisdom, to the advantages of the by-road, assuring them that it led to the Palace Beautiful by a more speedy and pleasant route than the highway, which, said they, was somewhat barren and uneventful.

But I saw also that at this point the King had caused to be set up a large finger-post, pointing along the highway and away from this by-road, on which was written, in letters so large and plain that even the near of sight could read them easily, this warning: "Beloved, believe not every spirit, but PROVE THE SPIRITS WHETHER THEY ARE OF GOD, because many false prophets are gone out into the world." These words I remembered to have read in that letter in the King's Guide Book for Pilgrims written by His well-instructed guide John.

But those loiterers did blandly explain to pilgrims that this warning was intended only for the careless and foolish, and that such evidently earnest and sincere pilgrims as themselves did not need it and need not heed it. So it came about, as I observed, that, in disregard of the King's words and beguiled by those of these cruel-eyed seducers, some were induced to enter the by-road. And as they entered I heard one say to another: Surely the King will not allow such sincere pilgrims as we are to be deceived. We have asked Him for bread and shall He give us a stone?

And truly for some little distance the by-road looked fair and promising; but as I gazed farther adown it—for it inclined rather downwards than upwards, a plain proof that it led other-whither than the highway—I descried many that were stumbling and tumbling in snares and pits artfully arranged for the feet of the unwary. Some indeed recovered themselves and returned to the highway, though torn and bruised; and many seemed not to regain their feet. But those following, for the more part, did not see all this, because they had closed their eyes and so walked on; and also a mist and darkness falleth over such as disregard the King's warning, and they see nothing clearly.

Thus I saw that Sincerity, though she be so sweet and helpful a companion, yet is no guide, nor can of herself assure the safety of pilgrims.

18

At Evening, Light

Unto the upright there ariseth light in the darkness. Psalm 112:4.

It was thus with A. N. Groves. For though sincerity cannot save us from the effects of our blunders, it commands the esteem of God, and He brings the upright forth to the light when they have learned the needed lessons in the darkness. How intensely black the darkness had been at times one passage from a letter to his wife shall show. It may encourage some other hearts walking in David's "valley of deep darkness," and enable them to believe that "all the days" of their life, including the dark days, goodness and loving kindness follow them, and that they shall yet dwell in the house of Jehovah (Psalm 23). The letter was dated April 1847.

> I expect this will reach you at Woolbrook, with your beloved mother and sister, etc. You will indeed be happy, but only if Jesus be there; it is His bright face that gilds even the dark places of despair with a ray of hope, how much more the dwellings of His happy saints. I felt today what it was to have a ray pass across my withered affections… It is like a ray from heaven illuminating and reviving me again. O, that it might not be as the visit of a wayfaring man! I had long been bordering on the depths of despair and hardly felt able to answer for my mind's stability; yet I know, though it be but a moment's joy, that there *is peace* in believing, and that there is a preciousness in Jesus that satisfies when *all else fails*. This very ray of light is to show what Jesus *can be* in all the *emptiness* of earth. He and He *only can* fill a *desolate* heart and satisfy a *craving* soul. How good of the Lord to allow me to feel that there is such sweetness in Him, when I was almost ceasing to feel after Him; I prayed, but I seemed to hear the Lord say, "I will not hear, though you make many prayers," and "what have you to do to take my name in your mouth?" But why do I tell you of this ray of hope, this moment's peace, to be followed, perhaps, by all the darkness and sorrow that I have so long known, and only increased by the brightness of these few happy

374

hours? …Hours before dawn I lay in an agony of mind that knew no alleviation; and when I called on the Lord He seemed as one deaf; yet from very misery, I called again from the very depths (see Psalm 130), and the Lord heard me, and, for the moment at least, in pity has restored my soul to a sense that even my heart can love Him, in whom is my life. I had almost thought that my obdurate heart, scourged by the clearness of my sense of what the Lord desired at my hands, would unseat my mind. … How sweet that passage in Isaiah sounded when Fewkes read it, "Let him that walketh in darkness and hath no light, trust in the name of the Lord, and stay upon his God." I felt I so *needed this;* for I have so long had more darkness than light; and I have yet to stand still and see the salvation of God… You know I have long told you that no *speculative* views of truth satisfied me… I am sure what we want to know is *Jesus personally;* and *this* knowledge sanctifies, because it *humbles.* To be by the Spirit *really* brought into communion with the heart and thoughts of Jesus; how it makes the soul loathe itself, and wonder at His matchless grace, and cry to the Lord that this odious disparity may, by His grace, be removed, and all our thoughts and wishes made to harmonize. I often wish you were here today, but I believe it is well you are away, and that I am left *alone with God* (414–416).

There can be little doubt, I suppose, that in Groves' case, as in very many cases, these extremes of despair and joy were physical at their basis. He had suffered very exhausting and long bodily and mental tax in Bagdad, and there and in India had endured a tropical climate, with much severe travelling. And though he seemed to stand the heat uncommonly well, any one who has experienced it knows that the gradual cumulative effect is considerable, especially upon a person of exalted sensibilities. Under these conditions the thought of having missed his Lord's mind as to the Chittoor service weighed upon him thus heavily. Perhaps also another factor was that, unperceived, the bodily conditions were already arising that developed shortly into the cancer that ended his life.

But darkness of spirit is not less painful for being mainly from the body, for the sufferer commonly does not recognize this factor. To the patient the trial is just as real and terrible, and such deserve only the keenest sympathy, even though often most helped by tender firmness of treatment.

But with Groves it was not to last to the end. That is a sweet figure in Psalm 30:5: "Weeping may come in to lodge at even, but joy cometh in the morning." As the shadows fall a sad-faced guest named Weeping seeks lodging; yet he stays but for the night, and with the morning light his place is taken by a radiant visitor named Joy, who floods the house with gladness.

> A downcast saint there was
> Who mourned his failure,
> And feared he ne'er had known
> The sinner's Saviour,
> And that, when Death's stern call
> He needs must hearken,
> Thick mists of doubt would all
> His sky o'erdarken.
> But as he walked at even mid the shadows
> The sun o'erpowered the clouds,
> And lit the meadows,
> And sank to rest in blaze of golden glory:
> The saint a-dying sang—the Old, Old Story!

It was thus with Groves. Even before the removal of the burdens the weight was gone from his spirit. He reached England on September 23rd, 1852, in very poor health of body, but manifesting that utterly supernatural experience of Paul, "though our outward man is decaying, yet our inward man is renewed day by day" (2 Corinthians 4:16), and therefore he fainted not. On the voyage he had written:

All we want is to see earth as it will be, and heaven as it is and ever will be; and then how easily we should be reconciled to much that now afflicts us (476) . . . I feel patient, quiet waiting is the thing in all such journeys; you cannot hasten matters by impatience, and it adds much to the discomfort not seeing the Father at the helm of all one's affairs. O! for an adoring, reverential, loving heart, that draws its deepest abiding happiness from the one overflowing fountain! (477) ... How slow we are to learn that all the discipline of life is to prepare us for eternity; that nothing that has not God in it, is either worth caring for or desiring (478).

From England he wrote in far other strain than that of the first extracts above, showing a fulfilment of that principle of the ways of God with the soul indicated in Psalm 34. In verse 4, David says:

> I sought Jehovah, and he answered me,
> And delivered me from all my *fears*.

In verse 6 he adds:

> This poor man cried, and Jehovah heard him,
> And saved him out of all his *troubles*.

The inward salvation is the more important, and it is blessed that it be given first, while the trial still presses, for thus the soul learns to be without fear when later troubles rise. Thus Groves could now say:

> I live in hope.

How far he had been brought from the darkness where he had written:

> I had long been bordering on the depths of despair.

now he writes:

> I live in hope that the Lord will yet let his goodness shine upon us, and round about us, and deliver us from every trial. Unbelief is ready to say "if He should open the windows of heaven, could these things be?" but faith says "yea; and far greater things than this can be accomplished by the breath of His mouth" (481). . . . Here I am, having reached another birthday—fifty eight of which I have seen; and oh, how little progress! yet this has dawned with a sense of that rich and unspeakable grace of God towards me, that makes my heart desire to be altogether His (485).

Then the external clouds also were completely dispelled, and, though his health failed steadily, and his wife was in distant India, he wrote this striking passage:

> The Lord be praised, I can truly say He lets me see brightness on every side from His love. I look through the cracks in my clay tabernacle up towards the everlasting hills, and have now just concluded all those little earthly cares that must be attended to; I only think on my precious ones and glory (489).

A Red Indian chief, a Christian, near his end, used a similar figure of speech. To the gathered tribe he said: "My body is like an old wigwam, and has many rents. But the more rents there are the more the sunshine streams in!" and thus he died in the sunshine. And so did Anthony Norris Groves.

The dread disease took its dire course, and he suffered terribly. Of the last days one wrote:

> The shock of corn was, indeed, fully ripe, and we had the solemn conviction that his life was quickly passing away. He felt nothing but *Jesus* could be his security, his hope, or his joy; and as he neared the gates, "discovered new glories in Christ and the resurrection," and felt that *now* was the season to prove the power and sufficiency of God's sure foundation (497).

Though in such pitiful weakness he exclaimed to those around his bed:

> Can't you *sing*? O, I could sing if I had strength (497).

And on the fourth day before his death he said:

> ...with my inexpressible weakness I have such *indescribable* repose; I never could have conceived such feelings... (499)

At another time he said, "it is a wonderful thing to come nigh to God—a *wonderful thing*. When we are about and well, outward things so interrupt our vision; but to be as I am now and find God so near, it is wonderful."

At another time: "I am sure I am not deceiving myself; who could give me such peace and joy? I could not give *myself* joy" (503).

Thus did he prove to the full, and exhibit to the glory of God and the strengthening of men, the truth of the words he had used by faith, that "in the midst of midnight darkness the believer knows that 'light is sown for the righteous and gladness for the upright in heart' (Psalm 97:11).

He died on May 20th, 1853, at 21 Paul Street, Kingsdown, Bristol, the house of his brother-in-law, George Müller. And thus, as Paul said of David (Acts 13:36) "after he had in his own generation served the counsel of God, he fell asleep," his last words being a fitting and simple revelation of his heart and summary of his life: *"Precious Jesus."*

The only infallible record and estimate of any man of God is preserved in the books on high and will be duly published. This present study may be fitly closed by the words of appreciation written by Dr. Alexander Duff in connexion with the memoir.

> I can simply say that my feelings of esteem, and reverence, and love, were greatly enhanced by increased converse and more familiar fellowship... I could not help regarding him as one of the most loving and loveable of Christian men, while the singular fervency of his spirit made it quite contagious; diffusing all around the savour of an unearthly sanctity and self-consuming devotedness. O, that a double portion of his spirit would descend upon all our drowsy and sleeping churches throughout Christendom! The Lord grant that the publication of the memoir of such a man... may be blessed to the awakening of many a soul steeped in the drench of carnality and worldliness, even in the bosom of our evangelical communions! The Lord grant that professing disciples in this luxurious age of self-pleasing and self-indulgence may at least learn from his example the lesson which they pre-eminently need, and which he was honoured of God pre-eminently to teach, and that is the lesson of real scriptural self-denial, the divine lesson of taking up the cross, forsaking all, and following the Lord! (538).

> He that *loveth* his life LOSETH IT:
> And he that *hateth* his life in this world
> Shall KEEP IT unto life *eternal.*
> If any man *serve* Me
> Let him *follow Me;*
> And where *I* am
> There shall also My *servant* be:
> If any man serve Me
> Him will My FATHER HONOUR.
>   John 12:25-26.

Appendix
(See page 310)

Statement by W. H. Cole

Concerning the following paper Mr. E. H. Broadbent writes: "A really instructive document. Mr. Cole was one of our first visitors after we were married: a delightful man."

The printed copy I have is prefaced as follows:

> The manuscript of this book was given to me by my beloved friend Mr. W. H. Cole. He was, from his entry into the first meeting at Plymouth to his death at Norwich, a capable, constant and gracious servant of the Lord. His ministry and example were of great value and much esteemed.

Beaumont,   E. B. ROCHE, M.D.
      Sheringham, Norfolk.

REMINISCENCES OF THE PLYMOUTH MEETING OF "BRETHREN"

Through the great mercy of our God, I was converted to Him in early youth in Plymouth, my native town, soon after which I was led to see the blessed truth of the personal coming again of our Lord from Heaven to take His church to Himself and personally reign over the millennial earth. And [I] was brought into fellowship with those, who I learnt, assembled upon principles taught in the Word of God, where no sectarian wall of division was acknowledged, and where there was the liberty of the Spirit of God, to minister the truths of Scripture by those who were gifted by Him for that purpose. At that time all was happiness and peace, unruffled by personal questions, undisturbed by jealousies or ambitions. The distinctions between rich and poor were lessened by holy, loving fellowship and unity which characterized their intercourse. Their social meetings, where rich and poor were alike the welcomed guests, were for the study of the Word, and religious converse. The homes of the wealthy were plainly furnished, presenting an air of unworldliness and making them more homely for their poorer brethren and sisters. Their dress was plain, their habits simple, and their walk distinguished by separation from the world. The meetings of the assembly were calm, peaceful and hallowed; their singing soft, slow and thoughtful; their worship evinced the nearness of their communion with the Lord; their prayers were earnest for an increased knowledge of God, and for the spread of His truth. Their teaching showed their deep searching of the scriptures under the guidance of the Holy Spirit, whilst the exercise of the varied ministry, under the power of the Spirit, testified to the blessedness of the teaching of God's Word on each important subject. It was into this scene I was privileged to enter in the year 1843. At that time the church had grown to a large number. It began in a small house in King Street, Plymouth, and soon grew in numbers, and finally settled in Ebrington Street [the copy reads Elerington Street] where there was accommodation for 1,000 in fellowship, and about 400 others. This was a large plain building, erected according to their own plans, without a gallery. The large table was placed in the centre, as the most prominent object, around which were ranged the seats on a gentle rise from the floor, so that everyone could look upon it. There were no pews, but plain and comfortable benches. The acoustic properties of the spacious hall were, however, very deficient, so that those who spoke, unless possessed of very strong voices, were compelled to stand at the table, and even Mr. Darby, on returning from the continent, had a desk placed upon it, that he might be the better heard. (See p. 102, Mr. Neatby's *History*.)

The leading ministering brethren were Mr. B. W. Newton, Mr. J. L. Harris, Mr. H. W. Soltau, Mr. J. E. Batten, Mr. W. Dyer. Dr. Tregelles, Mr. Clulow, Mr. McLean and others ministered occasionally, while several others, qualified for leading in worship and prayer, took part in the gatherings. Mr. Newton, who in King Street could only at first speak with diffidence to a small number for a few minutes, could afterwards hold, for two hours at a time, the interested attention of a mixed audience of from 1,200 to 1,400 persons from the sects around. He was the principal teacher of the church. His leading subjects were prophetic, yet by no means confined to these, for he had a large grasp of scripture, and seemed deeply acquainted with every part of that mighty volume of truth. He always dealt with high subjects, momentous to the mind, and sacred to the heart. His delivery was calm, orderly, lucid, captivating, such as became a great scholar, one deeply taught in the Word, and anxious to lead others on in the knowledge of that which he had himself learned from its close study.

The line of teaching pursued by Mr. Harris was of another kind. He was a very powerful exponent of the doctrines of grace, of the nature of worship, and the revealed counsels of God; an enthusiastic teacher of the Gospel, and an earnest exhorter of believers as to their daily walk. A man of rich and ripe experience in the things of God, he was a wise and loving pastor of the flock, whose interests seemed ever on his heart.

Mr. Soltau was the first, I think, who taught the meaning of the types and sacrifices of the Old Testament, and as he unfolded the teaching of those symbols concerning the manifold perfection of the person and work of the Son of God a peculiar awe brooded over the assembly, impelling to the silent worship of Him of Whom he discoursed. The strain was solemn, calm and clear; his voice a deep tone, yet melodious, as it seemed almost to sing of salvation and the glories of the Saviour. He was withal a great preacher of righteousness.

Mr. Wm. Dyer (elder brother of Henry) was a mighty man in the Scriptures. Mr. Clulow spoke only occasionally, but always as though the matter was fresh from the fountains of his loving heart; and others whenever they addressed the meeting, impressed one as speaking under the guidance of the Holy Spirit, who was present to call into exercise the special gifts He had distributed for the edification of the body.

The exhortation of these several teachers was to a holy life in fellowship with the Lord Jesus Christ, to the cultivation of love, to a walk worthy of our heavenly calling, and to animate the blessed hope of our Lord's return; that, in short, as we were called heavenly, and made heavenly, we should seek grace to walk in responsibility as heavenly.

I breathed what appeared to me the pure element of love; I was in the enjoyment of the liberty of home; I was enlightened by its teachings, cheered by its joys, comforted by its hallowed fellowship, strengthened by godly companionship, and encouraged by those who were over me in the Lord. Those were delightful times, so sweet for their simplicity. The fruits of the Spirit (Galatians 5:22) were in evidence. Whatever undercurrents were at work they threw nothing to the surface. But it was too fair a scene for Satan to contemplate, and he must by some means mar its beauties and desolate its loveliness.

This devastating work began soon after Mr. J. N. Darby's return from the continent in 1845. I was told that, when he left Plymouth for his mission there, he commended Mr. B. W. N. to the assembly as one qualified to lead on the saints in truth (although that ability had been abundantly proved), and to watch over, and guide them in all spiritual matters. But, when he returned he found him in a position of great influence, attracting to his teaching believers from various parts of England, many of whom took up their residence in Plymouth, to benefit by his teaching and that of others. What were the feelings this popularity stirred? It would not perhaps be difficult to suppose; but a personal attack was soon made, and the disastrous strife of the two great teachers, who then became rivals, broke up the peace of the assembly and almost stopped the progress of the work. The particulars of this sore contention have been partly set forth in Mr. Neatby's *History of the Plymouth Brethren* so that they need not be repeated. But no account, gathered merely from pamphlets, could describe the distress of mind, the poignant sorrow and heart-grief produced by Mr. D. as he ruthlessly pursued his course against his former friend. There was no question of evil doctrine in this antagonism, but only of ecclesiastical practice. I deeply regret to have to record that strifes, jealousies, wraths, factions, parties, works of the flesh, took the place, in great measure, of the fruit of the Spirit and loving fellowship of the saints.

About two or three years afterwards Mr. Newton's false teaching concerning the humanity of Christ came to light, and was exposed first by Mr. J. L. Harris, then by Mr. Darby and others. Mr. Neatby expressed his opinion that Mr. Newton did not trace out to their legitimate conclusion the inevitable results of his teaching, and that he would not have held any view which to his mind was derogatory to the person of the blessed Lord. I endorse that opinion most fully, and will give an instance. I had attended all his lectures on the Psalms when these new views were stated, but contrary to his former mode of teaching he was abstruse and ambiguous, and I was unable to grasp his meaning. Being in a town in Cornwall at the time of his visit there, I waited upon him, and desired he would give me as briefly as possible, an outline of his teaching. This he did. I replied that his views, in my estimation, dishonoured the person of Christ. He answered that on the contrary, in his mind, it greatly exalted Him; and that he would on no account think or say anything that would in the least detract from His honour and glory who was ever the delight of the Father, and who could, notwithstanding His relative position, as man, to God and men, which He took in grace, at any moment rightfully take His place in the glory with His Father. This short explanation gave me the clue to his teaching, for, although I had heard his lectures, and had copied for circulation the notes, taken by a sister, of these lectures (and if those notes could now be discovered, I believe they would be found to be in my handwriting) yet my mind was in a state of confusion, and could not clearly grasp the nature of his teaching; but when this mist was cleared away, I saw his error and repudiated his doctrine, and to this day I abhor it.

—oOo—

There are a few discrepancies in Mr. Neatby's book which, with your permission, I will make good from personal knowledge. Between July 1848, when "The Letter of the Ten" was known, and December, when the Brethren of Bethesda decided on a new course, Mr. Darby was in Plymouth and gave his opinion that anyone coming from Bethesda should be held under suspicion of holding Mr. N.'s teaching, or, to use his own simile, as the authorities treated ships coming from Alexandria, putting them into quarantine until it was known that they were in a healthy state. But after December, when Bethesda had declared "that no one defending, maintaining, or upholding Mr. N.'s views should be received into communion" he again visited Plymouth when he laid down another principle touching Bethesda, which I will explain presently. He had visited Bethesda, and having expressed his approval of their later course, demanded that "The Letter of the Ten" should be withdrawn, and that a statement of that withdrawal, and their more recent action toward the false doctrine, should he published, so that the circulation of it might be commensurate with the publication of "The Letter of the Ten." The Brethren of Bethesda declined this for the reason that they did not publish anything; that both letters were written merely for the guidance of the Church of Bethesda, and were so far private: that the former letter was published without their consent, and that he was welcome to publish the later letter if he wished. Upon this refusal being firmly adhered to, Mr. Darby threatened to make it a test of communion everywhere. This is what I want to make clear and prominent, that, upon that demand and refusal the division was made, and has continued to the present. That was the point of cleavage, although subsidiary matters might have contributed to it. On his visit to Plymouth, alluded to, he forced this test on us in order that we should have no fellowship with Bethesda. Many of us felt that that church had done all that could be reasonably claimed from them. I asked him what spiritual authority there was for cutting off a whole assembly of God's people. He replied to the effect "I grant there is none. But if some Godly men meet together to seek the guidance of the Holy Spirit, they may expect that guidance, although there be no scripture whatever for the course they consider they have been led to take." (Is not that the dogma which the followers of his discipline have taken as their rule ever since? Hence their many separations. They would have division then, they have reaped divisions in abundance since.) We had several meetings on the subject, and at last a division in Plymouth was forced and that solely, I repeat, on the question of the duty of Bethesda to withdraw "The Letter of the Ten." That was the issue, and division on division, upon that flimsy pretext, went on throughout this country and others. I allude to this as showing that this awful separation was made not on a question of doctrine, for that had been settled, but only on the question of subservience to an imperious demand. Can it possibly be of God? Or is it not the work of the adversary of souls who has for centuries made havoc of the church? And now, because we who are called "Open Brethren" refuse to acquiesce to such a destructive course, we are unrighteously charged with holding Mr. Newton's errors which we abhor, or of being in fellowship with those who do, which is equally untrue.

Mr. Neatby's book is called A History of the Plymouth Brethren. It seems to me that it would be more correctly termed the history of Darbyism, as Mr. Darby and his way are the theme of his book, and he almost ignores the position of those called "Open Brethren," or he says a good deal to belittle them. Now the principles we profess are those originally taught and maintained by the early "brethren" in Plymouth; from which Mr. Darby, and consequently his followers, departed, if not previously, certainly in 1848. We have simply continued to act upon these principles. We have not learnt them from, and do not imitate, Darbyism. We have gathered them from the pure fountain of truth; and the longer I live, and the more I know of the scriptures, the more sure I am that those principles are of God. I am thankful to say that they are still being carried out by thousands of the Lord's people all over the world. The testimony raised by the Spirit of God in the early part of the century has not therefore wholly failed, although much weakened by the strife; and we trust it will continue to be upheld by us in all humility and godly sincerity; with the fixed purpose of, by grace, following the mind of the Spirit, and obeying the commands of our risen and exalted Lord, to the honour of His word and the Glory of His great name. Oh! for a return of the loveliness and simplicity of the former days: but if that might not be, yet there is a path for the lowly and obedient heart. Let us therefore earnestly endeavour to keep the unity of the Spirit in the uniting bond of peace, doing our work of building up ourselves on our most holy faith, and seeking to gather in from all nations those who shall be the joy and rejoicing of our ever blessed Lord in the day of His glory.

Norwich, *April,* 1902.   W. H. Cole.

NOTE 1.—In 1928, on page 8 of *The Local Assembly,* speaking of the 1848 strife, I said: "… it is most important to understand that the cause of that lamentable division was not false doctrine, but a false principle of church order and discipline. The doctrine *all* parties condemned, including almost immediately the teacher thereof. Mr. Darby and his followers condemned it; the Bethesda church, by the church resolution quoted, condemned it; while already, one year before—in November 1847—Mr. Newton himself had condemned it, and had withdrawn and disavowed all writings of his in which it was to be found."

Also, in chapter 13 of this book, written before Mr. Cole's paper came to me, I had said that Open Brethren are the real continuators of the first principles and practice of the Brethren, and that Exclusivism was a surrender of most of them.

It is important that these two views are confirmed by Mr. Cole, seeing that he had personal knowledge of the meetings before the strife arose, that he went through the conflict at its centre, and then watched the outcome for over fifty years.

Mr. William Collingwood of Bristol bore personal testimony to the same effect. He united with Brethren in 1844, before the first disruption, and after fifty-five years wrote in 1899 as follows regarding those who followed Mr. Darby:

> They have taken a position as far removed from the original ground as they are separated from actual fellowship. As to either, they retain nothing in common with those they have left, except that they still have the same custom of "breaking bread" on the Lord's day and an open ministry. The latter being to the popular idea the distinguishing mark of the "Brethren," the two classes, different as they are in all other respects, remain confounded in the minds of those who see only the external form (*The Brethren,* 22).

Mr. Cole remarks that Darby departed from the original principles in 1848 "if not previously." In fact, the departure commenced within eight years of the commencement of the meetings, as has been shown above by Groves in his letter to him of 1836 and by Lady Powerscourt's statement therein mentioned. (ch. IX, 175, 177, 178).

NOTE 2.—Mr. Cole's remark, "They *would have* division then" (in 1848, 1849) is to be noted as the estimate of a contemporary actor in the then affairs. But the imputing of *intention* to another is ever serious. Had he warrant in this case? At the very time these pages had been sent to the printer the following confirmation has come to me quite unexpectedly. It is an instance of how facts from nearly a century ago may be transmitted reliably.

Mr. Whiting was a grocer at Nailsworth, Gloucestershire, and an Exclusive. He was a great friend of Mr. William A. Jones, who was born in 1831 and died in 1915, and was a respected public official, merchant, and Christian of the neighbouring town of Minchin-hampton. Mr. Whiting told Mr. Jones that a commercial traveller calling upon him had narrated that he was present at a meeting at Plymouth when, after the breaking of bread, Mr. Darby in his hearing had said that if Mr. Müller did not deal with the Newton matter as he desired, he (Darby) *would divide every meeting in the world over it*. Now at that very time Mr. Cole was in the Plymouth meeting with which Darby was associated, as is shown by his narrative above, and he may very well have heard, or certainly heard of, Darby's statement made thus openly.

My present host and informant was a grandson of Mr. Jones. The latter often explained to him as a young believer his questions concerning Brethren, and more than once he mentioned to his grandson this remark by Darby. Mr. Jones's daughter writes to me that to her also her father spoke of this and never ceased to deplore Darby's statement. Though, like many of us, he esteemed Darby in some aspects, yet his comment to his grandson was: "If that was not Satan working upon the flesh in Mr. Darby I don't know what it was."

It should be observed that the unnamed brother was evidently at the meeting at Plymouth with which Darby was associated, or he would not have heard the words he quoted. At that period Mr. Cole also was with that meeting. Mr. Whiting too was an adherent of Darby. Thus the statements before us come from members at that time of Darby's own circle, not from opponents.

This testimony confirms Henry Groves' statement that

> Shortly after the reading of "The Letter of the Ten," Mr. Darby came
> again to Bristol, and held an interview with both Mr. Müller and Mr.
> Craik, in which he again urged the taking up of the tracts by Bethesda,
> and passing a condemnation on them… Finding their judgments were
> not to be changed, he sought to intimidate by the threat of separating
> from them all those believers in other places with whom for years they
> had held Christian fellowship (*Neatby,* 161: *Darbyism,* 42).

With what characteristic energy and determination Mr. Darby
carried through his already formed intention history sadly proved.
The Bethesda church did not accede to his demands, and he forth-
with divided assemblies everywhere against them.

Surely the child of God needs ever to bear in mind the exhortations "Take heed to your spirit" (Malachi 2:15), "Be renewed in the
spirit of your mind" (Ephesians 4:23), "The grace of our Lord Jesus
Christ be with your *spirit*" (Philippians 4:23).

NOTE 3.—One other incident shall be reviewed, utterly crucial to
Exclusivism, and resolutely disputed by Exclusives, that is, the interview between Müller and Darby in July 1849, when, as is alleged, the
latter admitted that the reason for his separation from the Bethesda
church no longer existed.

The following is the history of the matter, as far as I can learn.

1. On June 29th, 1848 "The Letter of the Ten" was read to the
church at Bethesda and sanctioned, defining their attitude to the
controversy at Plymouth.

2. Shortly thereafter Darby visited Bristol and further urged Müller and Craik to get Newton's tracts condemned by the Bethesda
church. As they still refused he threatened to divide other assemblies
against them, and in August he issued his Leeds circular to that end.
See H. Groves' statement just quoted, p. 332.

3. In December of that year, on account of fresh circumstances,
the Bethesda church condemned the tracts, and decided that "no one
defending, maintaining, or upholding them or the views they taught
should be received into communion."

4. The following July (1849), as is asserted, Darby saw Müller and made the statement in question. No other person was present. Any account of what passed depends therefore upon the statements of one or other of them, and as these are irreconcilable we may believe one or other, but cannot both.

5. Fifteen years later, in 1864, Henry Groves wrote the first draft of his *Darbyism* above quoted. In his preface he tells that he read this to Henry Craik, who agreed with what was written, and it was then read by Müller. The latter therefore accepted the statements as to the interview now in question. The book was published December, 1866, again in September, 1876, and there was a third edition undated. The account of this interview is unchanged, thus continuing Müller's acceptance of it. It reads as follows:

> The last occurrence that need be noticed in connexion with this part of the subject is the interview that took place between Mr. Müller and Mr. Darby in the summer of 1849. We might not have alluded to this, had it not been that untrue statements have been in wide circulation in reference to it, some denying that such a meeting ever took place, others denying the tenor of the conversation that passed between them. The following is Mr. Müller's account of what took place: Mr. Darby called on him at the New Orphan House, No. 1, ten minutes before one o'clock, and Mr. Müller, on entering the room where he was, shook hands with him, and Mr. Darby said to the following effect: "As you have now judged the tracts, the reason why we should not be united no longer exists." To this Mr. Müller replied: "I have only ten minutes now free, having an engagement at one o'clock, and therefore I cannot *now* enter upon this subject; for you have acted so wickedly in this whole affair, that many things have to be looked into before we could be really united again." On this Mr. Darby rose and left, and thus ended their last interview.

6. Upon this account Neatby commented thus:

> Of all the incidents in Darby's chequered career, this is distinctly the most damaging to his reputation, for he left Müller's presence only to enforce to the last letter the decree that he had just declared obsolete, that is, his Leeds letter (*History* 176).

But Neatby does not mention Darby's denial as to the conversation nor J. S. Oliphant's paper giving that denial. Either he did not know of these, or he did not think the veracity or accuracy of such a man as Müller could be justly questioned.

Similarly Ironside did not know of Darby's denial, for in *The Brethren Movement,* issued 1925 and 1926, he says, after quoting Müller:

> There is no way now of getting Darby's side of this regrettable incident, as he had departed to be with Christ two years before the letter was written,

that is, Müller's letter of 1883 as below.

7. But before Groves published his book, in 1866, the interview was already known, for by 1864 H. W. Soltau had mentioned it to Oliphant, a devoted partisan of Darby, who submitted the statement to Darby, and next year published his reply in his *Bethesda Fellowship,* and mentioned it again in his second edition of 1871.

In 1929 in *The Local Assembly* I cited the incident from Neatby. An elderly Exclusive, whose memory went back to Darby's time, wrote privately some *Remarks* upon this as follows:

> In 1865 Mr. J. S. Oliphant published his *Bethesda Fellowship* in which is given in full Mr. Darby's comments on this allegation. He therein says: "It is a total and absolute falsehood in every part and parcel of it. I can only esteem it, as I do, a deliberate falsehood on the part of Mr. Müller. It is too precise and totally contrary in everything to the truth to be anything else." This denial was repeated in a second edition in 1871.

And in a letter from Exclusive Brethren in Switzerland, France, England, and Holland to certain German Brethren, dated March 15th, 1938, it is said upon this matter:

> Now here is J. N. D.'s own reply to this unfounded assertion: "As regards the statement of my interview with Mr. Müller, I had heard it before, and I have only to say: it is a total and absolute falsehood in every part and in all its details" (see Noel's *History of the Brethren*, vol. 1, p. 270, quoting from H. S.'s tract).

This American *History,* dated 1936, does not mention Müller's letter of 1883, with its categorical re-affirmation of his account of the interview, though this is given by both Neatby and Ironside.

The continued and one-sided use of this incident by both schools shows the need for the present attempt to set out the facts more fully.

8. Oliphant's original paper of 1865 I have not seen, but his *Bethesda Fellowship* (1907) repeats what bears upon the matter in hand, and, while these pages are printing, this has come to me by the courtesy of my Exclusive critic above mentioned.[1] It tells that in 1864 Oliphant had an interview with H. W. Soltau, of which he says that

> ...his [Soltau's] excuses for Bethesda and for the neutrality to Christ in the proceedings there, were of such a character that I was forced at the close of the discussion to refuse him the right hand of fellowship. He then wrote me a letter, saying that Mr. Darby went to Mr. Müller to say that he was satisfied with the decision arrived at by the Saints at Bethesda, and that they might consider all differences at an end. That Mr. M. refused to have the matter made up so easily, as he had questions with Mr. Darby himself. That on this D. went away in great dudgeon, and set Bethesda up again as a mark of attack. I sent this letter to Mr. Darby, and it is due to him to publish the reply which I received.

This account of the interview must have come originally from George Müller, and it agrees with that of Henry Groves in the particulars (1) that there was an interview; (2) that Darby expressed himself to the effect that separation was no longer required; (3) that Müller raised the question of Darby's personal conduct; (4) that Darby thereupon left. It adds the assertion that Darby was much offended, which has not been otherwise asserted.

Oliphant then gives Darby's reply to him, which ran:

DEAR BROTHER,

> I send back S.'s letter. It is all of a piece, the same egregious self-sufficiency which has always misled him. As regards the statement of my interview with Mr. Müller, I had heard it before, and I have only to say: *it is a total and absolute falsehood in every part and parcel of it.* I do not attribute it to Mr. S., but being given as coming from Mr. Müller, and having no reason to think it a pure invention of the relater, Mr. Müller and I having been alone, I can only esteem it, as I do, a deliberate

---

1. Note to this second edition: I now hold a copy.

falsehood on the part of Mr. Müller. It is too precise and totally contrary in everything to the truth to be anything else. You are at liberty to repeat my judgment if you wish. I am afraid sometimes that things are a great deal worse than I ever was inclined to think. The less you have to do with personal questions with them the better. Affectionately yours in the Lord. J. N. D.

It is not surprising that some have taken these strong and explicit words to mean that the interview itself never occurred. Moreover, H. Groves's statement in 1866 shows that some had denied the fact of the interview, and this is how a critic of Oliphant at the time of the first issue of his paper in 1865 understood both him and Darby. See paragraph 9 below.

But in view of other evidence on the point I prefer to take Darby's words as admitting the interview. To deny this he should have said: "the statement of my *having had* an interview," and "Mr. Müller and I, as *is asserted*, having been alone." The statements as they stand mean properly that the interview was a fact, and the denial is of that having been said which Soltau declared.[2]

It is pertinent to observe that Darby did not give the least intimation as to what passed at the interview. It would have been natural to have used this easy occasion given by Oliphant. Why did he not do so then, or on any other occasion that is known publicly? If his statement to Müller did not commit him adversely why did he not make it public?

Mr. Oliphant continued:

For further information as to J. N. D.'s sentiments about "Bethesda" and its supporters, those who desire to know the truth may refer to his letters published by G. Morrish.

---

2. Note to this second edition (1949).—I have lately read Oliphant's 1871 paper mentioned. It omits the Appendix to the first (1865) edition, which had given Darby's letter upon the interview, but the Preface gives this acknowledgment that the interview was a fact and confirms what is said above as to Darby's meaning: It is only necessary to remark that what Mr. D. denied to be true, in his letter to me as related on p. 34 [of the 1865 edition] was Mr. S.'s account of what had occurred at an interview between Mr. D. and Mr. M., though Mr. D. did not impute the falsehood to Mr. S. I mention this because one or two understood Mr. D. to mean that he had not had an interview with Mr. M., on the subject of separation from Bethesda.

I might quote from several private letters which I received from Mr. Darby in 1864–65, but it is sufficient to say that, before I printed and published my letter in October 1865, entitled "Bethesda Fellowship," I sent it to Mr. Darby who returned it to me saying: "I have read your paper and return it without engaging you to change anything." In both editions of this letter published in 1865 and 1871, I made public the denial by Mr. Darby of what was alleged to be his statement to Mr. Müller in 1849.

9. From the dustheap of a packet of ancient and controversial pamphlets lately received, I have, while this book is in the press, recovered the following statement upon this old yet still living issue.

Upon Oliphant's paper being published "W. C. B." issued three leaflets criticizing it, of which I have numbers 1 and 3. These show that the writer knew and conversed with Oliphant, as well as other persons prominent in those controversies. In tract 3 he wrote:

> Mr. Soltau, it appears, told Mr. O. that a meeting had taken place some time ago between Mr. Darby and Mr. Müller, in which the latter object-ed to matters being made up without confession; and Mr. O. having written to Mr. D. about it, gets for his reply: "It is a total and absolute falsehood, in every part and parcel of it." A total and absolute falsehood! And yet, I myself have seen a letter in Mr. Darby's own handwriting, admitting the interview, and giving his own version of it. Now, which is true? Mr. D.'s letter, that *I* saw, admitting the interview; or Mr. D.'s letter to Mr.O., saying, the report is "a total and absolute falsehood, in every part and parcel of it!" I should like to have a really authentic account of this interview; for interview *there was*, let Mr. O. write what he will."

This puts beyond question that the interview took place, and establishes the truth of that item of Müller's statement; for "W. C. B." would scarcely have dared to put in print his statement as to having seen a letter by Darby, if it were false, seeing that Darby was alive to deny it.

10. As to the accuracy of George Müller's memory, it was almost phenomenal. I myself heard him speak in Bristol two or three years only before his death, when he was about ninety years of age, and for one hour and a quarter he gave a *resumé* of his whole life, travels, and works of faith, with precise figures as to countries visited, orphans

supported, Bibles and books distributed, funds received, even down to farthings on various accounts, and all without notes. It cannot, therefore, be argued that he was cloudy in memory as to so specially critical, yet only brief conversation of but sixteen years before Groves wrote his book, and which indeed he had not previously kept to himself, for Darby had heard of it, and Craik accepted the account of Groves before it was referred to Müller.

Moreover, Darby himself gives no possible room for the idea that Müller was merely incorrect in details, for he affirmed categorically that the *whole* statement was "a total and absolute falsehood in every part and parcel of it ... and in all the details ... [and] a deliberate falsehood..."

On the other side, Darby's memory also was too fine to allow the supposition of a complete and utter failure to remember such an interview, which he himself had sought, or what took place at it. Had he been uncertain on either point he would not have been in the position to offer so unequivocal a denial or bring so serious a charge of gross lying. Moreover, his letter mentioned by "W. C. B." shows that he did have clear remembrance of the interview having taken place.

11. The desire of "W. C. B." for an account of the interview was answered, from Müller's side, in the year of his leaflet by H. Groves' book. Further, in 1883, the year after Darby had died, an enquiry as to the matter reached Müller, to which he replied as follows:

Breslau, Germany, April 30, 1883.

Dear Sir,

On my way back from a missionary tour in Russia and Russian Poland to England, your letter of Apr. 6, has been forwarded to me to this place. The reply to your question is this:

In July 1849 Mr. Darby came to me to the New Orphan House, No. 1, on Ashley Down, Bristol, and said:

"As you have judged Newton's tracts, there is no longer any reason why we should be separated."

My reply was, "I have this moment only ten minutes time, having an important engagement before me, and as you have acted so wickedly in this matter, I cannot now enter upon it, as I have no time."

I have never seen him since.

Yours truly,

GEORGE MÜLLER.

A facsimile of this letter is before me, with the following guarantee:

73 Ludgate Hill, London, 21st January, 1907.

The above is a Letterpress Print from a "Process" block—made by us by photographic process from an original letter placed in our hands, signed by George Müller.

A. Bourne and Co.

and with the following also:

NOTE.–The original of this letter is held by M. H. C. Crawley of Buxton.

12. In 1885, E. K. Groves, younger brother of Henry Groves, issued his *Conversations on Bethesda Family Matters*. In ch. 6., on the "Family Sorrow," that is, the 1848–9 controversy, he repeats what we have quoted from his brother's book. In the prefatory Note he says that, while he alone is responsible for the book, yet this chapter 6 "has been examined by four of those who passed through the Family Sorrow." Their names are not given, but George Müller was then only eighty years of age, and he was in the United Kingdom from June 6th, 1884 to November 4th, 1885, the year the book was issued. (See *Preaching Tours, etc. of George Müller*, ed. 2, 1889 "Contents.")

13. There is one further testimony known to me, and it is of much weight.

William Kelly was with Brethren before and during the 1848 strife. From the first he was intimate with and devoted to Mr. Darby, and was later the editor of his "Collected Writings." In *The Doctrine of Christ and Bethesdaism* he deals with this matter. When this was first issued I do not know. I quote from a New Edition dated 1906, the year of his death. A footnote to page 13 reads:

As much is made of J. N. D.'s visit to G. M. after these meetings [that is, those when Bethesda condemned the tracts of Newton], it may be stated that Mr. D.'s hopefulness was not shared by his brethren, who knew that Bethesda never owned its sin in receiving Mr. N.'s partisans, and never repented of the false principles in the Letter of the Ten (adopted by a formal vote of its constituents). Even after the seven meetings it never so much as noticed the sin of receiving back two of the Ten who had gone out and publicly supported Mr. N. before all Bristol. In the face of grave facts like these, what was the value of theoretic censure of the doctrine? Mr. M.'s rude repulse only compelled Mr. D. to feel, as others already felt, the hollowness of Bethesda throughout. Mr. D.'s power lay in expounding the word, not in disciplinary action, as he used to own freely throughout his life.

The last remark shows that the statement was written after Mr. Darby's death in 1882. The whole statement admits

(*a*) That the interview took place.

(*b*) That it was about the time Müller said, that is, soon after the tracts were condemned by Bethesda.

(*c*) The fact that Darby went with "hopefulness" implies that what he meant to say was conciliatory. This agrees with the tenor of what Müller declared Darby said, though it does not guarantee the words. Yet Darby asserted it was positively "*contrary*"[1] to the truth.

(*d*) The mention that Müller "repulsed" Darby likewise confirms Müller's statement as to the character of his answer to Darby.

Thus four essential features of Müller's statement are here implicitly confirmed by Darby's most illustrious friend and supporter, who was in his confidence at the time of the event. This by no means maintains Darby's sweeping and unrestricted assertion that Müller's statement was a "deliberate falsehood" and "*totally* contrary in *everything* to the truth."[2] It rather bears in the opposite direction.

Again we observe that Kelly also gives no direct report of what Darby did actually say, though it is highly probable he had learned it from him, seeing he knew how Müller answered. Alternatively, if it was from Müller's side he learned this last, still he admits the

1. My italics.
2. My italics.

truthfulness of that part of Müller's statement, though Darby had said it was false.

This recital establishes the following series of facts.

(a) That at least as early as 1864 Müller had given his account of this interview, for Soltau had mentioned it, and Groves gave it in his book, and Darby had heard of it.

(b) In 1865 Darby denied the account absolutely and charged Müller with deliberate lying as to it.

(c) In spite of this denial, indeed, because the incident was being challenged, the next year (1866) Groves published the account of the interview which had been passed by Müller.

(d) Five years later (1871) Darby's follower Oliphant republished his book with the denial.

(e) Five years thereafter Groves republished his book.

(f) It was thus that Darby allowed the matter to remain at his death six years later, in 1882.

(g) The next year (1883) Müller categorically and in writing repeated his assertion.

(h) And two years later again (1885) it was once more published, by E. K. Groves, one of the Bethesda church where Müller was.

(i) Thus the matter remained during the following thirteen years, and thus it stood when Müller died in 1898.

(j) Between 1882 and 1906 William Kelly tacitly admitted the essential elements in Müller's statement.

14. The reader has now before him material for forming an opinion upon this controverted matter. The painful, yet seemingly inevadible alternative which Darby forced by his charge is, that, in this matter, either George Müller was a deliberate and maintained liar, or if not, then Darby was. The Searcher of hearts knows which was the fact, and before His judgment seat they both have ere now appeared.

On the one hand, my esteemed Exclusive correspondent says:

God only knows the truth when two brothers' conversation, when alone, is called in question; but that J. N. D. should have said privately to George Müller the precise opposite of his every *known* word or deed during many years, is strong and overwhelming presumption that what G.M. alleged he said is false.

On the other hand, George Müller was the most renowned man of faith and prayer of later times, upon whom the seal of God's approval rested publicly. Explaining the conditions of success in prayer he used to emphasize Psalm 66:18-19: "If I regard iniquity in my heart the Lord will not hear"; yet indisputably the next clause was true of him, "but verily God hath heard, He hath attended to the voice of my prayer," and this on a magnificent and increasing scale all through that very period of thirty-four years from 1864 to 1898. Could this have been so if God had known that through those same years he was cherishing in his heart, and spreading by books and letter, what he would have well known to be deliberate and detailed falsehood involving another? Must not such hypocrisy, deceit, and persistent lying have been a secret cancer to destroy his unction and testimony? But these the Spirit of truth maintained undiminished to the end of his life.

But clearly the issue is far larger than the personal character of either Müller or Darby. If the former told the truth as to the interview, then the whole attitude and course of the latter, in relation to the Bethesda church, from July, 1849, and onward, was self-condemned in advance. It is this that makes the incident a vital issue still, or it would be happy to let the dispute fade and die. Hence this examination, and also because the important contribution to the facts of "W. C. B." is newly recovered and unknown, nor, I think, has the matter been before surveyed and set forth comprehensively and from both sides.

15. If a biographer were telling Darby's life-story he would rightly have much to say other than comes into this present book. Here Darby enters only in his relation to the "original principles and practices of the Brethren," which is the least attractive aspect of him. Another could justly describe the lover of children, the warm-hearted friend, the man of simple habits and utter self-abandonment to the cause of Christ. He would portray the strenuous traveller, with his portmanteaux not unpacked for thirty years, as is said, and the earnest seeker of souls and feeder of the sheep of Christ. And he would speak of the classical scholar and faithful translator of the whole of the Book of God into German, French, and English.

But Kelly's words last quoted singularly confirm the impression that may be gained from these pages. It is Darby's confidential and life-long friend that tells us that "Mr. D's power lay in expounding the Word, not in disciplinary action, as he used to own freely throughout his life."

Now it was precisely his measures of discipline that forced the 1848 and 1849 strife. I have read all his letters on Bethesda to which Mr. Oliphant referred his readers, and I say simply yet plainly that all his statements, and those of his followers, that Bethesda shielded error are, in my opinion, contrary to fact. The leaders of that church then and later were at least as devoted to Christ, and to the true doctrine of His person, as their assailants. Though never formally connected with that church, yet from long residence in Bristol I speak from personal intimacy with some principal leaders who grew up under George Müller's influence, and whose knowledge in some instances went back into the middle of the last century. To write as Darby did in 1864, "The evil at Bethesda is the most unprincipled admission of blasphemers against Christ, the coldest contempt of Him I ever came across" (*Letters*, 2. 254), was sheer misrepresentation. Only the second year after, he was writing to the quite unrepentant Craik in the brotherly strain before mentioned (p. 171).

The question in 1848 was NOT the false doctrine that had been taught elsewhere; *all* parties had condemned that: but the question was *how to deal* with the situation that had arisen. The Bethesda leaders took one line and Darby demanded another. It was the forcing of his method of discipline that compelled the division, and it was he who compelled it, not they. The strong man certainly revealed that discipline was indeed not his strong point; yet he insisted on his ideas of discipline being enforced, to the general disaster and at the price of fellowship. Hence in this sphere of his activities, and in this book, the ecclesiastic and controversialist are in evidence and the picture is not lovely. I doubt not that an account of him in other aspects and activities could be profitable for the people of God, if both the material and the writer were available, though as a biography it would be like a life of David without his mighty wars.

In 1837, before contention's withering blast had begun to blow, he wrote—

Rise my soul! Thy God directs thee;
Stranger hands no more impede:
Pass thou on! His hand protects thee,
Strength that has the captive freed.

. . .

Though thy way be long and dreary,
Eagle strength He'll still renew:
Garments fresh and foot unweary
Tell how God hath brought thee through.

When to Canaan's long-loved dwelling
Love divine thy foot shall bring
There, with shouts of triumph swelling,
Zion's songs in rest to sing,

There no stranger God shall meet thee,
Stranger thou in courts above!
He, Who to His rest shall greet thee,
Greets thee with a well-known love.

And after his death, forty-five years later, these lines were found:

Behind my back I fling,
Like an unwanted thing,
My former self and ways,
And reaching forward far,
I seek the things that are
Beyond time's lagging days.

Oh! may I follow still,
Faith's pilgrimage fulfil,
With steps both sure and fleet;
The longed-for good I see,
Jesus waits there for me,
Haste! haste! my weary feet.

—oOo—

FINIS

Index

Also from Kingsley Press:

AN ORDERED LIFE
AN AUTOBIOGRAPHY BY G. H. LANG

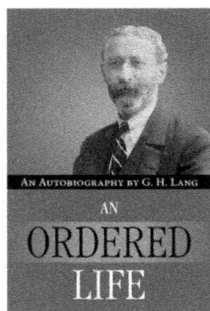

G. H. Lang was a remarkable Bible teacher, preacher and writer of a past generation who should not be forgotten by today's Christians. He inherited the spiritual "mantle" of such giants in the faith as George Müller, Anthony Norris Groves and other notable saints among the early Brethren movement. He traveled all over the world with no fixed means of support other than prayer and faith and no church or other organization to depend on. Like Mr. Müller before him, he told his needs to no one but God. Many times his faith was tried to the limit, as funds for the next part of his journey arrived only at the last minute and from unexpected sources.

This autobiography traces in precise detail the dealings of God with his soul, from the day of his conversion at the tender age of seven, through the twilight years when bodily infirmity restricted most of his former activities. You will be amazed, as you read these pages, to see how quickly and continually a soul can grow in grace and in the knowledge of spiritual things if they will wholly follow the Lord.

Horace Bushnell once wrote that every man's life is a plan of God, and that it's our duty as human beings to find and follow that plan. As Mr. Lang looks back over his long and varied life in the pages of this book, he frequently points out the many times God prepared him in the present for some future work or role. Spiritual life applications abound throughout the book, making it not just a life story but a spiritual training manual of sorts. Preachers will find sermon starters and illustrations in every chapter. Readers of all kinds will benefit from this close-up view of the dealings of God with the soul of one who made it his life's business to follow the Lamb wherever He should lead.

Buy online at our website: **www.KingsleyPress.com**
Also available as an eBook for Kindle, Nook and iBooks.

The Churches of God

by G. H. Lang

If you've ever wondered what the churches of the New Testament looked like—how they functioned, how they were governed, how they conducted their evangelistic and missionary enterprises, what ordinances they observed, what their liturgy consisted of, how decisions were made, how discipline was administered; if you've ever wondered how far modern churches have drifted from the New Testament pattern; if you've ever wondered what it would take for your church, and others like it, to return to the New Testament model, or if such a thing is even possible or desirable—then this book is for you!

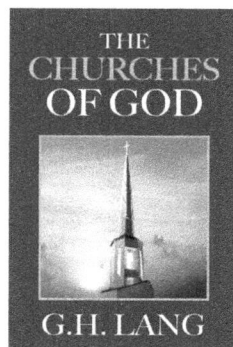

THE
CHURCHES
OF GOD

G.H. LANG

G. H. Lang's ability to elucidate Biblical truth was never more evident than in this small treatise on the constitution, government, discipline and ministry of the church of God. His gifts as a diligent Bible student, expositor, and precise thinker, together with his many years of experience as an itinerant Bible teacher in many different countries and cultural settings, all combine to make this a go-to reference on many issues relating to the local church.

About the Author

G. H. Lang (1874-1958) was a gifted Bible teacher and prolific author who in his early life was associated with the "exclusive" branch of the Plymouth Brethren but later affiliated himself with the Open Brethren. He traveled widely as an itinerant Bible teacher, depending solely on God for his support. Although Mr. Lang himself was a prolific author, it was his belief that "no man should write a book until he is 40. He needs to prove his theories in practice before publishing." In his own case, all but nine of his many books were written after he was 50. Kingsley Press has recently re-published Lang's amazing autobiography, *An Ordered Life*. More information can be found on our web site: www.KingsleyPress.com.

FIRSTFRUITS AND HARVEST

By G. H. Lang

Few writers have approached the subject of Biblical prophecy with more diligence and precise thinking than G. H. Lang. His purpose in studying and writing on the end-times and related themes was not to be controversial or sensational, but rather to encourage watchfulness and readiness. The serious reader will find much to challenge both mind and heart in these pages as the writer uses the prophetic Scriptures to give a strong call to holy and careful living.

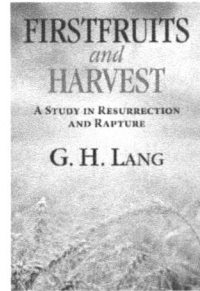

The secret of G. H. Lang's power and persuasiveness as a writer must surely be attributed to his lifelong dedication to searching the Scriptures, not for the sake of aquiring more knowledge, but in order that he might know God more intimately and follow Him more closely. His great passion was that God's children everywhere would press beyond the shallow and superficial and into a deep understanding of the ways and workings of God. In this respect he was the true successor to such spiritual giants as George Müller, Hudson Taylor, Robert Cleaver Chapman and Anthony Norris Groves.

One of Mr. Lang's contemporaries, Douglas W. Brealey, wrote of him: "I think I may truthfully say that he was the most apostolic man I have ever met; perhaps for that very reason he was a very controversial figure; a correspondent suggested to me that he was the most controversial figure in Brethren circles since J. N. Darby; yet it would be true to say that he himself was not a controversialist. A very close student of the Word, and an independent thinker, he was not prepared to take traditional interpretations unless he were personally convinced that they were right. . . . To be in his presence was to realize that one was in the presence of a true saint of God whose holy life gave weight and authority to all he taught."

Buy online at our website: **www.KingsleyPress.com**
Also available as an eBook for Kindle, Nook and iBooks.

The Revival We Need

by Oswald J. Smith

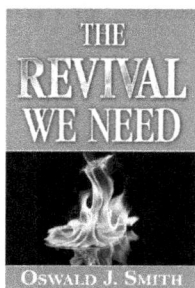

When Oswald J. Smith wrote this book almost a hundred years ago he felt the most pressing need of the worldwide church was true revival—the kind birthed in desperate prayer and accompanied by deep conviction for sin, godly sorrow, and deep repentance, resulting in a living, victorious faith. If he were alive today he would surely conclude that the need has only become more acute with the passing years.

The author relates how there came a time in his own ministry when he became painfully aware that his efforts were not producing spiritual results. His intense study of the New Testament and past revivals only deepened this conviction. The Word of God, which had proved to be a hammer, a fire and a sword in the hands of apostles and revivalists of bygone days, was powerless in his hands. But as he prayed and sought God in dead earnest for the outpouring of the Holy Spirit, things began to change. Souls came under conviction, repented of their sins, and were lastingly changed.

The earlier chapters of the book contain Smith's heart-stirring messages on the need for authentic revival: how to prepare the way for the Spirit's moving, the tell-tale signs that the work is genuine, and the obstacles that can block up the channels of blessing. These chapters are laced with powerful quotations from revivalists and soul-winners of former times, such as David Brainerd, William Bramwell, John Wesley, Charles Finney, Evan Roberts and many others. The latter chapters detail Smith's own quest for the enduement of power, his soul-travail, and the spiritual fruit that followed.

In his foreword to this book, Jonathan Goforth writes, "Mr. Smith's book, *The Revival We Need*, for its size is the most powerful plea for revival I have ever read. He has truly been led by the Spirit of God in preparing it. To his emphasis for the need of a Holy Spirit revival I can give the heartiest amen. What I saw of revival in Korea and in China is in fullest accord with the revival called for in this book."

Lord, Teach Us to Pray
By Alexander Whyte

Dr. Alexander Whyte (1836-1921) was widely ac-knowledged to be the greatest Scottish preacher of his day. He was a mighty pulpit orator who thundered against sin, awakening the consciences of his hearers, and then gently leading them to the Savior. He was also a great teacher, who would teach a class of around 500 young men after Sunday night service, instructing them in the way of the Lord more perfectly.

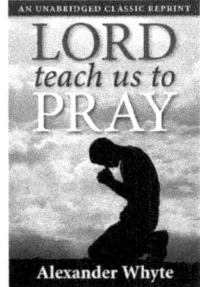

In the later part of Dr. Whyte's ministry, one of his pet topics was prayer. Luke 11:1 was a favorite text and was often used in conjunction with another text as the basis for his sermons on this subject. The sermons printed here represent only a few of the many delivered. But each one is deeply instructive, powerful and convicting.

Nobody else could have preached these sermons; after much reading and re-reading of them that remains the most vivid impression. There can be few more strongly personal documents in the whole literature of the pulpit. . . . When all is said, there is something here that defies analysis—something titanic, something colossal, which makes ordinary preaching seem to lie a long way below such heights as gave the vision in these words, such forces as shaped their appeal. We are driven back on the mystery of a great soul, dealt with in God's secret ways and given more than the ordinary measure of endowment and grace. His hearers have often wondered at his sustained intensity; as Dr. Joseph Parker once wrote of him: "many would have announced the chaining of Satan for a thousand years with less expenditure of vital force" than Dr. Whyte gave to the mere announcing of a hymn. —*From the Preface*

Buy online at our website: **www.KingsleyPress.com**
Also available as an eBook for Kindle, Nook and iBooks.

The Way of the Cross
by J. Gregory Mantle

"**D**YING to self is the *one only way* to life in God," writes Dr. Mantle in this classic work on the cross. "The end of self is the one condition of the promised blessing, and he that is not willing to die to things sinful, *yea, and to things lawful,* if they come between the spirit and God, cannot enter that world of light and joy and peace, provided on this side of heaven's gates, where thoughts and wishes, words and works, delivered from the perverting power of self—revolve round Jesus Christ, as the planets revolve around the central sun. . . .

"It is a law of dynamics that two objects cannot occupy the same space at the same time, and if we are ignorant of the crucifixion of the self-life as an experimental experience, we cannot be filled with the Holy Spirit. 'If thy heart,' says Arndt in his *True Christianity*, 'be full of the world, there will be no room for the Spirit of God to enter; for where the one is the other cannot be.' If, on the contrary, we have endorsed our Saviour's work as the destroyer of the works of the devil, and have claimed to the full the benefits of His death and risen life, what hinders the complete and abiding possession of our being by the Holy Spirit but our unbelief?"

Rev. J. Gregory Mantle (1853 - 1925) had a wide and varied ministry in Great Britain, America, and around the world. For many years he was the well-loved Superintendent of the flourishing Central Hall in Deptford, England, as well as a popular speaker at Keswick and other large conventions for the deepening of spiritual life. He spent the last twelve years of his life in America, where he was associated with Dr. A. B. Simpson and the Christian and Missionary Alliance. He traveled extensively, holding missions and conventions all over the States. He was an avid supporter of foreign missions throughout his entire career. He also edited a missionary paper, and wrote several books.

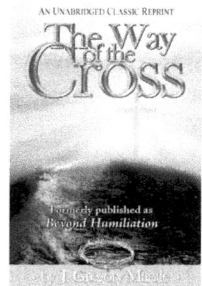

GIPSY SMITH
HIS LIFE AND WORK

This autobiography of Gipsy Smith (1860-1947) tells the fascinating story of how God's amazing grace reached down into the life of a poor, uneducated gipsy boy and sent him singing and preaching all over Britain and America until he became a household name in many parts and influenced the lives of millions for Christ. He was born and raised in a gipsy tent to parents who made a living selling baskets, tinware and clothes pegs. His father was in and out of jail for various offences, but was gloriously converted during an evangelistic meeting. His mother died when he was only five years old.

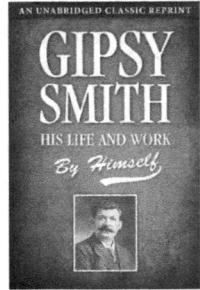

Converted at the age of sixteen, Gipsy taught himself to read and write and began to practice preaching. His beautiful singing voice earned him the nickname "the singing gipsy boy," as he sang hymns to the people he met. At age seventeen he became an evangelist with the Christian Mission (which became the Salvation Army) and began to attract large crowds. Leaving the Salvation Army in 1882, he became an itinerant evangelist working with a variety of organizations. It is said that he never had a meeting without conversions. He was a born orator. One of the Boston papers described him as "the greatest of his kind on earth, a spiritual phenomenon, an intellectual prodigy and a musical and oratorical paragon."

His autobiography is full of anedotes and stories from his preaching experiences in many different places. It's a book you won't want to put down until you're finished!

THE AWAKENING

By Marie Monsen

REVIVAL! It was a long time coming. For twenty long years Marie Monsen prayed for revival in China. She had heard reports of how God's Spirit was being poured out in abundance in other countries, particularly in nearby Korea; so she began praying for funds to be able to travel there in order to bring back some of the glowing coals to her own mission field. But that was not God's way. The still, small voice of God seemed to whisper, "What is happening in Korea can happen in China if you will pay the price in prayer." Marie Monsen took up the challenge and gave her solemn promise: "Then I will pray until I receive."

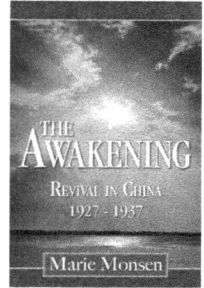

The Awakening is Miss Monsen's own vivid account of the revival that came in answer to prayer. Leslie Lyall calls her the "pioneer" of the revival movement—the handmaiden upon whom the Spirit was first poured out. He writes: "Her surgical skill in exposing the sins hidden within the Church and lurking behind the smiling exterior of many a trusted Christian—even many a trusted Christian leader—and her quiet insistence on a clear-cut experience of the new birth set the pattern for others to follow."

The emphasis in these pages is on the place given to prayer both before and during the revival, as well as on the necessity of self-emptying, confession, and repentance in order to make way for the infilling of the Spirit.

One of the best ways to stir ourselves up to pray for revival in our own generation is to read the accounts of past awakenings, such as those found in the pages of this book. Surely God is looking for those in every generation who will solemnly take up the challenge and say, with Marie Monsen, "I will pray until I receive."

A Present Help
By Marie Monsen

Does your faith in the God of the impossible need reviving? Do you think that stories of walls of fire and hosts of guardian angels protecting God's children are only for Bible times? Then you should read the amazing accounts in this book of how God and His unseen armies protected and guided Marie Monsen, a Norwegian missionary to China, as she traveled through bandit-ridden territory spreading the Gospel of Jesus Christ and standing on the promises of God. You will be amazed as she tells of an invading army of looters who ravaged a whole city, yet were not allowed to come near her mission compound because of angels standing sentry over it. Your heart will thrill as she tells of being held captive on a ship for twenty-three days by pirates whom God did not allow to harm her, but instead were compelled to listen to her message of a loving Savior who died for their sin. As you read the many stories in this small volume your faith will be strengthened by the realization that our God is a living God who can still bring protection and peace in the midst of the storms of distress, confusion and terror—a very present help in trouble.

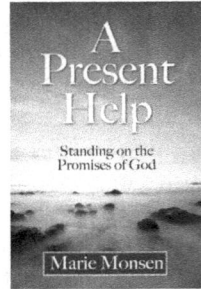